CANADIAN ISLAMIC SCHOOLS
Unravelling the Politics of Faith, Gender, Knowledge, and Identity

Religious schooling in Canada has been the subject of considerable political and academic interest, yet there has been little scholarship on Islamic education. In this ethnographic study of four full-time Islamic schools, Jasmin Zine explores the social, pedagogical, and ideological functions of these alternative, religiously based educational institutions. Based on eighteen months of fieldwork and interviews with forty-nine participants, *Canadian Islamic Schools* provides insight into the role and function that Islamic schools have in diasporic, educational, and gender-related contexts.

Discussing issues of cultural preservation, multiculturalism, secularization, and assimiliation, Zine considers pertinent topics such as the Eurocentricism of Canada's public schools and the social reproduction of Islamic identity. She further examines the politics of piety, veiling, and gender segregation, paying particular attention to the ways in which gendered identities are constructed within the practices of Islamic schools and how these narratives shape and inform the negotiation of gender roles among both boys and girls.

A fascinating and informative study of religious-based education, *Canadian Islamic Schools* is essential reading for educators, sociologists, and those interested in immigration and diaspora studies.

JASMIN ZINE is an associate professor in the Department of Sociology at Wilfrid Laurier University.

JASMIN ZINE

Canadian Islamic Schools

Unravelling the Politics of Faith, Gender, Knowledge, and Identity

UNIVERSITY OF TORONTO PRESS
Toronto Buffalo London

© University of Toronto Press Incorporated 2008
Toronto Buffalo London
www.utppublishing.com
Printed in Canada

ISBN 978-0-8020-9856-6 (cloth)
ISBN 978-0-8020-9572-5 (paper)

∞

Printed on acid-free paper

Library and Archives Canada Cataloguing in Publication

Zine, Jasmin, 1963–
    Canadian Islamic schools : unravelling the politics of faith, gender,
knowledge, and identity / Jasmin Zine.

Includes bibliographical references and index.
ISBN 978-0-8020-9856-6 (bound) ISBN 978-0-8020-9572-5 (pbk.)

1. Islamic education – Canada.   2. Muslims – Education – Canada.
3. Muslim girls – Education – Canada.   I. Title.

LC913.C3Z55 2008   371.0770971   C2008-905898-4

University of Toronto Press acknowledges the financial assistance to its
publishing program of the Canada Council for the Arts and the Ontario Arts
Council.

University of Toronto Press acknowledges the financial support for its
publishing activities of the Government of Canada through the
Book Publishing Industry Development Program (BPIDP).

Contents

Acknowledgments

This project grew out of my doctoral work in the Department of Sociology and Equity Studies at the Ontario Institute for Studies in Education of the University of Toronto. The study was made possible through support from a doctoral scholarship from the Social Sciences and Humanities Research Council (SSHRC) and a Summer Writing Fellowship from the Wabash Center for Teaching and Learning in Theology and Religion.

I am very grateful to the political and intellectual guidance I received from George Dei who continues to be a role model and source of inspiration for my academic career and political commitments. As a pioneer in anti-racism and anti-colonial perspectives in education, his brilliant scholarship and caring mentorship has provided me with support and important intellectual pathways to follow. I am also grateful for the support and friendship of Tara Goldstein. Her political dedication to a critical ethnographic approach to research has been inspirational and has contributed a great deal to the shape and form of the ethnography I present in this book. I would also like to thank and acknowledge Kari Dehli and Goli Rezai-Rashti for their support and thoughtful feedback on this work.

This book would not be possible without the generous support of the International Institute of Islamic Thought (IIIT). I am extremely grateful to Dr Jamal Barzinji, the IIIT Board and the reviewers at IIIT for their careful consideration of this book and their generous funding. Their commitment to developing research on Muslims and Islam has been an important gateway for promoting new scholarship and thereby having an important influence and impact on the field of Muslim studies. I am very grateful for their ongoing leadership and support to academic work in this field.

I am grateful for the support of Virgil Duff of the University of Toronto Press and his belief in this book. I am also indebted to the supportive and constructive comments of the peer reviewers that helped to further refine the draft manuscript. I would also like to acknowledge the careful editing work of Matthew Kudelka. His close editing has helped polish my words for which I am grateful.

I am supported by colleagues who are dear friends and sisters to me. I am forever grateful for the friendship and intellectual camaraderie of Maliha Chishti, Sonia James-Wilson, and Shabana Mir. Your sisterhood, humour, critical insights, and support have been a personal, professional, and spiritual lifeline throughout this project.

I am also grateful to my parents and to my brother for their support. In particular I want to acknowledge my grandfather Farogh Ahmad for his always open pride in my accomplishments.

This book is dedicated to my husband, Abdullah Zine (whose artistry graces the cover of this book), and my sons, Usama and Yusuf. I could not have done the work required for this book without their unwavering love, support, and encouragement.

Finally, I want to thank the Islamic school communities that participated in this study. To the students, parents, teachers, administrators, and community activists that shared their experiences, dreams, and struggles I offer this book as a testament to your hopes for the future.

CANADIAN ISLAMIC SCHOOLS

Unravelling the Politics of Faith,
Gender, Knowledge, and Identity

1 Staying on the 'Straight Path': A Critical Introduction to Islamic Schooling

Guide us to the straight path. Not the path of those who have earned your anger, nor the path of those have who gone astray.

Surah Fatiha, The Opening, *Holy Qur'an* 1:1

Walking along the right path, the path of the just middle, to remember God and keep in one's heart the sense of values and finalities. Always walking along despite the dangers and adversities, despite the injustices and horrors, trusting God so as not to despair of men and events ... The right path, at the heart of modernity: our spirituality, in our heart, is at the heart of life.

Ramadan, 2001, pp. xix–xx

Introduction

The opening verse of the Holy Qur'an and the passage quoted above speak to the practice of staying on the 'straight path,' *siratul mustaqeem* in the Arabic language – that is, on the path of righteous knowledge and behaviour. This is often termed in Islamic discourse a 'middle path,' one of moderation, balance, peace, and justice. This is the path that Muslims are enjoined to follow, and the invocation of being guided to this path is repeated more than twenty times a day during the opening verse of the five daily prayers. The repeating of this invocation and the search for divine guidance remind us of the difficulty of maintaining the balanced way and the need to keep the straight path constantly in focus.

For many Muslim parents in the North American diaspora, the way to help their children stay on the 'straight path' is through a spiritually centred education, one that from their perspective can only be acquired through immersion in an Islamic school setting. For Muslim students whose religious and cultural practices run counter to some of the norms of Western society, the secular, Eurocentric focus of public schools can be both alienating and culturally compromising (see Anwar, 1986; Murad, 1986; Parker-Jenkins, 1995; Rezai-Rashti, 1994; Yousif, 1993; Zine, 1997; Sweet, 1997; Berns McGown, 1999; Shamma, 1999b).

The difficulties of living between two cultures can lead to dissonance for these youth. An article in the *Toronto Star* quotes a Muslim youth describing the dilemma: 'Some friends have two different lives – one at home where they follow their culture, one away from home where they do what their friends do' (Scrivener, 1999). Attempts by youths to negotiate these dualities often result in what has been called the 'split personality syndrome': they develop a double persona in their efforts to resolve the cultural contradictions between home and school. Al-Jabri (1995), a young writer in an Islamic publication, refers to the clash between the norms of the dominant culture, where social acceptance is based on 'how flashy you dress, how cool you talk, how obscene you joke, whom you befriend – especially of the opposite sex' and what he characterizes as the 'other side of the planet ... the world of mom and dad – the world of Islam' (p. 28). To conform to both standards some youth begin living two different lives in two opposing worlds. In the end they develop a double personality, with one side tailored to the social/cultural demands of home and family, the other to the demands of the outside world.

Many Muslim parents fear the assimilative forces in public schools that threaten to 'de-Islamize' their children (Murad, 1986; Khan-Cheema, 1996; Parker-Jenkins, 1995; Sarwar, 1996; Yousif, 1993). Peer pressure, drugs, alcohol, dating, and violence in schools pose many challenges for Muslim students who attempt to maintain an Islamic lifestyle and identity while at school (see Jacobson, 1998; Shamma, 1999b; Zine, 1997, 2000). Issues such as racism and religious discrimination also inform the schooling experiences of Muslim students in the public education system (see Murad, 1986; Rezai-Rashti, 1994; and Zine, 2000, 2001b).

Muslim parents in Ontario have many concerns about the social and cultural milieu of public schools, as well as concerns regarding dominant policies, practices, and curricula (Azmi, 2001; Berns McGown, 1999).[1] Community-based Muslim organizations have been established that work with school boards and advocate for policies that would address the needs and interests of Muslim students in public schools. For example, these groups seek accommodations that would allow Muslim students to conduct their Islamic practices while at school – practices such as attending regular prayers and wearing Islamic clothing during physical education classes. They also call for halal[2] food to be provided in the cafeterias and for Muslim students to be exempted from subjects – such as music and sex education – that are problematic from some Islamic perspectives (see Zine, 1997, and Parker-Jenkins, 1995, for British examples of religious accommodation). A growing number of Muslim parents, dissatisfied with the status quo and fearful of the un-Islamic social and cultural milieu of public schools, are seeking alternatives to public schooling, such as full-time Islamic schools for elementary and secondary education and home schooling (Azmi, 2001).

Overview of Muslims in Canada and Canadian Islamic Schools

The Muslim presence in Canada had an unlikely beginning, with the arrival in 1854 of a Scottish family – James and Agnes Love and their newborn son. By 1901, Canada's Muslim community had grown to 47 members, who settled in Alberta and Saskatchewan. By 1911 there were 1,500 Canadian Muslims, most of them Syrian and Turkish migrants, many of whom worked on the construction of the Western railways (Abu Laban, 1983, Hamdani, 1999). By the early twentieth century, governments were enforcing policies of racial exclusion in order to stem the flow of Asian immigrants. Abu Laban reports that when the First World War broke out, many Turkish immigrants were classified as enemy aliens and sent back to their country of origin. As a result of these policies, Canada's Muslim population remained relatively small between 1911 and 1951. The 1931 census recorded only 645 Muslims – a figure that had grown to perhaps 3,000 by 1951 (Abu Laban, 1983, p. 76). After the Second World War, a time when the economy was shifting from wartime to peacetime production, Muslims began entering Canada as skilled labourers. By the end of the twentieth century, Muslims were the largest non-Christian religious group in Canada, having surpassed the Jewish population in 1996 (Hamdani, 1999).

In the increasingly multicultural landscape of Canada, a 2001 Statistics Canada report reveals that Islam is among the ten largest religions in the country. That year, 2 per cent of Canadians were Muslims: 579,640 lived across Canada, 352,525 of them (61 per cent) in Ontario.[3] During the 1960s and 1970s almost all Muslim children were enrolled in the public education system. By the mid-1990s the perception that Muslims needed their own independent religious schools was strong enough within the community that, in the Metropolitan Toronto region, a number of full-time alternatives had been developed in order to educate Muslim children (Azmi, 2001). According to Kelly (1997), there were 24 Islamic schools in Canada in 1997. Most of them (14) were in Ontario. According to Azmi (2001), that number had grown to 19 by the end of 1999. The Ontario Ministry of Education reported that 2,240 children were attending Islamic schools in 1999; estimates by the Muslim community suggest that this figure was even higher, perhaps as many as 4,000 (Scrivener, 2001).

The most recent count (from 2005), conducted by the Ministry of Education and Statistics Canada, reveals that approximately 3,500 Muslim students now attend Islamic schools – an estimated 7 per cent of all Muslim students at the elementary and secondary school levels (Memon, 2006). Many students are placed on waiting lists as soon as they are born, and some Islamic schools have waiting lists of 650 or more. Today there are 35 full-time Islamic schools Ontario, 18 of them in the Toronto region. All of these schools but one are part of the Sunni tradition; the exception is a Shia school (Sunni and Shia are the two predominant sects within Islam). Islamic education also takes place in mosques,[4] most of which provide weekend schools known as *madrassahs*;[5] these are usually attended by children who are in public schools during the week. In Ontario, full-time Islamic day schools are private and receive no government funding. Many Muslim parents cannot afford to pay the fees for private schooling but are committed to an Islamic education for their children. Some of these parents are choosing to educate their children through home schooling.

Research on Muslims and education in Britain has brought to light a difference between 'Muslim schools' and 'schools for Muslims.' The former schools set out to foster an ethos that is consistent with religious values; the latter schools base themselves on a common shared identity, one that 'aspires to be fully Muslim,' but because of staffing and funding constraints, they do not go the entire distance to developing Islamically oriented curricula or ethos (Parker-Jenkins, Hartas, & Irving, 2005, p. 40). In Canada, Islamic schools see it as their central mission to develop a knowledge base and ethos rooted in Islamic beliefs, traditions, and thought. These schools refer to themselves not as 'Muslim' but as 'Islamic' – indicating that they are organized according to Islamic principles as outlined in the Qur'an and in accordance with the behaviours and actions of the Prophet Muhammed as documented in the sunnah. The term 'Islamic' suggests adherence to a set tradition and is less open to discursive manoeuvring than the term 'Muslim,' which refers to adherents of Islam and not directly to the primary sources of the faith. The pointed use of the term 'Islamic' suggests a specific approach to education, one that is deeply rooted in traditional Islamic epistemology. By contrast, the term 'Muslim' can refer to a variety of orientations to the faith. Canadian Islamic schools, then, are faithful to the goals and purposes of Islamic education as a holistic enterprise – one that, epistemologically and ontologically, is grounded in specific notions of what is constituted as 'Islamic' and therefore rooted in divine principles and ordinances.

Dei (1998), writing in support of African-centred schools, states that Afrocentric knowledge is 'a legitimate way of knowing and understanding our world' (p. 200). In much the same way, Islamic schools in the North American diaspora have a vision of institutionalizing an Islamic epistemology as the basis for educating Muslim children. Religious knowledge is one of the multiple frames or lenses that people use to read and make sense of the world – though all too often a religious world view is held in contempt, as illegitimate, because of false dichotomies that privilege the 'rationality' of secular knowledge over the 'irrational' and 'mystic' knowledge that flows from religious or spiritual sources. Religious schools are often associated with intolerance (Sweet, 1997), and they are often viewed as anachronistic in matters relating to women or sexuality (Saghal and Yuval-Davis, 1992). These are difficult labels to transcend, and in some instances such criticisms are valid. It is not my intention to uncritically valorize all forms of religious education; I would, however, argue that religious schools – in this case Islamically oriented ones – should not be dismissed as intrinsically intolerant or inherently misogynistic sites for educating impressionable youth. Islamic schools are part of the Canadian landscape, and they need to be examined as viable, growing alternatives that many Muslim families are choosing for their children.

It is important to critically analyse any educational site. That said, especially strong scrutiny has been aimed at institutions that use the term 'Islamic' or 'Muslim' as a descriptor. Because of media images of 'militant *madrassahs*' as training grounds for religious extremism abroad, Islamic institutions in Canada can become unfairly suspect. With the recent hostage crisis and military assault on the Jami Hafsa madrasa in the Lal Mosque in Pakistan, which pitted security forces against radical clerics and their students, and with the barrage of media images of Al Qaeda schools in Afghanistan as terrorist training grounds or '*jihadi* factories' (Haqqani, in Hefner, 2007), Islamic schools abroad are being increasingly linked to violence and religious insurgency. Against this political backdrop, Canadian Islamic schools and their role in the Muslim community have come under greater scrutiny. In a climate of heightened security concerns, moral panic, and Islamophobic narratives, there is a need to understand the role of Islamic schooling in the diaspora. This can be an important means to dispel neo-Orientalist myths of a pervasive 'Muslim threat' while maintaining a critical focus on the social, ideological, and political dynamics of these institutions.

Because of the ubiquitous media tropes about *madrassahs* being hotbeds of religious radicalism and violence, it may be impossible to view Islamic schools without these negative referents hovering in the background. In a report on British Muslim schools, Mandaville (2007) notes that latent concerns about the efficacy of Islamic schools in preparing young Muslims as British citizens increased in the aftermath of the London bombings. The Muslim community's reaction was mixed: some community spokespeople rejected the criticisms; others admitted that certain reforms might be necessary and instituted programs of professional development. In the current climate of heightened fear and suspicion, Mandaville is sceptical that Islamic schools will escape public scrutiny: arguing that 'concerns about the impact of a parallel Muslim education sector – albeit one teaching the national curriculum – and its effect on conceptions of citizenship and belonging among young boys and girls socialized within an exclusively Muslim peer group are likely to endure for some time' (p. 233).[6] Notwithstanding this new reality, my intention is to provide a critical focus that will unravel the politics of faith, gender, knowledge, and identity in Islamic schools, always cognizant of the local and global socio-political contexts that also shape our attitudes towards these schools.

Locating Myself in the Discourse and Research

Part of my interest in Islamic schooling stems from the fact that my children attended a full-time Islamic school for their elementary education. For much of that time I was an active member of the Parent Association Committee and taught at a weekend Islamic school. These experiences have helped structure and inform the personal and political investments I bring to this research. My experiences as a community activist and Muslim parent in the Islamic school system have inevitably informed my ethnographic work. Writing ourselves through the discourses we produce is a part of the production of ethnographic knowledge. The situated nature of the researcher has strong political implications, whether 'insider' or 'outsider' research is being conducted. As a critical ethnographer doing fieldwork in my own community, my research intersects with my ongoing activism in education – activism that in this instance includes providing pedagogical and political support for Islamic schools. My children now attend public schools – institutions that I also strongly support. They, like many other children, have migrated in and out of various educational environments, all of which are valuable to a well-rounded education.

My personal experiences have framed my research in other ways as well. As a minority student growing up in the Canadian school system, I was well aware of the challenges entailed in trying to 'fit into' a dominant Eurocentric framework. I experienced a sense of invisibility by not being represented in the school culture or curriculum, on the one hand, and by being a racialized visible minority in a predominantly white school, on the other; this led to my disengagement, and I dropped out of school after grade nine. Later, I was involved in research exploring issues of student disengagement among Black youth in Ontario (Dei, Mazzuca, McIsaac, & Zine, 1997). During subsequent research on Muslim youth, I found that the pressures of race and social difference, coupled with pressure from peers to engage in un-Islamic activities, often lead to the loss of Islamic identity and practices (Anwar, 1986; Murad, 1986; Zine, 1997). However, as my research on Muslim students in the public schools has shown, some Muslim students are able to develop a resistance to conformity and marginalization through the social organizations that they develop in these schools (Zine, 1997).

Muslim Students and the Politics of Resistance

Muslim Student Associations (MSAs) in high schools have provided social and religious support to their members. Islamic subcultures in schools have developed from these associations. MSAs make possible a mode of 'formalized resistance.' Classical resistance theories in education focus on class as the catalyst for student dissent (see Giroux, 1983). By contrast, MSAs structure their resistance around religious identification as a site for social and political action and educational critique. Through strategies of 'formalized resistance' that involve developing a corporate base for political advocacy, Muslim students can gain the right to maintain their Islamic practices within the school. For example, they were able to advocate for accommodations such as prayer space, allowances for religious dress codes, and the provision of halal food in the cafeteria. Through formalized resistance, these students can also challenge courses and textbooks that present a biased and 'Islamophobic' perspective of Islam. In these ways, MSAs have helped Muslim youth negotiate their religious beliefs and identities within the secular framework of public schools. At the same time, they have had a role in transforming some of the structures of their schools to make them more inclusive of their needs and interests (see Zine, 2000).

My 1997 study, however, related to only a small percentage of Muslim students – to those who were able to structure their resistance and develop cohesive systems for social support through their schools and the community. Many students lack supports within a secular school system that at every step challenges their beliefs and their resolve to live according to those beliefs. Other students do not come from religiously observant or 'practising' families and therefore find mainstream conformity unproblematic. All of this suggests why a number of imams,[7] during their *khutbas* (sermons) at the mosques during Friday prayers, declare that sending Muslim children to public schools is like sending 'lambs to the slaughter' (Yusuf, 1994). Muslim parents' concerns about public schools are only exacerbated by news reports of school violence. These fears reinforce the sense of urgency in the Muslim community for an alternative school system.

The Case for Separate Schools

Gorder (1996) notes that while more parents are choosing home schooling as a response to issues such as violence, drugs, and poor student attitudes and performance, religion has been the number one reason for opting out of the school system. For parents who choose alternative religious schooling, a primary concern is the doctrine of secular humanism that has come to permeate school curricula. Accord-

ing to Gorder (1996), 'most people who have not studied home schooling assume that the teaching of evolution is a major concern to these
parents. It is to some, but it is not the only issue cited by most religious
home schoolers. It is a more widespread teaching concept that bothers
them, one that covers every subject in every grade. That teaching is the
concept of secular humanism, or putting people in every situation
before God. Parents object to this attitude in public schools. They want
their children to be brought up in a God-centred life instead of a me-
centred life' (p. 53).

Secular humanism is no less doctrinaire or dogmatic than religious-
based ideologies and should be viewed as an ideological position
rather than an unbiased or value-free set of assumptions. Religious
parents are disturbed that public education is based on secular human-
istic beliefs; they see this not only as a threat to their own values and
beliefs but also as leading to moral relativism and, inevitably, to a
moral vacuum in society (Gorder, 1996).

Islamic education, according to Bleher (1996), differs from secular
models in that 'everything focuses on the Divine element which is
always part of every situation. This differs greatly from a secular
world view within which, man [sic] is the master of his own fortune,
free to use his abilities as he pleases, for better or worse' (p. 61). He
goes on to argue that a secular education that does not attend to the
spiritual nature of learners is partial and fragmented: 'The secular education model cannot do justice to the human beings it serves to
educate, because it deals with various aspects of human nature in a
fragmented way, ignoring their inter-relationships and denying the
Divine origin in them all' (p. 62). Even so, Bleher is critical of the status
quo in Islamic schooling, which he regards as having 'short term' and
'backward looking' approaches that all too often seek only to preserve
the traditions from 'back home' instead of articulating a 'clear vision'
of sustained purpose for Islamic schooling in a diasporic context. He
argues that this approach in Islamic schools has undermined the transformative possibilities of these schools in favour of achieving only
material rewards. He notes that the result has been 'a younger generation who, instead of being at the forefront of the introduction of
Islamic principles into a non-Muslim society, have either lost part of
their Muslim identity in order to gain worldly opportunities or vice-
versa' (p. 61).

Alternative systems of schooling allow Muslim children to become
centred in their religious identity and spiritual growth. For Muslims

who choose a faith-centred lifestyle, Islamic education is essential to the development of self-awareness and a collective social identity. Independent, faith-based schools can foster this sense of identity and purpose. Yet these ideals do not necessarily encourage religious apartheid' – a charge often levelled by those who view independent schools as a threat to the public school system and the ideals of liberal pluralism (see Callon, 1997; Spinner-Halev, 1997; Sweet, 1997; Borovoy, 1996). On the contrary, as a Jewish parent quoted in Sweet's (1997) study of religion and education argues, being rooted in a sense of identity, history, and collective ancestry is an important anchor for individual and social identification and a sense of belonging in the world: 'The world makes you other, there's no getting away from that. But this [sending my daughter to a Jewish school] isn't about rejecting others. It's protecting a culture I see in jeopardy ... I am educating my child separately. But there's a paradox: the more I teach her who she is, the better she can live with others. She'll have a sense of herself, of her people in the context of Canada and the world' (p. 112).

For many families, religious education provides a spiritual grounding that is fundamental to identity development and societal health. Independent schools provide space for a religiously centred education – one that public schools cannot provide – and help instil a strong sense of identity, which, as I will argue, does not necessarily come at the expense of the 'common good' in a liberal society.

Despite the growing demand for full-time Islamic schools and the rapid development of these schools across the country, little research has been conducted on Islamic schooling in the diaspora. This research seeks to fill that void as it relates to Islamic education, the development and maintenance of Muslim identities, and the Islamization of knowledge in Islamic schools.

Mapping Objectives

This study offers a critical ethnographic examination of four full-time Islamic schools in Canada. It examines the social, pedagogical, and ideological functions of these alternative, religious-based institutions. This research is based on the following three objectives:

- To identify the role and function of Islamic schooling in a diasporic context.

- To understand the role of Islamic education in the development of Islamic identity.
- To examine the Islamization of knowledge and the politics of teaching and learning in Islamic schools.

The Role and Function of Islamic Schools

Murad (1986) has pointed out the need for Islamic schools in the diasporas to become sites for producing a potent 'counterculture' to challenge, resist, and ultimately transform the status quo cultures in which they are embedded. Similarly, Raza (1993) argues that Islamic schools must 'be political,' since nothing can be achieved within a democratic social order without knowledge of the political system and how to become active within it (p. 47). According to these two views, religious identification inculcated through independent religious schooling provides a site for counterhegemonic resistance and social transformation; furthermore, it provides the necessary 'cultural capital' or knowledge of mainstream politics in order to ensure that the Muslim community becomes a political agent for change. Thus it is important to examine Islam, and Islamic education, as a system of knowledge from the perspective of those who see it as an empowering alternative framework with possibilities for broader social transformation. In this sense, Islamic schooling needs to play a role in promoting conscious political action directed at issues of social justice and peaceful participation in civil society. This is part of a broader system of Islamic education known as *dawah*, which involves modelling Islam to non-Muslims and encouraging the spread of Islamic knowledge through open dialogue.

As a social and spiritually based alternative to the public education system, independent Islamic schools play multiple sociological roles. For example, they attempt to create a 'safe' environment that protects students from the 'de-Islamizing' forces in public schools and society at large. Transnationalism and the experience of migration lead to cultural dissonance for newcomers from Muslim countries, who are unaccustomed to culturally permissive social norms such as partying, consuming alcohol, dating, and premarital relations. Residing as they do in culturally incongruent spaces, migrant Muslim communities have sought to shelter their children and youth from negative outside influences. Cultural norms relating to family and religion are often enforced more strongly in the diaspora than they would have been 'back home,' as Berns McGown (1999) has noted in a study of diasporic Somali Muslim communities in Toronto and London: 'In Somalia parental pressure to conform to tradition would not have been so strong; it would have been accepted that they are still young and "practicing" to perform their religious requirements' (p. 212). In other words, immersion in a culturally incongruent environment has made parents fear more for their children and for the potential loss of their culture and religious way of life.

According to Nyang (2000), the challenge of self-definition and identity maintenance is a key one facing Muslim communities in North America. He argues that Muslims are beginning to assert their identity in the public square; in the past, new immigrants in particular had been more reticent to express their Muslimness openly and to facilitate integration they had engaged in 'survival strategies' such as the Anglicization of names. Nyang refers to people in this category as 'grasshopper Muslims': 'This type of Muslim is usually very eager to receive acceptance from the host society. For this and other related reasons, he or she may change his or her name to something else that is more familiar to the members of the majority community. This is why in the grasshopper category you find a Muhammed Jummah going by the name Michael Friday and Musa Abdulla changing his name to Moses Abdullah' (p. 2). Nyang notes that this survival mechanism helped many a Muslim immigrant 'weather the icy waters of racial or cultural prejudices' (p. 2).

The desire and need for Islamic schools emerges from the nexus of resisting cultural assimilation and promoting the salience of religious identity. According to Azmi (2001), Islamic schools are an attempt to assert a religious identity within a secular cultural and political landscape: 'The development and proliferation of these parochial institutions represents a determined assertion of religious identity in the context of a public educational framework of official secular multiculturalism, which de-emphasises religious identity in favour of Canadian national and secular ethnic identity' (p. 272). In addition to being a response to a secular multicultural ethic, Islamic schools provide many Muslim students with a culturally congruent space and a more seamless transition between the values, beliefs, and practices of home and those of school. They also provide a space free from racism and religious discrimination, which many students encounter within public schools (see Rezai-Rashti, 1994; Zine, 2000, 2001b). Yet Islamic schools, like other independent religious schools, are also accused of 'ghettoizing' students and of not socializing them to society at large;

moreover, they are considered inadequate arenas for civic engagement in a racially and religiously pluralistic society because of their 'particularist' orientation (see, for example, Gutmann, 1996; Sweet, 1997; Callon, 1997; Thiessen, 2001). These claims will be explored in the context of the narratives of Islamic school stakeholders.

Islamic schools play other social and ideological roles. For example, they function as sites for the social reproduction of Islamic identity. Also, they provide a spiritually based environment that allows the development of religious values and practices. In these ways they are discursive sites where religious knowledge forms the basis for personal and social growth and development. Some parents choose Islamic schools for children who have encountered difficulties in the public schools and who have begun engaging in un-Islamic behaviours such as alcohol or drug use, gang activities, or sexual promiscuity. The schools, then, serve as spaces to resocialize and rehabilitate wayward youth. Reshaping the mores and behaviours of youth who have deviated from the 'straight path' has emerged as an unwritten mandate of Islamic education. Discipline, in this sense, involves more than punishing prohibited acts; it is also a discursive process whereby students are resocialized into Islamically appropriate behaviour.

In addition to exploring the sociological and ideological roles Islamic schools perform, I will be examining school administrations as well as parent participation in schools. While parent involvement in public schools is expanding through the introduction of school–parent councils, the role of parents in Islamic schools is far more limited, despite the community-based nature of these schools. Very few Islamic schools in the Greater Toronto Area have a parent association. Where they do exist, parent activities include fundraising and the organization of sports programs and special events. There is also a more political element, with the parent association channelling parents' concerns with regard to leadership, curriculum, and teacher hiring. This often leads to antagonism between the administration and the parent body. Disagreements over school policies have been known to lead to schisms in the community at large, often along ethnic lines. Later I will make recommendations with regard to school governance and constructive input from parents.

A trend towards divisive ethno-politics and tribalism within the Muslim community is threatening to disrupt the goal of Islamic schooling stated earlier by Murad (1986) as the development of 'a potent counterculture.' Political posturing, nepotism, and ethnic divisions at the grassroots and leadership levels of the community are disrupting the solidarity that is needed to direct Islamic schooling, as a community-based venture, towards its intended goals, which are spiritual growth and social transformation. I will be addressing these tensions in this research, which I hope will become the catalyst for change and greater unity within the Muslim community by encouraging a critical re-examination of the goals and current practices of Islamic schooling.

Islamic Identity and Education

The second core objective of this research is to examine how Islamic schooling relates to the development of an Islamic identity among students. Some key questions emerge from this inquiry: What does 'being a Muslim' mean to Islamic school students? How do they construct an identity through their school experiences? How are notions of self and other articulated from their perspective? Does an Islamic education allow students to see beyond the binary opposition between believers and non-believers? What pedagogical choices do Islamic schoolteachers make to help students experience and interact within a pluralistic society? I address these questions and others in order to show how identity and knowledge of oneself and others are being articulated in Islamic schools and to help gain an understanding of the self-conceptions and world views of the students.

I also consider the students' sense of community identification through their links to the pan- Islamic notion of the *ummah* – that is, the global community of Muslims. Pan-Islamism is a fragile concept in the postmodern world of ethnic and political divisions, sectarianism, and fragmented and impermanent notions of identity. Increasingly in the post-9/11 world, the spectre of fundamentalism and extremism is the primary lens through which the Muslim community is viewed.[8]

In fact, the fundamentalists and the extremists are very much fringe groups within Islam. Often, their extreme views lack religious legitimacy and are entirely outside valid Islamic knowledge and praxis. Nevertheless, the insurgence and intransigence of these global extremist movements represented by infamous groups such as Al Qaeda have enacted a shifting narrative of Islamic identification for the majority of Muslims, who distance themselves from the political and epistemic violence of the extremes. Boundaries, concepts, and engagements of identity are being rethought as moderate Muslim groups coalesce to re-evaluate their positions within their homelands and the many diasporas they inhabit. New alliances and strategies are being forged to build a more unified sense of Muslim identity and purpose, one that centres on realizing a North American Muslim presence as being a positive constituent of the local social fabric (see also Ramadan, 2001).[9] This project of transcending differences to achieve a common basis for identification and collective social action underlies the concept of the *ummah* in Islam.

When we extend this engagement to the domain of education, we find ourselves facing some key questions: To what extent do Islamic schools promote global awareness and unity? How is this tied to the goals of social justice in Islam? Is the consciousness of a global community of Muslims displayed through community-based activism within Islamic schools? Such questions, and others, will help us address issues of collective identity building and the corresponding vision of Islamic schools as sites of social activism.

This study also explores gender dynamics in Islamic schools, especially in the girls-only school that was one of the four I investigated in depth. Between September 1999 and February 2000 I conducted preliminary research in an Islamic girls' school, where I had volunteered to teach a course on world issues. This allowed me to gauge the gender politics within the school. Later, when I asked my students about their experiences as Muslim girls, they trusted me enough to be candid, thus providing me with insights into what I saw as an emerging feminist discourse.

I will also be examining issues of gender and Islamic identification through discursive socialization and educational practices. For example, does Islamic education provide equal opportunities for boys and girls? Stereotypical notions of the status of Muslim women often assume that the education of Muslim girls is unnecessary or undervalued according to Islam. Ad-Darsh (1996) attempts to 'dispel the baseless notion that Islam forbids education for girls,' pointing out a famous hadith, or saying, of the Prophet Muhammed: 'Seeking knowledge is incumbent on every Muslim' (p. 26). Nevertheless, Ad-Darsh concedes that historically, certain scholars' interpretations (and in some instances falsifications) of Islamic *hadith* have betrayed a 'deep-rooted bias against women' (p. 26).

The hadith, or traditions and sayings of the Prophet Muhammed, are a primary source of traditional Islamic knowledge, after the Holy Qur'an, and represent the compilation of the oral tradition of prophetic wisdom in Islam. The narrators of the hadith were predominantly male, as the close companions or *sahaba* of the Prophet, though the most respected hadith come from Aisha, one of the wives of the Prophet, who also played an important role in authenticating hadith after the Prophet's death (see Mernissi, 1991, p. 77). The Qur'an is the primary source of Islamic knowledge as the revealed word of God. Historically and traditionally, Qur'anic exegesis has been the domain of male commentators. An androcentric bias in the interpretation of Islamic text is addressed by writers such as Fatima Mernissi (1986, 1991) and Amina Wadud (1992), who provide feminist reinterpretations of Islamic doctrines. Wadud's exegesis of the Qur'an is especially useful in examining the issue of how the 'prior text' of the Qur'anic interpreters, as part of their gender-based and culturally inscribed world view, can limit the meanings of the text. She argues that Qur'anic interpretation is 'never final' and that meanings must constantly be sought after and reinterpreted in order adapt the original, historically contextualized meanings of the Qur'an (p. 10). Miriam Cooke (2001) has examined how emergent forms of Islamic feminism are inspiring the development of a gendered epistemology as a critical counternarrative to prevailing male-centred religious discourses. Each of these scholars advocates the development of a feminist hermeneutics of religious knowledge.

These particular readings of the Qur'an and feminist methodologies of interpretation are new to mainstream Islamic discourse; thus their impact on Islamic education remains to be seen.

In this book I will be unpacking the ways in which gendered identities and gender roles among both boys and girls are negotiated in Islamic schools. Particular attention will be given to a high school for girls with regard to issues of gender equity, segregated schooling, and the creation and transgression of gendered spaces.

Islamization of Knowledge

Another focus of this research is the integration of Islamic knowledge into students' learning. Islamic schools strive to redefine curriculum and educational praxis by centring Islam within every subject being taught. Islamic studies is meant to be a seamless strand of knowledge that connects all subjects as they are taught from an Islamic perspective. However, few teachers are able to follow this approach effectively; most of the time, Islamic studies and Arabic (the language of the

Qur'an) are merely 'add-ons' to an otherwise mainstream Eurocentric curriculum. Thus the primary goal of these schools – Islamic immersion – is far from being reached. My investigation will also be considering ways to develop an Islamic focus in Islamic schools as part of an Islamization of knowledge. Besides examining the epistemological foundations for Islamically-centred education, I will be examining pedagogical practices and strategies, including methods of discipline and socialization, in order to better understand how they are informed by the religious and spiritual traditions of Islam.

Contemporary Islamic thought related to education has been developing over the past few decades. The hegemony of Western knowledge in Muslim societies – a consequence of European colonialism – has galvanized a movement towards the Islamization of knowledge. This intellectual project is geared towards reclaiming a space for Islamic knowledge in education and other academic disciplines. At the First World Conference on Muslim Education (held in Mecca, Saudi Arabia, in 1977), symposiums were convened to discuss the dilemma of Islamic education and to 'find new ways and means of evolving Islamic concepts and of creating Islamic methodology' that would pervade all branches of knowledge (Naseef, in Husain and Ashraf, 1979). From this point on, progress in Islamic thought on education included the North American Islamization of Knowledge project spearheaded by the late Ismail Al Farooqi of the International Institute of Islamic Thought (IIIT) in Virginia, as well as the work of the Association of Muslim Social Scientists (AMSS). The reconceptualization of Islamic epistemology and praxis relating to education is relayed in some seminal works produced in association with these academic societies.

The Islamization of knowledge involves more than simply remaking Western knowledge with a different 'spin' and inserting Islamic referents. It also involves examining the contributions and transformations that Islamic thought can make in mainstream public discourse and praxis. During the Golden Age of Islam in the Middle Ages, Muslim scholars developed a legacy of social, cultural, and scientific advancement that built the intellectual foundation for the European Renaissance. These scholars developed innovations in the arts and sciences that revolutionized culture and civilization globally (see Bammate, 1963). Yet the postcolonial Muslim world has languished in a state of intellectual paralysis. Recovering from the social, economic, and political legacies of colonization, Muslim countries in Asia, Africa, and the

Middle East were unprepared to deal with the challenges of modernity and the subsequent encroachment of an economic and political imperialist world order. This particular historical trajectory arrested the development of a long overdue Islamic renaissance. Muslim societies need to find renewed expression through the resurgence of the arts, philosophy, and scientific and spiritual reclamation rather than fundamentalist and extremist dogmas.

Speaking of the crisis in Muslim societies, Ali Mazrui (2002) points to the effects of 'lopsided globalization and its disproportionate economic and cultural effects on African societies': 'What passes for "modernity" in Africa is often superficial westernization which has not taken root. Africa has experienced urbanization without industrialization, western consumption patterns without western productive techniques, western tastes without western skills, western secularism without western science. The colonial experience has transmitted the wrong aspects of the western legacy to Africa' (p. 9). In other words, the colonial legacy has resulted in uneven patterns of development that leave countries in the South struggling with the social, cultural, economic, and political challenges of modernity. Mazrui applies this analysis to the broader Muslim world, highlighting the need for an Islamic contribution to the development of twenty-first-century politics and culture in order to resist Western mimicry and the homogenizing forces of globalization: 'If globalization is not to mean the westernization of the whole world, Islam is needed as a constant challenge to the cultural monopoly of the West. Islam is an antidote to the homogenization of the human race. But challenging the West need not mean being physically at war with the West. It should be a battle of ideas rather than an armed confrontation' (p. 10). Engaging in a 'battle of ideas' as part of an antiglobalization movement, as Mazrui advocates, places Islamic knowledge in a counterhegemonic role. A critically focused Islamic education is key to this level of global discursive engagement. In this sense, the Islamization of knowledge must revitalize intellectual thought, elevating it to the level of global cultural critique and then turning it towards the task of providing concrete alternatives to Western discourses based on Islam's spiritual principles of democracy and social justice. These aspects of Islamic philosophy are largely absent in most Muslim societies today that are governed by postcolonial dictatorships and monarchies. Such a critical counternarrative is necessary, to challenge not only the encroachment of Western cultural hegemony but also to the plague of fundamentalist extremism that has flourished in its wake.

According to Hofmann (2002), 9/11 has led to the laying of new charges against the Muslim world – primarily, that Islam has missed its Enlightenment. He notes that as a 'pre-Enlightenment religion,' Islam is increasingly accused of being archaic and irrational. He counters these accusations by invoking the Qur'an, which calls on us to 'observe, reflect, use one's mind and calculate advantages and disadvantages,' adding that Islam is the only Holy Scripture to make such appeals to human rationality (p. 4). He also challenges the legacy of the Enlightenment, which he views as a largely unrepeatable European phenomenon. While it did have some positive social and political outcomes such as liberal democracy, rule of law, and the market economy; other cultural products of the Enlightenment – products based on 'supreme confidence in human reasoning' and the shift from deism to pervasive agnosticism in the nineteenth and twentieth centuries – led to 'an extreme inhumane rationalism divorced from transcendental ethics.' The result was disasters such as colonialism, two world wars, fascism, and chemical and nuclear warfare (p. 7). Hofmann contends that 'long-term negative results of the Enlightenment continue to linger on, such as consumerism, the further decline of religiosity, wholesale environmental destruction, the widening gap between rich and poor, and neo-colonialist cultural domination globalization, all of which follow a commanding commercial or technological "logic"' (p. 7). Given this dubious legacy, Hofmann is galled that Muslims are expected to follow such a 'slippery slope' of social and political reforms. The task of living in a global postmodern condition is, in his view, not one of subscribing to 'outdated modernism'; rather, 'it means subscribing to the current wave of re-spiritualization of knowledge ... re-Islamization of knowledge' (p. 9).

The path of re-Islamizing knowledge is in some ways a path of ideological reform, one that requires us to reclaim the hermeneutical spaces of theology and Qur'anic exegesis from extremist and puritanical orientations. Many people view the project of reforming Islam as solely ideological or theological, but this is a narrow perspective that ignores the structural conditions that give rise to extremist movements. In many countries in the South, for example, the effects of the neoliberal economic policies demanded by the World Bank and the International Monetary Fund (IMF) in the 1980s and 1990s shifted modes of production from subsistence to cash crops. A goal of such policies was to integrate the South's economies with the world's free markets, but they had uneven consequences that led to drastic cuts in social spending. Discussing the effects of these economic 'reforms' in Nigeria and the rise of fundamentalist violence, Ayesha Imam, cofounder and executive director of Baobab, a Nigerian Women's Rights Organization, maintains that the economic 'immiseration' these policies brought led to social devastation that disproportionately affected the poor as well as women and children (in Landsberg, 2002, A2). These policies also created a vacuum in the social infrastructure that hard-line religious groups stepped in to fill, fuelled by resentment towards the West – as a direct result of the devastating impact of the 'invisible hand' of Western imperialism. Put simply, any analysis of fundamentalism or religious extremism must take into account the structural conditions that create the conditions for reactionary movements to flourish.

The development of the Muslim world has been heavily influenced by historical conditions of social, economic, and political oppression. Those same conditions are to this day part of the status quo in these societies. It follows that the intellectual project of fostering an Islamic 'reform' movement must first attend to broader social conditions of disenfranchisement of the kind that lead to rigid ideological responses. In the global arena, the Islamization of knowledge has to be situated as an anti-imperialist project; furthermore, that project must guide reforms by bringing forward economic, social, and political correctives based on new foundations. Islamic education must critically analyse global conditions in order to encourage a positive and proactive framework for this revisionist project; is so doing, it must also reclaim the historic roots of Islamic pluralism and tolerance (see also Abou El Fadl, 2002). The challenge for Islamic societies is to negotiate pluralism and democracy as a by-product of spiritual and religious discourse rather than seeking to contain or sanction those various forms of diversity that are seen as an additional 'threat' to an already threatened and compromised existence. The shifting ideological terrain of Muslim social politics is reflected in the discursive practices of Islamic schools. As independent, community-based institutions, these schools have limited resources, which of course affects how teachers teach and students learn. Ultimately, the confluence of ideological and economic factors affects the standard of education. Islamic schools struggle to cater to a cross-section of the diaspora community, many of whose members are newcomers and on the bottom rungs of the economic ladder. In responding to the diaspora's local needs, these schools are trying to develop new discursive foundations on which to build a pedagogical framework that reflects the culturally hybrid space in which they reside.

Historical Overview of Islamic Education and Schooling

Islamic education began in the home of the Prophet Muhammed. In the early seventh century, for the early Muslim community in Mecca, his house was the first informal site for Islamic education. As the number of Muslims grew, the Prophet moved the school to a site in Mecca called Dar Al Arqam ibn Abi al-Arqam. Little is known of how teaching was conducted during the Meccan period; however, Hefner (2007) notes that in later times, religious study was largely informal, conducted through *halaqas* (study circles) in mosques but also in homes and shops under the tutelage of a shaykh (master scholar) (p. 6).

As the Islamic state expanded, there was greater cross-cultural and civilizational interaction. As a consequence, in some sites the curriculum of Islamic education was expanded from religious subjects such as Qur'an, sunnah, hadith, and sharia to include what were referred to as the rational sciences, such as medicine and astronomy. During the caliphate of Umar ibn al-Khattab, (634–644) a number of religious schools known as *kuttabs* were established outside mosques. The caliphate's efforts to integrate diverse peoples into the expanding Muslim empire, as well as advances in scientific knowledge, led to the founding of independent institutes, organized schools, literary councils, bookshops, and libraries, all of which flourished throughout the Islamic Empire (Mutawali, in al-Otaibi and Rashid, 1977, p. 4). Historians of Islamic history have pointed out that during the Islamic Middle Period (1000–1500) Islamic education was still largely informal and lacked a standardized curriculum. Also, it did not offer examinations or bestow degrees. Thus the transmission of Islamic knowledge was more personal and informal as well as more flexible and inclusive (Berkey, 2007).

These early Islamic schools were largely independent of any central governing authority. By the eleventh century, however, because of ideological conflicts and the rapid growth of the Islamic empire, schools had come under the control of the central Abassid government. Though authority over education had been centralized, the administration of schools was left to local officials. Generally, teachers started up their own schools and established their own curricula. The government intervened only if there were reports that distorted information was being taught (al-Otaibi & Rashid, 1977, p. 5).

There were two types of *kuttabs* (schools): one for religious studies and memorization of the Qur'an, and the other for subjects such as reading, writing, and mathematics. The schools were open to both male and female students and would have catered mainly to elites rather than the rural classes. Women at this time were involved in Islamic knowledge production, albeit to a lesser degree than men. Aisha, one of the wives of the Prophet Muhammed, was recognized as the most learned scholar of Islam in her time (see Mernissi, 1991).

Berkey (2003) contends that the transmission of Islamic knowledge or *ilm* 'helped to draw towards the center social groups which in other circumstances, such as those of Medieval Europe, were marginalized by the expectations and demands of religious education' (p. 226). This meant that while women were forbidden to serve as *qadis* (religious jurists), they were not prohibited from gaining religious knowledge, as this would bestow on them *baraka* (spiritual blessings). Indeed, some women studied with and received *ijaza* (certification)[10] from experts in religious sciences and later themselves issued *ijazas* to other students who sought out their expertise on particular texts. According to Berkey (2003), this made them 'valued links in the chain of personal authority through which religious knowledge was passed on' (p. 227). This did not subvert the gendered hierarchy and male-dominated boundaries of religious knowledge production; it did, however, allow women a space (albeit limited) in Islamic education.

Education was offered broadly throughout the community and even in limited forms to slaves and prisoners of war (Quraishi, 1970). There were, though, some regional differences with respect to curriculum. In North Africa, no other books were taught in conjunction with Qur'anic learning. Only after students had memorized the Qur'an were other subjects such as literature and poetry introduced. However, in Muslim Spain, children were taught writing, poetry, grammar, and penmanship along with the Qur'an. There were diverse approaches to disseminating Islamic knowledge; generally, however, oral transmission of texts was central to all of them. Berkey (2003) notes that religious texts were often read aloud, and often in public spaces, these texts were 'performed' rather than simply being 'read' (p. 227).

According to Quraishi (1970), mosques were the only Islamic schools until the early ninth century, when separate educational institutions were introduced. The first *madrassah* separate from a mosque was founded in Nishapur in Khorosan. This *madrassah* was a private school that taught only religious sciences. With the shift from the

Abassid caliphate to Seljuk rule in 956, these private schools became public. Around this time, the mandate of the *madrassahs* was expanded to include the training of government administrators; thus they became centres of religious and political propaganda (p. 27). Financial endowments known as *waqf-i-khairi* provided for the maintenance of mosques and *madrassahs*. Renowned Muslim political leaders and scholars of the twelfth century, such as Nizam-ul Mulk and Salahuddin, made major endowments to educational institutions (p. 28).

During the Middle Ages, at the height of the Muslim Golden Age, one library in Cairo held more than 1.6 million books in more than forty rooms. Books, including those of the Greek philosophers, were available in a variety of languages. At the libraries, readers could borrow books, scribes could copy books by hand, and patrons could sit and read. By 1200 there were more than thirty-five schools in Baghdad, which was the centre of Islamic learning in the Middle Ages. Other famous centres of learning were Fez, Cairo, and Timbuktu.

The curriculum of the *madrassahs* expanded as epistemological traditions proliferated. According to Quraishi (1970), the ninth to eleventh centuries were an era when 'reason joined hands with faith' (p. 34). During this period, in the Muslim world's key cultural and educational sites – Damascus, Basra, Kufa, and Baghdad – the works of Greek philosophers, physicians, and mathematicians were translated into Arabic. As a result of this intellectual and cultural fusion, Muslim scholars made revolutionary advances in sciences, arts, mathematics, medicine, and astronomy.

Islamic knowledge was divided into the natural and the traditional sciences. The rational sciences included logic, arithmetic, geometry, astronomy, music, medicine, agriculture, and metaphysics. It is interesting that metaphysics was considered one of the rational sciences – a position at odds with modern-day notions of rational thought. During this same period, linguistic studies focused on grammar, philology, rhetoric, and literature.[11] Qur'anic sciences were the centrepiece of learning and included the study of *tafsir* (exegesis/commentaries), *qira'at* (oral recitation), hadith (traditions of the Prophet), *fiqh* (jurisprudence), *al-kalam* (theology), *tasawwaf* (mysticism) and *tabir-ar-ruya* (interpretation of dreams and visions).

Centres of learning in the Islamic world became renowned for their academic and spiritual sciences. During the ninth century, the Caliph Mamun established the renowned Bait-ul-Hikmat (house of wisdom) in Baghdad. It combined a large library with an academy and a translation centre and was reputed to be the most important educational institution of its time. In the Bait-ul-Hikmat library, scientific works were translated: logic, philosophy, geometry, astronomy, medicine, and alchemy. Attached to the institution was a large circular observatory. Bait-ul-Hikmat was the medieval world's first university, and the knowledge developed there paved the way for the European Renaissance.

During the eleventh century, Nizam ul-Mulk, the minister of the Seljuks, was a well-known patron of theologians and scholars. He founded institutes of learning in all the major cities of the Islamic Empire, the most famous being the Nizamiyah in Baghdad. Scholars were provided a generous stipend during their time at Nizamiyah, where there were six thousand students (Quraishi, 1970, p. 86). According to Quraishi, the most celebrated centre of learning was called the Mustansiriyah, named after the thirteenth-century Abbassid caliph who was its patron. Also located in Baghdad, this university's library boasted 160 camel-loads of books from the caliph's own library. Mustansiriyah had four schools of law, each specializing in a major branch of jurisprudence in the Sunni tradition. The school had a great kitchen that prepared food for students daily. There were storehouses for olive oil (for lamps) and cool water. A bathhouse and a hospital catered to students' needs. Beautiful gardens surrounded the building. All of this was a testament to the vitality of Islamic sciences and knowledge production that spanned several centuries. This brief overview has provided a historical context for our examination of the present-day tradition in Islamic education.

Traditional Concepts of Islamic Education

Husain and Ashraf (1979) have examined traditional concepts of Islamic education as a means of structuring current Islamic educational systems. They maintain that 'education is a process involving three references: the individual, the society or nationality to which he or she belongs, and the whole content of reality, both material and spiritual, which plays a dominant role in determining the nature and destiny of Man [sic] and society' (ix).[12] They argue that by infiltrating Islamic societies, secular Western thought – including Marxism and liberalism – has displaced spirituality from its central place.

Traditional Islamic philosophy of education is based on revelation. Sharifi (1979) contrasts this with modern Western educational philosophies, which proceed from secular epistemological theories such as idealism, realism, pragmatism, Marxism, existentialism, and scientism. Sharifi compares Islamic educational philosophy with the foundations of Western rational thought to illustrate the disjunctures between these ways of knowing as well as the fundamental incompatibility of these paradigms for Islamic education. Central to his critique is the neglect of the 'position of the heart' in Western educational philosophy. He argues that when this dimension of the self is neglected, 'the very centre of the human being, that which can realize the truth in education, amounts to the forgetfulness of the transcendental dimension of human life, to imprisonment in our limited sense perceptions and our worldly being forever, to confinement in areas which are by no means appropriate to our Intellect and real Nature (fitrah)' (p. 78). This aspect of spiritual knowing is also referred to as intuition. According to Muhammed Iqbal, the Pakistani philosopher, knowledge based on the senses deals with empirical reality and must be subordinated to divine knowledge, which is accessed first through sensory understanding and then through intuition: 'The knowledge of Truth is gained first through the senses and then through direct realization. Its ultimate stages cannot be encompassed within consciousness. Knowledge which cannot be circumscribed within consciousness and which is the final stage of Truth, is also called Love or Intuition' (p. 90, in Saiyidain, 1992). During the Middle Ages, Islamic philosophers and poets such as Rumi and Al Ghazzali wrote about the intuitive perception of the heart, which is to this day is a significant component of Islamic educational philosophy.[13]

Many writers engaged in the 'Islamization of knowledge' have pointed out that, because of colonialism and the imposition of Western secular education, revealed knowledge has been decentred as the basis of education in Muslim societies, and that the corollary aspects of spiritual development (such as intuition) have been decentred along with it (Al-Naquib al Attas, 1979; Ashraf & Husain, 1979; Qutb, 1979; Al Otaibi & Rashid, 1997; Safi, 1999; Shamma, 1999a). According to Safi (1999), 'the mission of Islamic education is to reintegrate the fragmented consciousness of modern man [sic] by once again repositioning divine revelation at the core of human consciousness, the binding and nurturing core which the secular project has managed to destroy' (p. 43). This, he argues, means that revelation must be reinstated as a source of knowledge. However, this must not involve relying solely on dogmatically interpreted texts; rather, 'both revelation and experienced reality should form the foundation for producing a body of knowledge dealing with modern social temporal challenges, while remaining true to the spirit, purposes and aspiration of transcendental truth' (pp. 43–4). Safi then writes that contemporary Islamic education must encompass responsibility for family, community, and humanity as well as a vision for social and environmental change based on empirical and spiritual knowledge.

This movement from knowledge to action can be understood as part of Islam's 'living curriculum.' In this sense, knowledge – both worldly and spiritual – is a catalyst for social, cultural, political, environmental, and individual change. As a path towards individual change, Islam as a 'living curriculum' relates to the ontological reality of being a 'Muslim.' This is echoed by Sahadat (1997), who contends that 'there is an existential challenge in Muslim education which seeks to lead the individual beyond the stage of "knowing" to the stage of. "being." Muslim education, therefore, poses an existential challenge with an ontological goal, when the state of comprehensive and total well being completes the process of knowing' (p. 25). The other existential challenge for Islamic education is to translate these epistemological goals into pedagogical possibilities. Much of the writing on the Islamization of knowledge in education examines the issue epistemologically rather than methodologically. The separation of secular and religious subjects in Islamic schools is antithetical to the goal of centring divine knowledge within every subject – an 'Islamocentric' approach – yet little work has been done to move this project forward. Safi (1999) points to efforts by the Council on Islamic Education (CIE) and the Council for Islamic Schools of North America (CISNA) in the United States to develop Islamically-centred curriculum, but adds that there is not enough community support to generate a more sustained and coordinated effort.

Shamma (1999a) examined the curriculum in the Sister Clara Muhammed schools in the United States, which were founded by the Nation of Islam. She noted that the Eurocentric curriculum of the state schools ran counter to an Islamic education, which should first and foremost be relevant to the lives of Muslim students. She pointed to the absence of Muslim writers in world literature texts; even more glaring, Muslims' contributions to Islamic history amounted to only 5.6 per cent of the 1,300-page textbook (p. 283). Shamma does not advocate removing all Eurocentric materials; she acknowledges that many Muslim-American children have European backgrounds that should be validated. However, she does maintain that a critical eye must be directed towards which materials are being used. For example, she critiques the representations of 'Othered' societies in many storybooks: 'Stories that take place in the home country are in clean, technological advanced, western garbed environments. Stories that take place in Africa, Asia or the Middle East are either non-existent or reflect "quaint" villages or wilderness areas like jungles, or fairy tale lands' (p. 285). In her view, creating a more culturally relevant Islamic curriculum requires that a *tawhidic* undercurrent be developed. In other words, in the textual materials being used, there must be a centring of an Islamic world view based on the consciousness of God. Such textual materials include storybooks, textbooks, and works of literature. She argues that 'culturally oriented reading materials should be included in order to include multicultural understanding and tolerance, which agrees with the tawhidic principle' (p. 291). She maintains that Muslim students in the United States need to be aware of their dual identity – American *and* Muslim – and in this regard she wants students to be provided with the required 'cultural capital' they need to negotiate these two aspects of their identity – capital that includes subjects such as civics and American history. However, the curriculum should be structured in such a way that it includes all the multicultural identifications of Muslim students,[14] while remaining centred on a *tawhidic* framework based on their identification, beliefs, and practices as Muslims.[15]

Selby (1992) examined teacher's experiences in an Islamic school in the United States, including the Islamization of the curriculum and the pedagogical practices followed to integrate Islamic knowledge into the curriculum. She found that while teachers selected less Eurocentric curricula for their classes and attempted to find materials that could be connected to the Islamic experience, the level of teaching ability at the school she observed made it difficult to implement the curriculum successfully. She called for more teacher development in Islamic schools and for the development of Islamic-centred curriculum.

In this study I will be taking up the need to bridge the gap between the Islamization of knowledge project, on the one hand, and actual school and teacher practices, on the other. This will help connect knowledge with praxis in the development of Islamic educational systems, on the basis that Islam is a 'living curriculum' and not simply an add-on subject or an abstract philosophy. In the following section I review existing research on Islamic schooling in diasporic contexts.

Muslims and Schooling: Research and Case Studies

Few studies of Islamic schools in North America have been published, and only a few relating to Britain. Ethnographic studies are even rarer. As mentioned in the previous section, Selby (1992) examined teaching practices in an Islamic school in the American Midwest. She focused on teaching methods, classroom management techniques, and the curriculum being followed. Selby found a 'mechanistic view of learning and teaching,' and she noted that the teachers 'were not operating from a single view of how Islam should revise the schooling experience' (p. 47). Some teachers attempted to Islamicize their courses; others treated Islamic knowledge as a footnote to standardized lessons. She concluded with a call for future research that would track the effects of Islamic education on students and that would reveal whether their education prepared them for life in American society or heightened their alienation from American culture.

In an overview of Islamic schools in the United States, Durkee (1987) examined the Sister Clara Muhammed schools, which at the time of her research comprised half of all Islamic schools in America. These schools are the oldest Islamic schools in North America, having been founded in Chicago by the Nation of Islam during the 1930s. Using the Qur'anic interpretations of their imam, Warith Deen Muhammed, Durkee noted that these schools provided the predominantly African-American Muslim community with a 'healthy, positive and moral Islamic environment,' in contrast to the crowded and troubled public schools in many large American cities. She found that the schools concentrated more on Islamic socialization rather than Islamization of the curriculum, primarily owing to the lack of time, knowledge, and money required to develop such curricula. These schools emphasized creating an 'Islamic ambience' through 'the teachers, the dress and behavioural codes, parent cooperation and the socialization of Muslim students with each other removed from the negative influences of public schools' (p. 72). In these schools, subjects such as Arabic and Islamic studies were taught alongside the standard curriculum determined by the state. She noted that African-American Muslims were the most marginalized Muslims in the United States, but that the community was proud of its Sister Clara Muhammed schools, regarding them as educational and social alternatives for youth who would have been disenfranchised in many public schools.

In her examination of other Islamic schools in the United States,

Durkee looked at the strategies that many Islamic schools under the auspices of the Council of Islamic Schools of North America (CISNA) were developing to integrate Islamic studies into subjects such as mathematics, science, history, and physical education. For example, geography was integrated with Islamic history so that as students learned the stories of the Prophets, they also learned about the region in a way that added a social geographical context to Islamic history. Science lessons used the many references in the Qur'an relating to the creation and structure of the universe as integral to the study of this branch of science. Durkee summarized the central goals of Islamizing education for Muslim youth in a diasporic context:

> We are attempting to instill in children certain traditional values which they may not find in many places in the modern world. Patience, through craftwork such as carpentry and weaving at an early age. Endurance, through long hikes and climbs in the surrounding mountains and along the river. Care, for both the environment and each other, taught often in science classes outside in the exploration of each stone and type of earth and bug and weed. Concentration, through the study of Arabic and the Holy Qur'an, through memorization and through the system of weaving together the materials of the different disciplines and making connections between them so the students can learn that knowledge is one thing. Reverence, through constant reference to the Creation and the Creator, through an ease and familiarity in speaking of all events as stemming from Allah ta'ala, through gratitude for their life, their families, their school, their din [religion] ... They begin their day with al-Fatiha[16] instead of 'I pledge allegiance to the flag of the United States of America.' They are Muslims first. (p. 80)

Durkee criticized the fact that many Islamic schools were hiring non-Muslim teachers. This, she argued, ran counter to attempts to Islamicize the curriculum in these schools, where teachers were expected to be role models as well as bearers of Islamic knowledge. Central to the educational goals of Islamic schools is the development of Islamic knowledge and praxis grounded in the Holy Qur'an and the sunnah (way of life) of the Prophet Muhammed. Islamic school teachers are expected to be exemplary models in both these aspects of Islamic education. According to Durkee 'the heart, light and soul of any Muslim school must be the constant and regular study of the Qur'an with a trained reader who can pass that tradition to the students. They must have knowledge *of* Qur'an not *about* the Qur'an. Without that study, the school is dead. With it no matter what else is taught or how, it is worth attending because of its light' (p. 75; emphasis in the original).

Islamic schools attempt to foster a social and cultural environment that is consistent with an Islamic world view and religious values. In a quantitative study of antisocial behaviour in Islamic schools, Abdus-Sabur (1995) found that drugs, alcohol, violence, and teen pregnancy were far less common in American Islamic schools than in public schools, and linked this to differences in values and moral standards between these school systems. Comparing American statistics on these antisocial behaviours with survey research conducted at eighty-seven Islamic schools, Abdus-Sabur made the following discoveries:

- Teen pregnancies were very unusual.
- Incidents of students carrying weapons were infrequent.
- Students rarely displayed aggressive behaviour towards staff or fellow students.
- Drug and alcohol use was very rare in Islamic schools (p. 57).

Such findings are attractive to parents who are searching for alternatives to the status quo of drugs, alcohol, violence, and teen pregnancy in most public schools.

Kelly (1997) conducted a qualitative research study that examined the social life of a full-time Canadian Muslim school in Montreal. A major theme of her study was the balance between 'community' and 'autonomy.' By this, she was referring to the role played by Islamic schools in developing a 'Muslim social identity' based on conformity with Islamic values and the concomitant desire to maintain some autonomy with regard to which aspects of that identity were emphasized (p. 114). She discussed the various ways in which members of the school community, including students, parents, teachers, and administrators, negotiated these boundaries. She cited, for example, the obligations of performing prayer. Students were required to attend the congregational prayers, yet teachers' participation was voluntary and often mediated by gendered cultural norms that made public prayer more obligatory for men to attend than for women. She also noted that the school's dress code required women to wear the hijab (headscarf);[17] teachers, however, were not expected to do so outside of school, though they were in some Islamic schools. Thus the negotiation between conformity and autonomy occurred at an ontological level, one that related to the different ways in which the epistemological precepts of Islamic practice were interpreted and lived.

Kelly also discussed the discrimination that Muslim students encountered in public schools, the lack of accommodation for religious practices, and the negative portrayals of Islam in the media, along with the reasons why many students opted out of public education in favour of Islamic schooling. And she noted the difficulties that Muslims encountered in their efforts to integrate with Québécois culture, as well as the dominance of the Christian religious orientation in schools, which left Muslims feeling both excluded and at the same time fearful of being assimilated, with the consequent loss of identity for their children. She found that in Islamic schools, parents saw greater opportunities for their children to develop the 'psychological strength' they would need in order to maintain their Islamic identity and lifestyle – something they could not do as a minoritized group in the public school system (p. 104).

Osler and Hussain (1995) examined the attitudes and values of twenty Muslim women in Britain towards their daughters' education, particularly with respect to their choice between a private Islamic school and a state primary school. Mothers who chose an Islamic school for their daughters felt a strong need for continuity between the values and beliefs at home and those promoted at school. Mothers who opted for state primary schools also felt strongly about Islamic values, but at the same time they felt that many core values, such as honesty, sharing, and caring for others in the community, were also espoused within the public schools. Even so, these mothers expressed certain concerns with regard to male/female interaction (which is usually limited in the Islamic context) and to the use of foul and disrespectful language towards elders, which some saw as a by-product of public schooling.

Yuval-Davis and Sagal (1992) and the organization Women Against Fundamentalism have criticized religious schools for concerning themselves only with 'bringing up dutiful wives' and compromising on academic standards for girls. She questions the notion that women from religious communities find a sense of empowerment in fundamentalist movements, suggesting that more consideration should be given to what the parameters of this empowerment are. The term 'fundamentalism', however, is considered a misnomer by some Muslims, who do not use it as a means of self-definition and in fact regard it as pejorative and as a signifier of Islamophobia (Parker-Jenkins, 1995). That said, there is a spectrum of beliefs among Muslims, ranging from conservative to liberal, and the same can be said of the ideological orientations of Islamic schools. Thus it is irresponsible to brand all such schools as 'fundamentalist' and antifemale. This highlights the need for more research to gauge the complexities of Muslim women's relationship to Islam in terms of the dynamics of Islamic schooling.

Yet Khanum (1995) did find some basis for Yuval-Davis's concerns about Islamic girls' schools with regard to academic standards and course choices. In 1985 she examined one school in particular that, one year after opening, still offered limited choices in subjects such as Urdu, child care, and religious studies. This would seem to corroborate Yuval-Davis's concerns that these schools were simply producing 'dutiful wives.' By 1990, however, the same school had added English and French and was promising that maths and sciences would soon follow. Khanum noted that the school lacked resources and properly trained teachers and argued that its students were not receiving an adequate education. In her interviews with the students, she found that girls saw education as a source of empowerment that would keep them off the marriage market: 'the education of Muslim girls has less to do with schooling than with the exercise of control by Muslim men over the lives of women in the family and in the wider community' (p. 282). This control, according to Khanum, translated into regulating and policing the interactions between unmarried men and women.

Other research on Islamic girls' schools in Britain provides different stories. Haw (1994) compared a single-sex state school and an Islamic school for girls and found that in the Islamic school environment, which was free from racialized tensions, Muslim girls were able to develop more 'feminist' subjectivities than their counterparts in state schools. She found that in the state school, 'Muslim students are less confident about being a Muslim student in an environment where being a Muslim woman is an issue' (p. 59). The fact that their identity as Muslim women was at issue had to do with the predominantly non-Muslim teachers, who found it difficult to deal with the 'complexities of difference' in their multicultural school. Haw reported that in British public or state schools, Muslim girls were subject to many negative preconceptions about their identity, religion, culture, and family life – misconceptions that sometimes inhibited them from developing strong notions of womanhood and selfhood as Muslims. She maintained that a more congruent and comfortable environment allowed

Muslim girls, who would have felt alienated in public schools, to concentrate more on academic achievement. Comparing the context for Muslim girls in single-sex public schools and Islamic schools, Haw noted: 'In this environment [Islamic school] it is "normal" to be a Muslim girl and this fact is celebrated. This means that there is a wider range of discursive positions open to them than their counterparts in City State and they are enabled to take these up because they receive an education couched in their own values. At any given moment, it is shared experience, shared knowledge and shared culture which is built upon' (pp. 58–9).

In her subsequent book, *Educating Muslim Girls,* Haw (1998) drew on the same data from two single-sex schools – one urban public school and one private Islamic school – and examined the relationship between teachers (often white and non-Muslim) and their female Muslim students, exploring how these relationships were affected by different educational settings and experiences. She used a Foucauldian post-structuralist framework to ground a feminist analysis of the two single-sex schooling contexts and their impact on Muslim girls' sense of identity and future aspirations, pointing out that this framework is useful in interrogating issues of power and discursive knowledge as it is implicated in the schooling experiences of these girls.

Written in collaboration with Muslim women (who co-wrote some chapters), Haw's ethnographic account described the cultural and historical background of these predominantly South Asian students and discussed the gender dynamics of Britain's South Asian diasporic community. She used 'insiders' to map out the social and cultural context that had given rise to the development of Islamic schools in Britain. These same people provided narrative insights into these schools' development, structure, governance, and pedagogy. According to these accounts, gender, religious, and cultural issues have driven the development of Islamic schools (p. 75). The same book discusses parents' expectations of these schools; these are framed by the norms and conventions of their own schooling in Pakistan and by their desire to recreate an *ummah* (Muslim community) in the diaspora. In comparing the public 'City State' school with the Islamic 'Old Town High,' the researchers found stronger formal and informal links between parents and the Islamic school. Minoritized Muslim parents with children in the public school system did not have the same level of comfort or confidence when dealing with school authorities. The narratives of non-Muslim teachers provided evidence of racism and frustration in dealing with parents owing to a lack of understanding of their cultural and religious backgrounds.

Finally, Haw analysed a fiction-writing activity she assigned to participating girls in both schools: she asked them to write an 'imaginative story' about the aspirations of a girl named 'Nazrah' who attended an inner-city comprehensive school. Muslim girls from both schools as well as some non-Muslim girls from the public state school were asked what Nazrah's life must be like and what she would be doing when she was twenty-five years old. The findings from this exercise – which was designed to reveal how these girls in the different school environments viewed their own social, cultural, and academic aspirations and possibilities, as well as how non-Muslim girls evaluated the life chances of Muslim girls – were that Islamic school students were more positive than the others regarding Narzah's academic and personal future. The second most positive assessment came from the Muslim girls in the public state school; the third most positive, from the non-Muslim girls. Haw regarded these variations as 'signs that the [Muslim] students were concerned about conforming to traditional stereotypes of femininity' (p. 138).

Haw used discourse analysis to analyse these stories, which spoke to the girls' hopes, fears, and struggles with tradition and conformity. Those stories provided different perspectives on how parents viewed girls' educational aspirations: some parents supported their participation in higher academic learning, while others discouraged it. Britain's Swann Committee report on education had criticized Islamic schools for not promoting higher academic learning for girls; Haw's research findings challenged this view (p. 135).

Finally, the stories Haw analysed expressed common themes such as identity, religion, the *bradari* (community) gaze,[18] arranged marriage, honour, and tensions within the community between Islamic precepts and cultural/patriarchal practices. They also provided evidence, according to Haw, of how Muslim girls and women negotiate their own personal and social contexts while at the same time 'being objects of the discourses which make up their lives' (p. 139). According to Haw, these fictionalized stories revealed the various 'discourses of Muslimness' operating inside and outside of school – discourses that were related to those of the family and *bradari*/kinship network, local and national politics, and the student's racial, ethnic, class, cultural, and religious positionings (p. 139).

As fictionalized accounts the stories provide interesting reflections, but they cannot be treated the same as other kinds of ethnographic accounts that focus on lived experiences. These stories were an exercise in creative writing, so it is fair to suggest that the girls used a good deal of literary licence when constructing them. Thus there is no way for us to correlate accurately between these accounts and what the writers actually perceived to be 'true' about their own social and cultural position. Furthermore, the stories written by non-Muslim girls were the least positive assessments of Nazrah's future aspirations and life chances, yet Haw did not publish these accounts. In this way she left out an important aspect of the discursive construction of Muslim girls' identities: the readings provided by non-Muslim peers. These accounts, had Haw provided them, would have rounded out the discussion to include how those from outside the community – who also wield the discursive power to inscribe meaning on the category of 'Muslimness' – developed their stories of Nazrah's life. Without access to and analysis of these stories, an important dimension is missing from Haw's discussion.

Halstead (1991) conducted research on Islamic girls' schools in Britain and reported that many feminists supported the idea of single-sex schooling 'as a means of countering a bias toward males and encouraging women to respect other women in an atmosphere free from male domination and harassment' (p. 262). Yet many feminists also suggested that Muslims use single-sex Islamic schools as a means to perpetuate traditional views of women's role in society. Halstead contended that some feminists may have 'unwittingly taken on board Western male prejudices about Islam' and that feminists and Muslims may have common ground on which to articulate common political goals for female-centred education.

The present study takes an ethnographic approach in order to provide a more comprehensive examination of the social and ideological formations of Islamic schooling. It takes a more holistic view than past research regarding (a) the role and function of Islamic schools in a diasporic setting and (b) the gendered social relations that develop in these schools. This study also explores the Islamization of knowledge in these schools. In this way, it contributes to the literature by building new empirical and discursive understandings of the social, ideological, and structural role of Islamic schools in Canada's Muslim diaspora.

Religious Education: Current Debates

Religiously segregated schools have often been criticized for promoting a form of 'religious apartheid.' Defenders of common schools argue that religiously or culturally segregated schools amount to a rejection of liberal democratic values and discourage the positive possibilities of cultural pluralism (Gutmann, 1996). Sweet (1997) also resists the balkanization of public schools along religious lines; she argues that this practice discourages the sort of dialogue and debate that can lead to effective citizenship in a pluralistic society. Yet she also realizes that governments' inflexibility in dealing with religion in public schools has forced many religious families to opt out of the public school system. She argues that the success of liberal multiculturalism lies in the development of more inclusive practices, including a funding formula to keep religious schools inside rather than outside public education.

In Ontario, equality of education funding has become an increasingly salient issue, especially since a 1999 UN tribunal found the Ontario government in violation of humans rights for funding only Catholic schools to the exclusion of other religious schools. In 1996, in *Adler v. Ontario,* the Supreme Court of Canada rejected the arguments of Jewish and Protestant parents that the Ontario Education Act, which limits public funding of education to non-denominational public and Catholic separate schools, violated their Charter rights. The legal challenge was then taken to the UN; meanwhile, religious communities continued to build alliances to force the Ontario government to respond to what they perceived as the violation of their right to religious freedom. The provincial government has since responded with a new controversial law that offers tax credits for parents sending their children to denominational or non-denominational private schools. This decision has been widely criticized by public education advocates, who argue that already limited funds will be siphoned from public schools and channelled into the private sector, including many elite schools.

Some Muslim groups had joined the multifaith coalition Ontario Parents for Equality in Education Funding (OPEEF) in order to advocate for funding for religious schools. Supporters of Islamic schools have long been on the defensive with respect to how Islamic schools are often seen as 'ghettos' for Muslim children and as denying their students opportunities to engage the broader society. The term 'ghetto' as used here has negative and racialized connotations. Yet the same negative terminology is not used against supporters of the publicly funded Catholic school system, despite past objections to these separate schools (see Sweet, 1997; Thiessen, 2001). Here, the term is being used strategically, to undermine the claims of other, more marginalized religious groups.

Liberal critics, such as Gutmann (1996), argue that all religious or culturally based schools are part of a 'separatist multicultural perspective' and are 'designed primarily to sustain the separatist cultural identities of minorities and to bolster the self-esteem of students on the basis of their membership in a separatist culture' (p. 158). Yet as Halstead (1991) noted in his analysis of Muslim schooling in Britain, Muslims in public schools face social isolation when white British parents refuse to send their children to Muslim-populated schools: 'A pattern now emerging in some cities is for White parents to stop sending their daughters to a girls' secondary school when there is a substantial proportion of Muslim girls at the school, so that the school then quickly takes on the nature of a "ghetto" school' (p. 275). Despite being part of the public education system, this process of racial exclusion and social distance therefore leads to these schools becoming de facto separate institutions for Muslims.

In liberal discourse, the debates on religion and education funding rage around issues such as multiculturalism, individual and group rights in a pluralistic society, and the dangers of religious fundamentalism. Some of the key questions that emerge from these debates will be addressed here: Are common schools and separate schools sites for competition, or can they develop a symbiotic co-existence? Can the balkanization of the public school system – which many argue will occur if religious schools are funded – be mitigated through greater inclusion of religiously minoritized groups in public schools? Within a liberal paradigm of education, can a case be made for state-funded separate schools? Is it possible to have liberal religious schools that produce good civic citizens? Do tax credits really serve the interests of community-based religious schools? How do we address the challenges of equity versus equality in education funding? Questions such as these are fuelling the ongoing public debates surrounding the issue of funding for religious schools in Ontario. The divergent perspectives on the nature of schooling and society in a liberal democratic society, however, are rarely debated from an antiracism perspective that includes Muslim voices.

Negotiating Pluralism and Religious Minority Rights in Education

Discussions framing the issue of pluralism and religious minority rights in education generally take place within the discursive framework of liberal multiculturalism. Proponents of this perspective argue that religiously segregated schools compromise a pluralistic society by creating separate cultural and faith-based enclaves. It is argued that balkanization of the school system robs public education of the diversity it needs in order to foster a truly multicultural society united under a common national narrative and socio-political framework (Gutmann, 1996; Callon, 1997). While the notion of a pluralistic common school system is to be lauded, pluralism in practice too often refers merely to the physical presence of students from culturally diverse backgrounds; it does not extend to accommodating a diversity of views within schools' 'official knowledge.' A truly inclusive school system requires that multiple centres of knowledge be represented as the basis for public education, not just the essentially Eurocentric and secular knowledge that dominates most public education institutions (Dei, James-Wilson, & Zine, 2001). In this regard, religious schools offer alternatives to the hegemony of secular,[19] Eurocentric education, by centring spiritually based knowledge and practice as a core component of learning.

A political counter-narrative to liberal multiculturalism's too often paternal treatment of the rights of racially and religiously minoritized groups flows from an antiracism perspective that squarely addresses the issues of social, political, and discursive power in public education and that also leaves room for alternatives to Eurocentric schooling, such as Afrocentric schools (see Dei, 1996). Gutmann (1996) argues that Afrocentric schools represent a 'separatist particularism' that is incompatible with liberal goals, since they (in her view) teach that 'African values are superior to Western values' (p. 158). Liberal educational thinkers like Gutmann view multiculturalism as a corrective to cultural bias in that it focuses on cultural diversity rather than cultural separatism. However, multicultural education has failed to move beyond a 'tourist curriculum' that features 'saris, samosas, and steel bands' as entry points into cultural knowledge. This 'events'-oriented approach to cultural diversity has done little to decentre secular Eurocentric knowledge as the privileged way of knowing in multiethnic/multifaith public schools. I would argue that secular Eurocentric knowledge represents the hegemonic way of knowing in public schools. Furthermore, it masquerades as a universal and neutral space, though in fact it is biased and culturally situated. Moreover, by virtue of its exclusivity it imparts superiority and invalidates other ways of knowing, especially those which are religiously centred.

By contrast, independent schools that are based on cultural values or religious beliefs are seeking to move the realities and experiences of their students from the margins of education to the centre. Gutmann (1996) would have it that separate schools that bolster cultural self-esteem do so at the risk of undercutting mutual respect among citizens. Her assumption is that these schools are teaching that the contributions of the students' ancestors are superior, which would contravene liberal conventions by imposing a particular view of the 'good life'. For an antiracist, a valid response to this critique is that in many mainstream Eurocentric schools, the contributions of marginalized communities have long been absent from the curriculum. This omission serves to secure the dominance of Eurocentric norms, values and history. Reclaiming these historical contributions hardly undercuts mutual respect; indeed, it reinforces respect while neutralizing the superiority of the dominant culture. Thiessen (2001) argues further that in a pluralistic society, religiously and culturally based schools enhance rather than hinder social harmony: 'Allowing for schools which are an expression of cultural/religious traditions, while at the same time ensuring that these schools teach liberal democratic values, will do much more to create harmony within a pluralistic society than the imposition of liberal values and multicultural programs within an environment that is alien to students from minority cultural or religious traditions' (p. 244).

Gutmann is opposed to independent schools; she does, however, support an inclusive curriculum in public education – one that represents cultural diversity in such a way that all individuals have equal civic standing. But when we are asserting the notion of 'equal civic standing,' we must do so in ways which address the reality that civic engagement is mediated by social conditions that are unequal in the present day. Forgetting this can only result in a bland, uncritical multiculturalism that does not address issues of power and privilege in society.

Also from a liberal educational perspective, Callon (1997) examines the argument that the common school operates as a vehicle of civic education by perpetuating the ideal of 'deliberative democracy,' which encourages 'open discussion in which diverse views are voiced and collectively evaluated, make, apply, and revise the norms by which their community lives' (p. 24). Callon argues that religious schools, though they inculcate positive values, are unable to provide the required approach to a good civic education and therefore cannot produce a good liberal citizenry. Callon goes on to say: 'Religious schooling may encourage much else that is laudable from a civic standpoint, but they *cannot* be arenas for inclusive deliberation by virtue of their exclusive religious identity' (pp. 24–5; emphasis in the original).

Yet it can be argued that mainstream public schools also impose a singular moral hegemonic point of view, based on secularism and Eurocentrism. As noted earlier, that point of view masquerades as a universal way of knowing when in fact it is culturally situated in opposition to faith-centred world views and also maintains fidelity to a particular partisan worldview or view of 'the good life.' McLaughlin (1992) argues that for various reasons the common school may not meet the needs of all students (be it on religious, cultural, or special needs grounds). He adds that from a social justice perspective, the liberal framework *can* support separate schools, provided that those schools develop critical rationality and independence. He argues that there can be more than one legitimate form of liberal education and schooling, that these various forms can all be starting points for a child's journey towards autonomy and liberal citizenship, and that these forms may start from a particular world view or cultural identity. Spinner-Halev (1997) refers to this as 'moderate separatism,' in the sense that early childhood and elementary education in religiously based schools can encourage greater knowledge of self without compromising the knowledge of others. Furthermore, this knowledge of others may develop in sites other than schools or through transition to common schooling in higher grades.

Debates on religious education within the Muslim community have also produced arguments against independent religious schooling. For example, Jafri and Fatah (2003) maintain that 'most Muslim parents wish their children to grow and become educated in a climate of diversity, where they can learn to respect and understand the faiths of others, while being exemplary ambassadors of Islam and peace. Muslims do not believe in the segregation and ghettoization of their communities' (A17). They further argue that tax credits for families who are sending their children to private schools only serve to isolate religious minorities from the mainstream by encouraging separate social and educational enclaves. In the run-up to the last Ontario provincial election, when Conservative party leader John Tory called for provincial funding for religious schools, the Muslim Canadian Congress (MCC) responded with the following statement against his plan:

> MCC insists that immigrant parents do not have the right to deny their children full access to the opportunities that are available to all Canadians. Every child has the right to learn with and from children of other backgrounds, to be taught the rights and duties of a Canadian citizen, to master Canada's official languages. Every child has the right to learn Canada's culture, which includes history, the rights and freedoms which are embedded in the Canadian constitution, our vast and unique geography, our music, sports, literature, how Canadians do business, and how we interact with each other formally and socially. Immigrants who have chosen Canada must allow their children to become Canadian.
>
> MCC cannot support schools which undermine the values that we and other Canadians cherish. If a school wishes to promote discrimination against women, or against people of other races or religions, if it is not totally committed to our democratic and pluralistic society, then MCC is vehemently opposed. Such schools should not even exist – let alone collect public money. Such schools are no place for the children of moderate Muslims. The values which are important to progressive Muslims are best taught and learned in public school systems. (24 July 2007, http://www.MuslimCanadianCongress.org)

It is ironic that as the self-proclaimed vanguard for 'moderate Muslims,' the MCC has been propounding a right-wing perspective on the need for immigrants to assimilate and become 'Canadian.' The MCC assumes, wrongly, that Canadian history, geography, and literature are not being taught in Islamic schools, when in fact these subjects are part of the required curriculum. The above statement frames the debate in black-and-white terms; it labels religious schools as inherently sexist, racist, and antidemocratic in a way that suggests that public schools are blissfully unencumbered by the challenges of these and other forms of discrimination. In addition, the MCC in that statement is branding immigrants as a pervasive threat to democratic values. It is saying that provincial funding for religious schools would reinforce racist and xenophobic ideologies about backward foreigners clinging to outmoded lifestyles and refusing to engage the body politic. In all these ways, the MCC is reinforcing Islamophobia and self-servingly playing the good 'progressive Muslim' against other 'bad Muslims.' Such narrow arguments locate injustices only in the camp of religious schools and institutions and allow public schools and institutions to remain unexamined and unaccountable.

Supporters of independent religious schools argue for greater inclusion in the educational funding formulas. A 1985 report on private schools in Ontario suggested a number of funding models, some of which would keep independent schools within the public domain as 'associated schools' – in other words, they would operate within the public system and be accountable to the province (Shapiro, 1985). Sweet (1997) has discussed multifaith schools in the Netherlands. In that country, they coexist with mainstream schools, receive full government funding, and in some cases share common complex; all of this reduces the barriers of isolation. Alternatives like these are worth considering when funding equity is being debated.

Mapping the Book

Chapters 1 to 3 of this book present the discursive and philosophical issues that are germane to contemporary dialogues and debates in religious education. They also address the methodological procedures I followed for this study, which takes a critical ethnographic approach. Chapters 4 to 8 present narrative analyses, which feature the voices of Muslim students, parents, and teachers. Here, key areas of the research are addressed – those that relate to the role and function of Islamic schools, the development of gendered identities and gender dynamics in schools, the Islamization of knowledge through curriculum and praxis, and the politics of teaching and learning in Islamic schools.

Chapter 2 presents four discursive paradigms that will be employed in this study to situate and guide the analyses of empirical findings:

• A critical faith-centred epistemology (Zine, 2001a) that provides a new discursive location for centring faith-centred knowledge, research, and praxis.
• An anticolonial discursive framework (Dei & Azgharzadeh, 2001) that identifies and counters colonial oppressions as they manifest themselves in the world today. The colonization of knowledge within the secular, Eurocentric public school system and the marginalization of religious and spiritually based ways of knowing

make the development of independent schools based on these subjugated knowledges part of an anticolonial discursive process.
• Integrative antiracism (Dei, 1996), which is used to examine the Eurocentric basis of public education. A demand for independent religious schools flows from this. This paradigm is a response to those
liberal education theorists who criticize religious schools for impeding the development of civic values and deliberative democracy.
• Foucauldian post-structuralism, which is employed to help frame
an understanding of how discourses structure subjectivities. In
particular, a feminist post-structuralist lens will be adopted in
order to examine the complex processes whereby gendered identities are constructed through socialization and schooling practices.

Chapter 3 offers an overview of the research methodology employed in this study, as well as an outline of the critical ethnographic
approach taken. The participants and the schools included in the study
are described. As well, a detailed account of the field research and
observations is outlined.

The narrative analyses of the ethnographic data begin in chapter 4,
which starts with a discussion of the role and function of Islamic
schools in a diasporic context. This chapter examines Islamic schooling
and the sociological and ideological role such schools play in the diaspora. The narratives of students, teachers, parents, and community
activists speak to the place of Islamic schooling in the Canadian
Muslim community.

Chapters 5 and 6 explore how gendered identities are constructed in
Islamic schools. Chapter 5 centres on the narratives of Muslim girls in
an Islamic high school and discusses their concerns about 'gendered
Islamophobia' and the politics of veiling. Chapter 6 explores the rules
of gender interaction in Islamic schools. In examining the various discourses that serve to structure the subjectivities of Muslim girls, the
analysis incorporates a post-structuralist feminist perspective.

Chapter 7 examines the Islamization of knowledge and practice in
Islamic schools. This chapter deals primarily with the narratives of
teachers and school administrators as they reflect on how Islamic
knowledge informs their pedagogy and practice and how they use
various methods to teach the otherwise secular Ontario curriculum
within an Islamically centred framework. Also discussed are transformative strategies for recrafting secular curriculum and for developing
more Islamically based methods for disciplining and counselling stu-

dents. Also examined are issues of social justice as curricular imperatives for a critical faith-centred perspective.

Chapter 8 continues to explore curricular and pedagogical issues in Islamic schools. Academic standards and teacher qualifications are discussed; so are the benefits and drawbacks that teachers associate with working in Islamic schools. Teachers, administrators, parents, and students address the politics of teaching and learning in underfunded independent religious schools. Also discussed are gender-based equity and access in the curriculum, teachers as role models, and approaches to discipline.

Chapter 9 contextualizes and deconstructs discursive practices in Islamic education. By means of those practices, knowledge is 'flowed' to students through the formal and hidden curriculum. Discursive practices shape the rhetorical and textual practices of both the school and the community; they also shape the pedagogy and socialization strategies, as well as schools' everyday practices; all of this impacts the discursive construction of the student's subjectivities as 'Muslims.' The chapter also addresses the challenges Islamic schools are confronting and provides some concrete recommendations for improving and reforming Islamic education. The recommendations, which are based on the grounded knowledge derived from the ethnographic research, are in accordance with the principles proposed for a critical faith-centred epistemological framework. These principles address the broader structural organization, including the roles of parents and school administrators in the social and political framework of Islamic schools. Finally, an examination of innovations of thought and practice in Islamic education leads to a mapping out of possible future directions.

2 Framing the Analyses: An Examination of the Discursive Frameworks

Discursive versus Theoretical Frameworks

The following chapters are informed by the discursive understandings presented here as critical frameworks for engagement with ongoing debates and dialogues in Islamic education, as well as for the narrative inquiry based on the empirical, ethnographic data. This chapter situates the analyses in this study within these specific conceptual and ideological frameworks. I use the term 'discursive frameworks' to indicate the particular lenses I have used for examining the data in this study. I use this term rather than 'theoretical framework' in order to highlight a difference in the epistemological approach. In contrast to the way in which theoretical frameworks are often operationalized, a discursive framework does not imply a rigid, a priori paradigm or set of presumed postulates that guide the research towards predetermined conclusions. A discursive framework *does* provide foundational principles and epistemic boundaries; but it also allows paradigms and conceptual constructs to develop through the process of creating a grounded theory from the empirical findings. Put more simply, an emergent theory evolves from a discursive framework, instead of being the construct from which the inquiry begins.

A discursive framework provides philosophical principles, as well as the foundations for building knowledge production through an inductive, hermeneutic process. In this type of discursive analysis, particular knowledge gained in the field is related back to the discursive frame as part of an epistemological engagement with the philosophical and ideological grounding the framework provides. This process of engagement allows for dialogical interface between the data and the framework. Discursive frameworks can therefore be conceptualized as fluid spaces that engage dialogically, resist academic closure, and provide an ideological context in which the data can develop into theories of the particular. This is not simply trading the universalism of grand narratives for the particularism of grounded theories; rather, it allows opportunities to examine the tensions as well as the intersections of particular historicized and contextualized phenomena in relation to general (albeit not necessarily universal) philosophical discursive foundations.

Employing Multiple Lenses for Critical Enquiry

The discursive frameworks used in this study's analyses emanate from four main epistemological foundations:

- A critical faith-centred epistemology (Zine, 2001).
- An anticolonial discursive framework (Dei, 2001a; Dei & Asgharzadeh, 2001).
- Integrative antiracism (Dei, 1996).
- A Foucauldian framework for analysing discourse, power, and subjectivity (Foucault, 1982). Particular attention will be paid to how these issues have been taken up in post-structuralist feminism.

The use of multiple frameworks reflects the variety of issues being examined, and their complexity. This approach will also help articulate the political perspective I have chosen in order to interrogate the issues emanating from this research.

Each of these frameworks attends to the various social, cultural, political, pedagogical, and ideological aspects of the issues under investigation. Given the range and scope of issues, the use of a single framework would only restrict the sociological critique and vision required for the task of interpreting the data. Multiple discursive frames will allow a more nuanced reading of the empirical data and provide opportunities for more fine-grained analyses. Fidelity to only one of these frameworks would have restricted the development of a more comprehensive analysis, one capable of integrating the philosophical standpoints provided by each of these discursive frames. Foucault suggests that in place of an underlying grand theory, the various discourses of a period may form an 'episteme.' The episteme is not that which unites the different discourses; rather, it is the space those discourses inhabit – a 'space of dispersion ... an open field of relationships' (McHoul & Grace, 1993, p. 45). I will be utilizing this notion of an open field of discursive relationships that can be used to define new epistemological vantage points when multiple yet complimentary paradigms are combined.

The political imperatives embedded in these paradigms reflect my deliberate choice to view the issues in this study from a particular vantage point – that of anti-oppression. Thus the frameworks chosen for this study are not just organically connected to the data; they are also connected to one another through their common fundamental purpose, which is to unmask how issues of knowledge, power, and social difference frame the pedagogical engagements being investigated.

Next I outline the philosophical foundations for each of these frameworks and how they are connected to the issues being investigated.

Introducing a Critical Faith-Centred Epistemology

In attempting to situate my analysis of Islamic schools in a way that would attend to the various religious, social, political, cultural, and gender issues under examination, I was constantly frustrated in my efforts to discover a single framework that would allow a complex analysis within these domains of inquiry. Most frameworks lacked a truly holistic engagement with spirituality and religious knowledge; nor were they completely amenable to the need – when dealing with a community defined on the basis of adherence to a common faith – to bring these issues and concerns to the centre of discursive focus. I would have to develop a framework capable of accommodating the required 'faith-centred' perspective, if I hoped to situate the issues relating to Islamic schooling within a broad paradigm that was organically connected to the way faith-centred people see the world and their place within it.

I developed this framework after conducting the field research and preliminary data analysis for this study and subsequently beginning a new project that sought to construct a new, faith-centred genealogy for Muslim women's feminism and praxis (Zine, 2004). In the course of these projects, I came to realize that I would have to build an epistemological framework that utilized faith-based knowledge as a lens for a particular reading of the world. Conventional paradigms of knowledge in the social sciences had never constructed that particular lens.

In political and discursive terms, developing such a framework involved creating a space from which faith-centred voices could enter critical academic and political debates and dialogues as valid sources of knowledge and contestation. Spiritual knowledges in the academy are subjugated knowledges delegitimated by the canons of secularism. Secular knowledge masquerades as a universal standard, though in fact it is merely one among many possible paths to knowledge. The dominance and perceived universality of this perspective silences other understandings – spiritual, metaphysical, and cosmological. Efforts to integrate spiritually centred ways of knowing as part of legitimate academic knowledge building and pedagogical praxis are being proposed as part of a broader challenge to Eurocentrism and the colonization of knowledge in education (see, for example, Dei, James, James-Wilson, Karumanchery, & Zine, 2000). According to Dei (2001, p. 2), 'the study of spirituality is appropriately captured within an anti-colonial prism which challenges and denies the imposition of knowledges through power, colonial and imperial relations.' Put another way, addressing the erasures of spiritual knowledge in academic and discursive contexts is part of an anticolonial politics of knowledge construction, reclamation, and inclusion.

Unpacking Spirituality

At this point, it is important to discuss the relationship between religion and spirituality, as well as the differences between these. Spirituality is intrinsic to religious beliefs and practices but is not confined to organized religion and theology. In a number of traditions and belief systems, spirituality is broadly defined and can even encompass the secular.[1] Thus, monotheism is a particular spiritual orientation that flows from a singular divine source. In many traditions, including Islam, spirituality has strong connections to social, economic, cultural, ecological, and political practices. Also, spiritual world views that operate outside religious dogmas often entail a more individualistic or 'self-styled' approach to moral issues: it is individuals, not religious orthodoxies, that determine moral behaviour. Conversely, within religious paradigms moral boundaries are constructed on the basis of doctrinal or prophetic sources.

Within the critical faith-centred paradigm, attempts have been made to develop broad principles that reflect various orientations towards spirituality and spiritual engagement. This perspective's emphasis on 'criticality' relates to the ways in which faith-centred people can identify, counter, and resist racism, classism, and sexism from a spiritually centred space – a space, however, that is at the same time attentive to the ways in which extremist or fundamentalist religious dogmas can become complicit in these constructions and in the structural relations and circumstances that sustain them. This epistemological framework will be applied in an Islamic context in this study, but can also be applied more broadly to other faith traditions.

Foundations for a Critical Faith-Centred Epistemology

Next I outline the philosophical principles for a critical faith-centred epistemological framework. The principles I elaborate are rooted in a specific moral terrain. As a guiding philosophy I identify four key elements of an Islamic epistemology; together, they will inform the principles of the critical faith-centred framework. All four are constituent elements of Islamic epistemology and as such transcend the various sectarian differences. This approach is necessary if we are to anchor this framework in common spiritual ground. The four discursive anchors are the following Islamic principles: peace, social and environmental justice, unity, and accountability. All four are central to Qur'anic knowledge and provide the moral grounding and discursive orientation on which the principles of the critical faith-centred epistemology can be constructed.

Peace, as a guiding moral imperative, is central to Islam; indeed, 'Islam' is the Arabic word for 'peace' and 'submission' to the Creator. Several hadith (sayings of the Prophet) highlight the centrality of peace and justice to Islam.[2] It follows that striving for peace is an important foundation on which to build the critical faith-centred framework, and that so is developing a critical understanding of the structural and ideological conditions that limit opportunities for peace and justice in the world.

Social and environmental justice is referred to a number of times in Islamic texts. Some of these occasions refer to the symbiotic relationship that must exist between people and the natural environment. For example, there are Qur'anic verses that refer to humans as the 'caretakers of the earth' and that warn Muslims against reckless exploitation of the environment. It is even forbidden to destroy fruit-bearing trees. Regarding social justice, Muslims are instructed by the hadith to 'neither suffer nor inflict inequity.'[3] Similarly, the Prophet in his final *khutba* (sermon) provides a clear basis for a spiritually centred antiracism paradigm: 'There is no White superior to Black, or Black superior to White. There is no Arab superior to non-Arab. People are differentiated only through their piety and good actions.' As Abou El Fadl (2002, p. 14) points out, the Qur'anic conception of justice is predicated on a high level of moral agency; Muslims are enjoined to stand up for justice even if it goes against their own interests. This is reflected in the following verse from the Qur'an: 'Oh you who believe, stand firmly for justice as witnesses for God, even if it means testifying against yourselves, or your parents or your kin, or whether it is against the rich or poor, because God prevails upon all. Follow not the lusts of your heart lest you swerve, and if you distort justice or decline to do justice, verily God knows what you do' (4:135). Perhaps it is this verse that inspired the great Muslim leader Malcolm X to declare: 'I am for truth no matter who tells it. I am for justice no matter who it is for or against' (in Myers & Jenkins, 2000, p. 32). These are only a few examples of Islam's strong support for social and environmental justice.

In its Islamic conception, *unity* has a number of meanings, which are all interrelated. For example, it can be applied to the *ummah* – that is, the supranational, supraterritorial community of Muslims. As a form of pan-Islamic identification, the *ummah* is the basis on which Muslims align themselves with their fellow believers spiritually and socially; it is their site of religious solidarity and as such transcends cultural differences. Unity also relates to the oneness of all humanity as the creation of God. For example, the Qur'an informs all humankind that 'you have been created as nations and tribes so that you may know one another' (49:13). This, then, speaks to the social aspects of unity. Another significant dimension of unity in the Islamic context is the notion of *tawheed*, or the Unity of God. The Oneness of the Creator is central to Islamic monotheism, for it speaks to the source of revealed knowledge.

Integral to all social and political paradigms is a mechanism of *accountability*, which refers to one's responsibility to a Creator or Higher Power, a responsibility that shapes one's ethics and the actions that flow out of them. In this sense, accountability is an especially important concept in indigenous epistemologies, which in spiritual terms are rooted more deeply in social and physical realities (see Dei, 2001b; Castellano, 1999). By contrast, secular humanist constructions

of accountability are shaped by individual moral and political conceptions.[4] Accountability is vital to a critical faith-based framework because it provides sustained moral grounding and purpose, not only as
an epistemological paradigm, but also as a means for situating specific
forms of liberatory social praxis.

The philosophical foundations I propose for a critical faith-centred
epistemology encompass seven key principles. These seven capture
the essence of this framework as an emergent paradigm for faith-
centred thought to be applied as a critical analytical tool for academic,
political, and social engagement. My hope is that the principles provide a concise yet comprehensive basis for examination.

*First principle: A philosophy of holism, or connections among the physical,
intellectual, and spiritual aspects of identity and identification.* In Islamic
thought the material, intellectual, and spiritual realms do not form an
artificial trichotomy; rather, they are seen as intrinsically connected
and mutually interdependent aspects of being. These essential aspects
of Muslim ontology are articulated by the renowned Pakistani poet
and philosopher Muhammed Iqbal: 'The evolution of life shows that
though in the beginning, the mental is dominated by the physical – the
mental as it grows in power tends to dominate the physical and may
eventually rise to a position of complete independence. The Ultimate
Reality, according to the Qur'an, is spiritual, and its life consists in its
temporal activity. The spirit finds its opportunity in the natural, the
material, the secular. All that is secular is therefore sacred in its roots
of being ... There is no such thing as a profane world' (in Saiyidain,
1992).

At the core of this conception of Islamic ontology is the primacy of
the spirit as it is actualized and manifested in the physical realm. This
understanding of the esoteric nature of being that synthesizes spirit,
mind, and body and that connects all existence to a fundamentally
spiritual essence involves the notion that we are 'spiritual beings on a
human path' rather than 'human beings on a spiritual path.' It emphasizes the physical incarnation of the spiritual rather than the dominance of material existence. Iqbal is also speaking of the element of
Islamic ideology and praxis whereby all mundane actions can be a
form of spiritual worship, or *ibadat*, provided that they are performed
with conscious intent of seeking the pleasure of Allah, the Creator.
Therefore, in this conception, there is no need to separate the spheres
of sacredness from the profane. That a spiritual essence is embedded

in everyday acts is central to maintaining the articulation of the spiritual, material, and intellectual states of being as holistic and mutually constituting elements of Islamic ontology. From an epistemological standpoint, this forms the basis of understanding of how faith-centred Muslims make sense of the world and their place in it.

Second principle: Historically and culturally situated analyses of religion and spirituality are an integral component of understanding human social, historical, and personal development. Religion and spirituality are woven into the history of human societies. Traditions of faith and spiritual practice are at the very core of human social and cultural development. Human societies have long been intrigued by cosmology and have evolved their understandings of life, death, and the afterlife according to particular spiritual and religious traditions. These understandings have come from pagan, animistic, and polytheistic as well as monotheistic beliefs in a higher power, goddess, Mother Earth, Creator, or God.

Whatever their particular cosmological or theistic orientation, belief systems have always been central to human societies everywhere. To understand a faith-centred reality, one must look to the sources of the meaning that is infused in a faith's everyday aspects, as well as in those rituals governing events such as birth, death, marriage, and religious ceremonies. These sources of meaning include oral traditions, prophetic knowledge, and religious doctrines, such as those that refer to the 'word of God' or that offer guidance from the Creator. A critical faith-centred analysis allows this level of metaphysical engagement so that we can understand how faith and spirituality constantly inform daily social life and personal development.

In the Islamic tradition, for example, prayers are offered five times each day. Thus the day is structured around the times when prayers must be offered. During these times, all worldly activities cease and Muslims perform ritual ablutions and stretch out their prayer mats to face the *kaaba* in Mecca. Muslims often have distinctive elements that indicate an Islamic lifestyle. Metcalf (1996) examined the Islamization of space in the Islamic diasporas of Europe and North America ranging from architectural design of mosques, to Muslim homes. She found that certain items within the home served to Islamicize the space, making it more conducive to worship. In addition to the prayer mats, beds were often aligned towards Mecca. Also, many Muslim families had invested in an *adhan* clock, which marks the traditional

Islamic calls to prayer. The creation of sacred spaces in this way is a distinctive aspect of Islamic praxis. According to Metcalf (1996): 'In the very act of naming and orienting space through religious practice, we see a kind of empowering of Muslims and a clear form of resistance to the dominant categories of the larger culture' (p. 12).

Fasting during the month of Ramadan also structures daily life by specifying the times when it is permissible to eat and drink: after sunset and before dawn. These sorts of religious practices establish a rhythm to daily life; though rooted in the spiritual, they organize more worldly practices such as eating, drinking, and waking (for dawn prayers). According to Berns McGown (1999) these rituals are especially important for Muslim newcomers to Canada, where they provide an 'anchor' and 'oasis of tranquility' during the otherwise tumultuous experience of migration and displacement: 'What was valuable about it [this anchor] was the very ritual of stepping outside the daily struggle, five times over the course of the day, to concentrate on the prayers that never alter, in rhythmic language that linked them to a community of believers that was theirs no matter where in the world they were' (p. 98).

To understand the realities of faith-centred Muslims in a diasporic context, we must first understand the central importance of religious practice to them. The critical faith-centred perspective attends to the saliency of faith and spirituality in framing the world views, beliefs, and practices of faith-centred people, and accepts this as a valid way of negotiating an understanding of community, selfhood, environment, and experience of trans-nationalism.

Third principle: Religious and spiritual world views and/or contestations of those world views continue to shape human social, cultural, and political development. The previous principle addressed how analyses of religion and spirituality are necessary in order to comprehend human historical, social, and personal development. This principle extends the framework to address the influence of religious and spiritual world views on the social and cultural development of adherents, and on how those same world views shape the politics of many societies. The previous principle attended to the importance of religion and spirituality for understanding human social and cultural development as it is affected by belief in the Divine, metaphysical, or incorporeal elements of being. The third principle expands this understanding to address how the ideologies that are drawn from these epistemological vantage points play a central role in shaping the ways in which societies are organized socially, culturally, and politically. This is not a deterministic view; rather it is one that recognizes the pervasiveness of religious and spiritual ideologies in many societies and the impact those ideologies have on everyday life as well as on social and political practices.

For example, in the Islamic tradition a variety of world views operate based on sectarian orientations among Sunnis, Shias, Ismailis, Ahmediyyas, and Sufis. And within the Sunni orientation – the predominant one – there are different schools of scholarly judicial thought based on the *mahdabs*, representing the Maliki, Shafi, Hanbali, and Hanafi legal traditions. These legal schools, which were founded in the ninth century, provide the theological-judicial grounds on which social and political policies and laws have been erected. Predicated on scholarly interpretation of the primary sources of Islamic knowledge, the Qur'an and the hadith, these systems of jurisprudence shape the social, political, and civic parameters of many parts of the Muslim world.

At the more conservative end of the religious spectrum there are more recent modernist orientations, such as the Wahabi and Salafi movements. It is within these more dogmatic and fundamentalist positions that extremism has flourished, owing to a narrow rigidity and a literal reading of religious doctrine. However, those who follow these more conservative traditions should not all be cast together with the violent forms of extremism. Groups such as the Taliban and Al Qaeda do not represent the majority of Muslims at either end of the religious spectrum. Within these very broad epistemological boundaries, a wide range of Islamic world views are represented. The more violent and extreme perspectives cannot be supported by a critical faith-centred epistemology, as will be discussed further on. The point here is that the multitude of views develop into various cultural forms that shape social discourse and praxis in many ways.

The organization of social space in the Islamic tradition provides a relevant example of how Islamically gendered world views shape social as well as physical and spatial contexts. Traditionally, sexual segregation during prayers is maintained so as not to allow either party to be distracted by the physical presence of the opposite sex. In Muslim countries such as Saudi Arabia, this segregation has extended to many spheres of activity, including employment, public transportation, and banking. The result has been a system of 'gendered apartheid.' This extreme practice has little validity in Islamic doctrine or history; for example, the women of Medina in the time of the Prophet Muhammed were active in business, medicine, and the military (see Mernissi, 1991).

As Muslim women contest and challenge these world views by developing counternarratives based on feminist readings of religious doctrine, they create a gendered Islamic epistemology that challenges the male-dominated status quo. These contestations challenge the gendered segregation of public space. As Cooke (2001) reminds us, Arab Muslim women 'have been left out of history, out of the War Story, out of the narratives of emigration and exile, out of the physical and hermeneutical spaces of religion' (p. vii). Muslim women intellectuals and writers are responding to this by challenging the erasures of their experiences in the public and discursive spaces of nation, community, and faith (see also Webb, 2000). Through these confrontations with existing static world views, social development and change move forward through dialectal shifts, which are initiated through the integration of material, ideological, as well as spiritual catalysts.

Fourth principle: Religion and spirituality occupy a central place in the understanding of various academic disciplines and subjects such as economics, politics, philosophy, gender, culture, education, and anthropology and are valid and legitimate sites for the analysis of social, existential phenomena. Issues of religion and spirituality have long been confined to the academic domains of religious studies or the social sciences. It is almost unheard of to apply a faith-centred lens to critical inquiry in these fields. In the academy, the dominant official knowledge is based on secular thought; religion and spirituality are merely subjects as opposed to critical frameworks. A critical faith-centred epistemology challenges this by maintaining that faith-centred knowledges and understandings can be valid ways of knowing and engaging in academic knowledge production.

Indigenous knowledges have made similar claims for recognition and inclusion in academia. As Dei, Hall, and Goldin-Rosenberg (2000) note, they resist the hegemony imposed by the canons of Western Eurocentric knowledge: 'Indigenous knowledges are a way to recover from the artificial split between mind and body brought on by the theorizing of the western European Enlightenment, and a challenge to the ways in which Western knowledges have become hegemonic. Such knowledges can be taken up in work on health, the environment, and spirituality and indeed at all levels of academic reflection' (p. 155). Indigenous knowledges are steeped in spiritual and cosmological understandings that structure thought and ways of knowing. They can provide critical vantage points for engaging in social research and praxis. For example, spiritually based indigenous knowledges are attentive to the holism of nature and the preservation of resources. They also provide the basis for political thought and action through anticolonial movements (see Tuhiwai Smith, 1999; Dei, 2001a). Simply put, these knowledges do not represent quaint 'folk knowledge' and should not be confined to non-academic public space. Indeed, they should be integral to the ways in which social, existential phenomena are read, theorized, engaged with, and contested.

Islamic frameworks are rarely used as analytical tools for the study of Muslim societies. Instead, they have long been regarded as elements of 'false consciousness' or as dogmas to be suppressed by 'rational' scholarly thought. The critical faith-centred framework is an attempt to situate spiritually centred epistemologies as valid locations for the production of academic knowledge. This does not mean that there should be an unequivocal validation of all forms of religious or spiritual thought from an academic standpoint, as the following principle will elaborate. To accept critical faith-centred voices as valid constituents of academic thought is not to support an uncritical moral relativism; the assertion here is that they should be allowed a place in the arena of legitimate academic engagement. The validity of these knowledges is open to contestation and challenge, in the same way that all other forms of knowledge are. Knowledges should not be invalidated simply because they are not secular. For example, Islamic perspectives on economics that place limits on capitalism generate alternatives to interest-based economies and provide for the economic redistribution of wealth from the rich to the poor. This can be a corrective to other systems of economic thought that lack an equivalent regard for economic justice. Clearly, then, faith-based knowledges can provide alternative understandings and solutions to the challenges societies face and offer new possibilities for social, economic, and political engagement.

It is possible, then, for faith-based knowledges and traditions to enter academic dialogues and inquiries not as static dogmas but as contextualized and historicized paradigms of thought and as ontological discourses that are referenced in metaphysical realities. They are not intended to operate as new grand narratives; rather, they can func- tion in a dialogical manner with other discourses and paradigms that have more secular foundations. Faith-based knowledges are not in- herently oppositional; they can, though, refine secular knowledges through a variety of empirical and ideological engagements (just as they can themselves be refined). In addition, intellectual alliances can be formed between secular and non-secular academic and philoso- phical perspectives, such as through struggles for social justice and through the pursuit of common liberatory goals.

Fifth principle: Religious and spiritual identities represent sites of oppression and are connected to broader sites and systems of discrimination based on race, class, gender, ethnicity, sexuality, and colonialism. However religion has at times been misused and become complicit in oppression. This framework accepts that various forms of social marginalization based on race, eth- nicity, class, gender, sexuality, religion, and ability form a system of interlocking and mutually reinforcing oppressions. To unravel and dismantle these systems involves addressing the multiple sites of oppression and challenging the hierarchies of racialized and class- based dominance that ideologically and structurally sustain social dif- ference and inequalities. As in critical integrative antiracism (see Dei, 1996), this framework enables the analysis of systems of oppression as they intersect within the lived experiences of marginalized groups. However, a faith-centred framework moves religious issues from the margins of discursive focus to the centre. Issues of religious difference and discrimination are central; the analytical approach attends to how religious differences intersect with other forms of social difference and in some cases contribute to the oppression of others.

Islamophobia is a pertinent example of discrimination and oppres- sion based on religion. The tragic events of 9/11 have brought this his- toric form of oppression into fresh relief. Since the attacks, Orientalist constructions of difference have permeated representations of Muslims in the media as well as in popular culture. Yet Islamophobia has a history that long predates the current times. In the early seventh century, adherents of Islam in Muslim society were victims of ostracism, humiliation, economic embargos, and verbal and physical abuse, all of which led to their exodus from the holy city of Mecca. The Crusades, which began in the eleventh century, were predicated on battling the barbaric and infidel Muslims in order to capture Jerusalem for Christianity. In the seventeenth century, the Spanish Inquisition resulted in the expulsion of the 'Black Moors' and the ethnic cleansing of the Arab and Muslim presence in Europe. The genocide against Bosnian Muslims during the Balkan wars in the former Yugoslavia and Kosovo, and the vilification of Muslims during the Persian Gulf War and the present war in Iraq, are contemporary examples of the persistence of anti-Islamic sentiments and violence.

The resurgence of Islamophobia after 9/11 resulted in hate crimes against Muslims, Arabs, Afghanis, and South Asians across North America and Europe. The incidents reported range from verbal abuse to physical threats, assaults, and the destruction of property.[5] In addition to these individual acts of violence, racial profiling and fingerprinting at airports and train and bus stations are now widespread and are compromising the civil liberties of Muslim citizens of Canada. This form of racial and ethnic discrimination can compromise the life chances of individuals in targeted groups by reducing opportunities for employment and housing (see Ornstein, 1996). For example, the Refugee Housing Task Force in Toronto reported that many landlords refused to rent to Muslims after 9/11.[6]

In the context of the present war in Iraq and continuing fears of Al Qaeda–style terrorism, Muslims in this new world order find themselves living under constant scrutiny and surveillance and in constant fear. However, Islamophobia and other forms of religious discrimination are tied to broader forms of social difference in a matrix of related oppressions. For example, 'gendered Islamophobia' targets Muslim women specifically (see chapter 5).

Religious discrimination against Muslims is pervasive. It is also strongly institutionalized and closely linked to the global clash of political ideologies. Moreover, there are situations where the misuse of religion helps construct oppression. I am thinking specifically of white-supremacist churches (such as the Church of the Creator), Third World missionaries who collude with colonial projects, the racial politics of the Nation of Islam, the suppression of women's rights in theocratic states, and the religious-based persecution of gays and lesbians. Al Qaeda and the Taliban are also examples of religion being abused to further political goals.

Abou El Fadl (2002) argues persuasively for a movement away from puritanical, literalist readings of Islamic doctrine, of the sort that that decontextualize and dehistoricize the faith. Fundamentalist readings, which are characteristic of the Wahabi and Salafi movements, inform the ideology of countries such as Saudi Arabia. In tracing the roots of religious intolerance in Islam, Abou El Fadl (2002) refers back to the puritanism of the Wahabi movement, which was founded in eighteenth-century Saudi Arabia by Muhammed Ibn Abd' al Wahab, who sought to purify Islam of liberal interpretations, which he saw as corrupting the faith. Abd' al Wahab advocated a strict literal adherence to the text and expressed extreme hostility to mysticism, intellectualism, and sectarian divisions within Islam. This narrow ideology was embraced by the ruling Al Sa'ud family in the late eighteenth century in their struggle to expel the Ottomans from the Arabian Peninsula. Abou El Fadl (2002) reports that the Wahabis 'indiscriminately slaughtered and terrorized Muslims and non-Muslims alike' during this bloody struggle and that their fanaticism and intolerance were condemned by the leading Islamic jurists of the time (pp. 8–9). Nevertheless, Wahabism became the prevailing creed of the Saudi Arabian state. According to Abou El Fadl (2002), Wahabism was a totalizing ideology that proponents regarded as the true 'straight path.' They maintained that their orthodoxy was the 'authentic' practice of *al salaf al salih*, or the Rightly Guided Predecessors – a term used to refer to the Prophet Muhammed and his companions.

Another narrow and puritanical orthodoxy took shape around the same time, though ironically, as Abou El Fadl (2002) points out, what is now known as the Salafi movement started out embracing a liberal theological orientation. Founded in the early twentieth century by leading progressive thinkers such as Al Afghani, Mohammed Abduh, and Rashid Rida, Salafism called for a resurgence of Islamic thought based on new interpretations of the Qur'an and the Sunnah, as a means to help contend with the challenges of modernity. However, by 1970 'Wahabism had succeeded in transforming Salafism from a liberal, modernist orientation to a literal, conservative and puritan theology' (p. 10).

Extremist and fundamentalist views based on literal, puritanical, and patriarchal readings of religious texts can lead to forms of gendered oppression. Thus, narrow and archaic interpretations of religious sharia law have contributed to Muslim women's oppression. Examples include the stoning of women suspected of fornication; the banning of women from schools, workplaces, and public spaces by the Taliban; and veiling by force in Saudi Arabia, Iran, and Afghanistan. The religious basis for gendered oppression has been developed through narrow, literalist readings of religious texts. That said, we must avoid ascribing women's oppression in religiously based societies solely to religion. Too often, the 'religious paradigm' has been used as a means to reduce the complexity of women's lives in theocratic societies to a singular religious *cause* for inequality as well as for underdevelopment more generally (Lazreg, 1994, p. 14). Other systems of oppression exist in these circumstances and intersect with those which are based on religion. Poverty, cultural politics, and imperialism can all be linked as part of a complex etiology of gendered oppression. When adopting religious and spiritually centred world views as a basis for social understanding and critical analysis, we must make sure not to overemphasize the role that religion plays in situations and sites of oppression.

Sixth principle: Religion and spirituality can be sites of resistance to injustice and oppression, providing a space for critical contestation and political engagement. Religion can be a site of oppression as well as, sometimes, a cause of oppression. But it can also be a site of *resistance* to oppression, as can spirituality. Foucault posited that power emanates from the microlevels of society and is not simply top-down (see, for example, Foucault, 1982). In a critical faith-centred framework, religion and spirituality are viewed as able to inspire grassroots movements to resist injustice and oppression. In Christianity, for example, 'liberation theology' connects religious and spiritual practice with emancipatory political aims. Challenging the notions of those who see religion only in terms of personal growth, Baum (1987) outlines the Canadian expression of liberation theology as reflected in the pastoral messages of Canadian bishops. These messages advocate the following:

- Attending to the experiences of the poor, the marginalized, and the oppressed.
- Developing a critical analysis of the social structures that cause suffering.
- Judging human values and priorities in light of Gospel principles.
- Stimulating creative thought and action for alternative social and economic models.
- Acting in solidarity with groups who are struggling to transform society. (p. 68)

These goals are embraced through the transformative philosophy of a critical faith-centred approach, which can be predicated on any number of spiritual or theological orientations.

Paulo Freire (1997) describes the connection between salvation and liberation in the context of liberation theology: 'Salvation implies *liberation*, engagement in a struggle for it. It is as if the fight against exploitation, its motivation and the refusal of resignation were paths to salvation. The process of salvation cannot be realized without rebelliousness' (p. 105). He describes spirituality and the struggle for salvation as a site of insurgence and rebellion against injustice. Similarly, Dei (2001a) argues that spirituality can be an active force, one that directs spirituality from intrinsic towards extrinsic manifestations through social transformation, revolution, and a collective struggle for emancipation: 'There are different spiritualities and the focus on reclaiming the spiritual is for an action-oriented, revolutionary spirituality. This approach moves beyond the liberal focus on compassion, humility and caring, to discussing how we evoke spirituality and spiritual knowledge to transform society and to challenge oppressive systems and structures. This approach thus focuses on questions of power and domination and role of spirituality in strengthening and empowering the self and the collective to resist marginality' (p. 3). Central to Dei's conception is the centring of spiritual knowledge as a means to build socially transformative movements that present possibilities for challenging oppressive structures and conditions. Muslim women, for example, are reclaiming the hermeneutic spaces of religious discourse as a means for developing a basis for Islamic feminist engagement. Some critics, such as Moghissi (1999), challenge the centring of feminist movements in an Islamic paradigm, arguing that Islam's inherent patriarchy cannot be transcended. Yet other faith-centred Muslim feminists see strategies such as feminist exegeses of the Qur'an as a means to articulate feminist thought and engagement from within the broad discursive parameters of Islam and to achieve greater gender equity and counter oppression (see Wadud, 1992; Cooke, 2001). This approach seeks to use the politics of hermeneutics as a means to generate alternative readings of religious texts, in this way building a discursive and spiritual basis for more equitable gender-based structures, systems, and practices.

Taylor (2002) refers to the development of spirituality as a revolutionary force as being a process of 'decolonizing spirituality' that refers to a 'spirituality that entails or creates decolonizing effects' (p. 1). Spirituality, in this view, is at the core of resistance and political engagement for social justice. Taylor (2002) examined the role played by decolonizing spiritualities in Latin American political movements; in that location they were expressed through cultural practices and formed 'a resurgent and insurgent vitality, a coming to life of times and spaces deadened by forces of (neo-)colonization. Especially through play-festival, music, dance, storytelling, street marches, rallies, vigils and more – this vitality acts up to not only bring a resurgence of life but also an insurgence, an aesthetic of resistance' (p. 2).

Dei (2001b) argues that we 'must eschew a liberal understanding of spirituality that separates the material from non-material existence' (p. 3). When we separate the spiritual from material practices, the result is an apolitical conception of spirituality. Taylor (2002) contends that when spirituality is treated as an anticolonial force, it is transcendent, resurgent, and insurgent. He describes its unifying and 'integrative reach,' which is 'evident in the visions and beliefs of those in struggle with (neo-)colonizing powers, who invoke and reflect upon alliances and unities, using myth story and history for some transcending of temporal and spatial horizons. This need not be a totalizing discourse replicating the universalizing paradigms of the (neo-)colonizer. It is a reach for unity, based in senses of 'one earth' or 'one cosmos' that can enable a reaching across national and cultural boundaries, as in Pan-African, Pan-Arab, and Pan-Maya resistance to (neo-)colonizing power' (p. 2).

Spirituality is, then, a site for resistance against oppression, one that provides a common language for articulating struggles. Dei (2001b) asserts a similar notion of spirituality as liberatory praxis, writing that 'spirituality speaks of the embodiment of the self as a necessary condition for political action' (p. 3). Spiritual education, then, involves implementing core values that lead to holism, solidarity, and empowerment: 'Spirituality is also understood in connection to humility, healing, the value of wholeness, self and collective empowerment, liberation and "reclaiming the vitality of life." In this sense then teaching sacredness, respect, compassion, and connecting the self to the world, self to others is spiritual education' (Palmer, in Dei, 2001b, p. 3).

Religiously oriented spirituality is not dissimilar to these perspectives, except that each of these virtues (respect, compassion, connecting the self to the world and others) is tied to a divine essence. In a religious conception, spirit emanates from this divine source; whereas in other traditions, spirit may reside in all forms of matter and living things. It follows that in a religious world view such as Islam, the political and transformative nature of spiritual practice is arrived at through revealed knowledge, just as it is in the decolonizing spirituality approach. Unlike revolutionary spiritualities, however, Islam has been demonized (especially since 9/11) as a religion of terrorist cult rather than as a 'liberatory theology' (which is how some Latin American revolutionary movements have been characterized). Extremist elements in Islamic society have come to be seen as the essentialized norm, ignoring the vast moderate majority of Muslims. Clearly, then, some spiritual traditions are seen as valid forces of insurgency and oppositional political engagement; whereas others have been delegitimated, their liberatory political imperatives unjustly vulgarized. We must never stop asking ourselves how this representation serves the interests of the forces of political imperialism and economic globalization.

Seventh Principle: Not all knowledge is socially constructed, but knowledge can emanate from divine revelation and can have a spiritual or incorporeal origin. Beliefs in prophets, revelation, messengers, angels, spirits, jinn, and so on must be incorporated into research and knowledge production as part of the way faith-centred people read and make sense of the world and their place in it. This principle speaks to the various sources from which knowledge is derived. As described in the earlier discussions of the foundational principles outlined in the critical faith-centred epistemology, the validation of religious and spiritual knowledge is important as a means to apprehend the non-secular ways in which people make sense of the world and their place in it. As we have seen, religion and spirituality are necessary for an understanding of human social, cultural, and political development, and these sources of knowledge can provide valid insights and commentaries for more secular forms of knowledge production. Also, anticolonial spirituality can provide a basis for liberation discourses that can help counter both religiously based oppression and the collusion of some religious ideologies with other sites of oppression. This principle seeks to validate religious and spiritual knowledge and the variety of traditions and sources from which it emanates, including these: divine revelation, prophets, messengers, angels, spirits, dreams, and visions. This principle acknowledges, then, that not all knowledge is socially constructed; rather, knowledge can have spiritual and incorporeal origins.

In indigenous epistemology, for example, knowledge is derived from a variety of valued sources. According to Castellano (2000), these include traditional teachings, empirical observations, and revelation. Traditional knowledge is preserved and transmitted orally down the generations through storytelling. Traditional indigenous knowledge, 'with variations from nation to nation ... tells of the creation of the world and the origins of clans in encounters between ancestors and spirits in the form of animals; it records genealogies and ancestral rights to territory; and it memorializes battles, boundaries and treaties and instils attitudes of wariness or trust toward neighboring nations. Through heroic and cautionary tales, it reinforces values and beliefs; these in turn provide the substructure for civil society' (p. 23). In this way, traditional knowledge serves a vital social, cultural, and political purpose in indigenous communities. This knowledge is rooted in the cosmological world view of indigenous peoples and is often transmitted by tribal elders, who are revered for their wisdom.

In Islamic epistemology, traditional knowledge is transmitted through the stories of the Abrahamic prophets and the *seerah* – that is, stories of the life of the Prophet Muhammed as the final messenger of God. Children in full-time or weekend Islamic schools acquire this traditional knowledge as the core of their learning. These stories may also be communicated to children by members of the extended family. Faith-centred historical narratives provide guidance in the form of allegories and parables, and well as through the examples set by the various prophets, who addressed a variety of social and political challenges as testimony to their faith in the Creator. Traditional knowledge is, then, an engagement with narrative history and is both orally and textually transmitted. This knowledge has physical *and* metaphysical aspects and provides a moral grounding for education within the faith tradition of Islam.

The second type of knowledge that Castellano (2000) suggests is central to the indigenous way of knowing is empirical knowledge – that is, knowledge gained through close observation. Castellano describes this form of knowledge as dynamic and as refined through constant observation. Unlike scientific forms of observation, which are based on theory and reproducible experiments, observation in the indigenous context refers to 'a convergence of perspectives from different vantage points, accumulated over time' (p. 24). This provides an active synergy in the collaborative development of knowledge based on observations of the natural world. Similarly, in the Islamic tradition, observation is a significant means for apprehending ritual practices and cultural codes of conduct. Also, observation of nature offers a testament to the powerful creative forces of Allah.

The third and final branch of knowledge referred to by Castellano is *revealed* knowledge, which is acquired through dreams, visions, and intuitions. These are understood to be spiritual in origin. Castellano points out that this knowledge is often sought after through vision quests, fasts, and ceremonies as well as through the wisdom of Elders. She notes that this knowledge is 'sometimes received as a gift at a moment of need; sometimes it manifests itself as a sense that "the time is right" to hunt or counsel or to make a decisive turn in one's life path' (p. 24). This kind of intuitive epiphany is seen in the indigenous world view as sacred guidance.

Revealed knowledge is the fundamental basis of many religions, including Islam. In this conception, knowledge emanates from the Creator and is revealed through intermediaries such as prophets, messengers, and angels. The esteemed medieval Muslim scholar Imam Al Ghazzali outlined in his treatises two main branches of knowledge: *ulum-i-sharia* (religious sciences), and *ulum-i-ghair-sharia* (non-religious sciences). In distinguishing between these, he wrote: 'By religious sciences I mean those branches of knowledge which are directly learned from the apostles of God. Reason does not lead us toward them, as it makes us learn arithmetic: nor are they learnt by experience, as the science of medicine is systematized; nor are they learnt merely by hearing, as philosophy is learnt' (in Quraishi, 1970, pp. 8–9). Here, Al Ghazzali is differentiating between systems of knowledge and thought and the methodologies for learning these. Revealed knowledge, he argues, is not arrived at through reason but is apprehended through the messages of prophecy.

In Islam, divine knowledge was revealed to the prophet Muhammed as he fasted and meditated in the cave of Hira in the Arabian Desert. The message was delivered by the archangel Gabriel (Jibreel, in Arabic), who ordered the prophet: 'Read! [*Iqra!*] In the Name of your Lord.' Other prophets from the Abrahamic tradition – which is shared by Christianity, Judaism, and Islam – are also represented as prophets of the Islamic tradition. Some of the prophets to whom Holy Scriptures were revealed are known as *nabi*; others are simply known as *rasool*, or messengers. Divine knowledge was often validated through various miracles that confirmed the authenticity of the knowledge and its source to the prophets and messengers.

Other metaphysical knowledges and realities are referenced in the Qur'an, such as the existence of magic and the 'evil eye' as well as the existence of *jinn*. *Jinn* are referred to in the Qur'an as a creation of Allah. They inhabit the earth alongside humans, but they are not visible. They do not represent spirits of the dead; they are living entities that have qualities and attributes similar to those of humans; however, they are constituted out of smokeless fire and are not generally visible to humans, though many people are reported to have witnessed sightings of *jinn*.[7] Belief in spirits or ancestors – and *jinn* – is integral to the spiritual world view of many communities and faith traditions. These metaphysical world views are part of the commonsense, taken-for-granted ways in which people make sense of their realities and reflect on the world and their relationship to the physical and social environments they inhabit. They are seen as valid ways of knowing and as alternatives to many forms of secular knowledge.

Spiritual knowledges can conflict with one another as competing truth claims. The point made here is that they are valid sites for debates about metaphysics of reality. They cannot be verified through objective inquiry. The conventions of rational thought would tell us that only verifiable truths are legitimate; however, spiritual knowledge cannot be fully comprehended through rational means. This does not necessarily mean that such knowledge is 'irrational'; it only means that it is beyond the limits of rational, scientific exploration. Even so, divine or cosmological knowledge is intrinsic to people's world views and has historically been a catalyst for scientific progress.[8] So, within a critical faith-centred framework, engaging with these knowledges is a valid approach to apprehending metaphysical knowledge and to linking social, cultural, and political practices to the physical realm.

Anticolonial Discursive Framework

The critical faith-centred epistemology can be linked to an anticolonial discursive framework in significant ways, including through the shared philosophy of holism, the inclusion of indigenous and marginalized knowledges in the academy (see Dei, Hall & Rosenberg, 2000; Dei et al., 2001), and an emphasis on identifying and countering colonial oppressions as they manifest themselves in the world today through a variety of conditions of domination (see Dei & Asgharzadeh, 2001). As Dei and Asgharzadeh remind us, the idea of a 'post-colonial' world is faulty, given the continuity of global imperialist social, economic, and political practices and their impact on local communities in the South. In my view, an anticolonial framework is situated in a different discursive space, one that seeks to move the discourse beyond the space of postcolonial critique towards active engagement in counterhegemonic knowledge production and corresponding political action.

Following the work of Dei (2001a) and Dei and Asgharzadeh (2001), the philosophical foundations of an anticolonial discursive framework include the following three processes of cognitive, academic, and political engagement: (1) processes of knowledge production and validation, (2) the understanding of indigeneity, and (3) the pursuit of agency, resistance, and subjective politics. A central goal of this framework is to 'question, interrogate and challenge the foundations of institutionalized power and privilege, and the accompanying rationale for dominance in social relations' (Dei & Asgharzadeh, 2001, p. 300). This approach attends to the neocolonial impact of global capital on the populations of the South as well as to the hegemony of specific forms of knowledge production that serve to rationalize such power relations. It also affirms the legitimacy of knowledge emanating from diverse sites and the need to validate the narration of lived experience as a form of knowledge production: 'The anti-colonial framework allows for a re-theorization of issues emerging from colonial relations. Specifically, an interrogation of the configurations of power embedded in knowledge production ... In this framework, knowledge is understood to emanate from multiple sites, sources and conditions (gender, ethnicity, culture, religion and language). Locally produced knowledge reflecting cultural history and social interactions is deemed important and knowledge is considered socially and politically relevant if it maintains a fit with people's aspirations, as well as their lived experiences' (Dei, 2001a, p. 3).

As a form of 'subversive pedagogy,' the anticolonial framework has certain elements in common with the antiracism perspective. Both seek to unmask the power relations that are embedded in the structures of schooling that reproduce social inequities, and to redress the marginalization of subaltern groups' knowledge and experiences within the 'official knowledge' of schooling: 'Like the anti-racist framework, the anti-colonial discursive framework acknowledges the role of the educational system in producing and reproducing racial, ethnic, religious, linguistic, gender, sexual and class-based inequalities in society. It acknowledges the role of societal/institutional structures in producing and reproducing endemic inequalities ... Further, anticolonial discourse problematizes the marginalization of certain voices and ideas in the educational system, as well as the delegitimation, in the pedagogic and communicative practices of schools, of the knowledge and experience of subordinate groups' (Dei, 2001a, p. 3). Where it challenges the colonization of knowledge in schools through the hegemony of the Eurocentric world view, the anticolonial discursive framework intersects with the critical faith-centred framework; both confront the privileging of secular Western knowledge as the exclusive vantage point for teaching and learning.

Also, spirituality is referenced in the anticolonial framework as a hallmark of indigenous ways of knowing. Spiritual knowledge is at the centre of many alternative epistemologies and world views. This represents a strong connection to the critical faith-centred approach, which seeks to reclaim a space in which faith-centred voices can become integral to social, academic, and political processes. To this end, it is necessary to situate anticolonialism not simply within a space of critique but also within a space of creation – a space where subjugated knowledges can be reclaimed and revitalized. In efforts to connect the anticolonial and critical faith-centred frameworks, Islamic schools can represent an anticolonial move, by centring subjugated knowledge in educational discourse and praxis.

The colonization of knowledge within the secular, Eurocentric public school system and the marginalization of religious and spiritually based ways of knowing make the development of independent schools based on these subjugated knowledges part of an anticolonial discursive process. I locate Islamic schooling within this project, as these schools produce a form of oppositional knowledge that seeks to subvert the dominant secular, Eurocentric discourses as the only valid basis for compulsory education and learning. Students from marginalized religious groups are subordinated by these dominant secular discourses; their realities are represented as stemming from sources of knowledge that have been deprivileged and that have no 'rational' basis.

Resisting this closure of the possibilities of alternative thought and non-secular articulations of knowledge and ontology is central to the project of decolonizing the intellectual spaces where knowledge is produced. This can be accomplished through processes of internal resistance as well as by developing more inclusive, multicentred orientations for public education (see Dei et al., 2001). Yet most schools are far from this reality, despite decades of struggles and advocacy by marginalized communities (see, for example, Wright, 2000). Centring the experiences of marginalized students can be more readily achieved through independent schools, which, in this situation, would provide a greater immersion in the discourses of faith-based communities. Reclaiming subjugated knowledges and engaging in educational politics that would decolonize those practices of schooling which privilege only dominant ways of knowing, teaching, and learning are parts of an anticolonial project in which the conscious creation of alternative and oppositional knowledge and praxis can occur.

Integrative Antiracism

The concept of integrative antiracism allows us to understand how race intersects with other forms of social difference based on class, gender, sexuality, ability, and religion. As previously discussed, these social differences represent mutually reinforcing systems of oppression. This approach to articulating the interrelatedness of various sites of social difference is not intended to suggest that there are 'hierarchies of oppression.' That said, Dei (1996) points out that there is a clear saliency of race and that conceptualizing intersections of difference does not preclude any one form of oppression from taking centre stage, given certain 'situational specificities' (p. 58).

In this study I will be using race and religious difference as a nexus for discussing the experiences of Muslim students in the public school system, as these factors provide a rationale for the development of Islamic schooling. My previous work (Zine, 2000, 2001b) identified racism and Islamophobia as factors mediating the school experiences of Muslim children and youth; another factor, however, is secular, Eurocentric knowledge and practices in the public education system that marginalize and exclude children who belong to faith-based communities. This Eurocentric bias and the resulting marginalization of minoritized Muslim students is what has led to calls for Islamic schooling.

This book's analysis of Islamic schooling will be borrowing from some of Dei's (1996) principles of antiracism education, which overlap with the critical faith-centred approach and the objectives of this research. Dei's principles include the following:

- The delegitimation of the knowledge and experience of subordinated groups in the educational system needs to be challenged, and a space needs to be created for alternative and oppositional knowledges (pp. 29–30).
- Also necessary is a holistic understanding and appreciation of the human experience in all of its social, cultural, political, ecological, and spiritual aspects (pp. 30–1).
- Identity needs to be linked to schooling practices (pp. 31–2).
- Canadian schools and society need to confront the pedagogic challenges arising from diversity and difference (pp. 33–4).

Dei views African-centred schooling as a means to 'provide Black students with the choice of an alternative learning environment and to develop their sense of identity and belonging to the school' (p. 108). Such schools, Dei argues, would provide opportunities to focus on Black/African-Canadian students' heritages. Ultimately, this would help them deal with the isolation they face in the public school system and the frustration that develops from this. I will be applying the same reasoning to Islamic schooling, which, as an alternative faith-based system, would expand the possibilities for Muslim youth by helping them to develop confidence and self-esteem and to grow spiritually (see chapter 5, on the purposes and goals of Islamic schooling in a diasporic context).

I will also be utilizing the antiracism discursive framework to challenge and contest liberal arguments against independent schools that are based on cultural or religious lines. Some liberal theorists argue that separate schools foster 'separatism' and that they create environments that discourage the development of civic virtues such as tolerance and respect for difference. They argue that these schools hinder the development of deliberative democracy by promoting singular frameworks based on specific cultural and/or religious ideologies. I will be answering these criticisms by applying an antiracism narrative that moves the debate onto a more complex terrain of racialized politics and social inclusion/exclusion.

Power and Discourse and Subjectivity

I will also be borrowing from Foucault's ideas on power, discourse, and subjectivity as well as from post-structuralist feminist theory. I do not claim strict fidelity to Foucault's post-structuralism; his theories do, however, offer some useful analytical tools for examining how discourses structure subjectivities. According to McHoul and Grace (1993), Foucauldian discourse analysis 'has intimate connections with how human subjects are formed, how institutions attempt to "normalize" persons on the margins of social life, how historical conditions of knowledge change and vary – how things "weren't necessarily as all that"' (p. 41). Thus, subjects – in Foucault's work, these include the mad, the ill, the criminal, and the sexual pervert – are produced as effects of discursive and power relations. Moving beyond modernist notions of an autonomous, sovereign subject, Foucault directed his analyses at the historical conditions that made possible various types of specific and differentiated subjects. Adapting an example from McHoul and Grace (1993), the questions to be addressed here would include these: How do historical and contemporary Islamic religious discourses produce a particular kind of social subject? How does this limit 'who we, as Muslims, can be'? And what strategies are available to broaden or defeat this limit?

I also borrow from post-structuralist theory in chapter 6, where I discuss how gendered identities are constructed. Many feminist scholars in the field of gender and education make use of Foucauldian post-structuralism in their efforts to unravel the complex processes of socialization and schooling whereby gendered identities are constructed and traditional gender roles are perpetuated (see, for example, Davies et al., 2001; Reay, 2001; Jones, 1993). In this regard, I will be examining the multiple discursive constructions of Muslim women's identities that are produced in both schools and the broader society. Muslim girls must contend, on the one hand, with competing and limiting constructions of identity based on popular Orientalist constructions of backward, passive, and subjugated Muslim women, and on the other hand, with narrow, puritanical Islamist discourses that rigidly circumscribe their participation in public space and regulate their physical and moral behaviour. Islamic schools are geared towards producing the 'Muslim woman' as a particular kind of discursive subject. I will be exploring Muslim girls' accommodations and resistances to these challenges through a narrative analysis, using the post-structuralist lens as well as the foundations of the critical faith-centred epistemology to develop a grounded theory of their lived experiences in Islamic schools.

The following chapter describes the methodology I employed for this research. It also explores the foundations of critical ethnography as the research paradigm I applied in this study. The discussion will encompass the politics, ethics, and framework of validity that together underpin critical ethnographic methods. In addition, some background will be provided regarding the specific Islamic schools that were investigated as well as the context for the ethnographic fieldwork in these sites.

3 Research Methodology:
A Crucial Ethnographic Approach

According to Anderson (1989), critical ethnography emerged as a result of 'the dissatisfaction with social accounts of "structures" such as class, patriarchy and racism in which real human actors never appear' (p. 249). This dissatisfaction led to the development of critical ethnography, which is 'sensitive to the dialectical relationship between the social structural constraints on human agency actors and the relative autonomy of human agency' (p. 254). Critical ethnography can also be a means to unsettle and unravel the status quo by invoking critical theory and political transformation (drawing on the work of Paulo Freire and others) and by focusing on the analysis of systems of oppression and 'unmasking the dominant traditions and the interests they represent' (p. 254). These were central imperatives behind this research.

Positionality, Reflexivity, and the Research Process

As a stakeholder, and as a supporter of the ideal of Islamic schooling (though not necessarily its present reality), I did not set out to uncritically valorize these schools but rather to interrogate their social and pedagogical processes from a critical faith-centred perspective. I knew full well that this interrogation might stimulate controversy within the Muslim community, but I also knew that to stay silent about oppressive structures and circumstances would be to help sustain these authoritarian systems. And I knew, as well, that I might be perpetuating Islamophobic stereotypes by revealing negative research findings.

Clearly, I was placing myself in a difficult political situation by taking up this research, which sometimes stagnated while I looked for ways to balance the goals of critical inquiry with the project of rupturing oppressive structures and conditions in my community, all the while struggling with the knowledge that in this racialized society, my findings could be turned against my community.

In interrogating power structures as a political and methodological process, I cannot ignore my own position of power as the narrator of other people's experiences. The power to label and define the realities of others is inherent in the research process whether or not one shares an intersubjective space with the research participants. I can claim a common identification and shared interests with my research participants, yet I cannot override the position of power and discursive authority I bring to the process. I am solely accountable for identifying research priorities and deciding which issues are to be privileged and/or deprivileged in the course of this work. I have the power to weave and fashion the narratives of my participants into a story and to editorialize on experiences borrowed from others. Though I try to highlight the voices of my participants as the architects and authorities of their experiences, I retain the power to frame those experiences as they suit my research objectives. Addressing the power imbalances that are inherent in the research process involves more than providing a political disclaimer. Efforts to become more reflexive and self-critical are an important means to develop more politically and methodologically equitable forms of praxis.

Reflexivity, according to Quantz (1992), is the 'hallmark of all ethnography' (p. 472). This is especially true of critical ethnographic work, in which reflexive practices are a fundamental element of praxis (Simon & Dippo, 1986). According to Anderson (1989), critical reflexivity is crucial to generating valid and trustworthy accounts; this in turn requires ethnographic work to attend to 'its own situated character' (Simon & Dippo, 1986). Critical reflexive praxis involves locating the researcher as part of that which is being researched (Hammersley & Atkinson, 1983) and identifying the process of knowledge production as being both shaped and limited by the personal histories of the researcher as well as the institutional forms within which such research takes place (Simon & Dippo, 1986).

According to Anderson (1989), this involves 'a dialectical process among (a) the researcher's constructs (b) the informants' common sense constructs (c) the research data (d) the researcher's ideological biases (e) the structural and historical forces that informed the social construct under study' (p. 254). Reflexive praxis in ethnography, therefore, requires the researcher to be attentive to the ideological orientation of the research, including any preconceived biases or meta-narrative constructs that contain rather than dialectically shift meanings. This approach responds to the informants' 'commonsense constructs' in such a way that social meanings are understood from the perspectives of the informants rather than imposed by the ethnographer. Patai (1992), however, in examining the inequalities and hierarchies that govern research situations and relationships among white feminist academics and their 'Third World' subjects, has asked this question: 'Is it possible, not in theory, but in the actual conditions of the real world today – to write about the oppressed without becoming one of the oppressors?' (p. 139). She argues that exploitation is *built into* the practice of research, in that the researcher and the subject are situated in unequal relations of power based on economics, class, and race privilege.

Entangled in this process, we find that developing textual accounts of the reality of others often involves transforming their subjective realities into an objectified discourse based on what Game (1991) has referred to as the researcher's 'politics, ideology and desire,' which together fuel the sociological imagination. This has important implications regarding the construction and representation of the realities of others. Dorothy Smith (1990), for example, has characterized this aspect of knowledge production as a process of discerning 'actuality and its representation'; she goes on to write that 'claims for the admission of accounts to membership in a textual reality depend upon establishing the proper relations between the original that it claims to represent and the account that has been produced' (p. 73). One could say that in ethnographic work, establishing these 'proper relations' hinges in part on processes of reflexivity. Addressing issues of positionality (i.e., how the researcher is located with respect to the subjects being studied) involves analysing the power relations underpinning the research process. This refers to the power to label, define, and locate the lived experiences of others within specific interpretive frameworks and ideological discourses that often have little relevance to the informants being studied.

Anderson (1989) alludes to this point when he refers to collaborative research as a strategy that allows researchers and informants to collaborate regarding how meanings are constructed and negotiated in textual accounts (see also Lather, 1986a). This is one way to address the issue of power and representation. However, the task of achieving consensus on meaning with participants is still mediated by the researcher's academic authority. Quantz (1992) maintains that the values that enter research do not necessarily have to be those of the informant. Ethnography, in his view, must not pretend to be value-free, and since the process cannot be construed as neutral, this invites the researcher to 'choose a position.' He remains unconvinced that 'one should present informant culture from the value positions of the group being studied instead of some other value position' (p. 472). He regards this as a methodological impossibility, given that the assumptions of reflexive inquiry hold that 'the researcher will always understand the cultural patterns in terms of the values of a researcher' (p. 472). The values held by a researcher are also mediated by his or her social location (in terms of race, class, gender, religion, ethnicity, and sexual orientation) as well as by the factors of politics, ideology, and desire, referred to by Game (1991). As noted earlier, Anderson (1989) refers to this feature of reflexive practice as the dialectical relationships among the constructs and biases of the researcher, those of the informant, and the structural and historical forces that mediate the research context (pp. 254–5). This points to a more negotiative framework regarding how meanings are *constructed* (dialectically) rather than *imposed* on the social realities being researched.

Quantz (1992), however, argues that, within the emancipatory goals of critical ethnographic work, merely accepting the meanings that informants assign to their actions is not sufficient to liberate them. Moreover, 'emancipation requires people to overcome their historically structured culture, which, in turn, requires that they step outside of their cultural views and reflect on their positioning in the world' (p. 473). It would seem that this mandate should equally be applied to the researcher. To step outside of one's cultural context and world view is also essential to processes of reflexive critical analysis. In the context of this research, though the cultural milieu was familiar to me, I was nevertheless challenged at times to understand the perspectives of others in ways that moved my thinking forward in new directions. In this sense, part of the process of reflexive inquiry involves derailing our a priori assumptions about those whom we intend to study *before* those assumptions become intellectual guides into the lived experiences of others. This leaves us open to engage with the transitions of thought we often experience 'out in the field.'

In examining our biases and political imperatives in the research process, we must also be cognizant of the meanings we may be imposing on the realities of others. Embedded in the textual accounts produced by ethnographers are certain claims to authoritative knowledge. It is essential to the work of critical ethnography that these claims to be ratified by the participants in ways that make sense to them, based on their own cultural and self-knowledge. As Simon and Dippo (1986) put it, 'we view all forms of knowing and all particular knowledge forms as ideological, hence the issue is not whether one is "biased," but rather, whose interests are served by one's work' (p. 196).

From all this, it follows that the political intentions of the researcher must be subjected to some reflexive consideration even before the research begins. It must be understood how politics, ideology, and desire guide the research process in terms of how they structure the method and mode of inquiry (research questions, choice of sample, etc.); also, the analytical implications in the textual account must be addressed. In this process, reflexivity is essential to maintaining the integrity of critical ethnographic research and, as Simon and Dippo (1986) state, to 'addressing the limits of its own claims by a consideration of how, as a form of social practice, it too is constituted and regulated through historical relations of power and existing material conditions' (p. 197).

Some researchers, however, see the emphasis on reflexivity as a form of 'navel gazing' that does little to improve the quality of the research. For example, Patai (1994) criticizes the overemphasis on reflexivity in research, which she regards as a practice that conflates politics with research She sees in this approach more romanticism than scholarship, and she asks whether postmodern considerations about self-reflexive practice actually lead to better scholarship: 'Becoming better human beings, more responsible, more self aware, may or may not make better scholars' (p. 68). I would, however, differ on this point and argue that it is precisely by becoming better human beings, more responsible, self-aware, and accountable, that researchers can be led towards investing in more ethical forms of practice, and hence become better scholars.

Text and Authority

In examining the politics of textual authority, Borland (1991) examines the interpretive dilemmas encountered in oral narrative research. She is sensitive to the need to preserve the meanings that subjects/informants ascribe to their stories and experiences; yet she also maintains that academic researchers, especially feminists, can provide narratives with a theoretical dimension that offers a strong social critique. The issue that concerns Borland is how researchers can 'grant the speaking woman interpretive respect without relinquishing our responsibility to provide our own interpretation of her experience' (p. 64). Abu Lughod (1991) makes a counterargument for limiting the researcher's authority in textual accounts; she articulates the need for more prosaic analyses in ethnographic writing – analyses based on 'ordinary experience' narrated in the terms in which the anthropological subjects operate (i.e., as opposed to the academic and literary conventions of the researcher). In other words, she favours engaging in a process that maintains the integrity of the subject's own authoritative voice.

These debates on ethnographic authority raise significant questions relating to the politics of representation in academic scholarship. Such concerns are especially salient when it comes to how Muslim communities are represented (see Said, 1979). For example, Moors (1991) presents a critique of Orientalist scholarship as it relates to Muslim women. She argues that the exoticization and essential difference constructed through these representations undermine the agency of the women represented (see also Lazreg, 1988; Mohanty, 1991; Zine 2002). She contests the ethnocentrism of writings on Muslim women, describing those writings as discussions of the 'intricate relation between politics and epistemology' in the production of cultural difference. These forms of feminist representation of the Muslim Other relate to what Stephens (1990) calls the 'unmediated association between representation and reality that surfaces when non-Western women are the object of feminism's gaze' (p. 93). Such accounts result in static representations of Muslim women, who become a category of analysis that is discursively mapped and defined by non-Muslim women, who are often subjected to essentialized characterizations of their identities. Stephens suggests that this sort of representational politics represents the point at which 'feminism collides and colludes with Orientalism' (p. 93). As a result of this type of academic imperialism, Muslim scholars – women in particular – are engaging in their own processes of knowledge production, claiming their own voices instead of allowing themselves to be *spoken for* (see Cooke, 2001; Zine & Bullock, 2002). My intention in this ethnographic account is to *speak with* the informants rather than appropriate their voices; in doing so, I hope to present an account of their experiences that does justice to their struggles *and* their accomplishments.

Research Strategies

The next section details the research strategies employed in this study. A critical ethnographic methodology was used; the strategies for inquiry included interviews, participant and non-participant observation, and action research as a volunteer teacher. Fieldwork and data collection were conducted over eighteen months, from September 1999 to July 2001. This section also describes the research 'path' and discusses the challenges and opportunities that presented themselves along that path.

Romancing the Field: Gaining Access to Research Sites

I am a parent of children who attended a primary Islamic school as well as a social and educational activist in the local Muslim community. These things allowed me easy access to the schools selected for this study. With each of the four schools, I approached the principal; all four were supportive of the research I was proposing. I was warmly invited into the schools to observe and interview teachers and students. At one of the schools, I was officially welcomed over the PA system during morning announcements, so that the staff and students would know I would be spending time in the school and in their classrooms. In each school, there were teachers and parents whom I already knew through my community work. In two of the schools, I was personally acquainted with the principal. This made access much easier, in that I was already known and trusted. At one school, as part of my preliminary research, I volunteered to teach a course. The school greatly appreciated this offer and reciprocated by cooperating fully with my research. This quid pro quo relationship allowed me to feel less parasitic, since I was 'giving back' in a tangible way. It also allowed me to become a school 'insider' and offered me a first-hand look at the practices and procedures as well as the staff and students. My presence also became less intrusive and more 'organic' to the environment.

Being a Muslim made access easier, since the participants felt safe around me. They were confident that since I was a fellow Muslim, their views and experiences would not be exploited or sensationalized. Rampant Islamophobia makes many individuals and institutions in the Muslim community wary of outside scrutiny. Muslims are constantly being misrepresented in the media and the popular culture, and as a result, many in their community are suspicious of all representational practices, including research. Being an 'insider' allowed a greater sense of ease in this regard; the participants trusted me to be fair and balanced, and they assumed that I had a vested interest in protecting the community from exploitation as well as from racialized and Islamophobic representational practices.

In one case, however, being an 'insider' did not help me overcome a school's resistance. This involved a girls-only school that taught kindergarten to grade twelve. I met with one of the male school administrators. As we sat in his tiny office, I provided him with the information letter explaining my research and told him about my objectives and methodology. I was asked to return the following day. When I did, he told me he did not have the authority to approve his school's participation. I was forwarded to another administrator, whom I returned to see the following day. I provided him with the same information about the study. I was asked to provide more information regarding my past research and writing. I came back a third time with samples of my earlier work, which I left with the administrator. When I did not hear back after a week, a returned to the school and explained yet again that I wanted to interview teachers and students and spend time observing classes. I also let them know that three other schools had agreed to participate, hoping this might ease any reservations. The administrator remained evasive; whenever I ran into him at the local mosque, he would only say in passing that they were still 'deciding.' Finally, I was told that they had decided not to participate. The administrator asked me to perhaps approach them 'next time.' I was not given a reason or explanation as to why they did not want to be involved.

My sense is that this resistance had to do, not with their fear of being exploited or sensationalized, but rather with their fear of having the school's status quo exposed to scrutiny. During the several visits I made to the school while pleading my case, it was apparent to me that the school's space, resources, and standards were substandard. Thus their reluctance. They were concerned less with how outsiders would see them than with how the Muslim community would see them.

Three of the four schools that had agreed to participate were also short of resources, yet apparently they trusted me to represent their circumstances fairly. In the school that declined to participate, I was a newer face, so perhaps they were less comfortable about having their circumstances 'exposed.' Also, I sensed that that school's environment was far more closed; the other schools, despite their shortcomings, were very open and correspondingly more cooperative. The participants at these schools told me that they hoped my research might suggest ways to improve. In sum, then, my access to these research sites was based on a shared religion, the trust I had already gained as a member of the community and an educational advocate, and the benefits the participants felt my research would bring to their schools.

The Participating Islamic Schools

The four schools that were selected for this study represent a cross-section of the eighteen Islamic schools currently located in the Greater Toronto Area. The participating schools varied in terms of length of operation, teacher certification, socio-economic level, students' ethno-cultural background, and physical space and resources. All of the schools were based in the Sunni Islamic tradition, as are most Islamic schools in the GTA.

During the fieldwork I visited a Shia school just outside Toronto; however, I decided to maintain consistency by focusing on Sunni schools. The four participating schools are described below (each has been assigned a pseudonym).

The Al Safar School

The Al Safar Islamic school is housed in a suburban mosque. The mosque was renovated to accommodate the school after the governing council, or *majlis as-shura*, conducted a community survey and town hall meeting in 1993 as part of a needs assessment to determine the demand for an Islamic school in the area. A school committee was formed. It founded a rudimentary elementary school in the mosque's basement while classrooms were being completed on the building's second floor. This approach met with resistance from the school governors, who wanted to delay opening the school until the renovations were completed. One of the school committee members, a retired elementary teacher, sister Mehrun (who would later become the school's principal),[1] was able to convince the school governors that the local Muslim community urgently required an Islamic school:

MEHRUN: I wanted to speak to them. I said it is like you have put your children in the water full of sharks and instead of trying to save them you are saying, 'Wait, we have to make a new boat before we can take you out. We can't use the raft or whatever we have.' And I said, 'We have the children in the kind of society where they are getting worse and worse and you are telling them no, we cannot start the school until you have some show piece there?'

The school governors voted, and the majority favoured opening the school quickly. Al Safar has since become one of the best Islamic schools in the GTA, despite its humble beginnings. A group of volunteer Muslim teachers who worked in the public education system put together a curriculum and helped organize the kindergarten and grade one class for the thirty-eight inaugural students. After the school building was completed, a grade was added each year. At this writing, the Al Safar school has over four hundred students, ranging from kindergarten to grade twelve.

All of the teachers at Al Safar have their Ontario Teacher Certification (OTC). Many of them are younger, second-generation Muslim Canadians who grew up and were educated in Canada. Overall, the Al Safar school has established a more professional environment than many Islamic schools, largely because of the vision of the founding teachers, who provided a strong pedagogical foundation. The school has a full-time principal with thirty years' experience teaching in the public education system. She is an efficient administrator who oversees all aspects of the school.

While I was doing fieldwork, the school had a Parent Advisory Committee (PAC); however, it was disbanded later on owing to 'parent fatigue' from dealing with the school administration. I served as a member of this parent committee, as both my children attended Al Safar from kindergarten to grade four. Generally, the parents at Al Safar were more highly educated and affluent than at the other schools included in this study. The school population is predominantly South Asian, but children from Arab, Somali, and Caribbean backgrounds also attend in significant numbers. Al Safar boasts a waiting list of more than six hundred prospective students, with many families registering their children as soon as they are born. There is no school bus service; instead, students are car pooled from across the city.

Al Safar students wear uniforms: grey dress pants and white dress shirts for boys; and burgundy tunics and pants for girls, along with a hijab. Female teachers are also required to wear the hijab. Classrooms are co-ed, but girls and boys sit in separate areas of the classroom starting in grade four.

The Al Safar school is housed in an architecturally impressive building. As a mosque, it has a beautiful prayer hall with a large domed roof. The classrooms are large and bright, with panorama windows and ample shelves around the perimeter. Most classrooms have tables and chairs arranged for cooperative work groups. Children's artwork and posters adorn the rooms and hallways, making an attractive presentation. The school has a state-of-the-art library, a gymnasium with a stage, and a fully equipped computer room. There is also a fairly large outdoor play area for recess and outdoor sports. Being housed in a mosque, the school is part of a larger public space, which connects it more closely to the Muslim community.

The Al Rajab School

I approached the Al Rajab school in 1999 with an offer to do some volunteer teaching in order to learn first-hand about life in Islamic schools. As an underresourced independent community school, it was grateful for the extra help, which I was offering free of charge. I agreed to teach an OAC World Issues class for one semester.

The school was operated as a family business by brother Nasir and sister Raeesa, a husband-and-wife team, who served as principal and vice principal respectively. They were originally from India but had lived in Canada for almost twenty years. All of their five children attended the school and also helped out. The school did not have a board or parent organization; all decision making rested with the owners/administrators, who were not themselves educators.

The school is located in a suburban plaza, surrounded by businesses such as a printing shop, a driving school, and a South Asian grocery. It occupies a fairly generous space, room enough for three hundred students from kindergarten to OAC. The school began as a girls' school, but after three years it began to admit boys as well. As a result, girls outnumbered boys while I was there.

The school opened in 1996, offering grades six to eleven, and had a starting enrolment of about 150. The high enrolment was owing to the fact that it did not initially charge fees. Most of its teachers were trying to accumulate 'Canadian experience' and to that end were volunteering their time. At first, the school grew by community word of mouth. Each year for the first three years, additional grades were added at the elementary and secondary levels until finally, all grades were being offered. By the middle of the second year, the financial burden was such that the more affluent families were asked to make voluntary donations. Later, school fees were introduced, but on a sliding scale that reflected family means. The teachers began to draw salaries, but these were minimal and left many living below the poverty line. Because of the low revenues, most of the teachers did not have an Ontario teacher's certificate, though all were university graduates and many had taught in their home countries. While I was doing fieldwork, most of the teachers were Muslim immigrants, mainly from South Asia; one or two were younger, second-generation Muslim Canadians who were seeking to gain teaching experience in order to apply for a teaching degree. A non-Muslim teacher of South Asian origin was teaching at the secondary level. This was the only non-Muslim teacher I observed in all of the schools in this study. Most schools prefer Muslim teachers so that all aspects of the curriculum can have an Islamic focus (see chapter 7 for a discussion of Islamically centred education).

The students were primarily of South Asian background, though many Somali, Afghani, and Arab students also attended. Many families were recent immigrants and earned low incomes, as opposed to the clientele of more elite private institutions. The school provided a bus service, and its students came from all parts of the city.

All students wore uniforms: black dress pants and a white dress shirt for boys; and maroon tunics or abayas (long overcoats)[2] for girls, along with a white or cream-coloured hijab. Female teachers were also required to wear abayas and the headscarf. Classes were segregated by gender after grade two. In the higher grades, boys and girls occupied separate spaces in the school.

The school occupied a large industrial space, which had been roughly partitioned into classrooms. While it was being renovated, the summer before I began teaching, the students volunteered to help paint and organize the space. Despite the construction, the facility was in disrepair and badly needed professional cleaning and renovation work. Decoration was sparse – only a few posters and sporadic pieces of children's art could be seen on the walls. There was an indoor gym but no outdoor play area for smaller children. The school did not have a library, but it did have a small reading room with donated books (most of them outdated). Many of the high school girls used that room as a study area. Few up-to-date resources were available, and many textbooks were old and used. For example, I was offered a textbook from 1989 to teach a World Issues course in 1999! The lack of outside funding and the large number of children from low-income families (who did not pay full tuition) made the school's financial situation difficult, with a corresponding impact on resources.

The Al Shawwal School

Like the Al Safar school, the Al Shawwal school was housed in a mosque. Unlike the Al Safar school, Al Shawwal did not have the benefit of experienced educators to guide its development. This was evident even in the physical space of the school, which was being added onto the existing mosque. Construction was still taking place at the time I approached the school about conducting the study. Though the renovations had been completed by the time I began my fieldwork, it was clear that the architects and school planners had not consulted with educators as to the appropriate dimensions for classrooms. Many of the rooms were windowless and far too small, and shelving and storage space were severely lacking. Some of the rooms were oddly shaped – one room was pie-shaped. There were few pictures or student works on the walls, which made for a sterile and unappealing environment. While I was at the school, the gymnasium was unfinished, and the students had to leave the building and enter through another door in order to reach it. The space, though new, was not big enough for the 250 students. The school included a small preschool. Though it was clean and nicely decorated, it did not conform to per pupil size guidelines for nursery schools.

The school also lacked resources and certified teachers. There was a small library where the school was organizing donated books. Members of the school's parent association volunteered at the school and helped raise funds to buy resources for it. Most members of the school community were recent Arab and Somali immigrants, though there were also some students from the Caribbean and South Asia. Many families were low income or on social assistance.

The students wore uniforms similar to those of other Islamic schools: black dress pants and white dress shirts for boys; blue-and-white tunics and pants for girls. Female teachers wore traditional Islamic dress: the abaya and the hijab.

Most of the teachers were also newcomers. Some, including the school principal, struggled with English. The principal, brother

Farrouk, was Egyptian and spoke little English. Though the school had been open for only eighteen months, he was its third principal. During my fieldwork at Al Shawwal, brother Farrouk left to start his own school; he was replaced by brother Yunus, who did not have any experience as an educator. A recent refugee, he had been a soldier in his home country. Bother Yunus had a difficult time, since he had no experience in school administration. Both principals were highly cooperative and supportive of my research, but neither spoke English well enough to be interviewed.

Total authority and decision making rested with the mosque's imam, who in effect was an oligarch. Since he had a day job, he was only available on Fridays, when he led congregational prayers at the mosque. Important school decisions were deferred until the imam was there to make them. The parent association primarily provided fundraising support but did not have any say in decisions affecting the school.

The Al Shaban School

Of all of the schools in this study, Al Shaban was the smallest and least developed. It was located in an industrial complex in a Toronto suburb and was in its second year by the time I began my fieldwork in 2000. There were about fifty students, from preschool to grade seven. The preschool was at the front of the building and was one of the only rooms with windows. The other classrooms were in the interior and were windowless, with overhead fluorescent lights. There was, though, an indoor gym and play area, which was a large carpeted space. The play area was too small to accommodate organized sports, and there was no outdoor play area for the smaller children.

The school administrator was a businessman who had no background in education. He conducted his business in an office above the school and viewed the school as community service. There were no school governors at Al Shaban, nor was there a parent association. Most of the teachers were recent immigrants from the Middle East and South Asia and were uncertified. In terms of the demographic make-up, there was a mix of Arab, South Asian, and Caribbean students. Their families seemed to be a mix: lower and middle income. There was no bus service; instead, students were car pooled from different parts of the city.

The younger students at the school did not wear uniforms, though the older girls wore the hijab and modest clothing. The female teachers wore the hijab and either modest, Western-style clothing (long skirt and blouse) or a *shalwar khameez*, a traditional, South Asian–style dress with a long, tunic-like blouse and baggy pants. One parent volunteer who had not worn a hijab began to wear it when she began teaching at the school. I saw this as a transition from being a volunteer to a teacher and, therefore, a role model for other young women to follow. All Islamic schools tend to require female teachers and staff to wear the hijab while at school even if they do not normally wear it outside school. This is encouraged in order to ensure that their attire is consistent with the overall school policy governing dress codes, but also because, from the Islamic perspective these schools advocate, it is seen as the normative standard for women's dress (see the discussion of gender and dress codes in chapter 5).

What struck me most about Al Shaban was the lack of resources and curriculum materials. Teachers were compelled to buy homework practice books from local shops in order to meet the curriculum's requirements, as no such books were provided. The classrooms displayed only rudimentary artwork, as art supplies were few. The teachers were eager to improve their pedagogy and skills, yet the school did not provide professional development workshops.

Overview of Participants and Sampling Procedures

In the sample I included students, teachers, administrators, parents, and a community activist. These categories allowed for greater triangulation of the data. There were thirteen parents, nine teachers, three administrators, one activist, eighteen female students from grade eight to OAC, and five boys from grades eleven and twelve. The activist had been involved in issues affecting the Muslim community at both public *and* Islamic schools and would be able to provide a global perspective. In all, forty-nine participants were interviewed for the study.

The participants represented a cross-section of the Muslim community. Twenty-six had a South Asian background (India, Pakistan, Afghanistan, Bangladesh); nine were from Africa (Somalia, Ethiopia, Sierra Leone); five were Arabs of Middle Eastern background (Syria, Palestine, Egypt); and six were from the Caribbean (Trinidad and Guyana). There were also three converts: respectively, an English Canadian, a French Canadian, and a Greek Canadian. All were from the Sunni community. Most of them were first-generation Canadian Muslims; they came from various socio-economic backgrounds. A few were relative newcomers; even so, they were proficient enough in English to participate in the interviews.

I identified the participants through snowball sampling, beginning with my own diverse personal contacts (including parents, teachers, and students from a variety of ethno-racial and social class backgrounds). These people then referred me on to other participants. I was mindful that if at all possible, the sample needed to be balanced ethno-racially and in terms of gender. Snowball sampling was a useful initial strategy, because it opened a gateway into the Islamic school communities that was based on referrals from insiders and allowed for greater trust. I found this recruiting method preferable to advertising for participants through flyers and other random approaches, which I knew from past experience would be largely ignored. However, if the initial contacts were not diversely represented this method might have yielded a more homogenous sample which would have been a potential drawback. When I entered the field (through teaching and other fieldwork activities), I was able to acquire new contacts; in this way, the sample became more random, as it was based on my observations and participation in the schools rather than on referrals.

For middle school students, parental consent was required for interviews, and I was only able to interview those who returned the forms. With the female high school students, I interviewed those who were over sixteen, who did not require parental consent. In the Al Rajab high school I began my search for participants with the students whom I knew and taught.[3] They later referred to me other possible interview candidates. Sometimes I simply approached a group of girls in the school hallway during lunch break and asked them if they wanted to participate. The high school boys were also accessed through referrals. There were fewer boys in the high school; therefore, proportionately fewer boys than girls are represented in the sample. I was also limited by the students' availability to participate in interviews, since all interviews were conducted on the school premises. I chose to do focus groups with students, as opposed to individual interviews, as a more efficient way of accessing participants. This also allowed for a more relaxed, conversational style of interviewing, as will be apparent in the narratives presented. I conducted student interviews during the month of Ramadan, since their lunch hours were then free, as they were maintaining their daily fast.

Parents were interviewed in the home on an individual basis as well as in groups, according to the participants' availability. Most parents were active in the school as volunteers or parent committee members; even so, I preferred to arrange interviews at home, to ensure greater confidentiality. Teachers and school administrators were interviewed either at the school during their breaks or after school. All interviews followed a set of predetermined questions to guide the conversation.

Fieldwork Activities

My fieldwork in the four Islamic schools followed a range of ethnographic research strategies, including participant and non-participant observation, interviews, and action research as a volunteer teacher. At the Al Rajab high school, between September 1999 and February 2000, as part of preliminary action research, I taught an OAC World Issues class for grade twelve and thirteen high school girls. This experience allowed me to become more of an 'insider' at the school and normalize my presence. All staff and students were, however, aware of the dual purpose of my presence at the school. I was also able to participate in school functions and field trips. For example, I served as a judge in the school arts and speech competitions and was a guest speaker at the school's annual science fair. I also participated in a school field trip to a protest staged at the U.S. consulate in response to the sanctions against Iraq.

To make my presence as a researcher more reciprocal, I taught three teacher development workshop sessions at the Al Shawwal school for sixteen teachers and the school principal. These workshops were based on the teachers' interest in furthering their professional development in the area of teaching towards multiple intelligences. Because these teachers did not have their Ontario Teacher's Certification (OTC), such strategies were new to them. This experience introduced me to the school's teachers; it also situated my research as a process of give and take, in that I was able to contribute to the school in a tangible way, just as the teachers contributed to this project.

Also, I offered a summer writing workshop at the Al Rajab school for grade ten to OAC girls. During this six-week course I taught creative writing skills and literary criticism to a group of ten girls. In the process I was able to further engage students regarding issues at their school as well as issues affecting Muslim women more generally. Through this experience, I gained further insights into these young women's lives and perspectives. During the summer course I shared with the participants some of my initial findings about the experiences of Muslim girls in Islamic schools. This allowed me to investigate the 'face validity' (Lather 1986b) of some of my initial theorizing by recycling meanings through this sub-sample of the stakeholders. In the process I refined and developed my ideas as the participants and I co-constructed them. The time I spent teaching in the community was an important opportunity to provide professional development and academic support to students and teachers from racialized communities. I saw this as an important means of furthering the social justice imperatives of my research.

I conducted fifty hours of formal classroom observation. In addition to this, I involved myself in other participant and non-participant forms of observation – for example, during school activities such as field trips, parent association meetings, and school assemblies. I also participated in religious festivities at the schools. And I continued some volunteer teaching in elementary classrooms, either assisting the teachers or leading lessons. In particular, I worked with a grade four teacher at the Al Shawwal school, teaching a social studies unit on the Islamic medieval world, which I co-authored. This allowed me to become more integral to the school culture and to give something back to the teacher and students; it also allowed me to model some interactive teaching strategies that represented a new pedagogical style for many teachers at this school. I also helped teachers at Al Shawwal develop positive discipline strategies and more democratic structures in the classroom. At each of the four participating schools, my position as a teacher/researcher allowed me to act as a much needed resource for the staff and students.

Challenges and Limitations

A researcher's findings are often characterized by a series of reflections prefaced by the statement 'if only ...' The research process seldom measures up to the goals it sets out to achieve: there are too many constraints to perfection. In the case at hand, the major culprits were time and resources: shortages of both derailed some of the specific outcomes I had hoped to achieve and ultimately framed both the challenges and possibilities of this research.

For example, because I was unable to employ translators, all interviews had to be conducted with people who spoke English well enough to be interviewed. Including non-English-speaking participants who are newcomers to Canada would have provided a different perspective. Also, given the time constraints, my sampling methods were more opportunistic than strategic. I would like to have interviewed more of the parents of the participating students, but time and scheduling constraints worked against this.

Also, I was sometimes limited by the circumstances within a given school. For example, I used my time at Al Shaban primarily in observation mode, or providing support and feedback to teachers who wanted my opinion on their teaching methods. During my fieldwork there, almost all the teachers were new to the school – they had only been there for one month. So I chose not to interview these teachers. Thus, this school was included in the study more as a site of observation.

Data Analysis: Developing a Grounded Theory

A critical ethnographic framework enabled me to focus on developing a theory that was grounded in the experiences of the research subjects. Glazer and Strauss (1967) refer to this process as developing a 'grounded theory,' where theory is inductively extracted from the data rather than predetermined through a particular grand narrative. Lather (1986a) notes that 'building empirically grounded theory requires a reciprocal relationship between data and theory. Data must be allowed to generate propositions in a dialectical manner that permits the use of a priori theoretical frameworks, but which keeps a particular framework from becoming the container into which the data must be poured' (p. 267). This speaks to the need to maintain an inductive process of inquiry that constantly correlates data and theory.

As discussed in the previous chapter, the use of multiple discursive frameworks provided various ideological contexts for the data to develop within and inform theories of the particular. The data analysis, therefore, involved extracting particular themes and conceptual categories of analysis from the data, which were then situated within and against the discursive paradigms employed.

As mentioned earlier, the contributions of stakeholders also helped inform and reform my analyses along the way by providing critical feedback. I spent several hours in discussion with various Islamic school students, parents, teachers, administrators, and educational activists regarding the pathways of my research and my theorizing of the experiences that were presented to me. These conversations took place in school meetings, in organizing sessions with educational activists, in Islamic teacher education seminars, in people's homes or offices, and in the form of heated conversations with other Islamic school mothers in the parking lot of the local mosque. This prolonged engagement with the issues represented a more organic process for discussing and debating the relevant issues in my research among the various stakeholders. This fostered a way of negotiating and co-constructing meanings that was more collaborative than would have been a formal and validation session designed simply to verify my predetermined conclusions. It led to a complex negotiation of the empirical observations, the textual data, the discursive frameworks, and the critical engagements of participants. The resulting synergy between epistemological and empirical dynamics has produced the ethnography I present here, not as a final authoritative account but rather as another entry point for apprehending the dynamics of Islamic schooling in new and provocative ways.

4 The Role and Function of Islamic Schools in the Canadian Muslim Diaspora

This chapter examines the sociological and ideological role performed by Islamic schools in the Canadian Muslim diaspora. The narratives of students, parents, teachers, and administrators provided insights into the various functions of Islamic schools. The salient themes that emerged from the interviews and participant observations I conducted over eighteen months of fieldwork showed that Islamic schools make the following sociological and ideological contributions:

- They provide a social and spiritually based alternative to secular public schools.
- They 'protect' students from negative influences (i.e., rather than isolating and 'ghettoizing' students).
- They rehabilitate and resocialize 'wayward' students (i.e., through a process of cultural reconstruction).
- They contribute to the social reproduction of Islamic identity and lifestyle.

These themes will be explored through a narrative analysis of how Islamic schools function in the Muslim diaspora.

Interviews with Muslim students, parents, and teachers revealed why Islamic schools are seen as a growing alternative to public schools. Islamic schools provide a culturally congruent environment; they validate religious values and practices and make them integral to the schooling experience and environment. In this sense, these schools are an alternative to secular public schools, where many Muslim students report feelings of alienation and often encounter Islamophobic attitudes (see Rezai-Rashti, 1994; Joshi, 2006; Zine, 1997, 2000, 2001b). Also, parents often fear that the social and cultural milieu of public schools will 'de-Islamize' their children as a result of peer pressure to assimilate (see also Berns McGown, 1999). Indeed, many students are channelled into Islamic schools because of their 'un-Islamic' behaviour. Some male students enter Islamic schools after being expelled from the public school system as a result of involvement in violence and drugs. Some girls have been sent to Islamic school after taking up with boys and violating the Islamic code of sexual abstinence before marriage. In this way, Islamic schools serve as centres for 'rehabilitation' and resocialization in accordance with Islamically acceptable values and norms.

Both parents and students often view Islamic schools as a safe haven, one in which students can learn in a faith-centred setting. The critical faith-centred perspective posits that holistic education that attends to the development of the body, mind, and spirit is necessary for individual and societal health. Spiritual education is absent from secular public schooling. Also, Islamic schools are sites where religious and spiritual knowledge is treated as an epistemologically valid way of knowing and engaging in intellectual activities; indeed, such knowledge is a focus of the curriculum. Many parents told me that they chose a religious education for their children so that they could learn about Islam and acquire the Arabic language, which is the language in which the Holy Qur'an is written and recited. They also wanted their children to absorb the values, norms, behaviours, and practices that constitute the Islamic identity. Islamic schools, then, are among the primary sites for social reproducing Islamic identity and lifestyle.

Students reported a greater sense of belonging – of 'fitting in' – once they entered an Islamic school environment. Many regarded the school's community of teachers and students as their 'family' and felt that it provided a more caring environment than the more impersonal secular schools. As community-based schools, Islamic schools are able to encourage greater cohesiveness, greater attachment to the broader Muslim community. Critics argue that this can lead to social isolation and 'ghettoization' – that independent schools foster a kind of 'religious apartheid' as well as an unhealthy insularity (see also Zine, 2007b). These issues will be explored in the narrative analysis that follows.

Public versus Islamic Schools: Racialized Encounters

As students compared their experiences in public schools with those in Islamic school, many themes emerged. They spoke of how public schools disenfranchised them and how Islamic schools allowed them to feel a greater sense of belonging. Rehana, a nineteen-year-old of Pakistani descent, was a student in my OAC World Issues course. She was born in England and had lived in Canada for ten years. At the time of our interview, her family had just returned from living in Saudi Arabia. In Canada she had mainly attended public schools; she had been attending Al Rajab for six months. She reported feeling isolated and excluded from her peers in public school because of how she dressed; also, her adherence to Islam meant that she did not date and avoided events such as school dances. (Some conventional interpretations of Islam forbid intermingling of the sexes in order to reduce the risk of premarital relations.) Rehana told me that she had felt alienated and socially isolated even before she began wearing the hijab:

REHANA: Well, yeah, at times it was difficult, because – I couldn't be like – I wasn't like them [other students] is the truth, I wasn't like them.
JASMIN: In what way?
REHANA: The things that they did, like for example, if you take dress, they dressed quite differently from the way I did. And they always used to question me: 'Oh why can't you wear this? Why can't you do this? Why can't you go out with guys? Why can't you come to our dances?' But it was hard for them to understand where I was coming from and what I was trying to say when I told them I wasn't allowed. And then they always used to exclude me from whatever activities that they did because I wasn't allowed to join in.

Rehana reports that during this period, she was not wearing the hijab, though she did wear very modest attire in comparison with the popular revealing fashions of other girls. This refusal to conform to popular clothing styles, and to 'normal' behaviours such as dating and partying, situated her outside the boundaries of social acceptance. Peer pressure both disciplined and excluded her.

It is common for Muslim students in the public school system to encounter social exclusion, discrimination, and Islamophobia. In my previous research, which examined the politics of religious identity among Muslim high school students in the public school system, similar accounts of alienation on the basis of race and religious identification were reported (see Zine, 1997, 2000, 2001b). So it is no surprise that students who had transferred from public schools to Islamic schools reported a greater sense of 'fitting in,' and social acceptance. The Muslim girls I interviewed often raised the issue of Islamic clothing when they evaluated their experiences in public schools. Aliyah, a sixteen-year-old grade eleven student of Afghani origin, spoke of how she felt more comfortable in a single-sex Islamic school environment, where the emphasis on being physically 'made up' was not as important a factor:

ALIYAH: You don't have to worry about what you wear. Like in public school you have to worry about your hair, what you're wearing, how you look every day. Here you just wear your abaya – everyone's wearing it, so it doesn't make a difference.

Aliyah found that wearing an abaya – which was part of the school uniform – resulted in less emphasis on keeping up with fashion and competing with other girls. The fact that all the girls wore the same uniform reduced the heavy emphasis on fashion conformity that is a strong part of mainstream public school settings.

The pressure to 'fit in' – to accommodate oneself to social and cultural mores – extended to other aspects of school life. For example, what kind of food was it 'socially safe' for Muslim students to bring to school? Nusaybah, a sixteen-year-old grade eleven student, Canadian born of Pakistani descent, talked about how she finally felt comfortable bringing the kind of food she ate at home to school without the judgment and negative reactions from other students:

NUSAYBAH: See here it's like Islam, so if you're Pakistani you can bring samosa, you can bring leftover food from the night before and it's like no one's going to care. It's like, 'Oh whatever.' But in public school, if you bring a sandwich and if it's like even slightly the weirdest thing they'll be like, 'Oooh … why are you doing?! Why are you eating that?' So you pretty much have to stick to peanut butter in public school.

Having to 'stick to peanut butter in public school' is a powerful metaphor for the dominance of Eurocentric practices in the culture of mainstream public schools, where any deviation from socially enforced norms results in being labelled 'weird' and, in Nusayabah's case, being forced to conceal any evidence of 'ethnicness.' Even mundane experiences such as lunchroom encounters have a profound effect on the identity and cultural self-esteem of ethnically minoritized students. In contrast, Nusaybah reported feeling greater acceptance and equality in an Islamic school environment:

NUSAYBAH: Here it's like you can do anything. Even like with different cultures' clothing, like you can wear it. See, like *shalwar khameez*,[1] like I'm wearing now, and like it doesn't matter and you don't need to wear make-up, you don't need to impress anybody. Everyone is so equal ... In this school it's like everyone is at the same level. There's no popular people and there's no nerds. Everyone is at the same level and so you feel comfortable because everyone is your friend, so you don't feel left out.

In Islamic schools, being able to fit in and be accepted was a significant theme in students' narratives. They reported feeling less social differentiation on the basis of race, class, or culture in the Islamic school environment in comparison with public schools. Socio-economic categories were not as visible since everyone wore the same uniform. Even though the school was strongly multicultural, in that the students were from a multitude of backgrounds (South Asian, Arab, Somali, and so on), the students reported that there were no 'colour-coded cliques,' as was the case in public schools, where students built affinity groups and social networks on the basis of race and ethnic affiliation. The politics of the colour line manifest in the practice of 'shadism' – a social process that privileges lighter skin colour within a given racialized group – did not seem overtly evident; it did not seem to be a factor in the girls' perceptions and evaluations of one another.

The students in my summer creative writing seminar referred to one another's skin tones as 'chocolate,' 'butterscotch,' and 'vanilla.' These descriptors were meant to be flattering, not derogatory or hierarchical. Shadism is a common practice within certain racialized groups, a result of the disavowal of racialization and the desire to attain the privileges associated with white skin (see, for example, Mire, 2001). Many racial communities have internalized the colonial politics of the colour line in this way, thereby reproducing the same practices (albeit more subtly) of skin colour discrimination. The experience of being among other racialized girls seemed to foster a greater acceptance of and comfort with physical and social differences.

The parents, too, spoke of their experiences of racism and exclusion in the public school system. These experiences informed their decisions to send their children to Islamic schools; they wanted to spare them from such negative encounters. Rumaisa, the mother of a four-year-old daughter attending Al Shawwal, had immigrated to Canada from England nine years earlier. Rumaisa was in her late twenties and was originally from Pakistan. When she came to Canada she went to a public school for two years after attending in an all-girls school in England. She reported the assumptions that were made about her identity and status in Canada:

RUMAISA: The very first time I went into a school here ... I mean, I didn't say a word. It was funny, but they thought I was a typical Indian person that came from India ... Off the boat. Fresh off the boat. 'FOB.' And then when the teacher asked me a question and I opened my English mouth and they're like, Wow! Usually people judge a book by its cover. They don't know what really is inside. So a lot people try to make friends because of my accent. It wasn't a big deal for me, but I wanted them to accept me for who I was.

It is interesting that the first reaction to Rumaisa was that she was 'FOB' or 'Fresh off the boat.' Then people heard her British accent, and she actually garnered positive attention from peers, who tried to make friends with her. Her accent allowed her to 'perform' her 'Britishness' – a social location that made her more 'acceptable' to peers than her status as an Indian immigrant. By occupying a space of hybrid cultural identification, Rumaisa was able to play out her British identity as a counternarrative to the more socially devalued location of 'South Asian Indian immigrant.' This trade-off is an example of how racially and ethnically minoritized groups are often forced to try to 'piggyback' off white Eurocentric privilege, whether through language or through other means of 'passing.'

Other parents reported negative encounters when they approached public schools to register their children. Qassim and Sobia were Canadian-born parents of a four-year-old son, also at Al-Shawwal. They were of Trinidadian origin and in their mid-twenties. Sobia had grown up attending Canadian schools; Qassim had returned to Trinidad for much of his schooling and had converted to Islam from Hinduism while in his teens. During our interview, Sobia reported experiencing a negative reception from public schools when she tried to enrol their son for kindergarten. They discussed how this had affected their decision to send their son to an Islamic school instead:

JASMIN: What made you decide to choose an Islamic school out of all the choices that you had?
SOBIA: Well, we just moved to the area and I went to the public school and I was rudely insulted there, and I was like, forget it!
JASMIN: What do you mean insulted?
SOBIA: They acted as if I had no knowledge of being in Canada in terms of filling out an application form or anything. And I was just like, if this is what the administration's like for this school, I can't imagine how the whole school would be run.
QASSIM: I think she was doing a lot of the fieldwork and was I sort of dealing with it from an ideological perspective. I think more and more I find that public schools are not meeting the needs of a diverse population. I think it pretends to be inclusive and it is in fact quite discriminatory. And I don't want my child to be placed in an environment where he is being discriminated against.
SOBIA: Exactly, but it's so difficult especially when they're in school. You don't know what they're exposed to and stuff. With me, I think going through the public system – like at the time Islamic school wasn't even an option, right? So you have to go through the public school. I guess in some ways it was hard being coloured and wearing hijab going through the public system. But I found I got a lot of support through my school in terms of like ...
QASSIM: You had peer support.
SOBIA: Yeah. You kind of were trying to find your identity then. And finding it within a group of people who share the same identity is a lot easier.

Sobia's experience was similar in some ways to Rumaisa's: she was treated like an immigrant, and the school officials perceived her as lacking the cultural capital required even to fill out an application form for her son. Sobia found this especially insulting: though Canadian born, she had been labelled a 'foreigner' because she was racially minoritized and wore the hijab. In discussing her own high school experiences, Sobia recalled how she had joined a Muslim Student Association (MSA) and had helped advocate for a more inclusive school environment, such as the provision of a prayer room. She had found a great deal of support for her religious lifestyle through the strong social network of Muslim students that developed. This is an example of how religious identities can be operationalized as sites of resistance to domination and oppression (see Zine, 2000, for more discussion on Muslim student organizations and the politics of religious identity). Based on their experiences with public education, Sobia and Qassim felt that placing their son in an Islamic school would allow him to build a strong sense of identity and self-esteem, free from racial and religious bias and discrimination.

Inclusive versus Exclusive Schooling

Both students and parents told me that public schools were failing to accommodate Muslim religious practices and holidays. They appreciated the centring of their religious knowledge, history, and practices in Islamic schools. Three grade eleven girls discussed this point with me. Zarqa and Nusaybah were both sixteen years old and of Pakistani descent, but both had been born in Canada. Both were relative newcomers to the Islamic school: Zarqa had been attending for four months, Nusaybah for two. Aliyah, also sixteen, was born in Afghanistan and immigrated to Canada when she was five. She had been attending Al Rajab for five years. In the following exchange among these girls, they discussed their feelings of alienation and exclusion in not having their holidays acknowledged:

ZARQA: Like in public school, you'd be like so whitewashed! You'd be like paying attention more to other cultures, you wouldn't really care about your own religion. Like it's Ramadan, you'd be like, 'Oh yeah.'
NUSAYBAH: But, guys, it depends on your school, if you go to a Muslim or like a Brown school, then you will be like a little more into your religion.
ZARQA: But if you go to a public school where there's all mixed cultures – like they care about their religion – but they don't give so much attention to the religion, like over here.
ALIYAH: Like they're more concerned about when it's their holidays, like when it's Christmas or Halloween.
ZARQA: When it's Halloween, they're like, 'Oh my God, it's Halloween! Are you guys going? I'm going!' I mean you feel pressure to go because everyone else is going. Or it's Christmas and everyone's like, 'Oh it's Christmas I just bought a gift, blah, blah, blah,'

and they don't give a ... they don't give a care about our holidays. They're more concerned about their holidays. Those are the ones that get celebrated more often. And like here you care about Eid. But in public school you feel like, you wouldn't even go home [for Eid], you'd just stay in school. I like it, like the way it is here.

ALIYAH: The other good thing is like during Ramadan and other religious holidays, you can actually get a chance to pray. You get a break. Like there, you have religious holidays for Christians, like they have Christmas holidays. They have all these holidays for those people but they have no holidays for us. Like we don't have Eid off in public school. Like here we have time off in Ramadan and it gives us a chance to pray more or like carry out our Islamic ways more, because then in public school you have to go to school the whole time. Even on Eid, you don't get a holiday; most people just come to school.

It is telling that the girls critically analysed the Eurocentric practices of schooling – those which centre the dominant culture as the norm and which do not equally commemorate the celebrations of marginalized communities – as a process of 'whitewashing.' Only in 'Brown schools' (i.e., public schools whose students were predominantly South Asian) was the school culture more inclusive (see Handa, 2003, for a discussion of South Asian students and cultural self-esteem in 'Brown schools'). The Islamic school environment did allow religion and cultural beliefs and practices to occupy a central place, both formally and informally. For students coming from public schools, this was the first time their experiences had ever been centred.

Qassim felt that his values and experiences as a Muslim would not be acknowledged or respected in the public school system. He was open to a pluralistic curriculum that would give his son access to other historical and cultural experiences, but he was sceptical that knowledge of Islam would be represented:

QASSIM: And I think that that was a big issue for me – what he was learning, what he would be exposed to in terms of what other people's values were – which I don't have a problem with because I am a convert, right? So I have no problem with them learning other people's values, but the fact that our values would not be shared as well and wouldn't be respected – that was a big issue for me.

Other parents commented on the lack of inclusive curriculum in public schools and the dominance of Eurocentric holidays and celebrations that conflicted with their Islamic sensibilities. Shahnaz, in her mid-thirties, was the mother of four children and had immigrated to Canada from India fifteen years earlier. She had originally placed her eldest daughter, Seema, in a public school. She later enrolled her daughter and her two younger sons at Al Safar. Having attended a British Catholic convent school in India, Shahnaz was no stranger to a Eurocentric school system; however, she was not prepared for traditions and celebrations such as Halloween and Valentine's Day, which were contrary to her Islamic beliefs:

SHAHNAZ: The other thing is I wasn't too pleased with the Christmas celebrations or the Halloween celebrations. Seema used to come home with Santa Claus and Valentine cards. For the first year, I was like, 'What is this?' I was new to Canada, too, and she was my first child. So even though in India I went to a convent school I never got exposed to these things. There were Christmas celebrations but not like these ones here. We never had Valentine's there. We never had Halloween there. So when she came home, I mean, I was, Seema, what *is* this? Oh, it's a Valentine card from a friend of mine. This is in JK and SK they're doing all this. It's telling them that it's okay to love someone like that. So I just didn't like it.

From the perspective of parents like Shahnaz, seemingly innocuous traditions such as Valentine's Day promote gender relationships that conflict with Muslim social norms. Promoting romantic notions among young children is seen as setting the stage for later forays into dating – a practice discouraged in Islamic traditions. Similarly, Halloween is seen as an essentially pagan celebration that glorifies the macabre, such as evil witches, demons, and vampires. Many Muslim parents, therefore, find it inappropriate to allow their children to participate in these school-based celebrations and the pedagogical activities related to them. At the same time, many Muslim parents (like Qassim) are concerned that their own traditions are glaringly absent from the curriculum and practices of public schools. In this vein, Muslim teachers reported that they preferred teaching in Islamic schools, for it meant they did not have to teach issues that compromised their belief system and made them uncomfortable.

From a critical faith-centred perspective, the exclusion of specific faith-based knowledges and experiences from the secular Eurocentric framework of public schools delegitimates the religious identity of students from outside that framework and forces them to deny this critical aspect of their identity. Conversely, faith-based schools enable expressions of religious experience as valid and normative. More inclusive practices are required in order to create a more multicentred curriculum in public schools, one that will validate religiously and spiritually based realities (see Dei, James, James-Wilson, Karumanchery, & Zine, 2001).

Islamic Schools: Protection or Ghettoization?

The challenges and debates surrounding religious education centre on whether religious schools ghettoize children and youth. On this question, many of the students, parents, and teachers responded to through counter-narratives of Islamic schools as 'safe' spaces that provided protection from negative outside influences such as drugs, gangs, violence and sexual harassment, and yet they rejected the notion that this constituted a form of 'ghettoization.' Others, though, did suggest that Islamic schools were not doing enough to prepare students to integrate with mainstream public schools and postsecondary institutions, and *were* concerned about social isolation. In particular, teachers felt that systems needed to be established so that independent and public schools could better share information and resources. The following discussion explores these issues and concerns relating to protection versus isolation as the by-products of independent religious schooling.

School as Family

Many of the students I interviewed described their school and the relationships among the students and teachers there as 'like a family'; they felt that Islamic schools offered a safer and more comfortable environment for them than did the public schools. In a study of a British Muslim school for girls, Mustafa (1999) found similar sentiments among the students he surveyed: they reported high levels of satisfaction with their school owing to the 'Islamic and friendly environment' (p. 296). Amal, an eighteen-year-old Arab student from Kuwait who attended my OAC class, described the welcoming environment she encountered at Al-Rajab and how 'kind' other students were when she began attending. Amal had been in Canada for only three years and had spent the first two years attending a public school. At the time of our interview she had been in Islamic school for one year. Her friends and teachers at Al-Rajab had become a surrogate family:

AMAL: Uh, what I like is ... or the most important thing for me is – friends. Like my friends, we have the same beliefs. We can get together; we all like the same things. And the thing is, like the teachers, they are more like sisters and brothers to us than teachers. We're like ... we're free here. We can talk and express our opinions because – of course we have the same beliefs and the same religion – and the thing is they understand. They are more understanding and we are like a community – like a small family. Not like public school. It's like I was really scared there. I had nobody there and the teachers were like strangers to me. Here it's more like a sense of community. I remember from back when I first came to this school it was like, OK, this is so familiar to me.

Saira, a fourteen-year-old of Indian descent, had transferred from the public school system to Al Safar two years earlier. She had similar sentiments, referring to her school as like 'a big family and a community, everyone can rely on each other, we can help each other.'

Other participants stressed that Islamic schools created spaces of solidarity and community among Muslims. Ibrahim, a community activist, originally from Sierra Leone, had cofounded a grassroots organization to provide educational support and advocacy for Muslim families dealing with the public school system and Islamic schools. He spoke of Islamic schools as sites where community solidarity could be fostered in ways that counteracted 'tribalism' – that is, the fragmentation of Muslims into ethnic enclaves – by providing mechanisms for fostering greater cohesion on the basis of a common Islamic identity:

IBRAHIM: Also, another goal of Islamic education, or Islamic school, is the reinforcement of the whole question of solidarity among Muslims – children as well as parents – because we're united in faith. And we're united in building the bond of brotherhood and sisterhood within Islam. I think most times, as it is in the mainstream, this is where these relationships are reinforced so that kids, teachers, identify more as Muslim – much more so than where we come from. Because we always say that, you know, Islam is one body and we are brothers and sisters. But I think we have not acted this out in our daily interaction and I think schooling allows that possibility to happen. You know, as kids grow up in these schools, the colour line is erased. They begin to see more and more of each other as children who are the same – not thinking about where they come from.'

Deqa, a sixteen-year-old grade twelve Somali student who had attended Al-Rajab for three years since arriving in Canada, also saw Islam as a force of social cohesion among her school's culturally diverse student body:

DEQA: We're all from so many different countries and different backgrounds and we all have different cultures. The only aspect that brings us together is Islam. So this makes Islam more pure to us.

Ali, an eighteen-year-old OAC student of Bangladeshi descent who had attended Al-Rajab for three years, described his relations with teachers and fellow students as a 'family' situation. He referred to his teachers as 'brothers' in a familial sense. This is a common term in the Muslim community, where people customarily refer to one another as 'brothers' or 'sisters' within Islam; but Ali's sense that the school was a 'true' family was even stronger than that. He felt that he was receiving more attention – including more *positive* attention – from teachers at the Islamic school than he ever would have in the public schools. Similarly, Deqa felt that the school was providing her with a more comfortable environment. When I asked her if she felt that she was facing any challenges in the Islamic school, she replied that there were greater challenges outside the school than inside:

DEQA: Challenges? Maybe you'd better ask somebody else because I can't think of any challenges. It's not too difficult, because it's actually more challenging to be outside because then you have to deal with more stuff. Around here all you have to deal with is being around fellow Muslims and just discussing faith, it's basically like a much more comfortable environment.

Clearly, the faith-centred environment provided comfort, familiarity, safety, and cultural congruence. Yet critics of separate schools argue that this sense of 'safety' and comfort breeds an unhealthy insularity by secluding these children and youth from non-Muslim peer groups.

Non-Muslim Friends

Many students spoke of their relations with friends from outside the community. Fourteen-year-old Saira, a recent entrant into the Islamic school system, noted that most of her friends were in public school and were not Muslim. Then she added that the friends she had made at Al Safar over the past year were closer to her. She felt that this was because they had more in common from an Islamic point of view and that they had a better understanding of her feelings and experiences as a young adolescent Muslim girl, since their experiences were similar. Fourteen-year-old Noora, a classmate of Saira's of Guyanese descent, had been one of the first students to enrol at Al Safar when it opened in 1993. She found it easier to socialize with Muslim friends, noting that non-Muslim friends were a more likely source of negative peer pressure and that they often questioned the religious lifestyle she had chosen:

NOORA: With your non-Muslim friends, they don't understand you, and they'll keep questioning you about your religion, and they might not only ask just to know, they might ask to try to shake you or to bend you.

Many students noted that their relations with their non-Muslim friends changed when they began attending Islamic school, owing to the shift in values and perspectives many of them experienced. They were not trying deliberately to distance themselves; they simply sensed that they were 'growing apart.' Iman, a seventeen-year-old grade twelve Somali student who had attended Al Rajab for three years, spoke of the changes in social practices that students underwent as they adjusted to the new values and mores of the Islamic school, leaving behind the often un-Islamic practices of their public school days.

IMAN: When you come into an Islamic environment, people tend to change a lot of the time. So it's like calling up an old friend and that person might have been the same or might have even changed worse, but you're, like, more on the positive side.

Deqa agreed, noting that since 'Islam was an everyday thing,' she found it more comfortable to share friendships with fellow Muslims.

The male students expressed a similar idea – that they needed to be around their Muslim friends in order to resist negative pressure from their peers outside the Muslim school. They also felt that the moral grounding provided by their Islamic school helped them resist negative peer pressure. Sabbir, nineteen, and Saadi, seventeen, were brothers and had been attending Al-Rajab for eighteen months. Both were born in Canada of Pakistani parents. They reflected on the friends they had left behind in public school:

SABBIR: Yeah, I still have non-Muslim friends who I used to hang around even before I was in the public schools. I still hang around them now, but you don't get influenced by their ideas. We don't get influenced by non-Islamic culture. But they are still my friends. They respect the fact that I'm Muslim. They always have. There are some people who don't accept you because you are Muslim, especially in the area that I live now.

SAADI: I have a lot of Jewish friends, too. We don't discriminate at all. Just because we go to a Muslim school, when we come out, it's not like we can only talk to Muslim people. It's not like that at all.

It is significant that Saadi and Sabbir maintained ties with non-Muslim friends from different cultural backgrounds and faith communities. This reminds us that religious schooling need not be a form of 'religious apartheid' and that it is possible to maintain cross-cultural and interfaith ties outside of school.

Ghettoization

Despite their concerns about negative peer pressure, Islamic school students were, by and large, open to maintaining ties with non-Muslim friends from outside of school. This does much to dispel the criticism that religious schooling breeds insularity among already marginalized groups. Students, parents, and teachers all confronted the notion that independent parochial schools are 'religious ghettos.' Farida and Shazad, Guyanese parents in their mid-thirties whose children attended Al Safar, pointed out, for example, that a certain amount of isolation was necessary in order to 'minimize the risks' of children falling into the temptations offered by the mainstream culture. Farida told me that the inculcation of values in a separate and culturally congruent environment was necessary in order for Muslim children to build a sense of identity; those values, having been absorbed, would enable them integrate into mainstream society without losing their Islamic values and identity:

FARIDA: I guess that some of the things they're being taught in the public school, and you have to, like, you know, just wonder what, because they teach them things that are non-Islamic, too, and you want to isolate them from some of that when they're young so that, not that you don't want them to be exposed, but if you give them too much of that, they will eventually be, you will have to, you try to isolate them and gear them into Islam as early as possible. Eventually they'll be going into the public system. You're preparing them for that too but they'll be stronger as their identity builds.

Yet it was also acknowledged that unless they engaged more with mainstream society, some schools risked socially and intellectually isolating their students. Even Muslims attached negative stereotypes to Islamic schools. Shahnaz noted that many of her family and friends from back home in India were opposed to her decision to send her daughter to Islamic school:

SHAHNAZ: My in-laws, everyone, they said, you know, 'Why are you putting her in an Islamic school?' My friends – they're calling from India, 'Why are you putting her in an Islamic school? You're in Canada! You should put her in the public school system. You know, why are you making her backward like that? And why are you doing this to her?' They weren't against the hijab or the Islamic dress code or anything, but they were just, you know, she's going to go out in the real world. Why do you want her to be just sheltered like that in the school system?

Shahnaz's family and friends back home saw social and cultural integration as the goal of schooling for their diasporic relatives in Canada. They felt that by sending her daughter to an Islamic school, Shahnaz was sheltering her from mainstream society and making her more backward. This suggests how, because of the colonial legacy and Western cultural imperialism and hegemony, Muslims equate Westernization with progress and view tradition and faith as anachronisms.

Rukhsana, a mother in her mid-thirties, had three children attending Al Safar. She had lived in Canada for twenty-eight years, having immigrated from Pakistan as a child. She felt that an Islamic education did not stand in the way of contributing actively to society, and she was critical of those who allowed themselves to become too insular:

RUKHSANA: Okay, they obviously should have the Islamic teaching but they should have to integrate in society. They can't be just Muslim. You have to be Muslim, obviously, but you can show that you can contribute to society. You can get involved in the community, you know, do something, volunteer. There's food banks. There's a lot of things that they can get involved in. They're an integral part of the society. We can contribute to the society. We can contribute with our academics. There are hundreds of ways to contribute but they're not contributing. They want to stay within themselves. They don't want to spread out. I don't know why.

Sister Mehrun, the principal of Al Safar, also disagreed with the perspective that Islamic schooling prevented Muslim children from interacting in healthy ways with children from different religious and cultural backgrounds. From her perspective, her pupils were engaged in activities outside school that brought them into contact with people from the broader community. Moreover, the confidence they were building *as Muslims* was just as important as cross-cultural interaction.

MEHRUN: We are living in the society – we are not that completely isolated – the children go shopping, the children are watching television, they go for picnics and all that, and you know they are aware. But at the same time, I think having a good self-concept, and being comfortable with who they are, is just as important. And after all, basically I came from another country and I don't think I had any trouble adjusting to the society. So those children that are growing up here, they are not completely isolated. *Insha'allah* [God willing], once they are older, they will have a good understanding, maybe a better understanding than what we have.

In sister Mehrun's view, then, her pupils were learning to embrace their Muslim identity. Having done so, they would be able to develop an understanding of others. A student I interviewed expressed a similar idea. Leila, an OAC student of Somali descent, had lived in Canada for five years. She had attended public school for four years before transferring to Al Rajab. She contended that a Muslim identity provided her and her classmates with the life skills that they would need in order to interact with others in the broader society:

LEILA: Well, you know ... not being out there, it's not such a big deal, cuz like you take the bus with everybody. It's like our lives interact with different people, but it's just that the school prepares us Islamically – giving us an Islamic perspective on how to deal with everybody – and in that sense they are preparing us, like, for the world.

Other students were offended by the suggestion that they were isolated – that they weren't aware of the outside world. Zarqa, Aliyah, and Nusaybah all defended their choice to attend Islamic school. They did not feel that it affected their ability to know about other cultures and ways of life. And they defended those who chose to focus on faith as a central aspect of their education:

ZARQA: But, like, you have a right to your own religion, and if you want to put yourself into a box and only do your religion and only know about your religion, it's your choice. It shouldn't matter. I know it's, like, a good thing to know about other religions and respect other religions and understand other religions, but how to explain it?
ALIYAH: You should also know about your own.

Liberal theorists argue that public schools, with their diverse student bodies, offer greater opportunities to gain cross-cultural knowledge. The students I spoke to countered that public schools focused on teaching Anglo-Canadian traditions and history to the point of excluding learning about other cultures:

JASMIN: What about the opportunity to, say, learn about different cultures?
ZARQA: That's good. I think that's a really good idea.
ALIYAH: But we've learned that. We've been learning all our lives before we came here. We've been learning about other people's religions, other people's holidays, other people's things. The teach-

ers, they'll be talking about what the Inuit did in the olden days, or what the Christians did. They talk about all that stuff, but you don't really hear them talk in a positive way about Muslims.

NUSAYBAH: But, like, Islam was never really talked about in public school. And only, like, the French holidays, or the English holidays, not Chinese holidays or Buddhist holidays. None of those are really respected or taught in public school anyway, so how are you supposed to know about other cultures? I only know about Christianity and Hinduism from Indian movies, right? But those are the only three religions that I know, they don't really teach you in public school, or you don't learn from other people.

In other words, they learned more about other religions from 'Bollywood movies' than they did from their public schooling. They also pointed out that opportunities to learn about other cultures and faiths from their peers were limited, given that most minoritized youth cared more about conforming to the traditions of the dominant culture (and going to malls) than discussing the finer points of theology:

ZARQA: I don't know that they really show you their culture. They all act that one culture, they all act that one Canadian, typical Christmas, Halloween, whatever.

ALIYAH: You won't have the Hindus talking about their temple or whatever, they all talk about malls, clothes, they don't talk about their religion anyways, so what's the point?

Students pointed to the cultural diversity of Islamic schools, where Muslims from South Asia, Africa, and the Caribbean could all be found, as well as North American converts. So they did not feel that Islamic school was 'cheating' them out of access to cultural diversity. Deqa, for example, did not feel that being in an Islamic school was an impediment in this regard:

DEQA: I think that's especially not true for Islamic schools because we're so, like, multicultural and in that sense we are very open minded and we accept each other's different cultures. And even though we have Islam as what is bringing us together, we also have many things that are different. And that's why we accept each other in that way. And we do deal with people – outside people, basically – and it's not like a big deal. And it's not like we get a shock outside later on.

Religious diversity was taken up at the high school level through World Religion courses, which were offered as electives, just as they are in public schools. I was very impressed by some of the projects that the grade ten World Religion students presented at an exhibition of the school's work at a local civic centre. One group of students had prepared a PowerPoint presentation on Buddhism; another group had constructed a model of a concentration camp for a presentation of Jewish history. This demonstrated to me that these students not only had access to knowledge of other faith communities but also had an interest in learning about other religions. They developed their presentations with both pride and respect.

In elementary schools there were fewer curricular opportunities to integrate knowledge of other cultures, since Islamic schools followed the same Eurocentric curriculum – mandated by the provincial government – as did public schools. However, individual teachers in these schools tried to make the curriculum more inclusive. Ruqayyah, a teacher of Pakistani descent in her mid-twenties, had been teaching for four years at Al Safar since graduating from teacher's college. Having attended public schools herself, she did not want her students to grow up as if they were 'living in a bubble':

RUQAYYAH: That's something [ghettoization] that I know myself – and I know some of the other teachers. We are scared sometimes that it might happen. But, *insha'allah*, I won't because I want them to realize that they have to learn about everything. They have to interact with everybody. So that's my main take. I personally have received criticism about teaching things like Olympics. Some parents think it's an un-Islamic thing. Not all of the parents, just a couple. But I said – without getting defensive – that I understood where they were coming from, but that to me is almost like living in a bubble. There are so many non-Muslims that know more about us than we do about them. I just think it's important for them to learn about everyone and everything. We're back to the Prophet of Islam. He knew about everyone. He knew about all the lifestyles and everything. And there's no harm in learning just for the sake of knowing and thinking, okay, this is what this group does, and this is what that group does.

Ruqayyah, then, was attentive to the need for students to have a broad education, one that included knowledge of other ways of life.

She situated this as integral to the practice of the Prophet Muhammed and thus as an example for all Muslims to follow. Yet she also had to contend with the narrow perspectives of some parents, who expected only Islamic knowledge to be represented – a position very much in conflict with Islamic traditions of pedagogy and knowledge production. Ruqayyah feared that such attitudes and the absence of a multicultural curriculum would lead to divisive social attitudes, as a result of which students would reproduce the 'us' versus 'them' dichotomy as a means of relating to the world outside the school:

RUQAYYAH: I hope, *insha'allah*, we're not ghettoizing them because – I know it's not just me, myself – I know a lot of the teachers are teaching them about different things, different projects. Last year I was teaching about Native cultures. So, *insha'allah*, I hope we're not doing that [ghettoizing]. It's scary because I don't want any child coming out of the school having an 'us versus them' approach.

That Islamic schooling might encourage 'us versus them' thinking is a significant concern. This is largely for two reasons. The first relates to post-9/11 geopolitics: the backlash against Muslims in North America, the wars in Afghanistan and Iraq, and the oppression of the Palestinians. As a result of these conditions, many Muslims feel victimized on a global scale, and their children are not immune to internalizing feelings of oppression and resentment toward those complicit in the causes. The 'the clash of civilizations' paradigm popularized by Huntington (1993) does have an impact at the psycho-social level, in that marginalized groups are 'Otherized' in dominant discourses and geopolitical narratives also return the gaze in equally distancing and pejorative terms.

The second factor relates to the many religious leaders who refer to non-believers in their *khutbas* (sermons) as *kafirs*. In the Qur'an, Christians and Jews are referred to as *ahl al-kitab*, or 'people of the Book,' in reference to the common theological heritage shared by Christians, Jews, and Muslims. *Kafir* refers to apostates or non-believers; however, it often used generically to mean anyone outside the Muslim community and is derogatory in that sense. The point is that some religious authorities use religious discourse in destructive ways to reinforce the boundaries between Muslims and non-Muslims.

Bilquees, a teacher of Indian descent in her late sixties, had lived in

Canada for twenty-five years and had been teaching at Al Shawwal for two. She had watched such attitudes trickling down from the religious authorities who were also the school's administrators. She discussed the inappropriateness of those attitudes and her resistance to seeing them reproduced within the school:

BILQUEES: I think they do get the feeling, oh, we are Muslims, they do get that identity eventually, but in a way, they are kind of discriminating [against] other kids, by saying that they are *kafir* and we are Muslim. That kind of attitude develops in them, between Muslims and non-Muslims, a lot. Oh, those are *kafir* and we are Muslim, more like arrogance and you know pride. Of course, we are supposed to be proud of our religion, but not in the way that they are doing it. Like, oh yeah, those are *kafir* schools or *kafir* this. And I said, don't say that, you know. It's not appropriate for us to say that. It's good to be a good Muslim, but you cannot put down somebody else.

Bilquees resisted the construction of a self-righteous or 'arrogant' Islamic identity, especially when it belittled non-Muslims. She argued that these attitudes, espoused by some community leaders, were themselves un-Islamic. She considered it important for schools to avoid reproducing this cultural ignorance in their students.

During my fieldwork I sometimes heard children use the term *kafir* to refer to non-Muslims. Because many of these children were often sheltered by their parents from interaction with non-Muslim children, fewer counternarratives were available to them. Using a critical faith-centred approach to counteract this negative practice, I would remind them that only Allah can judge what is in people's hearts; therefore, judgments of others and their beliefs are the province of the Divine. I would also refer them to prophetic hadith that relay the importance of kindness to our neighbours whatever their beliefs, in order to demonstrate the validity of this non-judgmental practice in the traditions of the Prophet Muhammed.[2] Ways must be found to bridge the gulf between the construction of Islamicized identities and the construction of 'Otherness' from a critical faith-centred perspective that is attentive to the ways in which religion can become complicit in the construction of other oppressions. Demeaning labels are contrary to Islamic ethos and praxis and must be resisted.

Other teachers spoke of the need to ensure that children grew up with an open mind and that they learned to tolerate social differences. Rima, a teacher in her mid-thirties of Egyptian descent, had spent most of her life in Canada. She had been teaching for four years, mainly in an Islamic school (having spent six months as a substitute teacher in a public school). She feared that an Islamic school environment sheltered children too much:

RIMA: We should equip them and have them open-minded to know what's going on out there ... not to live in that cocoon. That's another problem of having an Islamic school environment – having to live in this cocoon – in our school anyway.

Ruqayyah and Rima – teachers from two different schools – used enclosure metaphors when expressing fears that their students might become ghettoized. They described Islamic school students as inhabiting a 'bubble' or 'cocoon.' At the Al Shawwal school, where Rima worked, many families had recently arrived in Canada as immigrants or refugees, which contributed to their social isolation. Their social ties were mainly to the mosque and the school. As a consequence, their children had less exposure to other environments. Many newcomer families from Muslim countries find it difficult to come to terms with what they see as an overly permissive society – one, moreover, that legitimizes many practices which they see as contrary to Islam, such as drinking alcohol and engaging in premarital dating (Berns McGown, 1999; Shamma, 1999b; Zine, 2001b). These parents are attracted to Islamic schools because they provide a culturally congruent environment where family-centred values are reinforced.

At a forum on community education and activism, a Somali activist with a women's settlement organization described how Somali Muslim families saw children as their 'RRSPs'[3] – in other words, as an investment that would provide a 'return' to them in their old age, when they would be expected to provide for and look after them. She added that many families feared losing their children to the social mores of Western culture, which was based more on individualism at the expense of communal and familial responsibilities. For them, Islamic schools were a means of protecting their investment in family and community.

Desegregation and Integration into Public Schools

Some of those I interviewed acknowledged the 'ghettoizing' effects of segregated schooling that may make transitions to public secondary or post-secondary education more difficult. Bilquees, who taught at the Al Shawwal school, acknowledged the problems of integration without adequate preparation:

BILQUEES: If we are isolating our children from the rest of the world eventually when they go into high school or say even after high school, we have university that will not be an Islamic university or anything, so they eventually have to merge into some system that is not going to be Islamic. So if the child is not prepared from the beginning to go into these institutions, how is he going to progress? You know, I don't understand how we can do that.

Sakhina, a teacher at the Al Rajab girls' high school, was born in Canada of Pakistani descent. She had begun teaching one year earlier and planned to apply to teacher's college for certification. Having grown up in the public school system, she expressed similar concerns about making sure that students would be prepared to succeed in postsecondary schooling. She noted that ghettoization was a dual process: on one side were outsiders who viewed the students as culturally apart; on the other were the students themselves, who wondered how they would relate to the outside world:

SAKHINA: The people who were outside looking in would see these girls in their [Islamic] uniforms. And it's like, 'What goes on in there?' That sort of thing. The people who were inside looking out – like the students themselves – sometimes they don't know how to interact with our society and they have to learn. So I'm for the Islamic schools but I'm also afraid of that whole ghettoizing aspect. Are we going to be able to function in society?

In many ways, the students were living in a fish bowl, scrutinized from outside and at the same time afraid they wouldn't be able to adjust once they left the inside for mainstream schools and institutions.

Amira, who taught at Al Safar, was of Pakistani descent. She was in her mid-thirties and had come to Canada from East Africa when she was in elementary school. She had been schooled in the Canadian public system and had completed teacher's college after finishing a master's degree in science. She had been teaching at Al Safar since it opened. She agreed that students were somewhat distanced from the dominant culture but argued that they were not completely cut off from their social or cultural surroundings. She echoed the views of some students, who felt that for Muslim students living a faith-centred lifestyle, public schools were in many ways more isolating:

AMIRA: In terms of knowing what's out there, all of them, like, they live in a society where they see the kind of things that go on. They know, they are sort of aware of the things non-Muslims do. But it's sort of at a distance. It's not, like, when they're at high school they're put in an environment where they will feel like the odd-balls and there will be pressure to be like the others.

Peer pressure was also a concern regarding students who would be transferring from the 'safe' Islamic school environment into the public school system with all its social and cultural challenges. The desegregation process and the students' preparedness for resisting negative peer pressure – such as the pressure to date or to use alcohol and recreational drugs – were issues of concern to both parents and teachers. Amani, an Ethiopian teacher in her early thirties at Al Safar, said that some of her fears had been allayed by recent graduates from her school, who were succeeding in public high schools both academically and in maintaining their Islamic identity in the face of social pressure to conform to mainstream norms:

AMANI: I'm glad you brought that up because this is one of the concerns that all parents have. They constantly worry: are they going to be able to handle high school? Like last year we had our first graduates so in fact we want them to come back and tell us how they survived their first year, to talk to the grade eights that are about to graduate and to tell them, you know, I mean they were hearing lots of myths about how bad the high schools, public schools are … I always tell my students: If you know who you are and you feel confident about yourself and your identity and your place in this society, you can go anywhere and survive, you can go to the moon, you can go to Mars.

For teachers like Amani, faith-centred learning had the capacity to instil in students a strong sense of identity and purpose. Students would then have the strength to negotiate their identities and experiences in mainstream society while retaining their Islamic way of life. Amani felt that students needed guidance and support in order to make the right life choices:

AMANI: Even right now, as grade eights we keep telling them they're the role models and the ambassadors. So we're preparing them, psychologically we're preparing them that you know, you guys are now mature adults, you can make your own choices, you can be responsible. And the other thing also that we tell them is that you always know where to come when you need help. Like we try, we give them a support system.

She added that when these students reach puberty, they cross the threshold from childhood into adulthood, at which point they are considered accountable to Allah for their religious obligations. Because there are so few Islamic high schools, many Muslim adolescents transfer into public schools just around the time when the onus is being placed on them to be spiritually responsible, and just when they are newly accountable for maintaining their five daily prayers, fasting during Ramadan, and so on. She contended that students needed to begin developing life skills early in their schooling and that 'values education' would help guide them towards the correct moral choices once they left the more regulated environment of the Islamic school:

AMIRA: What we do, starting from grade six, we start teaching them, we start telling them, like you know, it's high school, this is what you're going to encounter ... And then also we start telling them that they're going to be their own decision makers, and that being in an Islamic school, there are teachers everywhere so there will always be someone there to pull you back and say, 'You know, you shouldn't be doing this' ... That will no longer exist in high school. So we tell them ... no one is going to tell you, your parents will probably never find out what you do in high school, so ... the onus is on them, they have to make their own choices. And that we have tried our best to show them the choices and what the consequences are for the choices. A lot of that starts in grade six ... you know, relationships, drugs, everything that is encountered. And we talk, openly and frankly, about all these things, especially the relationship with boys and girls and dating. We talk about the consequences and what can happen ... [sexually transmitted] diseases and things like that. So we sort of tell them that it's between you and Allah, and you have to seriously start saying to yourself, 'Oh what choice do I want to make? Do I want to make one that goes towards the straight path? Or do I want to make one that's going to lead me to the wrong path?'

Teachers described several strategies for helping students make the transition into public schools. Amira explained the steps taken at Al Safar to create dialogues and discussions regarding peer pressure. Most of the teachers at Al Safar had grown up in Canada attending public schools, unlike most teachers in other local Islamic schools, who were more recent immigrants. Al Safar's teachers had a greater understanding of the challenges their students would be facing and were aware of the need to develop proactive strategies to help them cope:

AMIRA: Like we have to, we just have to be very open about it. Because I don't think they're that open about it with their parents. We talk about gangs, being involved in certain cliques or groups in high school, or doing things because a group is doing it. We even had some seminars on gang violence, and things like that. We had the police come in and they were talking about consequences and the Young Offenders Act, and what constitutes arrest and so and so, so they have a better idea ... And that's all we can do, and just pray that they will make their life choice, because there's no longer someone watching you or someone telling you, or someone even enforcing ... Like if someone just goes and starts using foul language in every sentence, like who's going to enforce it? Whereas if they're with us, okay, yeah, they're going to be in trouble, it's a big deal.

Sakhina felt that the key to integration was community engagement through individual and school-based interactions:

SAKHINA: I think the key is community work. Not necessarily with Muslim organizations, but with non-Muslim organizations too. Like community service, where the school as a community goes to a senior citizens' home ... You know, because I think, like, 'Work within the community that way.' If you're working with senior citi-

zens, you're working with the elderly. You're helping them. Go to
the library and be part of a reading club for young kids who come
there.

Sakhina felt that Islamic schools needed to seek out opportunities
like these since they would provide interactions that were consistent
with religious values instead of simply being compromises. Some
Islamic schools interacted with the public school system through track
meets and science fairs. Teachers spoke of the need to develop more
such opportunities – for example, spelling bees and public speaking
competitions – in order to foster networks among local public and
independent schools.

Independent schools are not completely separate from the public
system; as we've seen, students often transfer back and forth between
the two systems, and Islamic school students eventually move on to
public high schools or universities. In this light, I was often told that
public schools have a vested interest in Islamic school students, many
of whom will at some point be returning to the public system. Rima
made some concrete recommendations for public schools with regard
to resource gaps and Islamic students' transition into the public
system. For example, she called for ESL support and for assistance
from public school guidance counsellors. She noted that Islamic
schools in New York could call on this sort of support from the public
system. But she added that because of racism and Islamophobia,
Islamic schools distrusted mainstream schools. For example, Islamic
schools feared that guidance counsellors might respond to community
issues by calling in Children's Aid and having children removed to
non-Muslim homes:

RIMA: Guidance counsellors or remedial help would be good. Maybe
  guidance helpers are limited, though, because if somebody gets hit
  or ... they get abused at home or somebody's going to complain,
  then it's going to be more of a problem for our community. We're
  being alienated in dealing with organizations like Children's Aid
  because of the way they're treating us ... And so that alienates us.
  You know, this is very important, but at the same time I don't want
  to make more problems for our community. I know the Children's
  Aid is very prejudiced so we feel that even though some kids
  might need their help, we don't tend to go to them because of
  what they might do.

Rima's fears about approaching guidance counsellors or Children's Aid are rooted in a history of negative experiences. These authorities have been known to remove children quickly from the home before abuse has been corroborated. For example, at Rima's school a son of one of the teachers was removed from his parents on allegations of abuse laid by doctors after the mother brought him in to seek medical assistance. Police came to the school and interviewed this teacher's grade one students to see whether she had been abusive towards them; her other children were removed from her care as well. Two weeks later, medical tests determined that the boy had not been abused; rather, he was suffering from a chemical imbalance in his brain. Members of the community accused the authorities of Islamophobia, insisting that they had acted against the parent and levelled suspicions against the school before other medical possibilities had been ruled out. The community's fears of differential negative treatment by the authorities are often a barrier to seeking professional help and services. Many prefer to deal with situations of conflict or distress internally, with the help of religious leaders, instead of risking exposure to mistreatment.

Local public schools, however, have provided logistical support for Islamic schools. Sister Mehrun, the principal at Al Safar, talked about the connections she had fostered with a local public school to provide various kinds of support, especially in a crisis situation:

MEHRUN: We invited the principal [from the public school] and we took them to dinner as well and showed the whole building, the office. Two years ago we went and borrowed some equipment for our play day, like ropes or whatever. And also we made an arrangement with them, in case of an emergency, you know, because they're on a main road and being a Muslim school and place of worship, in case of threats, or some kind of problem like that bomb threat, we made an arrangement with them to go to their school.

Evacuation planning became an imperative after the Oklahoma City bombing, when Islamic centres across North America – including Al Safar – received bomb threats (Muslims and Arabs had been falsely accused of the bombing; in fact, the terrorist was a white American). The alert shifted to high again immediately after 9/11. By the afternoon of that day, the community's Muslim men had left their jobs in order to form a security cordon around Al Safar (which is both a mosque and a school), even though it had not yet been announced who had carried out the attacks. The burden of collective guilt for 9/11 has profoundly affected the ways in which mosques and Islamic schools address safety issues.

The students I interviewed discussed the lack of government funding for Islamic schools and society's lack of knowledge of Muslims. For them, these were the main reasons why they were so often ghettoized. The following OAC students from Al Rajab explained:

DAOOD: Some of the challenges will be, like, the school, it's not government funded so there's a lot more, you know, involvement amongst the community and yourself, so in public school everything is basically given to you in your lap basically. You just come to school, write the stuff and then just go home, right. Here it's a lot harder than that, because like I said, the school is not properly equipped sometimes.

IMAN: See, we're not subsidized. Being segregated from different communities doesn't mean that we're not aware of the things that are going on, the social conflict going on around the world. But like, we pretty much know a lot of these things. We hear things but we're just not like in tune with them all the time.

SUMMAYA: And just because this is Islamic school, they might not think that we're well educated, right? And that's a problem.

IMAN: The Ministry of Education come in and they check out our school, the work that we're doing, you know, look at the binders and stuff. We're pretty much like normal people. There's no difference, just the religion, being tight with your religion, that's the number one key.

Rehabilitating and Resocializing Wayward Students

Cultural constructionists maintain that human behaviour and ideas are best explained as products of culturally shaped learning (Miller, Van Estenk, & Van Estenk, 2001, p. 13). Islamic schools provide a faith-centred environment that shapes student's behaviours and ideas in accordance with the religious culture. Students who are exiled from the public school system – either through expulsion or by parents out of concern that they are absorbing un-Islamic behaviours – are often channelled into Islamic schools to be rehabilitated and resocialized.

(One Islamic school reportedly used the slogan 'Save our children from hellfire' in its advertising.) In this sense, Islamic schools operate as systems of 'cultural reconstructionism'; that is, they are places where wayward students are disciplined to absorb the dominant cultural norms and values of Islam. Students commented on how Islamic schools provided a system of positive peer pressure that encouraged them to follow Islamic practices and ways of life.

Ali, Sabbir, and Saadi, OAC students at Al Rajab, told me that for them, Islamic school represented a break from their 'old ways' – that is, from un-Islamic practices such as taking drugs and engaging in gang activities (including street crime). Now, when they mixed with their old friends from public school, they realized that their values were no longer compatible with those of their former peers, even those who were also Muslim:

ALI: I have friends from other schools, too. Like the school I used to go to before. I still go see them, but the thing that's different right now is before I used to do everything that they used to do, even though it's wrong or whatever. Now the thing is that whenever I see them doing something wrong, it doesn't look good to me ... I see the respect that I had for them just going down. They started respecting me because they were looking at me ...

SABBIR: They're just jealous because they can't change.

ALI: They're jealous. Even though my friends are Muslim, they're different. They're doing lots of [bad] stuff. But when they're looking at me, they're like, if he changed so much, we should change too. But it's impossible to change at a public school. There's a one percent chance of changing at a public school.

JASMIN: So you think they're jealous when they see you and they wish they could make that change?

ALI: Yeah, but they like the other fun better, yet they want to change. But they're running after both ...

SAADI: *Shaitan* wants you to follow him basically ...

Saadi used the term 'following *shaitan*' (the Arabic word for Satan) to describe how his old friends had been turned from the 'straight path' of Islam by indulging in drugs, crime, and partying. Four of the five male students I interviewed at Al Rajab had been involved in these types of activities and had been sent by their parents to the Islamic school to be resocialized and 're-Islamicized.' The concern was not just that they were involved in illegal and harmful activities; it was also that they were involved in un-Islamic behaviour. Islamic school was seen as a means to steer these youth back to respectable Islamic modes of conduct.

Two brothers, Sabbir and Saadi, had entered Al Rajab eighteen months earlier. At a school basketball game, Saadi had got into a fight and Sabbir had stepped in to defend his younger brother; as a consequence, both had been charged with assault and expelled by the school board. Their parents then sent them back home to Pakistan in order to reform their destructive behaviour and resocialize them into the family's cultural values. Saadi and Sabbir spoke poignantly about this life-transforming experience:

SABBIR: For a year and a half we went to Pakistan to have a change of society and to basically learn our culture, heritage, and what our parents were trying to do for us. A child's first action towards what his parents are trying to teach him is rebellion because the child always feels that whatever his parents are telling him is not for the best of the child. And plus in the Western society, and in our Muslim culture, it wasn't exactly fitting. We were kind of confused. Am I supposed to do this? Am I not supposed to do this? It was really confusing but now, actually, after going there and seeing that society and this society and evaluating, you realize that over there in the schools and stuff, the person who is getting the best academics and stuff is the kind of person who is mostly respected by his peers. And over here the kind of person that has the most friends is the kind of person who is most intimidating. That's the kind of person that gets the most respect.

JASMIN: So going back home made it clear for you.

SABBIR: It turned around my life because I was always into crime. I was on the streets. I was doing stuff that my mom – if she found out – I don't know what she would do. All the time we were doing robberies and trying to make money. I asked my mom for money and she wouldn't give me money because she thought I am going to go out and do drugs and something and smoke and stuff like that. So basically I was on the streets. I was hanging around with all the bad guys that were older than me. So then I went to Pakistan and changed my life.

Saadi and Sabbir were dealing with negative peer pressure as well as with the 'double culture syndrome' that confronts many youth growing up in a culturally hybridized context. These youth find themselves having to contend with the competing cultural demands of home and the dominant culture (see Afshar, 1989; Al-Jabri, 1995; Haw, 1994; Basit, 1997; Zine, 2000, 2001b). Saadi and Sabbir described the 'lack of fit' between their Pakistani-Muslim culture and the dominant cultural norms of Canadian youth culture; for them, this had led to confusion and dissonance. In Pakistan they were able to witness a different set of standards for 'respectability' in the male youth culture – standards that were determined by academic merit rather than how tough or intimidating they could be.

Cultural constructions of masculinity revolve around various social determinants that lead to different constructs of a hegemonic masculinity. Saadi and Sabbir found that among youth in Pakistan, masculinity and 'respectability' were determined by academic success, which was broadly viewed as the path to economic and social mobility. Other dominant constructions of masculinity among youth often revolve around violence. According to Kimmel (1994), 'violence is often the single most evident marker of manhood' (p. 132). Saadi noted that in his circle of friends, 'physical violence is a normal thing. It's part of the behaviour.' For Saadi and Sabbir, then, acting tough and getting involved in gangs and violent behaviour was part of their socialization as young men – it was what gained them their peers' respect as well as a reputation for being 'cool.' The different cultural standards they observed in Pakistan opened up new possibilities for them to reconstruct their subjectivities based on alternative discursive constructions of masculinity and social prestige. By adjusting their norms according to these different standards, Saadi and Sabbir were able to return to the 'straight path' socially, academically, and Islamically.

Both brothers were disappointed that none of their public school teachers ever asked about them after they were expelled, even though they had maintained fairly good grades. By contrast, they described the teachers and administrators at Al Rajab as providing a more familial environment. Ali, an eighteen-year-old OAC student of Bangladeshi descent, had lived in Canada for nine years and had attended Al Rajab for the past three. Like so many other students, he described the school as a 'family':

ALI: It's different from other schools because in here, there's all Muslims and everything. In other schools there are fights and everything. In this school, everybody's like brothers. It's like less students and less trouble. So everybody's tied to almost everybody. Everybody knows everyone's family since we're all Muslim. At the regular school, we don't know each other. After school no one knows each other. In here each of us know everybody's parents. We talk, whatever. It's just like family.

The narrative of the family is invoked here once again to describe the sense of belonging and familiarity offered by an Islamic school environment. This metaphor extended to the school authorities, whose approach was more familial than formal. Ali and Saadi described how the principal, brother Nasir, approached the boys in the school in a 'fatherly way':

ALI: The way he treats us is ...
SAADI: Like his own kids.
ALI: Own kids. What we do and everything. Before we didn't appreciate it, that's the truth. Neither did I. I did not appreciate that. I never used to do that. I used to think different about it. But now since after the first year and a half I kind of changed, like totally. After six months I wanted to stay in the school but I wouldn't be saying that a year ago. Even right now, I just get more respect for everybody. Appreciating parents, everything.

Clearly, an Islamic school environment was pivotal in steering these youth onto the 'straight path' as far as un-Islamic behaviour was concerned; in addition, it framed their attitudes towards elders and their appreciation for their family members, from whom they had once been alienated. This illustrates how the Islamic school can provide a rehabilitative function in channelling wayward youth back to a faith-centred way of life.

Ali noted that there was little violence in the Islamic school he attended. This coincides with the findings of Abdus Sabur (1995), who conducted a quantitative study of eighty-seven Islamic schools in the United States and found significantly less antisocial or violent behaviour than in the public schools. He found very little violence or aggressive behaviour, and few incidents involving weapons, drugs, and alcohol. Also, teen pregnancies were rare. He attributed this to the inculcation of Islamic values and moral standards. In the study at hand, Ali noted that the school principal's approach to dealing with students made a difference when it came to meeting the challenge of the higher social and academic expectations, placed on them

SAADI: They want the Muslims to be ahead of other people. In terms of education they want us to be the ones getting the best marks and the ones that are getting the most successful jobs. They don't want us to be part of the low-class society.

SABBIR: We wouldn't be the same if we were in public school. It [Islamic school] changes your life.

Other studies of racialized students in Ontario public schools have found that teachers' low expectations lead to underachievement (Dei, Mazzuca, McIsaac, & Zine, 1997). Racism and Islamophobia have been implicated in school officials' perceptions of students – perceptions that result in differential evaluations and treatment programs for racialized youth, based on negative stereotypes (Zine, 2000, 2001b).

All of the students told me that Islamic schools placed strong emphasis on academic success and that they strived to live up to their school's strong work ethic:

SAADI: When exam time comes in the regular public schools, we wouldn't even care. We'd be like, 'So what. I'll study later.' As soon as we hear the word 'exam' here we're gone studying. I go to this guy's [Ali's] house and we're studying. Our old friends – a couple of girls – they're calling us on the phone: 'Like what are you guys doing?' We're like, 'We're studying.' Then they're like, 'Oh my god, are you guys feeling okay? You guys are studying? Are you sure?' We're like, 'Yeah, we've changed.'

ALI: [At public school] we didn't care about grades. To be honest, I don't know about everybody – I never used to open my binder.

Many students found that as a result of being in a more scholarly environment – one in which the youth culture privileged academic achievement – their grades had improved.

The female students told me much the same when they compared the social and academic values of public schools with those of their Islamic school. Zarqa described the public school environment as 'like a mall' – that is, as less about academics than about socializing and looking fashionable:

ZARQA: No, public school, it's all about like, talking, it's like a mall –
NUSAYBAH: Yeah, it is really like a mall!
ZARQA: You feel like, 'Okay, how do I look?' It's not about marks, it's nothing about your work, it's nothing about that. It's just all about the way you look, it's all about popularity.
ALIYAH: And competition there, if you get like a fifty, you're okay. Even 48 per cent.
ZARQA: There'll be a group of people in our school [public school] that have like 80 per cent and 90 per cent marks, but then there's the rest of them that all get 50 per cent, 60 per cent, and those marks. So it's not really a really big thing in public school about those marks.

For these students, then, Islamic school marked a shift toward more academically focused schooling.

Many students experienced cultural dissonance when they transferred to Islamic school from the public system Ali described how he felt out of place when he first arrived in the Islamic school. After being expelled from the public system, his parents had sent him home to Bangladesh in an attempt to resocialize him to Islamic values:

ALI: I used to call my mom and, 'Mom, I want to come back.' I was almost crying on the phone. I'm in this country I'd never seen before and I'm calling my mom and, 'No, you finish Qur'an and then come back.' My mom would hang up on me.

When Ali returned to Canada and enrolled in Islamic school, he was taken aback by the more studious atmosphere, in which there was far less opportunity to engage in negative behaviours such as truancy:

ALI: I was kind of forced to come here. I didn't really want to come down here or whatever. I wasn't happy. I didn't want to be in this school because guys here are different from the guys in public school or whatever because in public school it was just skipping out. And here, guys here, nobody's into skipping. Nobody's into nothing. It's just everybody's studying and I was the only guy who was different. So I was kind of left out because these guys are studying and whatever.

The female students noted that there were fewer opportunities in Islamic school to cut classes, owing to stronger surveillance and the smaller physical environment:

NUSAYBAH: Public school is like – I don't know how to explain it, it's like, people, they have other classes, too, so they really don't care. If you have like cooking or drama, it's like, 'Forget the English homework!' Or English class, 'I'll go to Drama.' That's the thing about public school. Here's it's like you gotta go to class. You start getting your act together – in public school it's like, 'I'll just skip English, cuz I've got Drama anyways.'

ALIYAH: You have places to ditch. Here we don't have places to ditch. The only place you can ditch is the bathroom.

NUSAYBAH: My old school was like four floors. This is like elementary school. It's a lot like elementary school. And the weird thing is like, you're so used to public school, cuz you used to skip. And if you'd skip, you'd make up the cheesiest lie and you'd get away with it! Here it's like 'Where were you? Why were you there? Oh da da da!' And you're not even skipping! You can't skip! You can't go anywhere.

In my earlier study of Muslim students in the public school system (Zine, 1997), the students reported that when they did cut classes, the teachers did not call parents; by contrast, when white students cut classes, greater concern was shown that they were wasting their future. The marginalized students viewed this differential approach to truancy as a function of lower expectations. The students in the study at hand talked about feeling more valued in Islamic school and being encouraged to succeed.

Saadi told me that there were fewer 'distractions' in the Islamic school than in public schools, which made it more conducive to study:

SAADI: The distractions [in public school] are drugs, alcohol, music, sex and that kind of stuff. And in Islamic school the only thing you can do is study and that's the whole point of school. So if all schools were like this then the people who want to study would be in the school and the people who don't would be out and there wouldn't be any people that are trouble makers. They wouldn't even attend school. Because that's what school's about, it's just learning.

Saadi seemed to be advocating a process of social selection to weed out students who were trouble makers. Such a system would be regulated by the social norms of the youth culture instead of by the school authorities. He seemed to be saying that if the normative discourses of the youth-based school culture changed so as to privilege academic diligence rather than social indulgence, students would regulate themselves, and this would encourage a stronger work ethic.

These youth found that the Islamic school environment had liberated them from the 'distractions' that were impeding their success in the public school system; they did not regard that environment as more socially repressive due to the strict regulation of un-Islamic social practices. Part of the reason for this is that male students enjoyed more freedom than female students to enter and leave the school premises; the female students faced stricter surveillance by the school authorities (chapter 6 discusses gender-based social regulation in Islamic schools). More generally, though, students in Islamic school developed a greater appreciation for academic success as a marker of achievement and social value and became more seriously focused on their educational aspirations as a result.

Ali remarked that after he got over the initial dissonance, he felt more encouraged and pushed to succeed. He found himself wanting to do well, to impress the teachers and principal and demonstrate that he was living up to their high expectations. He also remarked on the individual attention and encouragement he received from his teachers – something he did not receive in the more impersonal environment of the public school system:

ALI: They're telling me, 'You're a good kid. You're smart and everything.' They tell you that, and the next day you can't come to school without homework or whatever. In public school, before a test when a teacher's telling you, 'I want you to do good in this test,' it's not just that he's telling me, you know, he's telling everybody. For example, if he comes to your class and he goes, 'I want everybody to do well in the test,' it's not going to affect me. I'm going to be like, 'No, he's talking to everybody.' But in here he's going to take one by one. Whenever he finds each of us by ourselves, he says, 'You can't let me down. I want you to do well on this test.' Everybody knows what is going on. Everybody knows who is who and who is what.

Daood, an OAC student, was Canadian born of Pakistani descent and had been attending Al Rajab for eighteen months. He explained that the stricter surveillance in Islamic school reduced the likelihood that students would fall through the cracks by not taking their academic work seriously. He recalled standards in public school as less stringent:

DAOOD: At public school there were more factors like, you know, you had your friends in your class. They didn't care, they didn't have discipline there. You know, there wasn't that much action taken ... You can come there late to class, no one will say anything to you, you have your own choice. There's a lot more freedom there. You know, so when you get into that system then you start slacking, you keep continuing, and then you just get lazy and stuff. Here, it's more strict, so you respect the teachers a lot more. There, to tell you the truth I never respected any of the teachers. Here is the first time I'm respecting teachers and I'm cooperating with them. Like, back in public school the teacher would be talking, you don't care, you'd be talking to your friends, you'd be talking, doing something else in class, sometimes you don't even show up. But here it's a totally different environment, you know, that's what I like about it.

In terms of regulating and socially rehabilitating students in accordance with the school's religious culture, the students noted how the principal, brother Nasir, dealt with discipline in a positive rather than a punitive way:

ALI: The principal has the biggest effect on this. Like other schools, the stuff I did, like the first six months when I came here the stuff I did in this school, if he was any other principal – I wouldn't have been allowed to stay here. Because even myself, you know, if I was a principal and a student did that stuff I wouldn't allow him in my school. But the principal kept saying, 'You guys are Muslims. This is an Islamic school. I'm giving you a chance to do whatever.' It wasn't that he was putting us down. He was telling us positive stuff.
SABBIR: Like quitting smoking and stuff. Which teachers are going to go out of their way?
ALI: When I first came I used to smoke. The principal didn't call your parents and tell them that you smoke. It wasn't like that. He would

come not in front of everybody. He wouldn't make it a big issue in front of my friends. Alone, one on one, he used to tell me, 'Ali, I know you smoke. I can't stop you but you should stop smoking. You should cut down. It's not good.' Just explaining little stuff and when he puts positive stuff on and says positive stuff about you then you just want to change. You want to show him that you've changed. Every time I used to do something bad, he didn't say nothing bad. He used to still tell me good stuff about myself. like, 'You're a good kid. I can't believe you did it.'

SAADI: He would encourage us a lot.

SABBIR: In the public schools they kind of put you down.

ALI: They put you down.

SABBIR: They say, 'I'm going to suspend you. I'm going to expel you.' They have a negative attitude towards the students. They don't care about you that much, basically.

Clearly, these students felt more positively supported in the Islamic school environment, and eventually they began to regulate their own behaviours in accordance with the school's religious culture and its academic work ethic. They began to develop new social narratives based on the prevailing Islamically focused discourses, through which possibilities for reconstituting alternative subjectivities could be engaged.

Peer Pressure

Some parents were committed to an Islamic school education for their children during the junior years. Later they would enrol their children in the public school system, where they felt there were more academic opportunities. In this sense, Islamic schools were viewed as a temporary stage in the path towards Islamization. Other parents had a long-term commitment to Islamic schooling, feeling that it was the only system where their children would be safe from negative peer pressure that could steer them off the 'straight path.'

Negative peer pressure was a major reason why parents sent their children to Islamic schools. These schools were perceived as safe havens where social behaviours could be brought into accord with Islamic norms. Many parents spoke of the need for Islamic education, especially in elementary school, as a means to socialize children into Islamic beliefs and practices from an early age.

I sat with some parents from the Al Shawwal elementary school and discussed their concerns. They saw the school as a means to 'reform' students who were exhibiting un-Islamic behaviours and attitudes. Karim and Zahra, a husband and wife from Ethiopia, were active on the school's parent committee. They were in their mid-forties, had lived in Canada for ten years, and had two children, ages eight and nine, enrolled at Al Shawwal. Our discussion was joined by Zuleikha, another parent committee member, also in her mid-forties, who was from Guyana and who had lived in Canada for twenty years. Her nine-teen-year-old daughter had finished high school in the public system; her five-year-old son had been at Al Shawwal since kindergarten. All of these parents spoke of the challenges they faced raising their children in Canada and helping them resist assimilation into mainstream youth culture, which in many ways was contrary to the Islamic values they wanted their children to maintain. Swearing and other inappropriate language were among the concerns these parents had:

ZAHRA: They are getting wild, and the words they use! I mean, I see them whenever I go to drop the kids at school, the words they use at this age ... swearing! I don't want my kids to learn that.

KARIM: Just the general problem is that in this society there are so many things that are acceptable which are not in our own way, the Islamic way ... Before the kids they know what is wrong and what is right, they're bringing all these un-Islamic things home, before even they know what they mean.

ZAHRA: Yeah they were. Ayyoub was five years old and Yacoub was six.

KARIM: Already they were using 'f' words and they didn't know what they were, but they were using them.

Zuleikha had a daughter in high school and a son in elementary school. She had chosen Islamic school for her son so that he could avoid being exposed to some of the un-Islamic practices that her daughter had begun to take up:

ZULEIKHA: My daughter is nineteen now. So I had to deal every day with all kinds of behaviour. I mean, she has all kinds of friends, like they smoke, they do drugs – everything she was picking up. You know how some kids they could say no, but my daughter was a slow learner, so she obviously had to mix with friends who would accept her, so she started lots of times having boys coming to her. There used to be a bully in the schoolyard and they used to call her this and that and she couldn't handle it. So she had really low self-esteem. You see she's smoking, she's following around wrong company, one time she stole, because she was with some girls who were stealing. So lots of problems, lots of peer pressure, and I thought, when Anis came along I don't want to go through this, 'cause it was every day you're getting calls. Shazia was a good kid, but the company she kept forced this peer pressure, she couldn't deal with it so she just jumped into everything just to be friends.

Students also spoke of peer pressures that challenged their Islamic sensibilities and lifestyles. Rehana was an eighteen-year-old OAC student of Pakistani descent and been attending Al Rajab for six months. She described the challenges and exclusion she had faced in public school:

REHANA: There was a lot of peer pressure ... I feel that maybe those schools didn't have as many morals as the Islamic schools have. They [girls] were allowed to go out with guys, and you know, do whatever, basically whatever they wanted. So there was a lot of pressure on me because I was like the odd one in the group who didn't use to involve myself in any of that, so I felt a lot of pressure to do things that they did.

Nusaybah talked about how some Muslim girls negotiated the 'double culture syndrome' by 'performing' the social identity required to suit the cultural demands of the different social environments they inhabited. Their efforts to conform to the competing cultural demands of the dominant culture and the Muslim community, was seen as a negative example for other young Muslim women:

NUSAYBAH: Like Muslims in public schools, they like try to change themselves. It's so negative, they give you so many ideas. There will be girls who leave their house with hijab, they come to school and they take it off. And then it's like, okay, if my dad ever told me to wear hijab, I could do the same thing since she's pulled it off. Or it's like girls who leave their house with a sweatshirt and then they take it off [at school] and they have on like a tank top! And they're, like, Muslims! And you're, like, 'Well, if she can do it and she can get away with it, then why don't I do it? Even here [in Islamic school], I knew this girl, she used to go to the coffee shop and she'd go and get the washroom key and she'd like take off her hijab and sweatshirt and I was like, 'Whoa!' And then she'd come back, put it on and go home. And I'd be like, 'What the heck happened to her?!'

Young Muslim women who gave in to the double culture syndrome by surreptitiously adopting Western conventions of dress when they were at school or the mall were seen as 'hypocrites' by some of their peers and were accused of compromising their Islamic values. Yet most students understood all too well how difficult it is to maintain a faith-centred lifestyle in the face of a dominant youth culture that disciplined deviance from the existing social norms for dress and social interaction by ridiculing and excluding those who did not 'fit in.'

In the public education system, social practices such as dating and partying are common rites of passage. Many Muslim youth and their families find it a struggle to maintain a religious identity and to avoid practices such as drinking alcohol and engaging in premarital relations (see, for example, Zine, 2000, 2001b). Families saw Islamic schools as a more culturally congruent environment in which these challenges could be minimized:

ZULEIKHA: If you send your kids to Islamic school you erase half of the problems. Because [in public school] your child has to deal with different cultures, different religions, right, and obviously there's a whole different environment at home. So that's one of the most important reasons. No matter how bad the Islamic school is now – I mean, they're going to have the kids [mis]behaving sometimes, but not as bad what I've seen – in the public school, you're dealing with a whole lot more. So that's one of the most important reasons. I would send Anis right through to Islamic school because I know the problems in the public school.

Some of the students at Al Rajab reported staying away from friends whom they feared might still have a negative influence on them:

SABBIR: I tried for a whole year [to help my friend] to tell you the truth and now I just cut him off because he doesn't want to change.

He's still living that thug life if you want to call it that – jacking cars and smoking weed all day and doing all kinds of screwed-up stuff.
ALI: To be honest, you can't change a person by words. I can't speak for anyone but for me you can't change me by words. Like, I was changed by the Islamic atmosphere. That was the only thing that changed me and it took time. Even a week or a month wouldn't do anything to me. It took me almost two years.

There was nothing magical about the social rehabilitation that Islamic schools provided; rather, it was a gradual process that took time and patience. The students noted that many youth rebelled at first against changing their lifestyle and habits:

SABBIR: And the reason for rebellion is we had habits – Friday night and Saturday night you're supposed to be partying, you know what I mean? And you're supposed to be doing all kinds of activities which are non-Islamic. So over here they don't have those kinds of things. Once that came out of our life there was nothing left to do but study. You have to limit the amount of fun you have. You can give an example of water and oil. Like you can try and mix the two together as much as you want but it just can't mix together. It has to be separate, you know what I mean? There has to be a limit.

The change in school cultures and youth cultures was crucial to shifting the sensibilities of these youth towards more Islamically inclined behaviour, which focuses more on academic pursuits than on extracurricular temptations. Students appreciated being in a more faith-centred environment where they could maintain their daily prayers. Some public schools did have prayer rooms, but they felt that there was less impetus for students to break away from the flow of the school day to go and attend to their prayers, since it meant skipping other activities with friends, which they reported made them feel 'left out.' of the dominant social life and culture of the school. Other students reported abusing prayer privileges by treating them as an excuse to cut classes.

At the Islamic school, prayer was a normal and important part of the school culture. Students reported 'positive peer pressure' within the school that subtly encouraged them attend to their regular prayers and other religious obligations. This in turn made them more observant Muslims. The school's youth culture seemed to be self-regulating, with peers encouraging Islamic behaviour among themselves. Amal, an eighteen-year-old OAC student originally from Kuwait, discussed this:

AMAL: I have my friend Iman, she always reminds me, like, 'No that's *haram* [forbidden], you have to pray, like your praying is more important than these other things.' And she reminds me about this stuff that I don't know – like even though I'm from a country that I'm supposed to know more than her – she knows more. I'm really impressed and I'm happy with her, that she's my friend.

Amal was impressed by her friend's religious knowledge and Islamic practice. Amal had lived most of her life in Kuwait, in an environment that was more Islamically focused, yet her Canadian-born friend had a stronger faith and practised her religion more diligently. In this regard, Rehana noted how the example of other students who were more observant served as a form of positive pressure, in that it encouraged her to re-evaluate her own spiritual practices:

REHANA: For me like, uh, I pray really fast. My mom's like, 'You have no respect for your prayer.' Then I watch Muna and them praying and I think, 'Oh, they pray so nice and slow' and now I am trying to pray more slowly and, you know, just do everything much better than what I used to do.

Other students discussed how their peers served as a positive influence by helping them regulate their own religious practices and social behaviours, and how this was different from the negative peer pressure they encountered in public schools:

ALIYAH: Yeah! Like if you see a friend praying, we'll be like talking or hanging out and our friends will be like, 'Yo, guy, I gotta go pray.' And then you'd be like, 'Oh, well, she's praying, why should I sit here by myself? I'll just go pray with her.'
ZARQA: But in public school it's like, 'Let's go get a cigarette.' It's so different!
ALIYAH: And if everyone else is smoking, then you want to smoke. But if everyone else is praying, then you want to pray. [Others: 'Exactly!'] Everyone else is wearing hijab so you want to wear hijab, it's just that effect that you have.

UMBREEN: And over here there's less peer pressure and stuff and you don't have to be influenced into doing many wrong things. Cuz everyone over here prevents you from doing wrong things. Like they tell you what's right and stuff and when you're doing something wrong, they tell you it's wrong. Instead, other people would be, like, 'Oh come on, join us!'

SAHAR AND SAFIA: Yeah – 'Come on, let's do it.'

Noora and Saira, grade eight students at Al Safar, provided similar accounts of positive peer pressure at their school, where the youth maintained a faith-centred world view and avoided un-Islamic practices:

NOORA: Most of the girls that I am friends with, they usually encourage me to do better things. Like maybe not go to the movies, not go to the mall, or come to their house and do Qur'an or something.

SAIRA: Oh yeah, there's a lot of positive peer pressure. You're not forced into doing anything that you don't want to do, and you know that whatever you're getting pressured to do is good for this year, for this life and the hereafter, so really there's nothing to lose ... Because if we get together we can always have Islamic discussions, or, you know, discuss something that's good and will help us in our lives and maybe we can discuss issues on how to deal with other people and talk about our experiences, so its great. Maybe we can get advice, and we're pressured to do more – to go on the straight path.

Thus from these students' faith-centred perspective, the effects of the positive peer pressure they encountered at their school were not purely existential; those effects also prepared them better for the hereafter by encouraging them to stay on the 'straight path.' Here they were expressing the faith-centred view in spiritual terms that linked their physical practices – and the intentions that guided those practices – to broader metaphysical outcomes. They understood that their behaviour and lifestyle choices would affect their future in the *dunya*, or worldly plane of existence; in addition, they had the spiritual foresight to consider the effects on their life in the *akhira*, or hereafter. From a critical faith-centred perspective, it is necessary to understand this level of metaphysical engagement in order to apprehend how faith and spirituality inform the daily social life and personal development of these students.

The male students talked about how they were role models for some of the school's younger students. Al Rajab had students from junior kindergarten to OAC. The older students, then, saw the need to provide a positive Islamic example for the younger ones:

ALI: Since we're the older kids of the school, the younger kids are looking up to us so we can't do anything bad in front of them. Even though if we smoke, you know how we don't smoke in front of older people. In public school, I don't care if some kid is younger than me. Of course if he's younger than somebody you could smoke in front of them. In this Islamic school we can't do that.
SAADI: We care about them. It's like we're older brothers.
SABBIR: They're like our little brothers.
ALI: Because they respect us like older brothers. They see us. Whatever we do they follow. Especially because they're Muslim, one thing, and the second thing is that I see them as my younger brothers and if they see me smoke or do any kind of bad stuff around the school, of course it's going to influence them.
SABBIR: Whatever we do, these kids follow us.

Here, once again, they were invoking the narrative of the family in referring to the respect and brotherhood they wanted to foster in the school. This served as yet another motive for them to rehabilitate their own behaviour: they were aware of the influence they exerted on the younger students. This notion of brotherhood included a sense of camaraderie and fellowship among the *ummah*, the global community of Muslims, as it was represented at the school:

SABBIR: So here, even though he's from Bangladesh and I'm from Pakistan and he's from India, it doesn't matter because we're all Muslim. Somalia and wherever, it doesn't matter as long as they're Muslim. We're like a brotherhood.

These young men extended their school-based network of peer support into their extracurricular activities. They reported getting together often outside of school to engage in halal, or Islamically permissible activities, such as basketball. Ali remarked on the absence of cliques in the school and on the tight bonds of friendship that had developed among them so quickly:

ALI: Most of the evenings we go home and we stay with our families but almost every week – two or three days – everybody calls up each other. Everybody has cars. We meet up somewhere and we play. It's just that we see each other. These guys, I met them just for the past year but it feels like I've known them since I was a kid even though my other friends I've known since I was a kid. I don't respect them as much.

Other high school students from Al Rajab also reported a 'more positive vibe' than at the public schools they had attended. Muna talked about how the students themselves disciplined inappropriate behaviour among their peers when it disrupted the school's code of ethics and behaviour:

MUNA: Like somebody, OK, would go make fun of people and like put them down for how they look and stuff like that. And somebody else would jump in and say, 'Back off – if she wants to wear it let her wear it, you shouldn't be making fun of her.'

Overall, the students were protective of the youth culture they had helped negotiate and foster in their school. They understood that students who were new to the school, having just transferred from the public system, often experienced 'culture shock' and did not automatically adjust to the new ways. Iman had some sage advice for these students, based on her own experience as an Islamic school student:

IMAN: Be tight and do not drift away from your religion. It's like you have to practise your religion. It's what you grew up with. Basically you're not forced to, but you can open a door for him or her and if they want to come in it's open for them. And if they don't want to they can see whatever is going on in there ... It's a pretty modest place.

The Social Reproduction of Islamic Identity and Lifestyles

Islamic schools provide a means for disciplining wayward students through resocialization into Islamically appropriate modes of behaviour and action, and they encourage a positive youth counterculture. In addition, they are sites where Islamic social identities and lifestyles are reproduced. In a study of an Islamic school in Montreal, Kelly

(1997) discussed the role the school played in reproducing Islamically oriented social identities: 'I began to see that a fine equilibrium was maintained between, on one hand, families' desires to retain and reproduce not just piety and religious feeling, but also the degree of conformity within the community that could be called Muslim social identity; and on the other, their autonomy in emphasizing aspects of that identity' (p. 114).

Conceptions of Islamic Identity

This malleability of Islamic identity is a function of the disjuncture between how Islamic identification is socially mapped, enacted, and lived, on the one hand, and the religious conception of Islamic identity rooted within doctrinal texts, on the other. These two aspects of Islamic identity – the social and the religious – generate a dichotomy between the socially defined, ascriptive characteristics of Islamic identity and those which are divinely ordained and inscribed within the praxis of religious tenets, such as the Five Pillars of Islam. Adherence to these pillars is part of the essence of Islamic identity as a religious construct. That said, the social construction of a 'Muslim' absorbs many meanings and accommodates various sectarian and individual orientations to Islam (see Zine, 2007a).

The Islamic tradition is all-encompassing, in the sense that it governs and regulates the social, economic, and political practices of its followers, as well as other aspects of life, including values, etiquette, social relations, styles of dress, hygiene, and diet. Put another way, Islam constructs a distinctive culture or style of life. According to Abdul Rauf (1983), 'Islam is at once a religion and a culture. As a religion it covers three areas: doctrines, rituals and non-ritual activities. As a culture, it includes patterns of living its people may forge and assume in their efforts to meet the challenges of life within the framework of religious teachings. Its religious features are perpetual, but its peoples' cultural patterns may adjust to the changing needs of time and place' (p. 272). As a comprehensive cultural system, Islam provides moral and spiritual guidance; adherents structure and align their identity in terms of the sanctioned behaviours and beliefs outlined in the doctrinal texts (i.e., the Holy Qur'an and the *sunnah*). However, the interpretations of those texts vary in accordance with the socially mediated reading that occurs. That is, exegetical practices are implicated by the social, political, moral, and gendered location of the interpreter; this in turn leads to multiple vantage points for interpretation (see Abou El Fadl, 2002; Wadud, 1992).

Thus there are multiple orientations towards Islam based on individual, cultural, and sectarian locations. This makes it impossible to view Muslims and their communities in monolithic terms. Yet even allowing for this variation, there is a model for behaviour embedded in the Qur'an – a model rooted in the well-documented life of the Prophet Muhammed, whom all Muslims consider the living embodiment of Qur'anic principles. This suggests that there is a definitive 'essence' to Islamic identity as it is informed by religious doctrine; however, the degree to which that identity is adopted and emulated (along with the behaviours and attitudes flowing from it) is determined by more specific individual, cultural, and sectarian interpretations of Islam (Zine, 2007a).

By definition, a Muslim is 'one who submits to the will of Allah.'[4] Indeed, 'Islam' is the Arabic word for 'submission' or 'peace.' The guidelines for living one's life accordingly are outlined in the Qur'an; the actions of the Prophet Muhammed serve as a paradigm for believers. For Muslims who articulate their identity in terms of their faith, Islam is an embodied practice based on doctrinal referents. This is not to say that the theological foundations of Islam are not contested; there are competing discourses and sectarian differences that complicate singular definitions and meanings and that allow for epistemological and ontological pluralism within Islamic traditions. Within the culture of Islamic schools and the communities that comprise them, however, there is a stricter adherence to conservative interpretations of faith.

Regarding the participants in this study, their framework for constructing an Islamic identity was based on the dominant theological orientation promoted within the school and mosque community. All four schools were Sunni in orientation, but each followed a specific school of thought within that tradition. Thus, for example, Al Shawwal was guided by the more conservative Salafi orientation, whereas Al Safar followed the Hanafi tradition. Each of these schools was housed in a mosque, which made for a more specific theological orientation. Al Rajab and Al Shaban were family-operated schools, which meant that they were not guided by specific imams. Nevertheless, they were deeply conservative in their religious orientation and practices. Prevailing discursive norms provided the central organizing principles for the schools' social and academic practices. Students accommodated and sometimes challenged these norms as they constructed their own notions of what it means to be a Muslim; in that project, they both embraced and confronted their school's normative discourses (see chapter 6 for a discussion of discourse and identity formation).

The narratives revealed a sense of how the participants in this study understood and practised their identities as Muslims; those same narratives uncovered the role of the school as a site where Islamic identity was socially negotiated and reproduced. Students saw Islam as the most influential factor in their lives, and they valued and guarded their identity. Saira, for example, who had recently transferred into grade eight at Al Safar from the public system, saw Islam as pivotal to her life and as a foundation for her beliefs and practices:

SAIRA: Well, there's a very big difference between if I compare the two schools. I mean this school is just – wow, its great! I've been in public school for about eight years, and the reason I left there was basically to come to an Islamic environment, to be around people like me, to get closer to God and to learn about my religion. Because I believe that I need to learn more so that I know that I can go out into the world and be a strong Muslim. And I need to strengthen my roots so that nothing can shake me.

It is interesting that at the age of thirteen, Saira herself had persuaded her parents to send her to Al Safar. Her views clearly articulate the faith-centred lifestyle that she had chosen. Islam provided her with a moral compass in life:

SAIRA: Well, being a Muslim is like a gift for me, I don't know where I'd be without my religion, I'd probably be lost. Islam is basically not a religion to me, it's a way of life, it's something I can lie back on, something I can go to whenever I have problems, it has the answers to all of my questions, all I have to do is find the answer. And a Muslim is basically a person who completely submits ... to Allah, which means that basically everything you do, you remember Allah, and you do it in an Islamic way.

For students like Saira, secular education does not allow faith-centred understandings of the world; it does not accept that faith can be a valid parameter for knowing and relating to the world. Faith-centred youth can easily feel stifled when this aspect of their world view is denied in a secular environment; they find themselves unable to express their religious identity and sensibilities. Other students at Al Rajab spoke of what Islamic identity or 'being a Muslim' meant to them. For Saadi, Islamic identity had to do with righteous behaviour and conduct:

SAADI: Well, I guess just having, well, having *manners* is one of the main things I think about a Muslim. Like having good manners, like the way you talk to people, like respect for your teachers, respect for your parents. And basically everybody knows that Muslims have to pray and they have to fast. Those are essential things ... like you have to give to charity and stuff like that, but it's just your basic attitude.

Clearly, religion provided these young people with a path to personal and spiritual fulfilment. They framed their discussions about life's challenges in terms of the transitory nature of the material world, or *dunya*, which they contrasted with the eternal hereafter, or *akhira*, which Muslims view as the true goal of existence. Indeed, this metaphysical discourse was a salient factor in their constructions of identity and life purpose. Also important was their understanding of how life's hardships were tests of faith and spiritual fortitude:

NUSAYBAH: When I think of Islam, I think of love of yourself, love of your religion, love of your God. It's like, if you love yourself then you're going to be a proper Muslim, and that's what Islam really is.

ALIYAH: Yeah, because if you love yourself – well, if you want to go to heaven that means you love yourself. You love yourself enough that you want to go to heaven and that makes you be more pious. It makes you love Allah more.

NUSAYBAH: And it's like, you know there's no point of living in this world.[5] Like, Allah starts like doing stuff to you to make you realize how precious your life is and how important it is to follow Islam. Because He makes things in your life happen, and it's so unbelievable. He makes things happen, I don't know how to explain it – How do I explain it, guys?!

ALIYAH: Okay, Allah throws tests at you, right? He puts you through stuff, like either He'll make you break up with your friend. He's trying to test how strong your relationship is with your friend. And how you go about handling that test is how high your *iman* [faith] is. You know what I mean?

NUSAYBAH: Or it's like, Allah does things like, if you have a really close friend or family member and it's like, if they pass away. And Allah's testing you to see if you're strong enough to believe in him, or if you just go against God and say, 'Why did you do this?' And he puts you through tests like that to see if your love and your *iman* is true.

Parents saw Islamic schools as sites where an Islamic identity could be cultivated through immersion in Islamic beliefs and practices, as Qassim notes:

QASSIM: I think the goal would definitely be raising children who are strong and confident about their identity and their belief system but within their context. I think that's where it'll take a lot of hard work among all the Islamic schools ... so that they can develop the curriculum in a way that gives the kids an excellent standard of education but it reinforces their identity.

Nadia, a mother of Greek heritage in her late twenties, was a new Muslim, having converted to Islam after marrying her husband, who was from Pakistan. She had a five-year-old child at Al Shawwal and spoke of the role of Islamic schools in developing Islamic identities among children:

NADIA: Being a new Muslim, I want him to feel comfortable and strong in what he believes and what he practises ... I just want my children to grow up knowing who they are, what they believe in, and what their religion is all about. I don't want them to just have the identity of Muslim and not know what Muslim means or Islam.

As a new Muslim, Nadia felt that the Islamic school would be able to provide her child with a stronger foundation of Islamic knowledge than she could, given that she was still learning about Islam herself. Other parents talked about how they wanted their children to be grounded in Islamic *adab*, or etiquette, and about the school's importance in fostering an Islamic character. The students commented on how the Islamic school environment helped them develop their *taqwa*, or spiritual consciousness, which then framed their behaviour. Nusaybah explained how the faith-centred environment allowed students more freedom in expressing their *taqwa*:

NUSAYBAH: The people that come here, they've got this whole thing about them, they're stronger in Islam [Zarqa agrees in the background] and they'll be talking and they'll be like, *'mashallah.'*[6] I never used to say, like, *mashallah* or *jazak Allah.*[7] Now I'm like, *'mashallah! mashallah!'* or I'll be, like, *'insha'allah'!*[8] I say those things now. My parents even said, 'It's like you've changed.'

Rima, a teacher, saw Islamic identity as centred on specific beliefs and values, which she hoped to inculcate in her students. She stressed the need to recognize one's accountability to the Creator and to be responsible for one's actions as important aspects of *taqwa*, or spiritual consciousness. She also spoke of respect for elders and the need to promote communal rather than individualistic values among young people. According to Amira, this level of Islamic education had to begin with the intrinsic aspects of faith as opposed to extrinsic rituals and practices. For her, teaching Islam as a means to develop an Islamic identity started with inculcating core values that could be used to build an inner spiritual connection:

AMIRA: [The goal] is to teach the core values, to teach the children to practise from within. So not to force it. Like, not to do it in an intimidating or forceful way. You're trying to get the children to really see that, yes, Islam is the way, the best way of life, and I want to practise it, or I want to obey Allah, so to get it within themselves, that love for Allah within themselves. That's what we try to do through, you know, through the everyday values that are taught.

Ruqayyah talked about teaching Islam as a way of life and as a comprehensive system for living, rather than a form of practice restricted to attendance at the mosque. She felt that she was preparing students to develop their Muslim identity so that they could serve as 'ambassadors of Islam' and be role models for other youth. She saw herself as a role model for her students:

RUQAYYAH: [Islam] is a way of life. So I don't want them to think, like, 'Oh, it's only something we do when we go to the mosque.' I want them to realize when they go out there they have to be representing all of us the same way we have to be as well. We're accountable, too, as teachers, all of us.

Many of the narratives focused on the issue of representing Islam to others as a part of Islamic identity. Saadi noted that many people from outside the Muslim community were intrigued by the idea of Islamic schools:

SAADI: Nowadays, when you meet people and you're outside socializing or whatever, and they hear that you're from an Islamic school, just right away they get intrigued by the word 'Islamic.' They like to find out stuff, too – find out where it is, what we're doing, how is it in there. They're so curious about Islam.

So Islamic schools can be a means to confront negative stereotypes and Islamophobia by presenting positive counternarratives, as Zahra explained:

ZAHRA: Okay, I want my children to be a good example to the other society, I want the other people to see how the Muslims live, what they avoid. Because they have different thoughts about Muslims. They think *terrorist*, they think *bad*. No, really, I want them to know what Islam *is*. I want them to know what Muslims *do*.

Aliyah spoke of the public aspect of Islamic identity and how her friends at the Islamic school helped keep these goals in focus:

ALIYAH: They remind you of your religion. [Zarqa and Nusaybah agree: 'That's the most important thing.'] They remind how you have to be with others. They remind you that you're Muslim and this is how you have to be in front of non-Muslims.

Other OAC students at Al Rajab, like Umbreen and Safia, told me that Islamic schooling provided a space for culturally congruent counselling that reflected faith-centred values with regard to social practices such as dating. They preferred the Islamic school environment, where their values were supported and where they could receive counselling from a faith-centred and Islamically focused perspective:

UMBREEN: I feel that by coming to Islamic school, we gain a lot more Islamic knowledge. And in our surroundings, it's an Islamic environment, our teachers are Muslim and stuff and we don't have to feel uncomfortable talking with them. Because like, when you talk to them about your problems and stuff usually the non-Muslim teachers in public school, they wouldn't understand you. But ... when you're around people with hijabs on and everything, you don't have to feel uncomfortable. Like, you know that everyone – they don't judge you about how you look, because we're all the same.

SAFIA: And when you ask for help with something, like, 'Oh I have a so and so problem,' if you're in public school they'll mostly give the wrong information or the wrong advice, because they're not Muslim, so they don't have the Islamic knowledge. But in Islamic school they'll give you the Islamic knowledge and they'll guide you according to Islam.

Iman and Summaya, sixteen-year-old grade eleven students of Somali descent, also felt that Islamic schools were vital in helping youth maintain a faith-centred lifestyle. They saw this as the primary goal of reproducing Islamic identity and maintaining the continuity of Islam in the community:

IMAN: To keep the faith. That's the number one thing that we need to deal with. A lot of people before they come here, they lose faith, they lose track of their religion.

SUMMAYA: They get easily influenced. And so this is an easier way to get us together ... This way we can support each other so whenever somebody is weak they have fellow Muslims to help them. Because otherwise we'd all be scattered around and we'd lose our faith.

Iman had lived in Canada for nine years, Summaya for six years. Both had been attending Al Rajab for three years. Their experience with both the public system and their Islamic school allowed them to compare the circumstances of Muslim youth in both environments.

Some parents noted, however, that socially reproducing Islamic identities was not exclusively the role of the school – the home environment was also pivotal, as Shazad explained:

SHAZAD: In developing the child's identity, the Islamic school would aid in that process. [But] it wouldn't be the full solution. In developing the education background of the identity, it would be good. But at the same time, the home environment and other supplemental studying and training programs would make the healthy child

... Because usually training has to be multidimensional. It has to be in all phases of life. So, therefore, schools provide that education and training, say from nine o'clock to three o'clock, and that's about it. Training in the afternoon, at bedtime, playing sports, sleeping together, camping, dealing with others under different scenarios, and so forth, a school environment doesn't necessarily provide that. So you need other supplemental tools to build identity of the child.

Asma was a mother in her late forties of Anglo-Canadian background who had accepted Islam ten years earlier, after marrying her husband, who was from India. In her view, Islamic schools supplemented Islamic knowledge for children from families in which culture played a stronger role than religion. She saw Islamic schools as a means to sort out culture from religion and as providing the means to develop and promote a pan-Islamic identity that would move beyond cultural tribalism:

ASMA: I think with many parents who are immigrants, they may have lacked religious training themselves in their own homes when they were growing up. They went through the motions of it – a lot of cultural baggage intertwined with religious practices – and I would hope that the Islamic schools would sort the culture from the religious teaching because there would be a mix of cultural backgrounds in an Islamic school ... [An] ideal Islamic school ... would welcome all cultural backgrounds, and could accommodate them peacefully.

Yet like Shazad, Asma felt that Islamic schools should not be a panacea for the Muslim community and that parents should not become complacent in their own attempts to inculcate Islamic values and practices:

ASMA: But as we move forward, what we're seeing is new-generation Canadians, who were born here, but they're having their own children now. And I think the interest in those parents is to give a good foundation in religious training that definitely is not going to be provided in the public schools because public schools are not to teach religion. Parents have said to me, 'Well, if I can just get my children to go there for the first few years then I can send them to the public school and not worry.' But I think anybody who makes that statement is leaving the gate wide open because unless you, as a parent, are involved in support of your child, instilling Islamic values and thought and consideration every day, you're going to lose your child anyway. So the Islamic school must work with the parents.

In other words, while Islamic schools play a vital role in the social reproduction of Islamic identity and community, their success depends on the extent to which the home environment validates and reinforces those same values (see also Berns McGown, 1999). The construction of Islamic identity in Islamic schools and in Muslim homes serves to maintain the continuity of Islam in the Muslim community. This allows for Islamic identities to be reproduced down the generations, by resisting assimilation. This process, aided by Islamic schooling, is vital to the regeneration of the diasporic Muslim community.

5 Embodied Practices: Schooling and the Politics of Veiling

In this chapter, 'gendered Islamophobia' and the politics of veiling are examined through a narrative analysis of eighteen female students. Sixteen of the girls attended the Al Rajab high school, two attended middle school at Al Safar. They ranged in age from fourteen to nineteen and were of South Asian, Arab, Somali, and Caribbean backgrounds. Islamic school became a safe haven where these students had freedom from racialized and Islamophobic stereotypes. This was particularly important for girls who adhered to Islamic dress codes outside of school, which visibly marked them as Muslims. These girls constructed their identities in opposition to the stereotypes they encountered in the media and in their public school experiences that viewed them as 'oppressed,' 'backward,' and uneducated (see Rezai-Rashti, 1994; Haw, 1998; Bullock and Zine, 2002; Zine 2000 and 2002; McDonough, 2003a). Increasing Islamophobia, due to the tragedy of 11 September, has exacerbated these notions and encouraged Muslim women to develop positive counter-narratives. The discussion in this chapter will allow a deeper understanding of how gendered identities are constructed in the schooling experiences of Muslim youth, and will examine how the multiple identities they inhabit as social actors based on race, ethnicity, religion, and gender are connected to broader notions of diaspora and nationalism. The issues addressed in this chapter will also speak to the contested notion of gender identity in Islam and situate various orientations and articulations of identity that both challenge and affirm traditional notions.

Gendering Islamophobia

Islamophobia can be defined as 'a fear or hatred of Islam and its adherents that translates into individual, ideological, and systemic forms of oppression and discrimination' (Zine, 2003). 'Gendered Islamophobia' refers to specific forms of discrimination levelled at Muslim women that proceed from historically contextualized negative stereotypes that inform specific individual and systemic forms of oppression (see also Zine, 2006). For example, Orientalist images of backward and oppressed Muslim women often frame the Muslim girls' interactions in schools; those interactions have resulted in some girls being channelled into lower non-academic streams, owing to teachers' misperceptions that Islam does not value education for girls (Zine, 2001b). In France, Turkey, and Quebec, some Muslim girls have been exiled from the public school system for wearing the hijab (a phenomenon dubbed 'hijabophobia'), a practice viewed as an assault on dominant civic values of female liberty and as a denial of the dominant national identity (Misbahuddin, 1996; Gutmann, 1996; Todd, 1999; Lenk, 2000).

Banning Hijab in Schools: France and Quebec

These debates emphasize that balancing multicultural pluralism with religious freedom is a fragile act. A case in point is the French controversy known as *l'affair du foulard* (the scarf affair). In 1989 in France, three Muslim adolescent girls were denied access to public school because they wore the hijab, an act that defied a 1937 French law prohibiting the wearing of conspicuous religious symbols in government-run schools. This ignited nationalistic debates about perceived dangers of ethno-racial and religious diversity. The right-wing French politician Jean-Marie Le Pen urged the repatriation of all immigrants who had arrived in France since 1974. These xenophobic sentiments were echoed in the conservative newspaper *Le Point*, in which one provocative headline read: 'Should We Let Islam Colonize Our Schools?'

   The ensuing debate over secularism and religious freedom divided even the political left. Some French socialists allied themselves with the conservatives, defending the 1937 law on the grounds that 'the veil is a sign of imprisonment that considers women to be sub-humans under the law of Islam' (in Gutmann, 1996, p. 161). Many feminists concurred that the hijab is a symbol of gender inequality and therefore incompatible with French social values. In effect, feminists were denying the agency of Muslim women who wear the veil and reducing the multiple meanings associated with the veil to a single negative referent (El Habti, 2004). In the ensuing public debates, troubling discourses of fear, aversion, otherness, and even sub-humanness in relation to Muslim girls and the veil came to overshadow the fundamental issue of religious freedom as a human right.

In the Canadian context, the case of Émilie Ouimet captured national attention in 1994. Twelve-year-old Émilie, a French Canadian convert to Islam, was expelled from her school for not complying with a request to remove her hijab. This attempt to deny the right to wear the hijab received support from the largest teachers' federation in Quebec, which voted in favour of banning the hijab from French schools. The principal at Émilie's school justified his decision by saying that the wearing of distinctive markers such as the hijab and neo-Nazi insignias could polarize students. In other words, he was equating the hijab with racist authoritarianism and invoking a discourse of fear and repression. The social, cultural, and political context in which the hijab ban erupted was critical in understanding these debates. In 1977 the Quebec legislature passed Bill 101, which declared that all immigrant children in Quebec must attend French-language schools. This law changed the homogenous character of French schools and rapidly ushered in a new multicultural dynamic to these schools (Lenk, 2000). In the case at hand, the backlash to integration and ethno-racial diversity took the form of a controversy over religious dress in secular public schools.

Emilie's case also unfolded amidst a growing French nationalism in Canada and the hijab came to epitomize the challenge of defining a distinctive Quebecois national identity in a changing social and cultural environment. The French and English media were polarized in their representation of the issue and used the forum to further the broader contestations over the nature of French society and hegemony in Quebec (Todd, 1999; Lenk, 2000). The English language newspapers became the champion of Emilie's cause citing the need to value individual and human rights. Representing the anglophone minority in Quebec who were also subject to francophone hegemony, the English language press capitalized on Emilie's plight as a way to further their own political critique of French society and the failure of Quebec nationalism to conform to the laws of English Canada's discourse (Lenk, 2000). So in this political context, the hijab was not only a way of constructing the Islamic other as a threat to liberal civic values, but it also polarized French nationalism with anglophone federalism.

Lenk (2000) reminds us that an important racialized dimension to the debate was the fact that Emile was a white convert to Islam. She argues that Emilie's Islamization was viewed as racial transgression making her less sympathetic to the French nationalist constituency. As a result, she became racialized through her refusal to conform to the normative cultural standards and perform the dominant identity. What was seen as a disavowal of her dominant Francophone Quebecois identity was registered as a threat to the French nationalist goal of developing a 'distinct society' with a French character.

Lenk (2000) adds that the news media generally excluded the perspective of Émilie herself; moreover, they failed to include the voices of other Muslim women in the debate. As a consequence, the fact that Émilie's control over her body, dress, and ultimately her schooling were compromised by the ban became almost incidental to broader social and political issues. This unequal representation was also evidenced by the fact that while Muslim women's views were silenced in the media and the public discourse, a white female reporter received a great deal of attention when she donned the hijab and wrote about her 'experience' (Lenk, 2000). Throughout the media representation, political analysts and even the school principal who initiated the ban claimed the dominant narrative in a way that excluded and appropriated Muslim women's experiences. Émilie appealed to Quebec's Human Rights Commission, which ruled that public schools cannot forbid the wearing of religious headscarves (Khan, 2003). In the end, then, she was able to recuperate her agency and her religious rights. These landmark cases from France and Quebec are examples of the gendered Islamophobia at play when gendered religious identities are negotiated in secular educational sites.[1]

Hijab and Workplace Discrimination

Studies have found that Muslim women who wear the hijab suffer discrimination in the workplace (Parker-Jenkins, 1999). For example, a recent study in Toronto (Vashti Persad and Lukas, 2002) identified significant barriers to veiled Muslim women in their efforts to find work (Keung, 2002; Smith 2002). This study reported that twenty-nine of the thirty-two Muslim women surveyed said that an employer had referred to their hijab while they were applying for work in the manufacturing, sales, and service sectors. Twenty-one of the participants were asked to remove their head covers; one-third were told at least once that they would have to remove their veil if they wanted a job. ✓ Two sets of women were sent 'undercover' to apply for the same job. They provided almost identical resumes, ages, and ethnic backgrounds; the only difference was that one of the women wore the hijab. While 62.5 per cent of the women without a hijab were asked to fill out a job application, only 12.5 per cent of the women wearing it were given the same opportunity. These examples show how gendered Islamophobia operates socially, politically, and discursively to deny material advantages to Muslim women.

Examining the Politics of Veiling

Driscoll (1997) argues that 'both men's and women's bodies are important sites of cultural and religious inscriptions; yet these markings have particularly devastating consequences for girls and women' (p. 93). Here, she is speaking to the issue of how patriarchal standards of bodily acceptability drive women to self-denial and cosmetic augmentations through the 'violence of narcissism' that results in new cultural permutations of the female body, which she describes as 'the slender or starving body ... the tattooed body, the surgically corrected body ... the self slashed body,' to name a few (p. 94). In this way Driscoll is articulating a notion of the body as a 'cultural medium upon which is inscribed the politics of gender' (p. 94). Indeed, the politics of gender can be mapped onto women's bodies in various ways. Muslim women's dress, in particular, is a salient means of culturally and religiously encrypting the female body. El Guindi (1999) notes that as a form of religious dress, the Muslim veil (i.e., hijab) is located at the intersection of dress, body, and culture (p. xvi). Through the medium of the veil, then, Muslim women's bodies are gender coded to form a 'cultural text' for expressing of social, political, and religious meanings.

Multiple Meanings of Veiling

Hoodfar (2003) argues that dress codes such as the Muslim veil serve significant social, cultural, and political functions and constitute a medium of non-verbal ideological communication (p. 3). Clarke (2003) posits that Islamic dress is an important communicator of social and religious values (p. 217). From these understandings, we can conceive of the body as a site of variable inscriptions that visually mark and code religious, cultural, and gendered norms or, conversely, that resist and subvert those norms. Such corporeal inscriptions silently communicate social and political messages through specific forms and styles of dress. Through this process of social communication, meanings are mapped onto the body as it is presented and packaged for public consumption and spectacle. As a form of social communication and as a bearer of cultural and gendered norms, the Muslim veil is one of the most provocative and evocative forms of dress, eliciting as many diverse and conflicting reactions as there are reasons ascribed to its adoption.

Despite often static representations of veiling, multiple meanings are associated with the veil. These meanings vary across history and cultures as well as politically (Hoodfar, 1993; Kahf, 1999; Bullock 2000, 2002; Zine, 2002). Though women's practices of veiling predate Islam, this symbol has entered the popular imagination in Western societies as the quintessential marker of the Muslim world and as a practice synonymous with religious fundamentalism and extremism. In this conception, veiled women's bodies are cultural signifiers of social difference and social threat; furthermore, they represent fidelity to a patriarchal order that endangers women's autonomy (MacMaster & Lewis, 1998; Read & Bartkowski, 1999; Bullock, 2002). These notions can be traced back to their Orientalist origins, where depictions of veiled Muslim women in the colonial imagery ranged from oppressed and subjugated women to the highly sexualized and erotic imagery of the sensual, yet inaccessible, harem girl (Said, 1979; Alloula, 1986; Mabro, 1991; Hoodfar, 1993; MacMaster & Lewis, 1998; Yegenoglu, 1998; Khaf, 1999; Bullock, 2000). Historically, then, the veiled Muslim woman has been constructed as an object of fear and desire at once. Muslim women's identities are negotiated within the nexus of these ambivalent constructs, which mediate between the desire for and the disavowal of their social, racialized, and gendered difference (Khan, 2002; Zine, 2002).

For Muslim women who wear it, the headscarf or hijab is imbued with multiple and complex sociological and political meanings. For some women, it is an important marker of faith, modesty, identity, and worship (Zine, 1997; Read & Bartkowski, 2000; Bullock, 2002; Hoodfar, 2003). In some contemporary Muslim societies, the veil has also been used as a form of political protest and class-based signification (MacCleod, 1991; Bullock, 2000; Hoodfar, 2003). In its symbolic and practical form, it is also viewed as a means of maintaining the body as a space of 'sacred privacy' (El Guindi, 1999).

The multiplicity of meanings complicates the essentialization of the veil in ways that limit the scope of its social and political meanings. Remarking on the variability of the veil as a cultural signifier of difference, Todd (1999) notes: 'Clearly the *hijab* is no innocent "signifier" within such a volatile context. It has come to symbolize everything from Islamic fundamentalism, religious expression, women's subordination to women's empowerment and equality' (pp. 441–2). Therefore, as a political and discursive space, Islamic dress represents a mode of gendered communication that implicates how the body is narrated, read, and consumed both cross-culturally and within specific religious and cultural frames of reference.

The Veil in Religious Paradigms: The Hermeneutics of Dress

In a scriptural sense, the veil has been viewed as a divine injunction based on specific verses from the Qur'an and supported by some hadith. For example, the following Qur'anic verses address women's clothing: 'And say to the believing women that they should avert their gaze and guard their modesty, and they should not display their adornment except what is apparent thereof, and they should throw their veils over their bosoms, and not display their adornment except to their husbands or fathers' (24:31). 'O Prophet, tell your wives and the women of the believers that they should bring some of their cloaks closer/nearer to themselves, that is a minimum [measure] so that they would be recognized as such and hence not molested' (33:59).

During the seventh century in Arabia, when these verses were revealed, the customary pre-Islamic practice of women was to wear a long headscarf (*khimar*), which flowed loosely around their shoulders and left their breasts exposed. Some scholars view the verses related here as a corrective to this practice and as a means to signify Muslim identity (Hajjaji-Jarrah, 2003; Abou El Fadl, 2002). Significantly, there are no sanctions in the Qur'an for not covering, and in a survey of relevant hadith literature relating to dress, Clarke (2003) notes that only one report in the canonical collections clearly refers to the requirements of women's covering (p. 220). In this tradition it is related that the Prophet Muhammed stated that, at the age of puberty, women should cover all but the hands and face. Yet Clarke points out that this hadith is found in only a single collection and that this is not considered a strong account, since the *isnad* (chain of transmission) had been broken (pp. 220–1).

Given the complexities of interpretation and the divergences among scholars (i.e., some invoke more literal readings, others more historically contextualized ones), there is no juristic consensus regarding the areas of the body to be covered (Roald, 2000). Some of the early Islamic legal schools called for the entire face to be covered, others for all but the hands and face. Still other interpretations note that, since the Qur'an does not explicitly mandate that the hair be covered (rather, it refers to drawing the veil over the bosom), this is not an obligatory requirement, and that maintaining a dress code reflecting the contemporary cultural norms for modesty is all that is required (Hajjaji-Jarrah, 2003).

Both the Qur'anic verses and the various references in the hadith narratives have been subjected to rigorous re-examination by contemporary scholars, who have presented alternative contextualized readings. Some argue that the hijab is a historically specific form of dress that was used during the seventh century as a means to visibly mark Muslim women so that they could be identified as under the protection of the Muslim clan; in this way they could avoid being molested or harassed (Roald, 2000; Abou El Fadl, 2002; Hajjaji-Jarrah, 2003). The veil was also the marker of a free woman (as opposed to a slave or concubine); thus it established certain social and sexual parameters for the engagement of men with these different social and class-based categories of women (Hajjaji-Jarrah, 2003). These interpretations serve to offset other religious views that situate the hijab as a static symbol of religious practice and as a means for socially and legally demarcating women's bodies as part of private, non-public space. Feminist scholars rightly see this understanding as both contrary and detrimental to the Islamic ethos of equality and justice and as having arrested the development of true gender equity among Muslims (Mernissi, 1987, 1991; Ahmed, 1992).

Veiling as Feminist Protest or Fundamentalist Dogma?

Some feminists see the veil as a means to resist and subvert dominant Eurocentric norms of femininity and the objectification of the female body; it also protects women from the male gaze (Bullock, 2000, 2002; Read & Bartkowski, 2000). As a sexually politicized referent, the veil has also been identified as a symbol of the rejection of 'profane, immodest and consumerist cultural customs of the West'; in that sense, it is an anti-imperialist statement, one that marks alternative gendered norms (Read & Bartkowski, 2000, p. 398). These notions construct the practice of veiling as part of an oppositional political discourse that counters the 'tyranny of beauty' and that resists the objectification and commodification of women for the edification of patriarchal capitalist desires. When considered this way, wearing the veil can be seen as an empowering move because it resists sexualized representations of the female body. Halstead (1991) notes that such rationales have contributed to the saliency of the veil in the British Muslim diaspora: 'The Qur'anic requirements of modesty and decency in dress (Qur'an 24:30-31; 33:59) may be seen not so much as an exemplar of patriarchal domination as a practical attempt to defeat sexual exploitation and harassment, and as such it continues to be upheld by many second generation British Muslim women' (p. 274).

Narrations of Islamic womanhood both inside and outside Muslim ideological and ontological conceptions have long been linked to religious attire in highly reductive ways. On the one hand, conservative Islamic discourses see the veil as the key signifier of religiosity for women, and they emphatically reject alternative expressions of Islamic womanhood that do not include the veil. Many feminists use equally reductive paradigms to essentialize the veil as the universal marker of women's oppression; in doing so, they are negating veiled women's alternative constructions that locate the practice within spaces of social, sexual, and political empowerment (see also Lazreg, 1988, 1994; Mohanty, 1991). Muslim women must navigate between these reductionist and essentialized paradigms to claim their own representation over the discursive practices that determine how their bodies are narrated, defined, and regulated (Zine, 2004).

Driscoll (1997) has identified the body as a significant site of social control and regulation, arguing that 'our bodies are marked by the current cultural forms and norms by which the self, femininity, masculinity and desire are produced, not by way of ideology but by virtue of the manifold ways our bodies are organized and regulated' (p. 95). The ideological determinants that underpin socially constructed notions of gender and faith are themselves rooted in patriarchal systems of power, which regulate corporeal practices such as dress codes. She describes the mechanics of this regulation as operating through the ways in which the 'rules and regulations' of culture are written on women's bodies. In a Foucauldian sense, these mechanisms of social control construct 'docile bodies' that are subservient to the aims of specific structures of power and cultural authority.

In Islamic societies, Muslim women's bodies are regulated through patriarchal social rules on the one hand and through secularist reforms on the other. The veil (or the burqa)[2] is mandated in Saudi Arabia, Iran, and Afghanistan but outlawed in secular public institutions in countries like Turkey; in either case, however, the effect is essentially the same – state authorities are disciplining and regulating women's bodies and thereby challenging the political and spiritual autonomy of Muslim women to make reasoned choices about their bodies. In this way the hermeneutics of the veil as a religious dress code have generated a discursive terrain where multiple meanings, fears, and desires converge.

Veiling Practices in Islamic Schools

For Muslim girls who adopt Islamic dress codes such as the hijab, or headscarf, and the niqab, or face veil, and who wear the abaya, or long overcoat, these markers of Islamic identification often lead to social ridicule and ostracism. Negative stereotypes and discrimination in daily life relating to Islamic dress codes were among the most salient concerns among the girls I interviewed. At the Al Rajab and Al Safar Islamic schools, the dress code included a compulsory hijab as well as a burgundy-coloured abaya worn over street clothes. These dress codes were the school uniform and were enforced by the school authorities. Outside school, the girls were free to dress as they chose or in accordance with family expectations. Many of the girls chose to wear the hijab as an act of worship, as a show of modesty, and as part of their expression of Islamic identity. These girls wore the hijab outside school as well. Some also wore the abaya over their clothes outside school; however, many instead wore the hijab with other clothes, such as the South Asian-style *shalwar kameez*, or they wore Western-style clothes that conformed to traditional Islamic dress requirements and that were loose fitting and opaque. None of the girls reported that their families were 'forcing' them to wear the hijab outside of school; they had taken it up out of their own religious conviction. Only one of the two girls who wore niqab reported that her father had asked her to continue wearing it (they had come to Canada from Saudi Arabia). She had agreed to do so, and she felt personally comfortable with her identity wearing the niqab, though she was distressed by the discrimination she encountered in society as a consequence. Islamic school provided a safe haven from racism and harassment for many girls who otherwise would have been confronted every day with insults and humiliation.

Only one of the girls interviewed did not wear the hijab outside school, though during my tenure at Al Rajab as a teacher and later during my fieldwork there, I found that it was not uncommon for some girls take off their hijab and abaya right outside the school doors on their way home. Within the school, hijab requirements were policed by the vice principal sister Raeesa, and students were required to wear the burgundy abaya and a white or beige hijab. (Boys, as already noted, also wore a uniform: black dress pants and a white dress shirt). However, more surveillance was placed on the girl's clothing, since it was viewed as compulsory religious attire. Sanctions for violating the dress code for girls included admonishments that invoked references to 'hellfire'; such was the case in one conversation I overheard between a student and the vice-principal.

The girls also faced pressure from outside the Muslim community, where the veil has come to signify backwardness, oppression, and even terrorism (see Zine, 1997, 2001b, 2006). This form of discrimination or Islamophobia punctuates the experiences of many Muslim girls and women in mainstream society. In the following section I explore the concept of 'gendered Islamophobia' and examine the experiences of Muslim girls who find themselves having to contend with dual oppressions: sexism within their communities, and racism and Islamophobia outside their communities.

Unveiled Sentiments: Gendered Islamophobia and Lived Experiences of Veiling

Aliyah, Nusaybah, Zarqa, and Imrana were grade eleven students at Al Rajab. All four were sixteen years old and of Pakistani descent, except for Aliyah, who was Afghani. My interviews with them took place inside the school in an empty classroom during lunch breaks. Since it was the month of Ramadan, we were all fasting, which allowed time for them to sit and talk to me. The topic of Islamic dress arose often, especially when we discussed their experiences outside school and why they liked an Islamic school environment. During one conversation, when we began talking about who wore the abaya home and who took it off, they revealed experiences of racism, xenophobia, and gendered Islamophobia that they encountered journeying to and from school. Since Al Rajab was in an industrial park in a Toronto suburb, most students either took the bus to school or were car pooled. Most of the high school girls regularly used public transit, and it was there that they often encountered racist and Islamophobic attitudes. In the following exchange, the girls spoke poignantly about how this discrimination affected their sense of self and identity:

ALIYAH: Truly, I don't wear my abaya home. Honestly, I take it off.
NUSAYBAH: And I go home with mine on.
ALIYAH: Because the thing is, you take your car. I take the TTC,[3] see, and people look at me and they see me, and sometimes I'm treated rudely, seriously. Just with the hijab, sometimes I'm treated rudely.
JASMIN: By whom? The passengers or the bus drivers?
ALIYAH: The passengers and the bus drivers. Okay, like once this man, a passenger on the subway, called me an illegal immigrant. I think he was drunk. And I told him, 'I'm here legally! I didn't come here illegally! I came here legally!' Another time, I was wearing the hijab and I was standing right in front of the bus door, like I made it to the door but the guy [the driver] still shut the door on me and he drove off! And if I hadn't been wearing hijab I think he would have stopped.
JASMIN: Do you notice a difference when you go out without the abaya?
EVERYONE: [talking at once] 'Very much, yeah, Very much!'
ZARQA: Okay, I was going on the bus one day in Ramadan and I was wearing my hijab and my abaya. I was going to take off my abaya but then I didn't. And we were going past 5th Street and there was this lady on the bus, right, and there was a little girl and she was really, really cute and I love children and I was like: 'Oh hi, she's so cute!' and her mom, she like looked at me and she turns the daughter away from me and the girl just started crying. It makes you feel so bad!
ALIYAH: It makes you feel like, 'Oh if I hadn't been wearing this!'
ZARQA: That's exactly what I thought! The minute I saw that it was in my mind – I should have taken it off! Like, I know I shouldn't, but

at the time it made me feel that if I took it off it'd be different. It'd
be like … the girl wouldn't be crying.

ALIYAH: It's true. So many people do that. Like if you look at their kid
and you'd be like smiling at them, they'll just give you the dirtiest
look, like: 'Don't look at my kid!' But then when some white lady
looks at their kid, they're like smiling back at the lady.

Other girls in separate interviews recounted similar experiences of
being called 'illegal immigrants' and of being harassed on buses and
subways with comments like 'Halloween's over!' Many girls reported the same incident at a bus stop outside the school: the bus
driver often closed the door on them and drove off. Some of the
former students in my World Issues course spoke of people becoming 'afraid' when they saw them. Rehana, a nineteen-year-old OAC
student of Pakistani descent, wore the niqab, or face veil, covering
everything but her eyes. She reported that non-Muslim children were
often scared by her appearance and that she would have to reassure
them that she was not going to hurt them. Hawa, a seventeen-year-
old Somali OAC student, recounted the experience of her friend, who
also wore niqab:

HAWA: Like one friend of mine [who wears niqab], whenever we're
on the bus, all the little kids are looking at her and some of the kids
are like holding their moms and crying. And even the parents, they
look at her and they ask her so many questions, like 'Why are you
wearing that?' 'Aren't you hot in the summer?'

As the girls exchanged stories of their lived experiences of racism
and Islamophobia, it became clear that they had all encountered
similar experiences as a result of their bodies being marked as Muslim
through the practice of veiling. The veil located them as 'foreigners'
who did not belong to the Canadian social fabric, and the xenophobia
they encountered as a result cast as them as 'illegal immigrants' – tan-
tamount to a denial of their citizenry. This lack of social acceptance
created a fragile narrative of 'Canadianness' and belonging for these
girls, one that was easily ruptured by the open hostility they encountered in mainstream society. These were also experiences of social
rejection, of being excluded from the simple banal exchange of smiling
at a child, of being treated as persona non grata simply because of their

religious identity and the negative meanings imposed on the veil. During these encounters a specific discourse of 'foreignness' and Otherness emerged and framed the way in which they came to see their identities, as Muslims being socially evaluated and ultimately rejected. This process had woven its way into their narratives of identity, with implications for how they located themselves within the racially bordered spaces of nation.

The social contempt these girls encountered often resulted in greater insularity when it came to interacting with others. The girls found strength in numbers when travelling with other 'hijabis'[4] from their school. Despite the fact that they received more stares, they felt greater solidarity from being in the company of other sisters wearing hijab and felt that they could collectively stand up to the scrutiny and negativity their dress evoked in public spaces:

JASMIN: And does being here [in Islamic school] give you more strength with those kinds of situations outside of school?
ZARQA: It does.
ALIYAH: Yeah, because there [public school] you don't have as many Islamic friends. Here when you go out with all your friends, you'll all be wearing hijab and you'll be like, 'Yeah so what,' you'll be in a bigger group. And when you're walking like in the mall or whatever –
IMRANA: All of us – see those girls over there, and her and me, we went to the mall and we got stared at from every single angle! Cuz there's a whole group of us wearing abaya and hijab.
ALIYAH: But you don't care!
IMRANA: Hey! You were walking ten miles ahead of us – don't even bother! We were all getting stared at even though half of them had normal clothes on.
ALIYAH: See, but then I wouldn't care. I'd be like, 'Who cares?! I'm with them.'
JASMIN: Because you're with a group. Is it harder when you're on your own?
ALIYAH: I feel more positive then [with a group]. I don't care, but if I was by myself –
ZARQA: If I'd be like, by myself, I'd be like, 'Oh God!' I'd like go to the bathroom and take it off or something. I would feel so bad!

The pressures of conformity that are communicated through the social disciplining of a negative gaze were, therefore, strong enough to force some of the girls to consider removing their hijabs to avoid the negative attention from strangers. It is also telling that their reference to wearing western-style clothing is categorized as wearing 'normal' clothes. This speaks powerfully to the way they perceived their ethnic and religious identification as located outside the boundaries of social acceptance and their dress as being outside of the accepted norms of cultural expression. However, being within a network of support that they were able to develop through the connections they established with other hijabis in the Islamic school allowed them to feel a sense of security and the confidence that they did not have to deal with the negative exchanges alone. These systems of support and camaraderie were also important sources for resisting assimilation and maintaining religious identification among Muslim students in public schools (see Zine, 1997, 2000).

While these Muslim girls were socially located at the nexus of multiple sites of oppression based on their race, ethnicity, gender, and religion, they felt that their Islamic identity marked by their hijab, was the most salient factor of discrimination. They referenced this by comparing the reactions they received in public when they wore South Asian dress such as the *shalwar kameez,* as opposed to wearing their abayas. At these times they noticed a qualitative difference in the attention they garnered; they were recognized as South Asian but were less visibly marked as 'Muslim.' When they wore Western clothes, they were able to 'pass' simply as South Asians, without the added negative Islamic referent. Because they lived in a strongly multicultural district of Toronto, their race and ethnicity were easier to negotiate than their religious identification, which carried far more complex and reactive meanings. These differences in public reactions were reflected in the following exchange:

JASMIN: So do you think in *shalwar kameez* you would get the same reaction?

ALIYAH: It's the abaya and the hijab. Like I was so shy, like I wanted to wear *shalwar kameez* because they're so much more comfortable and they look nicer, too, than regular clothes, but then I was so shy, but after when I wore them the first day, like no one even said anything to me. No one even looked at me bad. And then I just started wearing them more. But then when I was wearing abaya, one day I wore it and everyone was staring at me. I wore it from the bus stop to the school and every single person that was standing on the street ... I could see them staring at me from everywhere!

NUSAYBAH: I don't know, I feel so weird. It was my first time going on the street wearing an *abaya*, and everyone was looking at me. Especially since all the public school kids were coming out and I heard some people talking, they're like, 'Oh look at that ninja!' And you're not even covering your face and they're calling you a ninja! Like, I don't understand that! Like, they say stupid things like that and I looked down. It was my first time looking down – I never look down! But it made me feel like, so low.

Feeling compelled to look down was clearly emotionally devastating for Nusaybah, as for her it signified 'giving in' to Islamophobia. The impact of this sort of trauma on the cultural self-esteem and construction of identity for these girls is significant, especially given their age.

I was constantly reminded, during my time teaching and conducting field work among these young women, how self-conscious and vulnerable they were to other people's perceptions of them. At times during the interviews, one of them would say something that her friends would good-naturedly tease her about, and she would fall silent for a time, embarrassed by the public critique. It reminded me of my own long-ago (and perhaps best forgotten) memories of being a teenager and similarly self-conscious of how I looked, what I said, and what my peers thought of me. This emotional instability associated with the traditional rite of passage from youth to adulthood is compounded for youth from racially minoritized communities, who have to contend with the added pressures of race and social difference alongside typical teenage angst and social awkwardness. Muslim girls in the geopolitical climate of the new millennium are also forced to contend with being labelled 'terrorists' as the result of global events they had no part in making – events that nevertheless have been inscribed on their identity.

Confronting Stereotypes

The girls were strongly aware that they represented Islam everywhere they went and that they needed to be careful what they said and did, since their behaviour would be essentialized to represent all Muslims. These issues emerged during my interviews with Safia, Sahar, and Umbreen, who were all sixteen years old and grade eleven students at Al Rajab. Safia and Umbreen were South Asian of Pakistani and Indian descent; Sahar was a Palestinian Arab. The following discussion highlights the scrutiny and surveillance they faced as young Muslim women and how they negotiated the burdens of representation and negative essentialism. This discussion is particularly salient in the post-9/11 world; so it is worth remembering that in fact, these interviews took place *prior to 9/11*. Even then, these young people were deeply troubled by being collectively labelled as 'terrorists':

SAFIA: There's so much pressure, especially for the female Muslims, because if we make one little mistake, the littlest mistake, they'll keep that as a stereotype about us and they'll make us look bad about that. Yet if another girl did it that didn't wear hijab or wasn't Muslim, it wouldn't be a bad thing for her. Yet for us we're, uh ...
SAHAR: Looked at greatly –
SAFIA: From every single point.
SAHAR: Exactly.
SAFIA: So that's why we have more pressure on us outside in public to act modest and respectfully with everyone. Even if, say, a stranger came up to us and started acting rude, right? If we responded back rudely to them, they would say, 'Oh look, she's so rude!' this and that, but they wouldn't remember that they started it. So that's why even if someone's rude on the street or whatever, I'll still give them respect just so they can't say, 'Oh Muslims are this and that.'
UMBREEN: Yeah, but if one Muslim does something, they'll think all Muslims are like that. Everyone is like that. They'll be, like, 'Oh look at these Muslim people, they don't have any shame, blah blah blah.' But then when they do it, it's an everyday thing. It's like, 'Oh who cares?' Yeah, like if a white man goes and kills someone they don't go and say *all* white men killed someone, they don't say, 'Oh my God, *all* white men kill people!'
SAHAR: Exactly.
SAFIA: But if it was ever on the news that a Muslim man killed someone –
SAMIA: They'd spend years on it!

SAFIA: It'd be on the news forever.

UMBREEN: And then Muslim people feel like more uncomfortable on the streets.

EVERYONE: Yeah, exactly.

SAFIA: And you think everyone's looking at you and they're thinking, 'Oh my God, this person's going to kill me!'

SAHAR: 'Oh God, terrorists!'

SAFIA: You know, she's going to start something, she's going to do this.

JASMIN: It's sort of more of a burden because you know your entire community is going to be judged.

EVERYONE: Exactly!

SAFIA: Especially in public school, let's say one thing happened and you come to public school and you're going to think EV-ER-Y-ONE'S going to think you're like that.

SAHAR: But here [in Islamic school] you come and they know it's not like that, so you feel more comfortable and more relaxed and more free and more open.

This discussion seemed to foreshadow the burden of collective guilt levelled against the Muslim community worldwide based on the actions of nineteen terrorists on 9/11. This particular discussion preceded these tragic events; nevertheless, the fact that any actions by Muslims would be held against everyone who shared the same faith (some one billion people worldwide) was seen as inevitable by these young women. They took proactive measures to ensure that their own behaviour would not be negatively essentialized to pathologize other Muslims, by monitoring their actions and consciously avoiding reacting to 'rude' behaviour levelled at them by others. They were acutely aware of the double standards imposed on them as racialized Muslims and that 'white people' did not have to contend with similar stereotypes and essentialized labels based on the actions of individual members of their group.

Umbreen recounted another incident: She was in a store with her baby brother, who started crying because he wanted a toy. She felt accusing stares from other people in the store, who seemed to have automatically assumed that she had hit the child, which was why he was crying. Safia recounted a similar experience: When her younger siblings had a crying fit on the floor of a shopping mall, she noticed people staring at her and whispering. She gave in and picked up whatever her younger siblings wanted in order to avoid the cold stares of the other shoppers. When I asked these girls whether these public reactions would have been different had they not been wearing the hijab, they replied that if their 'Islamic-ness' had not been self-evident, people would have viewed both situations as simply a case of 'bratty kids' and would probably have judged that it was 'the parents being abused.'

Some researchers would categorize these experiences as 'perceived' instances of racism – as opposed to 'actual', clear-cut, or verifiable cases – since they were based on how the girls interpreted the reactions of others. Since no overt racial epithets were uttered, some researchers might be inclined to dismiss these stories altogether. Obviously, it is difficult for those who have not experienced the visceral quality of racist experience to truly appreciate how people can not only perceive but also actually *know* and *acknowledge* racism in the form of a disapproving gaze. Many would call it paranoia, but those of us who have actually experienced the trauma of social alienation and exclusion are less likely to dismiss the qualitative knowingness of racialized experience, even when it seems merely reduced to a cold stare (see also Essed, 1991, 1996; Karumanchery, 2003).

Islamic Dress and Narrations of Muslim Female Identity

For many girls, Islamic schools provided a safe environment where they could feel comfortable expressing their religious identity. In articulating this sense of identity, Islamic dress became one of the most salient markers of being a Muslim woman. In Islamic schools, dress codes were a means to regulate female bodies so that they conformed to religious standards. Dress codes were heavily policed by school administrators. For Sakhina, however, Islamic dress was an individual matter of faith and choice, not something to be enforced:

SAKHINA: I wear hijab. I wear *jilbab*.[5] But for me, I will never, ever tell someone to put it on or force them to put it on. What I hated myself doing and I felt that I was doing there ... just because I was told by the administrators ... was [telling girls] 'Put on your hijab properly' or 'Your *jilbab* isn't buttoned properly.' The thing is, I know some of the students don't wear it normally. For them to even put it on their head there – because it's out of respect for the uniform in the school and whatever – it's a big step. You can't sit there and count every hair that's sticking out. Just kind of leave it. If they're not wearing the uniform hijab, at least they're wearing a hijab. You can't be chasing them down at the coffee shop when they take it off. Fine, it gives a bad image to Muslims, but they don't know and they wear it anyways. Certain things were so forced on them. This is not Islam.

From a critical faith-centred vantage point, the veil as a marker of Islamic identity or as an act of worship should be upheld as a valid choice for women who choose to take it up of their own free will. Similarly, when Muslim women choose not to veil, this should not invalidate their identities as Muslim women. To invalidate their identity in this way reinforces narrow, deterministic perceptions that Islam can be reduced to an article of clothing. A critical faith-centred view, while validating the veil as a form of religious expression, privileges a more holistic view of religious identification as it is actualized through broader forms of spiritual practice, which may or may not include practices such as veiling. Moreover, when veiling and other religious practices are imposed by force, they position religion as the cause of women's oppression – oppression that should rightfully be challenged from a critical faith-centred perspective. The Qur'an, for example, mandates free will in the practice of faith with the Qur'anic injunction that states: 'Let there be no compulsion in religion' (2:56). This provides a strong theological basis for contesting the regulation and policing of religious practice. However, within the domain of Islamic institutions, such as mosques and schools, there is a general consensus – among those who choose to participate in these sites – on how religious identification is lived and practised, including adherence to specific gendered codes of dress and behaviour. Therefore, the regulation of religious practice in some cases, such as with the hijab as school uniform, is based largely on consensually agreed-upon norms. The patriarchal nature of some of these norms is, however, rarely highlighted or challenged, and dissent is silenced by fear of bearing the impious label ascribed to those who resist conformity with these dogmas.

Negotiating the Discursive Norms of Dress

While there are spaces for dissent against such regulation within the broader Muslim community, those who contest these practices do not generally opt for Islamic schooling as a choice for their children, or they accept the hijab as part of the school uniform but do not extend the practice of veiling outside the boundaries of the school. Some Islamic school communities have been attempting to strengthen gender equity – for example, by allowing women and girls greater access to sports and other activities organized within mosques. Even here, though, religious dress codes and gender segregation are maintained. Overall gender equity is being negotiated within discursively bounded spaces that are framed by particular faith orientations and their corresponding beliefs about gender relations in Islam.

Muslim girls entering these discursive spaces are socialized to conform to the school's prevailing religious orientation and must, therefore, accommodate themselves to the social and institutional norms that affect how their gendered subjectivities are constructed. Therefore, even while Muslim girls resist the ways they are positioned by popular culture and by Islamophobic representations, they still find themselves accommodating to the prevailing discourse of the hijab; essentially, they are exchanging one form of discursive representation and control for another. As a result, they script their identities within and against these competing constructions, resisting or accommodating themselves to these discursive positionings. For many, the school's gendered norms were very much in sync with their own orientation to their faith. Reay (2001) refers to this acknowledgment as a process of 'discursive recognition' or 'feeling a better fit with one discourse than another' (p. 155). Therefore, I do not invoke the notion of 'false consciousness' to explain why Muslim women accommodate themselves to specific gendered codes such as dress style. Many women accept these codes as a matter of conscious choice and spiritual freedom.

Some young women did contest the policing of their dress in Islamic school, but even they recognized that it was a matter of school regulations besides being a religious injunction. However, as these young women develop greater political maturity and knowledge and gain the ability to act and engage within the space of Islamic discourse – where such issues are the subject of debate – they may just as legitimately choose to define their notions of Islamic identity and identification in alternative ways. Most of the girls I interviewed were spiritually centred and had chosen to express their faith within the acceptable bounds as determined by their Islamic school environment, though they often challenged these boundaries. That said, their notions of Islamic identity were largely constructed within the prevailing discourse produced by the school and local religious authorities. Among the young Muslim women in this study, these discursively and physically regulated aspects of identity were either strongly upheld or openly contested (see chapter 6).

Freedom, Sisterhood, and Articulations of Identity

It is interesting that though these girls attended a gender-segregated Islamic school, they actually felt *more* segregated in public school. In the public system, the lack of acceptance for their faith-centred lifestyle and religious dress meant that they were set apart and more socially isolated from other students. An Islamic school offered them greater freedom to express their religious identity without fear of ridicule or social exclusion (see also Haw, 1994). As Sahar and Safia note in the following exchange, being in an Islamic school meant greater equality vis-à-vis other girls, all of whom wore the same uniform. This led to less competition and distraction based on fashion styles. Also, the Islamic school environment was seen as a more familial setting, one in which bonds of unity and sisterhood were stronger:

SAHAR: I find that I have more freedom here. Because in public schools, like you walk around and you feel so segregated from everyone else. Because you have a hijab on ... I feel that I'm so different than other people. But when I'm in an Islamic school, I feel that everyone is equal and everyone's the same as each other so I don't feel different than other people. I feel like we're all one big family, like all sisters and that's what I like about it. I think that's very different.

SAFIA: And being in a private school there's a uniform that you wear so you really don't have to care about the clothes you wear. Yet in public school there's something that they expect of you to wear. Like for example, some girls will wear revealing clothes, things like that, yet here we can wear the abaya and not be stared at because everyone else is wearing it as well. And we don't look at anyone differently because everyone looks the same here.

Not having to conform to MTV-dictated standards of dress freed these girls to express their identity in more modest ways that accorded with their particular faith-centred orientation. Islamic schools also mandate dress conformity, but that standard was more congruent with the sensibilities these girls had already developed based on their religious convictions. Without the peer pressure to conform to more popular and less modest clothing styles, they felt a greater sense of fitting in. Girls reported that in public school they faced heavy social pressure to remove the hijab and be like everyone else. Iman, an OAC student of Somali descent, discussed the peer pressure she and her friends encountered while wearing the hijab in public school:

IMAN: I was wearing hijab and, you know, people ask too many questions. They'll be like, 'Why do you wear that on your head? Aren't you hot?' You'll feel kind of bad. You'll answer them and they'll be like, 'Take it off' and stuff like that.
JASMIN: So did you feel pressure to conform and take off the hijab and just be like everybody else?
IMAN: People, like a lot of my friends, don't wear the hijab right, and then I go, 'Are you like pressured?' and they go, 'Oh no, no, no, it's not peer pressure,' but it really is, right? Because then why wouldn't they wear it? Because they want to look like their friends. They don't want to be different. They don't show pride in themselves and the faith that they have.

For Iman, then, the hijab represented pride in her faith and identity as a Muslim woman. She had started wearing it in middle school, and because she did not have many Muslim friends, she felt pressured to take it off. Some friends, she reported, respected the fact that she chose to wear hijab, and when she later transferred to a school where there were more Muslims in the school wearing it, she felt more comfortable. Islamic school, however, was where she felt safest to express and live her Islamic identity.

Competing Constructions of Femininity

For girls in mainstream public schools, deviating from the dominant discourses of sexualized femininity by wearing the hijab and observing more modest dress codes means situating oneself outside socially accepted norms of behaviour and dress. The Muslim girls I interviewed viewed wearing the hijab as an act of resistance and non-conformity that often resulted in exclusion and social isolation. Peer pressure is a powerful form of social control that sanctions transgressions against socially constructed norms of feminine identity. Girls who do not subscribe to the latest fashions and who do not wear revealing clothes to attract male attention are operating outside the dominant discourse that regulates representations of the female body.

For the girls I interviewed, swimming against the tide in this way was exceptionally difficult, given the social conditioning and limited narratives available to young girls in developing their identities. The normative standards of femininity that are available to young Muslim girls have already been discursively marked and produced within the dominant Eurocentric paradigms. They can either accommodate to these articulations of identity or challenge and resist the positioning of their bodies in this way. According to Jones (1993), 'girls perceive (in their wide observations from media, family, everyday life) the positions – including the silences – available to "normal" women, and usually regulate their own desires and behaviours within those parameters. This is not simply false consciousness which can be altered with some feminist education; it is not a choice between being liberated and being oppressed. Rather it is a choice between being "okay" or "normal" and being "weird"' (p. 162). In the same way, the construction of normativity relating to Muslim women's identity as it is articulated within the social and discursive boundaries of the Muslim community is based on conformity to a homogenized religious and social identity. The category 'Muslim woman' has been scripted as an a priori construct and is imbued with the weight of religious authority and divine sanction; thus, many religious leaders or school authorities do not view it as open to social negotiation. Even though there are competing perspectives regarding 'legitimate' articulations of Muslim women's identity (see, for example, Khan, 2000; Bullock, 2002), the views that are more challenging to the conservative status quo interpretations of gender issues in Islam are often marginalized and invalidated by patriarchal religious authorities (see, for example, Abou El Fadl, 2001, Barlas, 2002; Wadud, 1992, 2000).

Muslim girls in Islamic schools confront more conflicting standards for femininity and womanhood than they would encounter in public schools. The dominant hegemonic religious views on gender, faith, and identity circumscribed their choices for expressing their

sense of self and womanhood in radically different ways than do
secular (albeit also powerful) discourses of femininity in public
schools. However, many girls found the Islamic constructions more
conducive with the way they articulated their own sense of religious
identity and gender than the prevailing discourses of femininity they
encountered in public schools. For example, from a feminist standpoint, they were opposed to the sexualization of women in the media
and popular culture and felt that this objectification of women made
it more difficult for their intellect and spirituality to be taken seriously. They embraced the veil as a marker of identity and as an act of
worship, but they also appreciated the way in which it gave them
control over the male gaze. As Bullock (2002) notes, 'Hijab when
viewed from this perspective, is a way of saying "treat me as a
person, not as a sex object." It is a tool to counter the male-gaze
aspects of the patriarchal capitalist culture in which we find ourselves' (p. 192). From this standpoint, Muslim women take ownership of the veil as a way to regulate visual access to their body and to
limit unwanted male sexual attention, which they feel detracts from
other aspects of their identity. Yet at the same time, one could argue
that the emphasis on covering the female form actually *limits* the
construction of women's bodies to a singular sexualized referent.
In other words, covering the body as a means of protection from
the male gaze actually *constitutes* women's bodies as solely sexual
objects.

I was often troubled by the degree to which some girls attached their
identity to the practice of veiling. For example, when I asked Zarqa
what it meant to be a Muslim, she immediately referred to veiling:

ZARQA: I think it [being a Muslim] means to cover yourself. The main
thing is to cover yourself, because, um – where did I read it? A
woman is a jewel. And when I hear Islam I think it's the most religious culture. Like the Christians in every single culture, they
don't cover themselves. I never used to see ladies wearing niqab
and abayas and hijab and scarves. And now I see them so much.
Like I see them everywhere, like on buses. And when I see that
person, I see 'That lady's Muslim.' But you can never tell if you're
not wearing hijab.

Here, Zarqa was highlighting the visibility of the hijab as a marker
of Islamic identity and applying the rationale – often heard during

lectures in mosques about women and the hijab – that a woman is like a precious jewel that one conceals because it is so valuable. A Muslim woman participating in a recent study of Muslim veiling in North America emphasized this notion: 'A woman is not a commodity or an object, but she is like [a] precious pearl. The oyster is the hijab that covers and protects it from the dangers of the sea. The pearl remains pure and untouched by any corruption. But it is the brutal nature of mankind that strips this treasured gem from its covering and places it for display or sells it for a price' (McDonough, 2003b, p. 110). Here, this woman is arguing powerfully against the commodification of women's bodies in society; yet she seems oblivious to the fact that she may be trading one discourse of subjugation for another, in that she is rationalizing a similar attempt to regulate women's bodies and sexuality to suit a different set of patriarchal norms and expectations. Whether women are exhibiting their bodies to satiate the male gaze or covering their bodies to inhibit male desires, either way they are being compelled to cater to specific patriarchal demands.

Nevertheless, the veil-as-resistance discourse (El Guindi, 1999; Bullock, 2000, 2002; Read & Bartkowski, 2000) presents a more empowering contrast to other views of hijab that see women's bodies as causing *fitnah* (i.e., social discord and chaos) and which mandate that women's bodies and the sexuality they exude be disciplined by hiding them from the male gaze (see chapter 6 for further discussion of *fitnah*). Read and Bartkowski (2000) argue that rationalizations of veiling that liken women to jewels and precious objects are rhetorical strategies for inverting traditional gender hierarchies that privilege masculine qualities and attributes over feminine ones. For them, this inversion is the reason why 'women's inherent difference from men is perceived to be a source of esteem rather than denigration' (p. 402). Yet both views can be challenged for the limiting ways in which they narrowly reduce Muslim women's identities to the practice of veiling.

By conflating the saliency of the veil, these discourses also reduce religion to its extrinsic elements, placing less emphasis on inner spiritual development. For example, there is no social policing of women's or men's engagement in more vital acts of worship, such as attending to regular prayers. Prayer is one of the Five Pillars of Islam and is viewed as central to Islamic practice, yet it is left to individual regulation and is viewed as part of a Muslim's private sphere. The exception is when prayers are public and congregational; then there is greater social pressure to attend. However, since women are not required to pray during periods of menstruation, they are never questioned if they do not attend a congregational prayer. Women's dress, however, is part of the public sphere, in that the hijab is worn only when women are in the presence of men outside their immediate family. Thus, within this public/private dichotomy, the hijab is subject to greater social control than prayer, which is of greater religious significance. This highlights a sad irony regarding the various ways in which religious practices are regulated and how this regulation is differentially applied in the context of gender.

Wearing Niqab: Choices, Constraints, and Consequences

Despite attempts to develop a homogeneous, universal category of 'Muslim woman' – something that is promoted in many conservative hegemonic Islamic discourses and purveyed in Islamic schools – many of the girls I spoke to applied their own understandings of Islam to the process of constructing a religiously gendered identity. For example, while the hijab was the minimum requirement for Islamic dress, some girls chose to go beyond the standard code of dress and adopt the niqab, or face veil, as an expression of faith and identity. Those who made this choice reported receiving positive feedback from other girls in the Islamic school, even the ones that did not wear the niqab and that did not wear the hijab outside school. They did not encounter negative evaluation and treatment of the sort they would have had to face in public schools, and they appreciated the unqualified acceptance they received from their fellow sisters in the Islamic school. Even the girls that I spoke to who did not wear the hijab respected the choice of the girls who adopted the niqab; they were impressed with the level of *iman* (faith and personal strength) that they felt it represented.

Rehana had been wearing the niqab for three years, beginning when she was fifteen years old and living in Saudi Arabia. She felt that wearing it was an act of *ibadat* (worship), and she maintained that it had been a personal decision: 'I don't think that force is the idea, but I wanted to go ahead and do it.' She wanted to continue wearing it in Canada, but she felt that it embarrassed her friends from public school who did not wear it when she saw them outside school. She reported sitting far away from her friends on the bus so that they would not have to feel uncomfortable about the stares and comments she received. She had even declined an invitation to attend a friend's high school graduation because she did not want her friend to feel uncomfortable about the negative attention she would attract:

REHANA: Like I'm supposed to be going to my friend's school to attend her graduation next Monday. I told her, 'Are you sure you want me there?' Like she wears a scarf and everything, but I thought, 'Are you sure you want me there?' Because I cover my face and I don't want to embarrass my friends. And she told me, 'No! You're my friend! What do you think?!'

Rehana did, however, note that when she attended a public school that was more multicultural in terms of the student population – and, therefore, more accustomed to religious and cultural differences – she did not encounter the same stereotypes as in other schools:

REHANA: Like before, I usually tried to leave early so I could beat everybody home, avoid the rush hour so I didn't have to hear all the stupid comments. It was new to me so I was getting kind of embarrassed, but now I'm more used to it [wearing the niqab in Canada], so I'm more comfortable. Before, like all the students were standing at the bus stop from public school and that's where I'd have to get off. And they just looked at me and they didn't say anything. Because I know I used to go to that school and it's really, really multicultural and they don't have any of those stereotypes there. I loved it. I loved going there.

Rehana's experience seems to make the case that if public schools fostered more plurality and inclusion, marginalized communities would feel less impetus to splinter off and create independent schools. Certainly, Rehana experienced more comfort being in a multicultural environment that was more accepting of religious and cultural differences, one where she was not perceived as alien or 'strange.'[6] However, while antiracism education and more multicentric modes of education do create more inclusive spaces for minoritized students, the need for religiously based schooling also flows from the desire for faith-centred learning, which cannot take place within secular school settings.

The Muslim girls I interviewed told me that Islamic school provided for greater religious empowerment through both the spiritually centred environment and through the solidarity created among fellow Muslim sisters. Rehana remarked that she felt more comfortable and 'free' wearing the niqab at Islamic school:

REHANA: I like the feeling of wearing my *niqab* and nobody's telling me anything about my niqab, and, uh, just the environment is very nice. It's nice to be in all-girls, its just like we're all alone, uh, that's what I like, basically – the religious environment, and being all together with only girls, and having no problems of putting on my niqab and, you know, I can just walk around freely. .

Leila, a Somali OAC student, had been in Islamic school since grade five. She had begun wearing the hijab in grade three and wearing the niqab in grade ten. For her, the transition to Islamic school provided greater acceptance for her religious attire. Also, the environment was conducive to the more foundational aspects of faith, such as prayer.

Challenging Gendered Islamophobia

The Muslim girls I interviewed consciously and actively challenged some of the stereotypes governing the ways their identities were represented. When I was a university undergraduate, after I had spoken out forcefully on a particular issue in anthropology class, the professor remarked that he was 'surprised' I had spoken so strongly, since he had expected me to be 'shy and demure.' Obviously, his assumption was based on the way he read my body as a veiled Muslim women and on the negative connotations with which my body had become discursively inscribed. Muslim women were not *supposed* to be intelligent, forthright, and outspoken; my back talk had generated dissonance in the mind of this professor, who had expected me to be 'oppressed' and without voice or agency.

Some Muslim girls at Al Rajab were challenging such essentialized constructions. While I was teaching the World Issues course, I arranged for some of my students to make oral presentations to the rest of the school on topics related to the issues we were studying. We were examining historical situations of women and migrancy and the sexual violence and harassment that many female refugees often face when they flee their homelands. Rehana delivered a powerful talk on this subject, which addressed issues of rape as well as topics like female circumcision. While she was preparing the talk, I asked her if she felt comfortable speaking about these issues, since the assembly would include male students and teachers. I was being sensitive to the fact that some Muslim women feel it inappropriate for them to raise such issues in a mixed audience, owing to the overt references to sexuality, which here involved difficult references to subjects such as 'female genital mutilation.' I thought Rehana might feel uncomfortable raising these issues, since the gender segregation in the school made girls self-conscious around boys. This reticence silently mediated such encounters so as to reinforce rather than disrupt appropriate decorum. But Rehana assured me that she would not have a problem raising these issues, since she felt strongly that they needed to be addressed and that we could not afford to be shy about it. She added that her mother had some concerns over the content of her talk, but that she (Rehana) argued it was necessary for her to go ahead, since as a 'niqabi,'[7] it would always be important for her to challenge people's preconceptions of her:

REHANA: Like my mom, she said, 'Why do you have to talk about this?' And I'm like, 'No, you have to be open about what you want to say, or else you are just like the stereotype: quiet, you just see two eyes, you don't see anything else. But you have to go against the stereotype!'

The gendered Islamophobia that Muslim women encounter structures particular counter-responses: some women openly challenge Islamophobic attitudes, as was the case with Rehana; other women adopt a more laissez-faire attitude when dealing with those attitudes.

Noora and Saira were both fourteen years old and in grade eight at Al Safar. Noora, Canadian-born of Guyanese descent, had been one of the first students to enrol at Al Safar, and she was now to be among its first graduates. Saira was Canadian-born of Pakistani descent and had been attending Al Safar for only one year, having transferred in from the public system. To attend Islamic school was a choice Saira had made herself; she had convinced her parents to enrol her at Al Safar. I asked Saira and Noora whether the school was doing anything to prepare them for public high school the following year – in particular, whether the school was preparing them for the racism and Islamophobia they might encounter in mainstream schools and in the broader society:

SAIRA: Of course they [the teachers] tell us how to deal with these
issues. For example, if they tell us that racism is something that
happens – I mean, you can see it happening especially toward
Muslims and girls who wear hijab – and you know, we know how
to deal with that, so we don't feel too bad about it. I mean, you
can't really stop people from doing it because it's out of your
control, but at least you won't feel … at least they won't get to you
and you won't feel like you don't belong here. You'll be strong,
and you will be able to tell them, 'This is who I am and if you can't
accept me, that's up to you.' But I'm going to wear my scarf wherever I go, and you know, you can be nice to them and deal with
them nicely.

NOORA: And I would say that people who are racist, they don't know
what they're talking about, most of the time. So if someone told
me, why am I wearing my hijab, or they started making fun of me
because I look different than them, I would probably tell them that
this is my way of life and you can go on your road and I'll be on
my road. So we'll be on different roads, but if you have a problem
with that, then I guess that's your problem.

I was deeply impressed by the strength and conviction of these two
young girls, who wanted to maintain their identity despite the challenges they knew they would be facing. It was admirable that at such
a young age, they had a strong sense of who they were and how they
wanted to express their identity. Both girls seemed prepared not to let
society's politics of racial or religious exclusion challenge their sense of
belonging or their identity and faith. They would be opting to address
any social tensions they might encounter through polite dialogue and
a 'live and let live' philosophy. As Saira pointed out, they were not
strangers to gendered Islamophobia. She and Noora seemed committed to confronting discrimination by using their identity as a source of
strength.

Muslim girls face multiple challenges relating to how their gendered
identities are constructed. On the one hand, the Muslim community
subjects them to patriarchal forms of regulation relating to their body
and dress; on the other, mainstream society subjects them to negative
stereotypes and gendered Islamophobia. Competing frameworks
attempt to structure their identity in conflicting ways; sometimes they
resist and challenge those frameworks, other times they adjust to

them. All the while, these young women struggle for a sense of agency, spirituality, and belonging within the discursive parameters of faith, community, and nation. They consistently locate their strength and resistance within a faith-centred paradigm; and, as the following chapter describes, they learn to construct alternative understandings of Islamic identity and gender from within a religious framework that is often critical of the patriarchal norms that have long defined the ontology of Muslim womanhood.

6 Islamic Schooling and the Construction of Gendered Identities and Gender Relations

This chapter focuses on Islamic schools as sites for the construction of gendered Islamic identities and sensibilities. It also explores how Muslim girls construct notions of gender and religious identity from within Islam. The conceptual/discursive framework used for this aspect of the study borrows from a post-structuralist feminist analysis that is informed by Foucault's interest in how subjectivities are discursively constructed. Post-structuralist feminist theorizing however often seems to circumvent issues of race, as if spaces of subjectivity are somehow transcendent of racialized ontologies. By not interrogating the intersectionality of race and gender, such analyses have a limited and ultimately impoverished vantage point. In addition, I include a critical faith-centred perspective to help make sense of the specific context of girls in an Islamic school environment and in order to add an important dimension for understanding their lived experiences. To this end, anthropologist Saba Mahmood's (2005) ethnographic research into a women's piety movement in mosques in Cairo, Egypt, has been useful in allowing for a transnational perspective on the ways religiously conservative Muslim women negotiate faith, patriarchy, and agency in religious settings.

Post-Structuralist Feminism: Narrations of Gender and Identity Construction

Following Foucault's lead, post-structuralist feminism has engaged in identifying and dismantling the structures of power and domination that operate through discursive practices. We can understand discourses as systems of knowledge, supported by institutions and practices that both enable and constrain social conditions and possibilities (McHoul & Grace, 1993; Mascia-Lees & Johnson Black, 2000). As McHoul and Grace (1993) inform us, discourses are not simply ideologies; they are also part of a more diffuse system of signification, representation, and meaning: 'Both "the world" and our consciousness of it are effects of the kinds of representations we can make of it. But at the same time, discourse is not just a form of representation; it is a material condition (or set of conditions) which enables and constrains the socially productive "imagination." These conditions can therefore be referred to as "discourses" or "discursive conditions of possibility"' (p. 34).

Therefore, in this view, discourses are not disembodied ideas; rather, they are the products of social actions and interactions that create the possibilities for certain kinds of social conditions. From a feminist post-structuralist perspective, identities are produced through complex interactions with prevailing discursive paradigms or 'regimes of truth.' Identity is, therefore, seen as a site of power operating as a 'locus of domination through which people are controlled' (Mascia-Lees & Johnson Black, 2000, p. 83). In relation to the social and cultural production of specific ontologies, discourses create categories of identity that sustain relations of power, privilege, and domination in society (Mascia-Lees & Johnson Black, 2000, p. 82). Post-structuralist feminists follow Foucault's interest in understanding how individuals are produced as particular kinds of subjects through discursive practices and power relations. This is also of interest in the following analysis of Muslim girls and the religious and cultural discourses that shape their identities through their experiences in Islamic schools. Davies et al. (2001) suggest that 'experience' in post-structuralist feminist theorizing is not conceived in the sense of people *having* experiences; rather, it relates to 'subjects who *constitute themselves and are constituted as experiencing subjects*' (p. 168; original emphasis). I borrow this understanding as a means to locate 'experience' as an active and creative process through which identities are always being constituted and negotiated. This involves moving beyond modernist notions of an autonomous sovereign subject in order to investigate the historical and cultural conditions that make specific types of differentiated subjects possible in the first place (McHoul & Grace, 1993).

Subjectivity can be understood as the ways in which individuals give meaning to themselves, to others, and to the world (Davies & Banks, 1992, p. 2, in Jones, 1993, p. 158). The process of constructing these meanings and making sense of the world and one's place in it is shaped by the discursive realities that frame our experiences. In the following analysis of Muslim students' experiences, religiously and culturally based discourses (often related through a largely patriarchal prism) are the prime movers shaping the ways that young Muslim girls are produced as subjects in Islamic school settings. Yet this is not a deterministic view of identity construction. As Jones (1993) notes, a 'useful post-structuralism ... seeks to understand how children are both made subject by/within the social order and how they are agents/subjects within/against it' (pp. 58–9). In other words, one is not passively 'subjectified' through various discourses; rather, one *claims* 'subjecthood' by contesting, negotiating, or affirming prevailing discursive conditions. As Davies and Banks (1992) aptly point out: 'People are not seen as actively shaped by others including "social structures"; rather they "actively take up as *their own*, discourses through which they are shaped"' (in Jones, 1993, p. 158, original emphasis). This highlights the agency with which one engages in discursive processes as well as the critical discernment that is necessary in order for us to understand our complex negotiations as we socially and culturally produce self, identity, and Other.

Schooling and the Construction of Gendered Subjectivities

Schooling is a powerful discursive site through which young people, male and female, become constituted as specific kinds of subjects. Using discursive constructions as means to comprehend the structuring of subjectivities in the context of schooling is an important approach to realizing how gendered identities are constituted and lived. As Jones (1993) notes: 'The language of discourse and subjectivity offers ways of talking about complexities and contradictions in understanding girls' schooling' (p. 157).

In examining gender constructs, it is important to recognize how these signifiers of difference are culturally mediated and open to change, struggle, and negotiation. There are varying 'cultural scripts' that implicate the ways in which gender roles are performed. Our identities are scripted within these socially constructed categories, and we either accommodate them or challenge, subvert, and redefine them. Within the socializing practices of schooling, girls take up gender roles in multiple and contradictory ways, simultaneously accommodating and resisting them (see also Francis 1999). According to Proweller (1998): 'Female identities are constructed discursively through active struggle and negotiation, pointing us in new theoretical orientations that open up the possibilities for girls to design complex discursive constructions of who they are becoming on a daily basis in school' (p. 198). The process of being in a state of 'becoming' is a powerful notion of identity construction as a fluid, dynamic process in which we are constantly engaged. Throughout this process, identities operate as active sites of creation; they are not simply a priori subject locations that are 'acted upon' by various social forces. Proweller rightly points out that 'theorizing that students are simply shaped by available discourses has effectively denied youth culture agency over the processes of becoming "somebody"' (p. 198). Thus, youth are entangled in various discursive arrangements in their social and cultural lives, but at the same time they actively engage with these positionings in ways that can disrupt and challenge the discursive boundaries that are imposed – or, conversely, they may comply with the normative standards made available to them.

Proweller describes the utility of a post-structuralist perspective in engaging with the social and cultural dynamics of discursive positioning within the process of schooling: 'Post-structuralist discourse is helpful here to the extent that it can inform ways of understanding school culture in its multiple and complicated forms, so that students are not seen as simply positioned by existing discourses but importantly re-position themselves in response to available meanings and practices in schools and in the broader society' (p. 205). Jones (1993) provides a powerful explanation for why such a mode of inquiry may be especially meaningful: 'A focus on the discursive production of subjectivities might offer possibilities for how we as researchers might help construct and make available new subject positions which resist the dominant forms' (p. 162). Therefore, as Jones describes it, understanding the saliency of discursive practices is significant in the struggle to identify and resist the ways we become positioned within dominant discourses. This is also the transformative political motive behind the use of this analysis here. The discussion that follows will explore, in particular, the effects that the schooling experience of Muslim girls has on the construction of gendered identities as well as the role of specific discourses in structuring their sense of subjectivity and womanhood in Islam. The discussion will also explore issues of socialization and how they differentially affect gender equity and gender interaction in the context of Islamic schools.

Applying Post-structural Analysis to Muslim Girls' Schooling: Two British Case Studies

Preceding work in this area was undertaken by Parker-Jenkins and Haw (1996), who conducted an ethnographic case study of six single-sex girls' schools in Britain that examined three issues: patriarchy in the governance of the school; the different discourses of Islam among school leaders, teachers, students, and parents; and the relationship between gender-segregated schools and the contested position of women in Islam. In a later study of the educational experiences of young Muslim girls in Islamic schools and state schools in Britain, Haw (1998) contends that 'the educational experiences of the Muslim students and their teachers in each school could be seen as a set of *discursive relationships* (*discursive fields*) consisting of a number of different and sometimes contradictory discourses, such as those of "race," gender, class, culture and religion' (p. 31; original emphasis).

Parker-Jenkins and Haw (1996) found that there were different and often competing discourses of Islam and of the role and function of Islamic girls' schools among the various stakeholders: the elders (school governors), parents, teachers, and students. Elders' views were perceived as patriarchal and paternal: they saw Islamic schools as a means to protect girls. Parents saw such schools as a way to preserve values and identity (see also Shaikh & Kelley, 1989; Basit, 1997). Teachers' views, on the other hand, were couched in what Parker-Jenkins and Haw referred to as the 'educational discourse of Muslimness,' as opposed to the 'patriarchal discourse of Muslimness' expressed by the school governors – though the educational discourse, they argue, was marginalized vis-à-vis the patriarchal discourse since the school governors acted as the school's decision-making body even though none of them had a background in education. Student discourses were defined as 'the most challenging and different discourses of Muslimness' (p. 31). Students challenged the conventional patriarchal notions of 'Muslimness,' viewing them as products of culture and not the religious discourse of Islam. These students were able to use their knowledge of Islam to argue for alternative understandings that they felt better represented the status of women in Islam.

Discursive Constructions of Gendered Islamic Identities: The 'Pious Muslim Girl' as Guardian of Public Honour

The girls I interviewed for the present study combined many of these discourses into their own identity scripts. The canonical discourse of what I term the 'pious Muslim girl' was a salient archetype for young Muslim women to model themselves upon. This discourse is rooted in largely conservative and patriarchal views of Muslim women's identity. The result is an overemphasis on extrinsic shows of faith, such as the dress code, which is regulated more in accordance with conservative cultural norms than with Islamic injunctions. This promotes specific cultural expectations relating to the behaviour, dress, and actions of young Muslim girls – expectations that are presented as reflecting Islamic norms and religious requirements. These cultural codes of conduct are enforced as legal narratives; thus they frame the actions and interactions of the 'pious Muslim girls' who adhere to them.

Behaviours and dress codes are regulated in accordance with the socially constructed paradigm within which many girls are socialized as part of their religious duties and obligations. These normative standards form the basis for what I term the 'public performance of piety.' For example, maintaining specific dress codes such as the hijab and the *jilbab* from the time of puberty, shying away from make-up and nail polish, and avoiding unnecessary contact with boys are all hallmarks of the notion of piety ascribed to Muslim girls. These social aspects of behaviour are often regulated more within the community than are the spiritual aspects of behaviour such as adherence to the Five Pillars of Islamic belief and practice. In this way, a preoccupation with dress and modesty overshadows the spiritual dimensions of Islamic identity. Mahmood (2005) argues that bodily acts, including veiling and modest comportment, are 'critical markers of piety as well as the ineluctable means through which one becomes pious' (p. 158). She maintains that while modesty is presupposed by the act of veiling, it is not necessarily constituted prior to donning the veil but is inculcated through the act itself whereby 'the outward behaviour of the body constitutes both the potentiality and the means through which interiority is realized' (p.159). This may be the case in some instances, yet we cannot underestimate the way that socialization into religiously defined notions of piety, modesty, and appropriate gendered behaviours are inculcated at an early age within the pedagogy of the home and school.

The issue of *izzat*, or honour, as it is ascribed to women was a salient component of this discourse that regulates the behaviour and actions of young Muslim women, so as not to compromise family honour or the reputation of the school. In a study of young Muslim women in Britain, Afshar (1989) noted that these women 'are the public face of the community and it is they who are burdened with guarding the honour of the family by their behaviour, their garments, and their attitudes' (p. 271; see also Basit, 1997). The regulation of Muslim girls through this paradigm of honour and piety is a function of the puritanical belief that women's bodies create *fitnah*, or discord, by sexually enticing men. Mernissi (1987) describes this social disciplining of the female body as society's fear of the 'disruptive power of female sexuality' (p. 45).[1] The notion of *fitnah*, then, leads to the demarcation of gendered spaces within many Islamic societies and institutions, so as to avoid unnecessary contact between men and women.

Commenting on the erroneous assumptions and dubious doctrinal referents on which the notion of *fitnah* is based, Abou El Fadl (2001a) argues against these puritanical misconceptions from a legal standpoint:

> The most profound feature of the legal determinations that exclude women from public life is the obsessive reliance on the idea of *fitnah*. In these determinations, women are persistently seen as a walking, breathing, bundle of *fitnah*. One can hardly find a *response* that deals with women without the insertion of some language about the seductions of womanhood. So, for instance, according to the C.R.L.O.[2] women may attend mosques only if it does not lead to *fitnah*; women may listen to a man reciting Qur'an or give a lecture, only if it does not lead to *fitnah*; women may go to the marketplace only if it does not lead to *fitnah*; women may not visit graveyards for the fear of *fitnah*. (p. 235)

Abou El Fadl's point is well stated regarding the outrageous assumptions (and their detrimental implications) about women that are derived from such faulty reasoning. Speaking as a legal scholar, he notes that, 'importantly, these traditions become the vehicle for symbolisms placing women in the role of the distrusted or treacherous and for associating them with the construct of a menace that must be restrained' (p. 236). Clarke (2003) refers to *fitnah* traditions as constructions of the 'dangerous feminine' that lead to traditions of female seclusion and *purdah* (p. 254). Mernissi (1987) argues that this negative discourse has provided an ideological justification for exiling women from public non-domestic space, out of fear that their presence may lead to chaos and disorder.

Abou El Fadl (2001a) further notes that ascribing the notion of *fitnah* to women's bodies unduly places on them the burden of public morality and the responsibility for curtailing the desires of men: 'Most *fitnah* determinations rely on the dubious logic that women should pay the price for the impious failures of men. Furthermore, in these determinations, as far as women are concerned, *fitnah* emerges as the core value of Islam. Therefore, women's education, mobility, safety and even religious liberty should be restricted in order to avoid *fitnah*' (p. 235). He also emphasizes that the fear of *fitnah* is at the core of discussions on the necessity of veiling, as some interpreters would have it, despite the fact that the Qur'an provides no such evidentiary basis (p. 232; see also Mernissi, 1991; Bullock, 2002). Traditions attributed to the Prophet Muhammed include alleged statements that support the idea that women are bearers of seduction and physical temptation. However, the veracity of these statements has been challenged by Abou El Fadl: 'In the science of *hadith*, any tradition that contravenes human experience cannot be accepted as valid' (p. 237). In other words, the notion that women are an irresistible enticement to men and unequivocally dangerous to the social order, unless secluded, cannot be empirically validated, and thus is not defensible as a valid tradition. Abou El Fadl notes that some argue that the *fitnah* traditions are not describing an empirical reality per se but are, rather, establishing a normative principle. He rightly draws attention to the danger that these propositions are self-fulfilling: 'By prophesying that women are dangerous and treating them as dangerous, we are never able to realize any reality other than women are dangerous' (p. 237). Rational thought and Qur'anic texts do not bear out the negative assertions embedded in such puritanical notions of gender; even so, these perspectives have maintained their currency among conservative and fundamentalist circles.

Maintaining a critical yet faith-centred approach involves attending to the ways in which puritanical religious sensibilities allow patriarchal discourses to prevent the more balanced and egalitarian Islamic ethos from becoming the normative referent for Islamic discourses on gender. These perspectives allow religion to become a complicit factor in the subjugation of women by selectively, narrowly, and literally interpreting doctrines through the lens of patriarchal supremacy. From the standpoint of a critical faith-centred epistemology, oppressive male power and privilege must be interrogated and challenged as inconsistent with the values of Islam. The destructive impact of this gendered oppression on the development of a just Islamic society or community must be relentlessly exposed as an inauthentic dimension of true Islamic faith.

Examining the Narratives: Gender Interaction and Gender Equity

In Islamic schools, specific discourses regulate and control different aspects of social behaviour. The following discussion examines the Islamically oriented gendered discourses that implicate the types of gender interaction and the contexts of gender equity that exist in the Islamic schools I am examining. Along with the narratives of Muslim girls, this section includes the narratives of teachers, parents, and male students from the Al Rajab school. Through their lived experiences, we explore the dynamics of gender interaction as well as the construction and regulation of gendered spaces within the school. The discussion examines the boundaries of social interaction between female and male students with respect to how those boundaries are circumscribed and policed. As Muslim girls navigate a complex social and ideological terrain that situates them within specific narrations of gender, religion, culture, community, and nation, they find themselves having to negotiate within and between various contradictory and competing discursive paradigms that structure their subjectivities. How they resist and accommodate the discourses and identifications they face will be explored in the following narrative analysis.

Gendered Socialization

The teachers discussed gendered socialization in the school – a process that was viewed as necessary in order to acculturate students into

Islamically appropriate modes of behaviour and conduct, especially with regard to gender relations. According to Amira, an elementary teacher at Al Safar, this process was especially important during puberty, when students learned the social rules relating to male–female relations:

AMIRA: There is definitely a difference in the way they're socialized. Especially Islamically when they reach puberty there's a big difference. And what we do is, before they reach puberty, which is when they reach around age ten, we start teaching them social rules, not only just teaching them, but trying to make them understand why, especially the interaction between the boys and the girls. Because when they reach puberty then there is a separation. Starting from grade four in the classes, they are physically separated. So the boys sit on one side and the girls sit on one side. So, it's sort of slow, the aim is to slowly, slowly bring it in, so that when they do reach grade seven, you know, the girls are all covering, they know that they have to cover. The boys know dressing rules, language, behaviour with the girls. They're taught it little by little.

At this stage in their social and emotional development, young Muslims are socialized into patterns of gender segregation and conformity with modest Islamic dress codes. Puberty is a significant milestone in social and spiritual development for Muslim youth. At this stage in life, as they cross the threshold towards adulthood, they become accountable to Allah for their actions, including obligatory prayers and fasting. Most Muslim children from observant households are socialized into these practices from a much earlier age, but it is at puberty that they become responsible for maintaining these practices. Islamic dress codes, such as the modest dress and *hijab* worn by girls and the covering of males from the navel to the knee, are already part of the school uniform, but by this stage they are also seen as obligatory (see, for example, Al-Qaradawi, 1960).

Typically, it is also around this time that gender segregation is instituted in classrooms. At three of the schools in this study, gender segregation began in grade four, with girls and boys seated separately in the same class; at Al Rajab, this process began in grade two. In the high school setting, all classes were single-sex only, and young men and women were relegated to separate spaces in the school. The purpose was to limit social interactions between the sexes that might lead to un-Islamic practices such as dating and premarital relations. In the Islamic tradition, close physical interactions are confined to marriage. Thus the social construction of gendered space is instituted early on in Islamic school settings as a precautionary measure, to avoid possibilities for inappropriate encounters or distractions caused by members of the opposite sex.

According to Amira, students often have difficulty reconciling the social norms of the school with those they encounter in the mainstream culture. She would encourage her students to talk about their feelings, especially during the health periods, when the classes were gender segregated and the students found it easier to discuss relationship issues. For example, she spoke of how the girls had crushes on boy bands like The Backstreet Boys and N'Sync and would bring their pictures to school. Her approach was to validate their feelings but to place them in an Islamic perspective that reinforced marriage as the appropriate venue for expressing romantic feelings. Because of the focus on eventual marriage (rather than boyfriends), Amira reported that girls as early on as grade six would fantasize about a future husband rather than a future boyfriend. She reported that boys seemed less concerned about romance or future marriage than girls of the same age; occasionally, though, they would seek advice on what they should do if they liked a girl. At these times, teachers counselled students according to Islamically oriented social norms pertaining to gender relations and gender interaction. The students saw this as a positive feature of Islamic schooling: the advice teachers offered reinforced rather than contradicted Islamic values (which was not the case in the public system).

Socializing for Gender Equity

Amira also pointed out, however, that she always tried to make sure that the modesty Islam inculcates between members of the opposite sex did not translate into reticence when it came to academic pursuits, especially with girls. She made a conscious attempt to promote gender equity in the classroom, where boys had the tendency to dominate:

AMIRA: I really try to make a special effort to make sure that both their voices are being heard. Sometimes the boys get dominant in discussion time. So I have to pick, deliberately pick, one girl and one boy. And this time I have to pick two girls and a boy because I have to balance that ratio. I have to remind myself, it's something where I have to make an effort because it's usually the boys who raise their hands and who take the dominant role in the discussion ... because the girls are very self-conscious at this age, they don't want to be laughed at. I think it's not only an Islamic problem, it happens in public school, too, with girls at this age. And in Islamic school I believe it depends also on how they're treated at home, so they're not afraid when it comes to having discussions. There's some of them, they're very shy, maybe by nature, and I tell them, 'Look, you know shyness is encouraged in Islam, like you know modesty is part of *iman, hayah*[3] right.' But I tell them when it comes to knowledge there is no modesty. And I have to constantly be reminding them. And I say, 'As long as, you know, you're both here to learn and don't be afraid to ask questions.' But sometimes there's sensitive issues that they don't want to talk about in front of the boys. Then we deal with it.

Nawal, an elementary teacher at Al Rajab, agreed that though there may be certain socially conditioned gendered differences, these should not result in differential treatment in class:

NAWAL: Of course, I mean I think the girls and the boys are two different genders ... they can't be equalized in that sense. The rules and policies could be the same but the expectations of course will not be. Also, the way they're raised at home is different. In a lot of things I try to do, for example, in my class tidying up – sometimes I take my boys, sometimes I take my girls.

Thus, while certain patterns of differential socialization were recognized as emanating from the home culture, within the school these teachers were committed to ensuring that there were equal opportunities for participation and responsibilities among boys and girls. However, even very young students often questioned differences with respect to religious practice for males and females. Nawal offered an example from her JK/SK class:

NAWAL: When I'm doing some sort of a lesson like a *salah* or the *dua*,[4] sometimes I pick boys and sometimes I pick girls. A lot of my girls complain because they never get to be the imam[5] during the *salah* time and they also have problems because boys are always at the front. So it's hard to explain to those little ones why those things are there because they can't understand them. The first thing they [girls] question is, 'How come we never get a chance to be in the front row?'

During congregational prayers, males are often positioned in the front and females in the back in gender-segregated rows, though they can also be situated on either side of a room. The purpose of separating men and women is to maintain focus and concentration on the spiritual aspect of prayer without worldly distractions, such as members of the opposite sex. The gender-segregated spaces need not be hierarchized; nevertheless, many Islamic schools and centres situate women's prayer areas outside the main prayer hall, which is dominated by men, or in curtained areas behind or beside the men. In addition, the role of imam, or leader of the prayer, is traditionally reserved for males. Clearly, these religious rules were being questioned and challenged by girls at a very young age, though they are generally socialized to accept the status quo.

Constructing Gendered Spaces

The social organization of space within Islamic schools, even outside prayer areas, was also gendered. During my fieldwork in the elementary Islamic schools, I noticed that the children from a young age seemed unconsciously conditioned to situate themselves in gender-based groups. For example, when the teacher asked students to sit down on the carpet, automatically the girls would sit on one side and the boys on the other, without being instructed to do so. Rukhsana, a parent from Al Safar, complained that during the taking of attendance in kindergarten, the boys usually sat in the front and the girls in the back. She felt that this organization of space privileged boys and imposed an unwarranted gender-based hierarchy in the classroom. She did, however, notice that on some occasions girls were also sitting up front, but she felt that boys were more often given this featured spot.

The teachers I interviewed did try to consciously promote gender equity in their classrooms; some parents, though, had concerns that this was not a uniform practice. Rukhsana, for example, had concerns regarding differential access to physical education. Such activities were always gender segregated, with boys and girls sharing the gymnasium and sports equipment. She noted that during gym periods, more attention was paid to the boy' activities, whereas girls seemed to be left with a non-structured program:

RUKHSANA: The girls don't have a chance to do anything. In kindergarten it's not a problem. But I've heard from the older classes that the girls just sort of have a free play type of thing. It's not as structured. The boys always get the balls for basketball and soccer. The girls, it's sort of run, or do whatever they want to do.

Another mother, Khadija, who was of French-Canadian background and who had accepted Islam when she married her Egyptian husband fifteen years prior, also felt that boys were privileged in classrooms and during gym. As the mother of five daughters and one son, she noted that boys in physical education enjoyed certain advantages:

KHADIJA: It happened a few times where during gym, the girls are usually left in the supervision of a volunteer – someone who does not have qualifications to be teaching them. Then the boys get the full attention of the teaching staff. I cannot talk about all the instances. There are instances when the girls ask questions like, 'Why is it that they [boys] always get the right spot, the right time, the right person, and we are left outside?'

Rukhsana and Khadija both felt that girls were not being encouraged to excel in sports and that this was reinforcing the negative gender stereotypes that isolated girls from physical activities.

Rukhsana had observed other gender-based socialization practices that reinforced traditional roles for females, such as play kitchen or dollhouse areas for girls and trucks and tools for boys. This type of gender-based role play is not exclusive to Islamic schools. In any case, Rukhsana complained that it was 'sexist' and felt that while segregation was required during prayer, it should not extend to other aspects of young children's socialization. She described how her seven-year-old daughter Anisa had been questioning her about issues such as whether a woman could deliver a speech at a mosque. Even at this young age, Anisa was exploring the kinds of narratives that would be available to her in the future as a Muslim woman. According to

Rukhsana, she was committed to ensuring that her daughter's opportunities would be the same as her son's:

RUKHSANA: I, as a parent, try to make sure she does everything my son does. But I also make sure my son does everything my daughter does. I don't want this sexist thing to be happening.

Gendered Opportunities

Sakhina, a teacher at Al Rajab, described the different types of cultural expectations that some families held for boys, who were expected to study further than the girls in the family. She lamented the narrow perspectives of some Muslim families, and she looked back to the 'Golden Age' of Islam – the Middle Ages, when Islamic knowledge was at its pinnacle – as a time when women were intellectual leaders. She often encouraged her girl students to advance in their academic pursuits:

SAKHINA: I found it really rewarding because I was able to go one-on-one with the girls and say, 'Educate yourselves. Become strong women. Okay, fine, get married, have kids. That's beautiful. But what are you going to teach your children? Because you're their first teacher.

She noted, however, that this bias was not evident in the school and that girls were equally encouraged to succeed academically. According to Jones (1993), this encouragement is necessary in order to enable girls to pursue a broader range of possibilities in their lives: 'Constructing girls as powerful in the ways in which we talk about them is part of the process of enlarging the possible discourses on/for girls and thus the range of feminine subject positions available to them in practice' (p. 162). During my fieldwork at Al Rajab, I found that education was highly valued for both girls and boys. Indeed, because girls were the majority at the school, they had more course options available to them and, therefore, better academic opportunities. They were encouraged to excel in academic *and* religious sciences. In a study of a British Muslim all-girls' school, Mustafa (1999) reported that the students felt supported and encouraged by teachers to pursue their career aspirations, which included medicine, the law, science, dentistry, and nursing (p. 296).

Other parents, like Shazad and Farida from Al Safar, were less concerned about gender equity issues, feeling that boys and girls were being provided for equally in both academics and physical education. They felt that, while academically there should be no gender-based differences in the delivery of education, with respect to physical activities, as girls matured, the school authorities needed to make more deliberate efforts to maintain Islamically appropriate dress codes and standards of modesty. Another mother from Al Safar, Shahnaz, felt that girls actually received *better* treatment than boys at the school, since the school kept 'more of an eye out for them.' It comforted her to know that there was greater protectiveness of girls and more surveillance over them. As the discussion continues, however, we will see how this surveillance was a means of regulating girls rather than protecting them.

Single-Sex Schooling and Feminine Empowerment: A Corrective to Male Privilege?

Leila felt a strong desire to be in a single-sex school environment, where she could experience a greater sense of sisterhood in the company of other young women and female teachers:

LEILA: Being around sisters, that's the number one thing. And having women teachers. And like, when somebody does something bad, like they tell you, 'This is wrong, don't do it.' Plus, I can pray here. And I can stick to wearing whatever I want Islamically without hiding anything.

Other case studies of Muslim girls' schools have reported similar reactions with respect to solidarity and sisterhood (see, for example, Haw 1994, 1997; Parker Jenkins & Haw, 1996). For example, Haw (1997) compared the experiences of Muslim girls in public schools and Islamic schools, and found that they were more 'feminist' in Muslim schools, in that it was easier for them to explore their identities and to question and challenge their discursive positioning from within an Islamic framework. Haw also noted that Islamic schools provided a more comfortable venue for girls to begin this journey of exploration and challenge:

In Old Town High [Muslim school] the students feel comfortable and confident in their more monocultural setting and are therefore enabled to pursue explorations of what it means to be a Muslim woman operating within the Muslim community. In this environment being a Muslim women is not an issue. Whereas the students of City State [public school] are marginalized because of the multicultural nature of the school, where staff felt confident in their abilities to deal with the common issue of being female but not confident in their abilities to deal with the complexities of difference. This means that the Muslim students in City State are less confident about being a Muslim student in an environment where being a Muslim woman is an issue. (p. 59)

Haw (1997) concluded that Muslim girls were better able to negotiate ways of 'dancing with the discourses of gender and race' in the Islamic school; conversely, in the public school their racialization was a prominent social barrier and their identities as Muslim women were often stereotyped and challenged.

Many of the girls at Al Rajab actually preferred a gender-segregated academic environment: there were no boys to distract them, and they could express themselves without feeling self-conscious. Halstead (1991) notes that in single-sex Islamic schools, 'Muslim girls have more freedom to develop a balanced understanding of (and confidence in the presence of) the opposite sex with much less danger of sexual harassment or the unhelpful accentuation of gender characteristics' (p. 265). In this sense, he contends that Muslim views regarding single-sex schooling for girls may have some commonalities with radical feminist arguments. He argues that, while there are obvious ideological divergences, the focus on creating female-centred spaces may connect the political imperatives of Muslim groups with those of feminists in significant ways.

Freedom from sexual harassment and scrutiny by boys has been cited as an important rationale for single-sex schooling for girls (Burgess, 1990). Zarqa and Aliyah described feeling 'freer' in the single-sex Islamic school environment than they had at the co-ed public high school:

ZARQA: In public school there are guys and then there are some girls that are really rude. And if you ask questions they just give you attitude and stuff and then the guys … like, you don't feel comfortable.

ALIYAH: Like here, you can ask personal questions. If the class had
guys in it we wouldn't be able to ask as many questions about girl
stuff. So you can ask here more freely.

For these girls, then, single-sex classrooms offered an environment
that was more supportive and female-centred. Like Halstead (1991),
Haw (1998) argues that this construction of Muslim girls' schooling
has its roots in a 'radical feminism' designed to place women's experiences more firmly at the centre of the schooling experience (p. 167).

Iman, Summaya, and Deqa described what it was like to transfer to
a single-sex school from the co-ed public system. They spoke of the
support and camaraderie they encountered in female-centred spaces,
and they reflected on the tensions inherent in speaking out in class and
being judged by boys:

IMAN: It's a bit different [in Islamic school] because then you don't
have to run into guys all the time, but it's more comforting because
if basically you have a girl problem then you have a bunch of girls
to be surrounded by if there's any issue or any problem in your life.
And I don't see a big difference, because even though the guys are
next door to us there's nothing different because we go outside and
we see a lot of them. And in high school I felt a bit uncomfortable.
SUMMAYA: It's more comfortable, you can put your hand up and like
say things and like, everybody will support you on that, but like, if
there's guys in your class, you'd be like, thinking and rethinking
what you're going to say and analysing everything you do.
JASMIN: Yeah, I find a lot of the girls say that. Why do you think you
have to be more self-conscious about what you say in a class in
front of boys? I'm trying to remember when I was sixteen but it
was a while ago!
DEQA: You're thinking what they're going to say, how they're going to
judge you.
IMAN: Oh yeah, it can be judgmental at times. It's pretty tough
because I personally feel uncomfortable even – most of my life I've
been in a co-ed school and now that I finally came to an all-girls'
school I felt so comfortable.
DEQA: Like, girls, they can associate with each other, they can understand each other, while guys, they've got a different mentality! It's
a whole different thing. And you're afraid of how they're going to
interpret it, what are they going to think?

It is clear that, for these girls, being in a female-centred space was more empowering. They felt less reticent and self-conscious now that they were free from the judgmental gaze of boys. Yet according to Robertson (1997), while many argue that single-sex girls' school allow for greater expression and mitigate the silencing of girls that can occur in co-ed settings, which are often dominated by boys, true self-expression for girls and young women is impoverished if the audience is limited to other women and to the exclusion of males who need to learn to 'hear' these voices. She makes a powerful point relating to the need for reciprocity in the process of claiming voice and empowerment for girls: 'I do most fervently want my daughter to find her voice and to express it clearly, but perhaps more importantly, my son must learn to listen and to hear. She must learn to take up her space, but he must learn to make room. She must learn how to assert, but he must learn not to aggress. How can he learn to yield the prerogative of male "voice" if he is excluded from the conversation?' (p. 6). Robertson's quite cogent point is that male privilege cannot be challenged when males are not in the room. Subverting the saliency of dominant voices, therefore, cannot be accomplished in the absence of other marginalized voices that are necessary to the task of de-centring and making room for themselves.

Other girls spoke of the reduced pressure to keep up physical appearances in the single-sex school environment. They did not have to worry about attracting boys or being distracted by them. Thus they could focus more on academics:

UMBREEN: The girls that I've noticed that come from public school, they never used to care about their grades, because they were like, so distracted by other things, like boys and stuff. But now, when they come here, they're so like, changed in their interests and their studies.

SAFIA: Because you don't have to worry about how you look. You don't want to look nasty, obviously, in front of girls either. But you don't have to worry, like, 'Oh what if I do this, they're going to think I'm stupid.' It's not really a big deal.

SAHAR: But then usually if there are guys there, everyone watches what they do and they, like, put their attention on the guys.

SAFIA: I've seen girls that go outside and they act so dumb. And they'll like, jump in front of the guys, they act so desperate!

UMBREEN: And like, you feel so uncomfortable in front of guys. You feel like you're being stared at sometimes.

Nusaybah noted that just because they were in a single-sex school, it did not necessarily mean they were 'sheltered.' She did not want the different boundaries that she and other young Muslim women maintained in their interactions with boys to mark them as 'abnormal,' however out of sync those boundaries were with the dominant youth culture:

NUSAYBAH: Like, I don't know, [girls in public school] all talk about, like, who's going out with who, or whatever. And it's not like we're all sheltered. Like, if we see a guy, we think he's cute, but like, we're not going to go as far as them. Yeah, it's not like we're all locked up and all strange and abnormal! Like, if we see someone – like, we'll find Indian actors attractive, or TV actors. It's not like we're abnormal ... we have our limits.

The boys had similar views with respect to their own single-sex environment. As Ali explained, that environment was less distracting in terms of the sexual tensions that often arise in co-ed settings; as a result, it was easier to focus on academics. He described how his school's process of cultural resocialization had helped him develop a new attitude and respect towards girls, who had become more like 'sisters' to him:

ALI: Public school, like ... the other thing with me was girls. I couldn't study because of the girls. I used to skip because of girls. But at Islamic school they taught us that we should see girls as our sisters and we should respect them. And after learning that, you can't go up to a girl – you know, like in public school – you can't do that if you go to Islamic school after what they teach you. You see them as your sisters.

For boys like Ali, Islamic school helped them reframe their attitudes towards girls in more respectful ways.

Honour and Surveillance: Policing the 'Pious Muslim Girl'

Male interactions with female students were disciplined by reframing those relationships in an Islamic context. For the young women, inappropriate gendered interactions held negative social consequences bearing on their reputation and 'honour.' Safia, Sahar, and Umbreen discussed the social consequences for women who transgress the boundaries of gender-based social distance through Islamically inappropriate actions such as dating:

SAFIA: I keep using the same example all the time of boyfriend – I can't think of anything else – but, okay, here if we had a boyfriend and anyone found out, our whole reputation would be ruined.
SAHAR AND UMBREEN: It'd be gone!
SAFIA: Yet in public school, they wouldn't care. It wouldn't be known as anything.
SAHAR: It'd be known as something normal.
SAFIA: There's more pressure on us to be good than in public school. And that's a big challenge, because you have to show yourself that you're really good and anything can break you, like, in one second. It's like, as they say, you're like glass and if anything gets broken it's really hard to repair.
UMBREEN: Yeah, and especially girls, they say that girls are really fragile and stuff.
SAFIA: Yeah, one thing can ruin their whole reputation.

Safia added that actions (dating) construed as positive social behaviour in public schools were strongly sanctioned in Islamic schools, and noted the dissonance some students experience when they transfer from one system to the other. Dating was unheard of among the girls at Al Rajab. One of the teachers confided that a girl who had recently transferred in was pregnant and that the school authorities were not yet aware of it. Such instances are extremely rare in Islamic schools, in which the status quo is based on gender segregation and social distance between the sexes.

Rehana noted the double standard with regard to male behaviour, which was not as heavily scrutinized or policed as that of the girls. She felt that, relative to most Canadians girls, Muslim girls were subjected to more surveillance by family and community, adding that unmarried Muslim girls in particular needed to be careful in their actions:

REHANA: Women have a lot freedom in here in Canada. But sometimes when girls do something it gets talked about and I don't think that's fair. Guys do tons of worse things, but nobody talks about them. But it's better here than anywhere else, like in our own countries. Like, they don't talk about you as much here as they would if you were in Pakistan or Bangladesh or India or Islamic countries like that. But you still have to be careful about what you're doing because you don't want people to think this way. Especially if you're unmarried.

In her study of Muslim girls and schooling in Britain, Haw (1998) found that there were double standards in the community when it came to the moral behaviour of young Muslim boys versus girls: 'Significantly, boys are not being stopped from manifest violations of Islamic teachings. They, it seems are forgiven for keeping girlfriends, indulging in dating, illicit sex, alcohol and gambling (the last three explicitly forbidden in the Qur'an), and what they do does not seem to be perceived as a threat to Islam by the community' (p. 157). Muslim girls, on the other hand, were subject to more stringent standards of conduct, and their actions more heavily policed. Haw refers to this invisible scrutiny as the 'bradari gaze,' referring to the regulation that Muslim girls are placed under by their family and ethno-cultural community. She likens this surveillance to Foucault's notion of a Panopticon: 'The bradari gaze disciplines the girls like a Foucauldian Panopticon. These girls exist in a Panopticon, and wherever they move they are watched by the invisible gaze, which only "frames" and any "captions" can be put into those frames by the watching eyes' (p. 157). This notion of panopticism refers to the disciplinary structures of social surveillance that regulate behaviour within specific culturally determined physical and ideological parameters. In this case, the disciplining gaze was an ordinance of power that operated through the apparatus of the family and the ethno-cultural community.

The social regulation and disciplining of female sexuality occurs through what I have described as the discourse of the 'pious Muslim girl,' which constructs specific boundaries for culturally acceptable behaviour. The subjectivities of young Muslim women are structured in terms of this archetypal discourse, which is rooted in the social, cultural, and ideological constructs of femininity and womanhood promoted within conservative patriarchal Muslim communities. For example, in the preceding exchange the reputation of a Muslim girl was described as a 'piece of glass' that, once shattered, is difficult to repair. This speaks to the fragility of women's honour, or izzat, should

they transgress the discursive norms of 'piety' and the socially and culturally sanctioned rules of conduct laid down by patriarchal authorities. Women in the community are disproportionately affected by this;
men are less stigmatized by aspersions that may be cast on their character owing to inappropriate behaviour.

According to Quraishi (2000), this double standard is rooted in the
patriarchal nature of many societies: 'In nearly every culture of the
world, women's sexual morality appears to be a particularly favourite
subject for slander, gossip and insult. The tendency of patriarchal societies, in fact, is to view a woman's chastity as central to the honour of
her family, especially the men in her family' (p. 112). Speaking from an
Arab context, Abu-Odeh (2000) discusses the patriarchal construction
of female honour and its relationship to social perceptions of male
'honour': 'Throughout the Arab world, male honour derives from the
struggle to retain intact the chastity of women in the family, and this
makes male reputation insecurely dependent upon female sexual
conduct' (p. 374). In the local diasporic Muslim community, patriarchal
fears for the sanctity of women's honour are exacerbated by the more
sexually permissive norms of North American society. This accounts
for the profusion of Islamic schools, where girls are seen as being
better protected from external influences. In her study of Muslim girls'
schools in Britain, Haw (1998) noted that 'in Muslim girls' schools
there is a safe environment, devoid of any threat to their value system.
Parents, even under economic constraints, would pay for their daughters to study in these relatively poorly resourced schools if they
believed that these schools were the only safe, infiltration-free zones'
(p. 157). Clearly, then, the desire to create 'safe spaces' for young
Muslim girls, spaces that are free from the dangers imposed by the
opposite sex, is doing much to fuel the development of single-sex
Islamic schools.

Regulating Gender Interaction

Amira talked about an incident at her school during which the gendered boundaries of social etiquette were breached. A female
student passed a note to a male student; its content was inappropriate and objectionable from an Islamic perspective. The boy's father
was told, and he reacted by removing his son from the school,
furious that such things could happen in such an environment.
Amira sympathized with the father's expectations of the school, but

she also noted that such expectations were not always realistic, given the competing cultural norms of the dominant society, which cannot but affect children and youth as they begin to construct their views on relationships:

AMIRA: I myself feel like ... it is an Islamic school, but it's just like other schools; we have the same problems. I mean, we don't have drug problems or violence to the extreme, but we still have some problems that are natural to the culture that we live in. These kids go home and watch TV, they see people their age dating, writing notes to the boys ... You can't tell them to shut that whole thing down, saying that you want them living in a very isolated environment. You have to let them know right from wrong. But we can't put a partition, like this is one of the suggestions that one [parent] said, we can't just put a partition and ask them not to see each other.

Amira told me that some parents responded to violations of Islamic conduct by calling for harsher restrictions. For example, one parent suggested that a physical barrier be placed in the classroom to separate boys and girls. Amira rightly pointed out that this was unrealistic and that it would not remedy the underlying problem.

Muslim youth in Canada inhabit culturally hybrid spaces. This can lead to the 'double culture syndrome,' discussed earlier. The politics of cultural hybridity confront Muslim youth with various challenges as they attempt to construct their sense of identity; they are pulled between two conflicting sets of cultural expectations. In turn, Islamic schools must compete with the dominant culture over which will be the defining referent in the lives of these youth. Narratives of gender relations are structured by the prevailing discursive formations that circumscribe appropriate modes of behaviour. Muslim youth are influenced (often heavily) by the dominant culture's mores, which promote dating and premarital sexual behaviour as the norm, just as they are by the strictures of religious authorities, which mandate abstinence and gender segregation. As they attempt to negotiate these conflicting boundaries, some youth may test them by occasionally stepping out of bounds.

For teachers like Amira, guiding young people to maintain Islamically appropriate boundaries for gender relations involves providing them with the skills they will require to navigate through a society in which they should expect to be equal partners. She explained that, especially in the co-ed environment at her school, this involved socializing youth into 'proper' etiquette for interactions with the opposite sex. This included using a 'business-like' tone of voice:

AMIRA: They [girls] say: 'Oh, I don't want to talk to the boys,' and I say, 'Well, what are they going to do to you?' And I tell them, 'Look at their face and talk to them, it's business.' So I do encourage them to have debates, to talk, but I say, 'Use a business tone, we have to learn … you're living with them and you have half the population that are male and half female. You have to know how to interact properly in a proper manner.' Instead of telling them, 'Don't look at each other,' you know, face to the wall. That's very unrealistic.

Clearly, Amira does not advocate reticence on the part of Muslim girls in their dealings with boys. Rather, she attempts to frame their interactions so that they focus on necessary issues without unnecessary socializing. Students have, indeed, taken this approach in their interactions. Noora talked about how she dealt with boys:

NOORA: Well, if I had to be in a group with a boy, that's the only time I would communicate with him. So if I had, like, a lab assignment with them, I'd tell them at the beginning, 'This is only confidential, we're only doing this on business. Any other matter, I can't talk to you about.'

Noora has internalized the discursive norms of piety that restrict gender interactions to 'businesslike' relations as opposed to more friendly and relaxed conversations with boys. The purpose of inculcating these social manners is to prevent any Islamically inappropriate types of interaction. However such attitudes have the unhealthy impact of constructing even the most banal encounters between boys and girls or men and women as being potentially sexually charged. Such innocent encounters are sexualized by the emphasis placed on gender from the outset, no matter what the actual nature of the encounter. This is neither recognized nor challenged; indeed, it is upheld as the Islamic norm. The result is a hypersexualizing of all gender interactions, which is counter to Islamic ideals. Rigid interpretations of faith and gender then ensure that this consequence is ignored.

Some girl students noted that in the single-sex school environment, where contact with boys was limited, they felt uncomfortable talking to them. Students like Tasleema, an OAC student at Al Rajab of Pakistani descent, were concerned that a co-ed college or university setting would pose challenges for them, since they had been so isolated from boys:

TASLEEMA: You have to get used to the idea of talking to boys as well, like, you have to talk to them no matter what. If I go to college, I'll come to, like, to meet those boys and have to work with them. It'll be harder for me in the beginning, because I'm used to this environment now. So I think that's a little negative point. I had to work with boys before and I was fine there, now I came here and I have difficulty talking to them.

Rehana told me that, having lived in Saudi Arabia – a highly segregated environment – and then having enrolled at a single-sex Islamic school, she was now uncomfortable dealing with boys, whom she had once befriended in public school:

REHANA: Before, when I was in public school, like in high school, my friends used to be the guys, like, I didn't usually hang out with the girls, I didn't get along with them. And then I went to Saudi Arabia, it was a girl's school, and I don't know how to talk to boys any more.

Some parents and teachers worried that gender distancing would result in reticence and a lack of confidence, especially among the girls. Shahnaz described her concern for her thirteen-year-old daughter Seema, a grade seven student at Al Safar, who was facing the challenges of adolescence coupled with the demands of conforming to the discourse of the 'pious Muslim girl':

SHAHNAZ: It's just that they are so conscious of themselves – their own body, their own selves. They are just so conscious of … talking to them [boys]. They just don't want to talk. They're just so shy. They just feel that, 'Oh, we are girls and in Islam you're supposed to be covered and you just cannot talk.' I haven't talked to Seema about it but I think that's the kind of feeling she gets – 'Oh, I just can't go near them and talk and look in their eyes and talk or stuff like that.' But it [Islam] doesn't say that you can't ... because they have to go out in the real world and talk to people. She'll have to talk to male teachers when she goes to school – to peers in a class in high school. What is she going to do?

Shahnaz's daughter is attempting to conform to the appropriate standards for female behaviour as dictated by the community's religious authorities and promoted in mosques and Islamic schools. The discursive construction of the 'pious Muslim girl' involves adherence to rules that limit being in the company of males for fear of creating *fitnah* within the community. As discussed earlier, women's bodies are especially regulated to guard against this possibility (see Abou El Fadl, 2001a).

Young Muslim girls develop their subjectivities within this discursive space, sometimes accommodating and sometimes resisting the standards that are being imposed. These standards largely conflict with social realities, which require gender-based interaction as part of daily life. In an attempt to reduce un-Islamic influences, some schools and communities erect more physical barriers between women and men, or they isolate themselves further from the mainstream. Usually, though, efforts are made to negotiate a space of identity that allows for full participation in mainstream society, albeit with more limited types of engagement or socializing between unmarried men and women.

Protection versus Freedom

The Muslim girls in this study viewed Islamic schools as sites that 'protected' them, that promoted values they embraced, and that encouraged sisterhood and empowerment (see also Haw, 1994; Parker-Jenkins & Haw, 1996). Their notions of empowerment flowed from their religious understanding of women in Islam. They were also based on a strong sense of religious identity and spiritual fulfilment and on the bonds of sisterhood that developed in the single-sex school environment.

In other respects, though, these girls recognized to some degree their physical and social disempowerment. They expressed varying degrees of discontent regarding the surveillance that had been placed on their activities both inside and outside school. With respect to gender interaction, they were well aware of the 'double standard' with respect to boys. In discussing the policing of gendered spaces, the girls both affirmed and contested the parameters within which they lived their lives; they did so in the context of Muslim women's lot within an Islamic paradigm.

During my fieldwork at Al Rajab, I found that the girls' movements were heavily policed. As noted earlier, Shahnaz felt comforted as a parent that the school was 'protecting' the girls and 'keeping an eye out for them.' However, other teachers and students were critical of the degree of surveillance placed on girls, viewing it as regulatory rather than protective. Sakhina spoke candidly of her concerns regarding this surveillance. Girls were not allowed outside of the school during school hours, even if accompanied by a teacher. This unwritten school policy was seen as a means of 'protecting' the girls. Yet it was clear that this policy was underpinned with sexism, as many of the following narratives describe. Sakhina spoke of the difficulties she encountered when trying to bend the rules even to take the students out for an activity:

SAKHINA: I taught art. There are two trees outside the school just on the front area. I wanted them to draw the trees. I had to go through this whole process of even letting the girls come outside with me. Like, we would just be on the sidewalk in front of the school, drawing. But it was such an issue – a 'girls can't come out' kind of thing. But eventually I won.

Girls were also forbidden to walk down the street to the mosque, a short walk from the school, to attend Friday prayers. Congregational attendance for Friday prayers is not compulsory for women, as it is for men. Sakhina, though, argued that Friday prayers were an important part of Islamic learning and would have tied the girls more closely to the broader Muslim community.

Female students at Al Rajab also complained about the close scrutiny over their whereabouts, which limited their ability to come and go without seeking permission from the school authorities. This, even though they were over sixteen and otherwise considered adults. Many argued that even their parents were more lenient and that they faced fewer restrictions at home. Especially for those students who had transferred from public high schools and who were accustomed to more freedom of movement without the consent of school authorities, these conditions were stifling. Especially during exam times, students were expected to have notes from their parents allowing them to leave the school:

ALIYAH: Oh my God, we have to have notes. They have to call our parents to make sure we're allowed to leave the school during that time. The coffee shop at the corner, we're not allowed to go there because the guys go there. And we have no place else to hang out.
NUSAYBAH: Like we need to go *some*where, usually after school we're hungry.
ZARQA: I told my mom I went there for lunch and my mom was okay with it. But then brother Nasir found out and he's like, 'You're not allowed to go there. You're not allowed to be there.'
IMRANA: Wasn't there one time somebody spying on us all the way home? There was this person that brother Nasir hired to spy on everybody.
JASMIN: Was that for real?
NUSAYBAH: A couple of days ago they sent someone to the coffee shop because they thought the girls went there. They sent a teacher over there.

I was unable to determine whether anyone had actually been hired to 'spy' on the students. It is more likely that Imrana's suspicion was a consequence of the 'panopticon effect,' discussed earlier in this chapter. The sense of being under a constant gaze was produced more through the discursive disciplinary constructions of 'piety' imposed on Muslim girls with respect to what the school authorities deemed to be the appropriate physical and spatial boundaries for their behaviours and interactions, especially in public domains. In this sense, the disciplinary gaze or panopticism created through the school's discursive practices allowed the social regulation of these girl's activities to occur without having to resort to 'spies' or other, more tangible forms of surveillance. In other words, the watchful gaze was always assumed to be there, and its effect was to make the girls conscious of their behaviour whether or not anyone was truly monitoring them. The panoptical effect, in this way, becomes self-regulatory as Foucault (1975) explains: 'He [sic hereafter] who is subjected to a field of visibility, and who knows it, assumes responsibility for the constraints of power; he makes them play spontaneously upon himself; he inscribes in himself the power relation in which he simultaneously plays both roles; he becomes the principle of his own subjection' (pp. 202–203). Driscoll (1997) notes that the invisible disciplinary power of the panoptical gaze 'serves as a larger system of social control whereby women internalize the normative gaze to which they are subject' and, therefore, become 'self-policing subjects' (p. 102). She further situates this type of surveillance as a form of 'obedience to patriarchy' (p.103).

A panoptical system of power operates through these tacit measures, rather than imposing overt and rigid constraints: 'The panopticon ... must be understood as a generalizable model of functioning; a way of defining power relations in terms of the everyday life of men [sic] ... In short it arranges things in such a way that the exercise of power is not added on from the outside, like a rigid, heavy constraint, to the functions it invests, but is so subtly present in them as to increase their efficiency by itself increasing its own points of contact' (Foucault, 1975, pp. 205–6). Along with this form of regulatory power, the girls were subjected to other formal and explicit restrictions. Besides not being free to move about in the public spaces outside the school without written permission, they were cloistered within the school, where the windows were coated with green paint to conceal the girls from public view. Some of the girls complained about being shut in like 'prisoners' and about the double standards that allowed boys freedom from the restrictions imposed upon them:

IMRANA: Sister Sakhina took us out for a winter walk. And that was because we begged and begged.
ALIYAH: We had to beg. Sister Sakhina and I had to ask so many times. Like a lot of begging. They don't want us out at all. And I think we need fresh air because there are no windows in the school. They're all covered up, we're not allowed to go near the windows or open them a crack.
JASMIN: That's why I was asking, because I do notice the guys out.
NUSAYBAH: They're like always out. They can like, go whenever.
IMRANA: They come and go as they please. [Everyone agrees: 'Yeah!']
NUSAYBAH: And we go near the door and it's like a big issue. Or the windows open and it's a BIG issue. It's like, 'Why'd you open the window!?'
ZARQA: That's why, like, all the little kids, they have windows, but ours are covered up with that green paper.
IMRANA: We felt like ... prisoners. Like, you sit there and you look

out the window and think, 'Can I just like, breathe some fresh air?'
Then we eventually got caught for that so we couldn't use the room.
ALIYAH: The windows are shut. You're not allowed to open them.
NUSAYBAH: And if you are, you open them this much [demonstrates
an inch opening with her fingers] and if you open them any more
than this much it's like a BIG issue.
ALIYAH: Everyone's just like, 'Close the window! Close the window!'
They think that we're going to be looking outside and the guys are
going to look at us.
NUSAYBAH: I asked a teacher when I first came here, 'Can you open a
window?' and the teacher's like, 'No.' I mean, it's not like we're
going to like, jump on top of the guys! We're just going to sit there
and do our work, but like, fresh air is coming inside, right?

Another group of girls had similar complaints about double standards as they related to male students having free access to public
spaces denied the girls:

REHANA: Well, I notice they [the boys] go out and have lunch. They
leave school in their cars and go out and have lunch or whatever in
a restaurant. Now if I would want to go there..
AMAL: We can't even go to the coffee shop, we're not allowed to.
Even with sister Assiya [a teacher], we decided once we had a
spare and we wanted to go with her to the coffee shop and brother
Nasir was like, 'Don't leave, don't go.'
REHANA: I think it's a problem. That's not fair. This is Canada. This is
not like any other Islamic country, like maybe Saudi Arabia, where
women are all hidden away.

From her perspective as a teacher, Sakhina reported that the school
administrators had made it clear to her that girls required more protection than boys:

SAKHINA: It was said to me point blank: girls need to be protected
more. And I'm just like, they need to learn how to protect themselves. That's just my philosophy.

For Sakhina, then, the issue was one of empowerment, and all the
sheltering was preventing these young women from developing
autonomy. They were young adults, yet they were being treated as

children, with no power to exercise freedom of movement outside the
school, not even during lunch hour or spare periods. I asked the girls
if they felt that this rigid surveillance was conducted out of concern for
their safety:

JASMIN: Help me to understand. What you think this is about? Do
  you think they do this out of a sense of protection?
ALIYAH: It's out of the reputation of the school.
NUSAYBAH: Every time we get in trouble he [the principal] says,
  'You're ruining the reputation of the school!'
ALIYAH: But as a matter of fact, in a way it's good that he protects us,
  because he tells us, 'You girls are like my daughters.' Like, the
  girls, we're really close, and like, his daughters are our best friends
  and ever since I've been here, he's really cared a lot about my education, how I am. And he told me so many times, 'You're like my
  daughter and I don't want to see anything bad happen to you.' So,
  like, I admire him for doing that. But sometimes it can be a little
  overboard.

Thus, they were somewhat ambivalent on this matter. Aliyah and
Nusaybah agreed that the policing was done to preserve the school's
reputation, though Aliyah felt that it was framed in a fatherly or protective manner. And clearly, concern for the school's reputation did not
extend to the boys, many of whom, as we have seen, had troubled
pasts.

Sakhina complained that while boys were not reprimanded for
smoking outside the school, the girls were strongly chastised for
having an innocent snowball fight outside or for wearing make-up or
nail polish. She had once asked a student to go out after school to the
coffee shop and bring her a hot chocolate. When the girl returned, the
school administrators reprimanded her for venturing into a forbidden
public zone. It angered Sakhina that the school was unwilling to
acknowledge that it was restricting the students' liberty, as well as
treating them unfairly and with disrespect:

SAKHINA: She got yelled at! I'm like, 'What?!' So I went to the administrators and I was like, 'You have a student in the bathroom crying
  just for stepping outside and doing me a favour? I really think you
  should apologize.' They were like, 'Why should I ...?' It's that

whole 'Those in authority do not apologize to those who are below them' kind of thing. I sense that so much. You're in authority. How do you keep your class disciplined and controlled? Sometimes I would literally let my students go loose just because they've got pent-up energy.

Sakhina was clearly upset about the position that the administrators had taken in relation to their authority over the students, especially when it came to enforcing the rules that restricted the girls to non-public spaces.

As El Guindi (1999) notes, 'the paradigm public/private and its corollary honour-shame, is the one most commonly imposed on Arab and Islamic cultural space to describe the division between the sexes' (p. 79). Islamic cultural standards relegate females to the non-public arena yet allow males to navigate without sanction between private and public spaces. Those standards are linked to the notion that women's bodies create *fitnah* and can attract and allure negative male attention. In the case at hand, the only difference is that the need to preserve family honour has been replaced by the need to preserve the school's honour. In both contexts, the burden of creating or destroying honour and social status is inscribed onto the bodies of women, who are forced to conceal themselves from the gaze of public scrutiny and aspersions.

Sakhina had fought many battles with the administration at Al Rajab, trying to convince them to ease some of the restrictions imposed on the girls. She lamented that the problem of excessive policing of Muslim girls saturated the entire community. In her view, part of the reason was that Muslim women are more visible because of the clothes they wear, which make them easier to scrutinize than men, whose visible markers of Islamic identification, such as a beard, are less overt. Worth noting here is that the beard is considered more 'optional' for Muslim men who follow the sunnah (i.e., the example of the Prophet Muhammed), whereas women's Islamic dress codes are largely seen as *fard* or obligatory, based on certain interpretations of the Qur'an. There has been a tremendous amount of debate regarding whether the hijab is religiously mandated; so far, though, that debate has not reached Islamic schools, where the hijab is the unquestioned status quo. Another reason for the overemphasis on policing Muslim girls was based on the notion that girls needed it:

SAKHINA: I don't know why ... It's something that's bothered me
throughout ... since I started wearing hijab and stuff like that. I'm
being policed myself. I think because girls can be more visibly
policed. Do you know what I mean? You can obviously spot a
Muslim girl who's not wearing a hijab. You can't spot a guy who
doesn't have enough hair growth to grow a beard. I think it also
has to do with ... they think that girls should be policed. There
are certain attitudes ... Guys, well, they're supposed to go out in
the world, and girls are supposed to sit isolated? And so these
were arguments that I'd have. Because you're basically against a
brick wall, I would have nothing to say more than the fact that
it's wrong.

Sakhina's frustration came from her many attempts to reason with
the administration at Al Rajab and to intervene on behalf of the girls.
She resisted the rigid public/private dichotomy that relegated the girls
to the cloistered spaces of the school and that allowed the boys unre-
stricted access to the public domain. After hearing many such complaints from female students and teachers regarding the restrictions, I
asked one of the administrators, sister Raessa, to account for these
double standards:

JASMIN: Are there the same rules for boys and girls in the school? Some
of the girls say that the boys have more freedom to come and go.
RAEESA: No, I've heard that too. Why? Because, you know, the boy's
school area has a smaller space and they don't have the facility of
the cafeteria, and, you know, boys normally don't bring lunch from
home like how girls do, so they just want to go out to buy their
lunches, so that's how we allow them. Otherwise boys' schedule is
the same thing. They get forty minutes of lunch, and – this is in
higher grades – they are allowed to go buy the lunch around the
corner. Otherwise, you know, up to grade eight no one is allowed
even to cross the road. We have a cafeteria here for them, so the
smaller boys, they will come and buy whatever they want. But for
the older grades ... the place is small, other boys they just have to,
you know, goof around, that's why we just allow them to go out
for lunch, that's all.

Here, sister Raessa was trying to couch the reasons for the dispar-
ity between the girls' and boys' access to public space in practical and

pragmatic terms. She was arguing that the space within the school was too tight, with the cafeteria located on the girls' side of the school, and that to maintain appropriate gender segregation, only the primary schoolboys could be allowed to have lunch there. Since the senior boys could not be allowed to go to the cafeteria with the girls, and because they were the smallest group in the school, they were allowed to leave the premises for lunch. Yet she also noted that boys have a need to 'goof around' – that is, blow off steam – something that is seen as completely unnecessary and inappropriate for girls in public spaces.

Affirming and Contesting Gendered Boundaries

These double standards demonstrate the different sets of expectations that exist for boys and girls with regard to accessing the public domain. The school saw it as a paramount duty to guard the dignity and honour of the girl students. Also, the school's reputation was inextricably linked to the girls' behaviour, which, it followed, had to be disciplined in accordance with 'pious Muslim girl' standards. Sexism, therefore, operated as a means to protect the reputation of the school as a place where young Muslim girls could be isolated from negative social influences and 'illicit' interactions with boys. In this way the girls' honour was kept intact, and so was the school's.

Foucault (1975) regarded such mechanisms of social control as a means of connecting the body to the discursive formations of power. Through these mechanisms, various disciplinary regulations are enacted, leading to the construction of 'docile bodies.' As Foucault explains, 'what was then being formed was a policy of coercions that act upon the body, a calculated manipulation of its elements, its gestures, its behaviour. The human body was entering a machinery of power that explores it, breaks it down and rearranges it' (p. 137). For Muslim girls, this form of regulation is a powerful strategy of discipline that exercises control over their very gestures, behaviours, and movements. Some of the girls I interviewed conformed to both the physical and discursive boundaries that circumscribed their behaviour, identity, and freedom as young Muslim women; other girls resisted and challenged those boundaries.

Some girls had been in the public system and contested the policing of their movements; others viewed this surveillance as 'protection' and denied that it was inhibiting their freedom. In a sense, then, these girls saw 'spiritual freedom' as superior to 'physical freedom' and did not feel constrained by the school's surveillance. Iman, Deqa, and Summaya discussed how they had accommodated themselves to the school's regulations. The discussion begins with a complaint that the school doesn't trust girls (hence the rigid controls on their behaviour); but it goes on to affirm the school's restrictions on the basis that they reflect Islamically appropriate gender differentiation:

IMAN: The disadvantage part is like, being controlled too much and setting the boys free in a way. And not trusting us. So it's not a good thing.

DEQA: In my opinion you can only compare two things that are similar. Like the way they treat us is different from the boys. That's why you can't even compare it. Because in Islam, women are women and men are men. You can't compare them and you can't say they are equal because each of them has a different role. And like, us in the school for example, the reason we're not allowed to go out as often is because we don't have to. The guys, they have to go to *jumuah* prayer, they don't have a cafeteria so they go out. It's obligatory on them and it's not on us, that's why we can stay. So in my opinion I don't think there's much difference in the treatment and I do think they treat us equally, but just different.

Deqa, here, was applying an 'equal but different' discourse to rationalize the girls' repression. When I related the objections that other girls had expressed about the restrictions on their freedom of movement outside school, these students challenged their reasoning:

DEQA: It depends like, why we'd want to go out. Like, obviously if we'd want to go out and pray in the mosque, they'd have to let us. But why are we going to go out? To sit in the coffee shops? To do what? Like, for example, I don't think it's right for a guy to do that either. But it's just that, if the guys are doing it, that's fine with us. Like, just because somebody's doing something doesn't mean that we have to say, 'Oh my God, we have to do it too.' We have our own rules and they have their own rules and whether they're going to go by them or not, it's up to them. But we, as women, we're going to do our job and, you know, fulfil our duty.

SUMMAYA: But it's, okay, like their side of the school is much smaller, it's crowded. And here it's more open space and we could go sit somewhere and eat, right? But they don't have that space.

JASMIN: Some girls talked about needing fresh air, because it gets a little stuffy and just being able to go out for a walk or get fresh air. Do you feel like that at all?

EVERYONE: Not really.

IMAN: But I've never heard of a school where in the middle of the school day you could just go out for a walk.

DEQA: I don't think fresh air is like, a valid reason to go out. Like, if it's against the school rules to leave then I don't think fresh air is like, such a big deal that you should make a discussion about it and argue about it.

These students disagreed with those of their peers who contested the rules that differentially governed the girls' actions in the school, based on what they believed to be appropriate standards of Islamic 'propriety.' They had been scripted by the school authorities, their families, and the community as 'pious Muslim girls,' and they maintained that script as the normative discourse through which their identities as Muslim women were to be constituted, even though doing so reinforced the dominant patriarchal hegemony.

Deqa in particular was adamant regarding gender roles. In her view, the boundaries were part of an 'Islamic order' and it was her 'duty' as a Muslim woman to maintain them. This speaks to the power of gendered discourses to structure these young women's subjectivities according to prevailing Islamic norms as promoted at schools and mosques and in many Muslim homes. The fact that these discourses have been attributed a seal of Divine ordinance, giving them unquestionable authority, makes it easier for many young girls to uncritically accept them as their religious duty. Yet I would argue that from a critical faith-centred perspective, we must attend to the ways in which religion can help construct oppression, in this case on the basis of gender. There is an imperative need to challenge the discursive authority of puritanism and to examine the perspectives of those religious scholars and Islamic feminists who have created cogent arguments against these rigid gender discourses from alternative faith-centred perspectives that promote the Islamic ideals of social justice (see, for example, Abou El Fadl, 2001; McCloud, 2000; Al Hibri, 2000; Ahmed, 1992). For more critical faith-centred perspectives to flourish, a plurality of views must exist so that young Muslim women can have a variety of discursive opportunities available to them through which they can begin to frame their identity and womanhood.

Other students did contest and challenge the school's boundaries. They regarded the restrictions as an expression of the administration's distrust of them:

ZARQA: There is a lot of surveillance on what you do. You'll have teachers follow you.

IMRANA: Parents may think it's good, but for us, we're teens and we have to have our rights. We're teenagers. They think it's our job to do bad stuff at this time, but we're not going to do bad stuff like that.

EVERYONE: Yeah!

ALIYAH: We *can* be trusted. Like, even if we do see a guy and we talk to him, it's not like we're going to go and like, kiss him!

These girls were challenging the constraints that had been placed on them, arguing that the school's lack of trust was unfounded, since they had already internalized the boundaries of propriety that they felt were important for them as Muslim women. They wanted to be able to exercise their right to navigate society, guided by their own Islamic sensibilities and parameters.

The lack of trust evident in the rules imposed on girls at Al Rajab may have broader sociological implications. In her study of Muslim girls' schools in Britain, Haw (1998) noted that being 'marriageable' was of key importance to the predominantly South Asian Muslim families whose children attended those schools. Their daughters' honour and respectability needed to be maintained to ensure their eligibility for marriage. School was allowable only to the extent that it did not interfere with those prospects. Haw notes: 'As I perceive it, the main issue at present for the Muslim community in Britain is not the education of girls or concern for their careers, but the unproblematic movement toward marriage. The girls are allowed access to education and to career as long as these do not disturb institutions like marriage and family' (p. 157). I disagree that this is the 'main issue' facing the Muslim community in general, but I agree that it is key to explaining the emphasis on Muslim girls' respectability, and why Islamic schools work so hard to protect the status and reputation of girl students, restricting their movements and limiting their opportunities to mingle with boys.

Transgressing Gendered Spaces

Even innocent actions that breached the school's gendered boundaries led to sanctions. Imrana, Zarqa, and Aliyah had been reprimanded because one of them had crossed over to the boys' side to offer condolences to a male student who had just lost a brother in a car accident:

IMRANA: There's this guy in our school, right? His brother passed away in a car accident.
EVERYONE: It was in the paper.
JASMIN: Oh, was it that awful car accident on Fourth Street?
IMRANA: Yeah. They found out that I was talking to him and I got in so much trouble it's not even funny!
JASMIN: And you were just extending your condolences?
ZARQA: That's what she said.
IMRANA: I said, 'I'm sorry about your brother' and stuff. And he was fine with it. It's like, okay.
ALIYAH: And it was only her.
IMRANA: It was only me and they [the other girls] still got in trouble. You know, when the principal asked me, I said I was just giving my condolences to him and I felt sorry for him. So then he goes, 'Yeah, well, I'll go and give you a list of the guys you should feel sorry for and you can go and give your condolences to them too.'
ZARQA: That was mean. That was so mean.
IMRANA: It's not my fault his brother passed away and I had the heart to go and say sorry to him. Because the guy lost a brother! It's not like a normal thing, right? I'm not just going to sit there and act dumb about it.
ZARQA: If we know. It had been on the news and stuff.
IMRANA: You get *sawab* [blessings] for saying sorry.
JASMIN: Absolutely.

Significant here is that Imrana transgressed the school's gendered boundaries and violated a social taboo (i.e., crossing over to the boys' side) based on her religious conviction, which guided her to seek out the male student and offer him condolences as an Islamically appropriate action. In her view, the blessings she would receive for this action would outweigh any sanctions by the school authorities, since she was carrying out an act that was required of her as a Muslim. In defying the school's rules, she was asserting her own Islamic imperatives and rejecting the school's imposed standards in favour of carrying out a duty of compassion to a fellow Muslim, irrespective of gender. Through this small act of subversion, she was establishing and asserting her own Islamic standards and beginning to script her own identity as a Muslim woman based on Islamic ethics and values that were not constrained by gender.

A question arises: Can such actions be viewed as exercises of agency and resistance? If we agree that a moment of political consciousness and critique must be embedded in actions for them to qualify as resistance (see, for example, Giroux, 1983), it is difficult to say whether Imrana saw her actions as politically derived and motivated. Yet Mahmood (2005) reminds us that it is more useful to examine how agency operates through multiple modalities and through 'the grammar of concepts in which its particular affect, meaning and form resides' than to propose a specific theory of agency (p. 188). She goes on to argue that 'insomuch as this kind of analysis suggests that different modalities of agency require different kinds of bodily capacities, it forces us to ask whether acts of resistance [to systems of gender hierarchy] also devolve upon the ability of the body to behave in particular ways. From this perspective, transgressing gender norms may not be a matter of transforming consciousness or affecting change in the significatory system of gender but might well require the retraining of sensibilities, affect, desire, and sentiments – those registers of corporeality that often escape the logic of representation and symbolic articulation' (p. 188). Mahmood, then, contends that to understand the various mediations of agency within gendered acts carried out by subordinate bodies, we must look beyond consciousness and political motivation as the hallmarks of resistance and examine the cultivation of specific dispositions, sensibilities, and desires that undergird the discursive and material relations of piety and performativity.

Islamic Schooling and an Emergent Islamic Feminism

Female teachers and students were keenly aware of the repressive structures in the school that limited the freedom of girls. In a study of a private, single-sex girls' school, Proweller (1998) noted that these schools act as sites where girls 'actively engage in counter-hegemonic moves both in accommodation and resistance to school structures and sex-stereotyped messages' (p. 8). Regarding this study, the resistance of the female students and teachers to these structures was part of a critical feminist stance through which they were beginning to articulate an alternative set of possibilities that would still be consistent with their Islamic outlook. They challenged some of the puritanical and patriarchal notions of the school administrators and religious leaders through small acts of defiance – for example, when Imrana transgressed the school's gendered spaces in order to fulfil what she viewed as a religious obligation. Through contestations such as these, the girls were beginning to assert alternative understandings of their role as Muslim women, counter to the limiting discourses presented to them in the school and the community at large.

The restrictions placed on the girls were designed to inhibit their opportunities to mingle with boys and to preserve their reputations and that of the school in accordance with their role as 'pious Muslim girls.' Yet it is significant that those restrictions did not extend to the academic opportunities the school provided (see chapter 8). For example, the girls were very much encouraged to excel in subjects such as science and math, which have often been seen as male intellectual domains. Researchers have found that girls are often not challenged by teachers and society to venture into traditionally male-dominated academic spheres (see, for example, Smith, McCoy, & Bourne, 1997). This was not the case at Al Rajab, where girls were equally encouraged to excel in all areas of learning. In other words, the restrictions they faced were linked to their social practices, not to their academic pursuits. Nevertheless, the rigid regulation of gender-based structures created a limiting paradigm that worked against gender equity, notwithstanding the Islamic schools' efforts to provide equal access and academic opportunities for both male and female students.

Rehana resisted the limiting discourses imposed on her by conservative and sexist ideologues in the community, who saw 'freedom' as a path to excess, especially for women:

REHANA: Well for me, I want to run my own business, but that gives me lot of freedom, and you know how it's like, 'Muslim women shouldn't have that much freedom,' because they're going to go astray.

JASMIN: Do you agree?
REHANA: No! I don't, because I just want to have my freedom, but
  I'm not going to go astray.

Rehana, who wore the niqab, was aware of the conflicting standards
to which she was held in the society at large and within the community. She had to contend not only with the 'gendered Islamophobia'
she encountered in the dominant society but also with the narrow fundamentalist dogmas espoused by certain sectors of her own community. She was attempting to negotiate between these equally limiting
paradigms in order to construct her own notion of womanhood from
her specific faith-centred vantage point.

Sakhina saw her role of teacher as a powerful space from which
she could present her students with alternative possibilities for
resistance and change that would decentre some of the patriarchal
norms that were uncritically accepted by the community. She noted
that many Muslim women find their sense of empowerment by
gaining a critical education and then examining Islam's original
sources and messages:

SAKHINA: It's so very male ... like, culturally, Islam is very male dominated. But the funny thing is ... I've actually read articles about
  women in Muslim countries who are going back to orthodox Islam,
  to what Islam *was*, and that's where they're getting their empowerment from. That's what I try and teach these girls. It's like, if the
  system's not good then fight it and try and change it. Do it properly and respectfully. Don't do it so [that anyone] can point a finger
  at you and say you did something wrong. You do it within the.
  system to change it, right? But work for it. And the only way you
  can do that is if you educate yourself.

From a post-structuralist feminist standpoint, the type of critical
empowerment that Sakhina is attempting to impart to these young
women is vital in opening up the discursive realm of possibilities for
young girls.

Through these contestations of patriarchal practice, and through the
development of a critical consciousness that will enable young Muslim
women to become change agents in their societies, a discourse of
Islamically centred feminism is emerging. Cooke (2001) describes how
Muslim women are 'claiming Islam' by challenging the erasure of their

experiences in the public and discursive spaces of nation, community, and faith. By reclaiming their voices and redefining their identities in more politicized ways, Muslim women are contributing to a burgeoning Islamic feminist movement based on a gendered Islamic epistemology (see also Yamani, 1996). The quieter acts of subversion by the women at Al Rajab, who were seeking to transform the narrow and inequitable parameters of the gendered social space available to them, can be viewed as a contribution to this nascent feminism. While these students were not making explicit claims to being 'feminists' per se, as that term is discursively constructed and produced within Eurocentric paradigms, it was clear that their goals were both faith-centred and emancipatory in relation to the advancement of Muslim women's rights.

As bell hooks (1993, in Haw, 1995) notes, it is not the enunciation of a feminist stance that indicates actual feminist praxis; rather, it is the actions that lead to expanding the opportunities and critical consciousness of young, racialized women. She further notes that while many Black teachers during her childhood did not use the word 'feminism,' their lived pedagogy was based on a liberatory mission: 'Though those Black women did not openly advocate feminism (if they even knew the word) the very fact that they insisted on academic excellence and open critical thought for young Black females was an anti-sexist practice' (p. 58). It is clear that many Muslim girls and teachers at Al Rajab were cognizant of the inequality of their status as women in the school, and they were committed to challenging those disparities from within an Islamic paradigm. In this vein, in a study of a British Muslim girls' school, Parker-Jenkins and Haw (1996) found that students challenged patriarchal discourses and were 'seeking equality within Islam not without it' (p. 31). Haw (1995) adds that girls in Islamic schools have available to them greater 'discursive flexibility' through which 'the processes of exploration, questions and challenging from within an Islamic framework can begin' (p. 59). So it is within the discursive terrain of the Islamic school as a site of knowledge production and dissemination that alternative possibilities for Islamic womanhood can be imagined and created, at the same time as other, more limited discourses are resisted and challenged.

Sawicki (1991) reminds us that agency and freedom reside within the complexities of identity formation: 'Freedom lies in our capacity to discover the historical links between certain modes of self understanding and modes of domination, and to resist the ways in which we have already been classified and identified within dominant discourses' (p. 43). For Muslim girls, this means resisting the dominant ways in which they have been scripted both within the dominant racialized and Islamophobic discourses in mainstream society and within the limiting patriarchal discourses in certain sectors of the Muslim community. Their narratives are a powerful reminder of the multiple oppressions that confront them. Their voices serve as testimony to the desire and ability of many of these girls to transcend the victim-centred images of passivity and complicity in their oppression and, instead, position themselves within the struggle to seek and assert agency over their lives and identities from a critical faith-centred space.

7 The Islamization of Knowledge and Social and Political Praxis in Islamic Schools

This chapter explores the Islamization of knowledge and praxis in Islamic schools. Issues related to integrating Islam into the largely Eurocentric secular curriculum mandated by the Ontario Ministry of Education are examined through the narratives of Islamic educators, administrators, parents, and students. Teachers at Islamic schools share their strategies for Islamizing knowledge in their lessons and discuss how Islamic knowledge and values inform other areas of educational praxis. Particular attention is paid to how current global events and social justice concerns are addressed in the curriculum of Islamic schools as a means to promote spirituality through social and political activism. The discursive practices embedded in the current diasporic orientation of Islamic education are explored in order to uncover both the tensions and the possibilities that emerge in this context.

Grounding the Discursive and Epistemological Frames

The discursive frameworks that provide a lens for examining these curricular and pedagogical issues are based on the anticolonial paradigm discussed in chapter 2 and on the critical faith-centred epistemology. As discussed in earlier chapters, both an anticolonial discursive framework (Dei & Azgharzadeh, 2001) and the critical faith-centred epistemology challenge the privileging of Western secular knowledge as the exclusive vantage point for teaching and learning. Furthermore, the critical faith-centred approach recognizes that religion and spirituality are central to the understandings of various academic disciplines and subjects and are valid and legitimate sites for analysing social, existential phenomena. Islamic education, therefore, provides an entry point for faith-centred knowledges and understandings to become valid ways of knowing and making sense of the world and for faith-centred voices to become integral to social, academic, and political processes.

In challenging the colonization of knowledge by Eurocentric hegemony, I situate anticolonial thought as a space where subjugated knowledges can be reclaimed and revitalized and where new discursive knowledge can be created. The marginalization of religious and spiritually based ways of knowing in public education makes the development of independent schools based on these subjugated knowledges part of an anticolonial discursive process. Islamic schools represent an anticolonial move in that they offer a central place to subjugated knowledge in educational discourse and praxis. Islamic schooling generates a form of oppositional knowledge that seeks to subvert the dominant secular, Eurocentred discourses as the only valid basis for compulsory education and learning. In that way, they allow the development of alternative thinking and of non-secular articulations of knowledge and ontology.

Independent religious schools provide a greater immersion in the discourses of faith-based communities; they also provide a pedagogical medium for faith and spirituality to inform daily social life and personal development. The knowledge base for teaching and learning in these schools recognizes the importance of religion and spirituality for understanding human social and cultural development. The ideological world views that are drawn from these epistemological vantage points do much to shape how diasporic Muslim communities (including Islamic schools) are organized socially, culturally, and politically, given the strong impact of religious and spiritual ideologies and culture on faith-based communities in terms of social and political practices as well as everyday life.

In Islamic schools, these effects are discursively produced through the Islamization of knowledge. The first part of this chapter explores how Islamic knowledge is integrated with the secular Eurocentric curriculum in Islamic schools. Teachers' approaches to integrating Islamic knowledge and transforming curricular imperatives are examined. Islamic education as a means for liberatory social justice education is also examined through specific social and curricular initiatives instituted in Islamic schools to address global inequality and oppression.

Integrating Islam: Strategies for the Islamization of Knowledge

As discussed in chapter 4, the importance of Islamic knowledge and learning was a major factor in parents' decisions to send their children to Islamic schools. Many Muslim parents want their children to have a spiritually based education alongside more secular learning; for them, immersion in an Islamically centred curriculum is a drawing point. These parents regard a spiritually centred curriculum as a means of instilling Islamic values and identity in their children. Karim notes that for Muslim parents, this means setting priorities for their children's education:

KARIM: When you do something you have to set your priorities. We're not sending the kids to be scientists or the top-of-the-class students ... because if they're at the top of the class, they're a genius and all that, they don't have the Islamic background, the Islamic education, they could be lost and they could forget it.

For Karim, Islamic knowledge is preferable to more worldly knowledge. In his view, learning is about spiritual growth, devotion, and enlightenment, as opposed to a more existential rationale promoting only academic knowledge and material success as primary goals in life.

Ibrahim, an educational activist, advocated a holistic approach to integrating Islamic knowledge, one that used the Qur'an not just as scripture for students to memorize but as a basis for making curricular connections:

IBRARIM: There tends to be an emphasis on Qur'anic memorization. I said earlier on – it is not enough for kids to memorize Qur'an unless that Qur'an is then taken and then integrated into the secular curriculum. Then the kids can make the connection. If you teach biology, there is so much you can draw from the Qur'an that you can bring into biology. The same thing for physics. You know, every subject in the curriculum, if you have teachers who are well trained and who can make that connection, they can pull those elements from the Qur'an and feed them into the curriculum, I think it would make our Islamic schools so entertaining and so exciting for the children.

In this way, Qur'anic knowledge becomes a 'living curriculum' that is infused through all subject areas. According to Ibrahim, this approach to integrating Islam allows children to understand the beauty and saliency of its message. When secular knowledge is decentred as the primary basis for teaching and learning, Islamic education begins to generate new epistemological possibilities:

IBRAHIM: Islamic knowledge ... can be allowed to permeate throughout the curriculum. And the children can come to appreciate the beauty of Islam. Because the notion now ... and I see a lot of this even from our own upbringing ... where secular education is given prominence because it has benefits. We don't see possibilities in reading Qur'an, but if you see it within the curriculum in every subject, you can.

Therefore, for Ibrahim, moving beyond the memorization of the Qur'an to finding ways to apply Qur'anic knowledge to the curriculum and daily life allows students to have a greater sense of how Islam can be beneficial to them and their learning.

Islamizing Early Childhood Education

As we saw in chapter 5, Islamic education provides a system of socialization for Muslim children. For families who are spiritually dedicated, inculcating Islamic values, beliefs, and practices begins early in children's lives. Only one of the schools in this study had an early childhood education program. I spoke with Maha, the preschool teacher at Al Shawwal, and spent time in her classroom observing the strategies she used for introducing Islamic values and behaviour to small children:

MAHA: In circle time, we sing, 'We love Allah, Allah He gave us everything, he gave us the sky, the moon, the *qamar* [moon].' I try to say it in both [English and Arabic]. I have some pictures about the sun. 'Allah gave us this, who gave us honey? ...' So they know that Allah gave us everything. So we love Allah, we say, 'La Illaha Illallah, Muhammadur Rasullallah'[1] ... And when they enter the class, we should say, 'Assalamu Alaikum wa Rahmatullah.'[2] We don't say 'hi,' we don't say 'bye,' we say, 'Assalamu Alaikum' if we go out.

Maha's pedagogy was based on helping the children develop a sense of *taqwa* (consciousness of Allah). To that end, she implemented traditional methods of learning, which featured Islamic songs and games. She also emphasized the development of *adab* (Islamic etiquette) in the children's daily interactions. Also, she introduced them to the Arabic language, on which Qur'anic studies are based.

Bilquees, a kindergarten teacher at Al Shawwal, discussed her methods for introducing young children to Islamic knowledge and practice. She had created a 'God-centred classroom' in which students could develop reverence for divine creation and learn proper Islamic etiquette:

BILQUEES: Usually we have circles and things like that, and we talk about Allah and what is Allah's creation and everything. The curriculum is the same as the board of education is teaching, but we have our Islamic studies, too. Like, we sing Islamic songs, and we tell them it's raining, what do you say when it rains? And it's snowing, what do you say? '*Alhamdulillah, subhanallah,*' you know, 'mashallah.' These are the things we try to tell them, how to appreciate things. And if something happens, if you're mad, what do you do? So this is how we try to tell them. We teach them how to make *dua* before eating, going to the washroom, coming out of the washroom, and when somebody gives something to you what do you say? Thank you. What else do you say? You know, things like that. So we start teaching them in the young age, and they respond to that very well, actually.

During my fieldwork at Al Shawwal, I participated in the preschool's 'circle time,' teaching the children songs and dances that had been part of my own childhood in mainstream Canadian culture. This was new both for the children and for Maha. Maha was from Kuwait, so Canadian children's songs were new and somewhat foreign to her, and she was eager to learn them so that she could pass them on to the children. There was an openness to mainstream culture as long as it did not conflict with Islamic values.

Except in early childhood education, teachers generally avoided music. In some schools of Islamic thought, music is limited to specific instruments, such as the drum, and to special occasions, such as weddings and Eid festivals (see Al-Qaradawi, 1960). As a result, Islamic schools do not include music in their curriculum, and the use of music is restricted to Islamic songs. Also, schools do not begin the day with the Canadian National Anthem as in public schools; rather, they begin with Qur'anic recitation. When a new principal in one of the schools in this study suggested incorporating the National Anthem, the parents had mixed feelings; some of them objected that this would be overemphasizing nationalism. These are issues where Islamic schools are often bound to the views and interpretations of the most religiously conservative ideologies within the community and generally tend to cater to these views.

Art was another area where religious dogmatism hindered broader educational opportunities for the children. Some schools of Islamic thought forbid figurative drawing. In elementary education, figure drawing is part of children's natural expression. Some of the schools in this study did allow children to draw figures, but I noticed that when such artwork was displayed on the school walls, the eyes were cut out or taped over. In this way the images were rendered less 'human-like' and more in accordance with the school authorities' religious sensibilities. In the kindergarten classroom, even the snowmen had had their eyes cut out – a bizarre and disturbing sight. I often felt that these types of dubious prohibitions were leading to a paralysis in artistic development in the schools. Other art activities were structured around religious festivals or seasonal themes. Occasionally, Islamic art and tessellations were introduced as well. Historically, Muslims have been renowned for their artistry, so the schools' efforts to disregard this longstanding tradition were especially unfortunate.

From an early age, students are taught the fundamentals of the Islamic faith – for example, the correct performance of the five daily prayers. In all Islamic schools, prayer times are maintained and all children participate. In schools that are housed in mosques, such as Al Shawwal and Al Safar, students in the higher grades pray in the prayer halls with other members of the community. On Fridays, congregational prayers are held and the children attend as part of their spiritual education. Younger children pray in their classrooms and can hear the call to prayer and the *imam* (prayer leader) over the PA system. Learning the proper methods for praying is integral to Muslim children's spiritual education. Prayers are offered in different positions – standing, bowing, prostrating – while specific verses from the Qur'an are recited in Arabic. Ruqayyah, a teacher at Al Safar, explained her strategies for helping young children concentrate during prayer times. She wanted her students to develop a love for prayer, instead of regarding it simply as a ritual action:

RUQAYYAH: I tell them I want them to love *salat* [prayer] … The only way to calm them down during *Salat* is not to keep telling them, 'Well, if you don't pray properly, you're going to get in a lot of trouble.' No, I say, 'This is your special time. This is like your phone call between you and Allah. Like, this is your time to talk to Allah, so don't ruin it.'

By characterizing prayer time as their 'special time' to have their 'phone call' to Allah, Ruqayyah was able to frame spiritual practice in a way that the young children in her class could relate to and appreciate. In each of the strategies discussed so far, spiritual knowledge is made relevant and accessible to young children through a variety of age-appropriate pedagogical strategies.

Besides inculcating ritual religious behaviours and practices, teachers socialize children into Islamic values. Ruqayyah discussed some of the values she reinforced in her classroom:

RUQAYYAH: Not just in terms of *salat*, but like in everything, I go, 'Be the best you can be,' in terms of education, finishing their work, being neat and tidy, being clean. I think I even mentioned having clean socks and everything. Sure, a lot of kids giggled, but it needed to be said. Hygiene is a very important thing.

Therefore, these guidelines for good social, physical, and academic practices are seen as a part of the student's religious obligation and moral training. The early education provided by Islamic schools, therefore, focuses on developing Islamic behaviours and practices among young children as a means for developing their identities and 'life skills' as Muslims.

Curricular Strategies for Integrating Islam in Elementary and Intermediate Schooling

Mehrun, the principal at Al Safar, explained how teachers, especially those with strong Islamic knowledge, connected that knowledge to the curriculum:

MEHRUN: Okay, let's say the water cycle. The teachers, especially the ones that are more confident and more aware, they try to find hadith or *ayat* or the verses that have something to do with the water cycle in the Qur'an. They say, 'Look, Islam does not oppose science, Islam is not a seventh-century religion, it is a modern religion, and all this so-called modern information is already in the Qur'an.' That makes the children feel happy that oh yeah, this is what is in the Qur'an. And they realize that Islam is, you know, it's a modern religion.

For Mehrun, this strategy of connecting curricular themes to Islamic knowledge was a means for children to see how science actually validates knowledge from the Qur'an rather than contradicting it. In this way, Mehrun argued, they could see that Islam is a 'modern religion,' that it has currency, and that its relevance transcends time and space.

For Amira, who taught the elementary level at Al Safar, the Qur'an was the starting point for planning lessons:

AMIRA: Okay, in my teaching what I do is whenever there's any unit, or if we're starting a new unit, whether it's math or science, what I usually do is I'll look into the index of the Qur'an, and it's divided into subject topics, and I always try to find any other information in the Qur'an and hadith about what we're learning. And if there is, then I always introduce that or incorporate that into the unit. And I try to give it in an Islamic perspective, especially in science. Like, for example, with the grade six diversity of living things, that's the unit for life systems. And the first thing we do is, I mean the Qur'an talks about the diversity, and how everything is so different, the variety of everything, so you teach that first.

Amira also noted that this involved a lot of extra research on the part of teachers, who had to make connections to the secular Eurocentric curriculum mandated by the Ministry of Education. Undertaking the process of integrating Islam involved a great deal of extra time, and required a certain level of proficiency and knowledge in Qur'anic studies. The Islamic schools in this study hired only Muslim teachers; even so, not all teachers felt comfortable enough with their Islamic knowledge to develop integrated strategies. Teachers do not receive any formal training or skills in order to learn techniques for the Islamization of knowledge in the curriculum, and many schools, in fact, hire specialist teachers for Islamic studies and Arabic language. Occasionally, some teachers would 'trade' classes with another teacher who was more proficient in Islamic knowledge, who could take on their Islamic studies curriculum while they took over a different subject area in that teacher's class. Therefore, the extent to which the Islamization of the curriculum took place was left up to the interest and volition of teachers, based on their feelings of proficiency with this knowledge.

To avoid ad hoc attempts by teachers to Islamize their curriculum, more training is required for Islamic schoolteachers to develop integrative strategies, especially since they are all at different levels of knowledge and experience. To date, no school in Ontario has attempted to develop a formal curriculum that blends the ministry's expectations with Islamic knowledge, which would make the Islamization process easier for all teachers to follow. Limited resources may account for why this has not yet been done. Meanwhile, Islamic studies remain a compartmentalized area or an add-on to the standard curriculum (see Shamma, 1999a).

Teachers who were proficient at Islamicizing the curriculum provided important insights into their methods. Amani, who had been trained as a secondary school teacher but who was teaching at the elementary level at Al Safar, felt confident in her ability to integrate Islamic knowledge in the curriculum. Originally from Ethiopia, she had studied at the Al Azhar Academy in Egypt and was deeply learned in both Islamic studies and Arabic. She spoke enthusiastically of her strategies for linking Islamic studies to other parts of the curriculum. She noted that there was greater flexibility in the elementary curriculum, which allowed for the integration of Islamic knowledge in key areas. In her view, Islamic studies were a seamless strand of the curriculum that had no beginning, middle, or end. Even though the period for Islamic studies was no longer than for any other subject, Islamic knowledge was seen as integral to all subject areas. She described the various ways that she incorporated Islamic knowledge and teaching into science, math, social studies, and language in ways that met the Ministry of Education's curriculum expectations. She shared some of her strategies, focusing on the links between math and Islamic art and the science of the Qur'an:

AMANI: I say in patterning, 'Where do you see patterns?' In lots of Islamic art we have these patterns. I try to integrate that. Science is one of my favourite subjects. I mean, I tell them, again in science, basically the natural phenomena – all these are already in the Qur'an. In fact, like, you know, sometimes I like just saying *subhanallah*[3] and they know, I just have this huge enthusiasm when I tell them, 'Look at the Qur'an, there are verses in the Qur'an that talk about the creation of the earth and it's very nicely tied to the science.' And in fact there is a book written by a French scientist, Maurice Bucaille, *Qur'an Science and Bible*, so ... I try to make them do research ... so I'm constantly bringing the Islamic studies into science.

Amani saw Islamic knowledge as completely complementary to the subjects such as science and math. (Teachers often spoke of how science actually lent credibility to the Qur'an and verified much Qur'anic knowledge.) She also looked for opportunities to rupture the curriculum's Eurocentrism, with its strong emphasis on Western hegemonic knowledge, by highlighting the contributions of Muslim scholars to scientific knowledge and civilization:

AMANI: I'll give you an example, let's say in math. We talk about patterns. So I give them a little bit of history about ... algebra and about Al-Khurizmi. I just want them to know that we have Muslim mathematicians ... So I give them a little bit of history ... Like Al-Jibr Al-Muqabalat is written by Muhammad Al-Khurizmi. The word Al-Jibra [algebra] was taken from his book. And this numerical system, it was the Arabic numerical system ... there were lots of Muslim explorers who, you know, came up with geography and mapping. So I try to bring those up in the classroom.

For many Muslim students, lessons like these were the first time their histories and knowledge had occupied a central place in the school curriculum. Saira and Noora appreciated the value added to their education by learning about how Muslims had contributed to arts, sciences, and the development of civilization:

SAIRA: That's the thing about Islam: it's such an amazing religion! It ties in with everything that we learn. I mean, we just have science lessons, which is another advantage with this school, by the way – when we come here, we know how our religion is related to the rest of the world, to the rest of the fields of study. And so many of our Muslim scholars have contributed to, you know, science and math, and it's amazing to learn how things are getting discovered now that have already been in the Qur'an and already been explained so many years ago.

NOORA: A little while ago we were learning about the water cycle and we were also doing some verses in the Qur'an that also stated where and how it was described before. How sometimes scientists say that they have discovered it first, but in reality Muslims did and it's already in the Qur'an.

The information these students received decentred Eurocentrism as the predominant system of knowledge. They learned that many 'Western discoveries' had in fact been appropriated long ago from Islamic scholarship. For example, the grade four class at Al Safar learned about the medieval scientist Ibn Al Haitham, who conducted the first experiments with optics and light refraction centuries before Isaac Newton, who nevertheless had been credited with these 'discoveries.' This is one example of how Islamic education contributes to the decolonization of knowledge and presents an anticolonial methodology for reclaiming historical narratives from Eurocentric discourses.

Amani talked about how she helped students understand that there was no inconsistency between science and the Qur'an, though Muslims might not validate all scientific theories:

AMANI: I tell them, 'Some people think when you are a scientist you are going against your belief.' And I tell them, 'Your aqeedah and your belief is a totally different thing. Science is all about theory that is explaining this natural phenomenon, so if you love and are interested in science and you believe in that theory, that doesn't mean that your beliefs are going to be affected.' In fact, we have an article called 'Islam and Dinosaurs.' It talks about evolution and how we as Muslims always take the middle way. We don't reject all the theories and we don't blindly accept all the theories. Whatever is according to Islam we accept, whatever is against it, clearly against it, we refuse. And we believe the whole universe is created and controlled by Allah, no questions. It doesn't mean that I don't teach them the other perspectives, I do teach them, because I say, 'You have to know these issues.' And the kids are very responsive, they understand. And we try to do so many, you know, activities and research work on that.

Amani was trying not just to centre the Islamic perspective but also to examine how it intersected with or deviated from other, more secular forms of knowledge. She saw empirical knowledge as a means to further both knowledge of science and knowledge of Islam. For Dr Ghulam, the administrator of an Islamic school that I visited during my research, there was no need to integrate Islamic knowledge. He contended that the facts pertaining to the Qur'an and science were self-evident:

GHULAM: Oh there's no need to integrate, there is already integration if you make a rational observation of the facts and figures. If you study Islam you will see that science has proved everything that is there in Islam. If you study the Holy Qur'an you will see that science is proving everything, so there is natural integration.

Other teachers used strategies that involved the students themselves linking the Qur'an to the subjects they were learning. Instead of making the connections for them, Ruqayyah would have them use the Qur'an as a primary source to complement their understanding of core subjects. In a unit about insects, she used the Qur'an to promote respect for these creatures and the environment by asking the students to examine the Qur'anic verses relating to bees and ants. Those stories reinforced the role of these insects in nature and their utility to human beings. This is an effective approach to connecting spiritual knowledge to environmental justice and sustainability. It is also a critical faith-centred approach.

For skilled teachers like Amira, who also excelled in Islamic studies, integrating the curriculum was a way to meet ministry guidelines for specific subject areas. This approach enabled students to meet those expectations in new ways:

AMIRA: What I do is I integrate the Islamic studies period and the language period. To me they're almost the same thing and I always have them back to back. Because Islamic studies, a lot of it is reading and writing, and we do a lot of vocabulary building with the words in the Qur'an, sentence structure, synonyms of words, using the dictionary, thesaurus, just things like that. They do a lot of oral reading when they read the verses in the Qur'an. It really gives them a lot of practice in reading and writing.

There is a pragmatic reason why such integration is important for Islamic pedagogy. Islamic schools add two extra subjects to the mandated curriculum: Islamic studies and Arabic language. As a result, teachers have more subjects to cover in a given school day. Integrating Islamic studies with other areas of the curriculum is, then, a holistic means for handling curricular demands, besides being more efficient.

Amira used opportunities provided in the curriculum to help students demystify knowledge from an Islamic perspective:

AMIRA: Now when they do the language program and we're reading stories, we always read the story and you know the children are asked, like, 'From what the Islamic perspective, if this person or character was a Muslim, what would they have done, or what should they have done?' When we look at stories in mythology, there's a lot of stories in the grade five and six program, so we talk about them, they read them, and then we talk about them from the Islamic perspective, like, 'Okay, according to Islam, can Allah change the creation of man to an animal or an animal to a man?' ... So we talk a lot about that, and then sometimes they even go back to the verses in the Qur'an and they talk about how Allah has created man [sic] and how Allah has created animals. So they get the both. And, you know, you teach them both, this is the belief of the Christians, and this is what some cultures believe in. So, they're made aware of that, okay, this is what some people believe in.

Rather than 'ghettoizing' students' knowledge, as many critics of separate religious schooling claim, Amira demonstrates a commitment to providing access to broad discursive knowledge, which she helped students filter through an Islamic lens. Islamic education provides students with an epistemological frame of reference through which they develop an understanding of the world, including traditions and beliefs different from their own. This knowledge is presented alongside Islamic knowledge as a means to examine the plurality of social and spiritual ideologies and beliefs.

Multicultural knowledge is integrated into Islamic schools in conformity with ministry guidelines for specific strands, such as the grade two social studies unit on traditions and celebrations. When I asked Mehrun, the principal at Al Safar, how diverse knowledge systems were brought into the children's education, she reminded me of what was happening in my own son's classroom:

MEHRUN: Your child is in Ruqayyah's class. As you know, they did multiculturalism, because in Islam there is no better race, everybody is equal, it's just the behaviour that sets them apart. If they are nice and kind, they are better people, if they're fighting and not cooperating, they need to improve.

Here, Mehrun is linking multicultural education to a broader spiritual imperative rooted in the Islamic tradition that promotes racial and ethno-cultural equity. This faith-centred perspective imbues antiracism with the power of Divine sanction, making it more imperative than purely existential understandings would be. In my son's class they did projects on diverse cultures; they also had a 'multicultural day,' during which other classes visited their class and viewed their projects and shared in different foods that the students had brought in as part of the project. Children generally focused on the various cultures represented in their families; thus there were projects about Pakistan, India, Malaysia, the Caribbean, the Middle East, and North Africa. While the emphasis on 'special days' in liberal approaches to multicultural education further compartmentalizes marginalized cultures, truly inclusive or multicentric practices are also not apparent in the public system. In this way Islamic schools are on par with the current status quo in education, although a more critical antiracism perspective is needed in both systems (see Dei, James, James-Wilson, Karumanchery, & Zine, 2000).

Yet not all teachers had such well thought-out ideas and methods for making relevant curricular connections. Rima, who was teaching the elementary level at Al Shawwal, discussed how she sometimes connected lessons about the physical environment to the divine Creation, reminding students of their social responsibilities as caretakers of the earth. But she agreed that her strategy was ad hoc in the sense that it exploited 'teachable moments' as they arose. She did not preplan specific lessons on this basis:

RIMA: No, it's not in my plan ... I'll plan it generally and then when I find the opportunity in the class, I'll bring it up right away and something clicks ... It's spontaneous for me. I feel that I'm more free to do that in an Islamic school than I would be in a public school.

Rima also raises an important issue here that several teachers also spoke of, that is, the freedom of being able to teach from a faith-centred perspective. For many teachers, this is the primary reason that they decide to teach in Islamic schools, sacrificing the higher pay and benefits they would receive in the public school system for the freedom to teach according to their values and religious ideology. For Rima, having the freedom to draw on Islamic epistemology to capture specific teachable moments in her class had even more personal satisfaction for her since she was unable to do this when she had taught back home in Egypt in a private British school. She spoke of how her attempts to integrate Islam were rejected by the British school authorities, even though she was teaching in a Muslim country:

RIMA: I had this problem even when I was in Egypt because the school was not made to be a Muslim school though most of the kids were Muslim. When I was in Egypt I had some Islamic songs and they did a concert every year. I wanted to bring in these Islamic songs and they refused it.

For Rima, then, integrating Islam was a means to challenge the Eurocentric colonization of knowledge in her homeland as well as in Canada.
Yet in one parent's view, Islamic knowledge was often centred to the detriment of more secular knowledge. Asma, an English-Canadian parent who had converted to Islam, felt at times that the school did not maintain an appropriate balance between religious and secular subjects:

ASMA: I think the school was missing the boat in that there were a lot of things in the curriculum that were not covered because the administration felt that it was not relevant to Islam and I felt that the administration should not be making that judgment. Very possibly the reason that subject matter – like medieval studies, for example – was not covered was because the teacher was not in complete control of the class, again, through no fault of his own. He ran out of time and he had to chop. That kind of thing would be the first to go because there isn't a lot of material that has an Islamic perspective on medieval studies.

The new Ontario curriculum required a great deal of material to be covered. Asma's concern was that Islamic schools would 'chop' certain mandated areas when they ran out of time, as opposed to sacrificing religious subjects.

Arabic: The Key to Islamic Literacy

Other parents did not highlight this concern; indeed, they worried that their children were not learning enough in subjects such as Arabic. Because it is the language of the Qur'an, Arabic is an important part of Islamic education. While all Islamic schools provide Arabic-language classes, some focus more on Qur'anic recitation, which doesn't necessarily involve understanding what is being read. Many Muslim children, especially those from South Asian families, attend classes for Qur'anic recitation in addition to what they learn in school. The goal is to finish 'reading' the Qur'an, which is more of a practice of 'decoding' the language, since they do not actually understand the words. Generally, Islamic schools with a higher number of Arab-speaking students place more emphasis on learning Arabic as a second language. Other schools – the ones that cater to a more South Asian population – place greater emphasis on reciting or memorizing the Qur'an.

Two of the schools in this study, Al Safar and Al Rajab, now offer *hifz* classes for memorizing the Qur'an. A person who has memorized the entire Qur'an is known as a *hafiz* and enjoys particular honour in the community besides gaining spiritual rewards. Many children take a two- or three-year sabbatical from their regular schooling in order to focus entirely on memorizing the Qur'an. Some *hifz* programs offer a half-day program of Qur'anic memorization; the other half-day is spent on math and English. Children who attend *hifz* classes occupy the prayer hall or another area of the school, where they are able to concentrate on memorization. Students sit in a circle on the floor with their Qur'an in front of them and rhythmically rock back and forth as they recite. These classes are overseen by a shaykh who is also a *hafiz*. In Islam, women are permitted to become *hafiz*; yet by tradition, only boys attend these classes. I have yet to see a young girl training to become a *hafiza* in any school program. This is another gender barrier that is erected out of the dominance of patriarchal standards rather than being referenced in any legitimate religious prohibition.

It troubled many parents who were not Arab speakers that they could not help their children with homework in this area. For Nadia, who was of Greek-Canadian heritage and a convert to Islam, it was important for her son and daughter to learn Arabic as part of their Islamic education; but as she did not speak Arabic, she found it difficult to support them in this. She found immersion in Arabic difficult without English translation:

NADIA: I don't know the Islamic curriculum very well. I just know what's in his homework. But the main concern for me about the Islamic curriculum is they don't have the English translation for most things. And like the Sister said, Arabic is not spoken at home. Greek, English, and Urdu's spoken at home so it's very hard for me and my husband sometimes to explain to him what the handouts mean, what the handouts are trying to say, or what he's writing when it comes to writing skills. Personally – being a new Muslim – I would like to have these (translations) for my learning experience, too ... To have the Arabic and then the English at the bottom like most material that the bookstores offer. Plus I will find that the children will more likely pick it up, too, when they have the English translation.

While coming from a multilingual home, neither Nadia nor her husband were proficient in Arabic. She was frustrated that the Arabic language materials her children used did not have translations in English. Many parents have tried learning Arabic alongside their children as part of their spiritual growth and also to help their children acquire the language.

According to Amani, children in Islamic schools whose parents do not adhere to Islamic practice at home experience dissonance and confusion between the conflicting standards of home and school:

AMANI: So Islam is taught through example and practice. So, this is one huge area where we have problems. The children whose parents don't practise Islam at home give us so much problem. Because they feel conflicted, they are saying, 'Who's right? My teacher or my parents? Because my parents don't do it this way.' So we are having this constant issue that we have to deal with these students. But those students whose parents practise Islam at home, it is very easy to teach them because they see the same example at home and they see the same example at school. For them it's a continuation process, you know? I mean, nothing is conflicting. So, these kids find it so easy being in this environment. For the others, they feel as if, and I tell you this from experience, they feel as if they have two identities.

To avoid another form of the 'double culture syndrome,' there must be congruence between the practices at home and those at school. Islamic schools cannot help children develop an Islamic identity unless this learning is reinforced and supported in the home.

Another aspect of the Islamization of knowledge that must be addressed relates to the criticality required when implementing Islamic teaching methodologies. As I emphasized earlier, moving from a faith-centred perspective to a *critical* faith-centred perspective involves rejecting rigid dogmatism and opening spaces for contestation and debate. Some teachers do integrate a variety of perspectives – albeit privileging and centring those which are rooted in an Islamic framework, this is not necessarily a uniform practice. Further, I would argue that, in order to be faithful to a critical faith-centred approach, this would involve re-examining many taken-for-granted aspects of the Islamic tradition, based on new scholarly perspectives, many of which have not yet gained currency in the traditional mainstream of Islamic thought. Broader discursive practices in Islamic epistemology and intellectual scholarly dialogues and debates have not filtered down to the level of Islamic schools. So it is not enough to simply integrate Islamic knowledge, but it is critical to be attentive to what *kind* of knowledge is being imparted and whether it sustains the core values and ethos of justice and equity in the Qur'an or whether it has become subservient to patriarchal or authoritarian orientations.

Teaching about Global Social Justice Issues

Extracurricular opportunities tend to be limited at Islamic schools. However, during my fieldwork at Al Rajab the female students in grades ten to twelve were bussed downtown to the U.S. Consulate in order to join a protest against economic sanctions against Iraq. I accompanied the students on this trip, as I was about to begin teaching a 'World Issues' class that focused on the Persian Gulf War. The field trip was organized by Sakhina, and after the school administrators were convinced that it was important for them as Muslims to speak out against injustice, they relented and supported the excursion. I will explore the views of the some of the students who participated in this event which represented the promotion of a politicized spirituality that was the basis for expressing solidarity with other disenfranchised Muslims as part of the global *ummah*. Before doing so, I examine the broader discursive context for addressing issues of global injustice in an Islamic school curriculum.

Islamizing Social Justice Education

All of the teachers I interviewed situated their approach to social justice issues within an Islamic framework. Amani told me that addressing social and environmental concerns is integral to Muslim identity:

AMANI: So this is one thing that I constantly tell the students about. Know what's going on, because being a good Muslim is not just praying and fasting, and dressing Islamically. Being a good Muslim is being a good human being, being a humanitarian, it's being a good citizen, following the laws. For example, we just finished a unit in life science about ecosystems, about waste management and conserving energy, and I say, 'These are Islamic things, this is not just science.' I bring them verses from the Qur'an, you know, Islam teaches us to conserve, to save, not to waste. So by helping the environment you are being a good Muslim. You know, when you are wasting you are hurting the environment and you are also being a bad Muslim.

Thus, Amani's pedagogy involved politicizing spirituality and Islamic identity within a framework of social and environmental justice. This kind of educational praxis negates the charges of 'intellectual ghettoization' often levelled against parochial schools. In fact, parochial schools open spaces for projects of social and political change. Amani went on to describe the efforts she had made to counteract the reticence that some students develop about issues affecting the broader society:

AMANI: I encourage the students to think about what's going on in the world. I constantly ask them to bring issues that are happening outside their community and their religion and to discuss this and be concerned about it. We live in the same country, the same world. Last year, when there was a controversy about pledging allegiance in the public school, I brought an editorial page and we discussed it, and I said, 'Why do you think people are angry and protesting this?' And they said, 'Why should we care, it's not for us, it's going on in the public school.' And I said, 'Well, these are your cousins, your friends, and you know, you will be going there in about two years

... It's an issue that concerns you and you should know about it.' So I do try to bring that perspective. Because you can't make changes working alone, saying that what's going on in the outside world is not going to affect me. Because everything is going to affect you ... Yes, you can think you're different, but you have to work to bridge that gap by helping the outsiders understand you, so you can't help them understand you unless you make an effort to understand them.

According to Amani, Muslims cannot afford to isolate themselves socially or politically. She argues for broader cross-cultural understanding between Muslims and Canadian society. She feels that developing a sense of social responsibility and civic engagement is integral to Islamic education. She has found that when she looks at education from this vantage point, it opens up opportunities for learning 'beyond the textbook.' She often ties analyses of contemporary social issues to examples from Islamic history and the life, or *seerah*, of the Prophet Muhammed. She roots her study of social justice issues in a critical faith-centred framework, and she does not valorize the Muslim world by presenting false dichotomies polarizing the 'angelic East' and the 'demonic West.' Instead, she critically examines the social conditions in each society:

AMANI: So I really enjoy those moments, because teaching is not just a textbook. There is a lot of teaching that goes on outside the classroom. I mean, whether it's affecting the Muslim countries or affecting humanity as a whole. That's what I mean by social awareness. The good thing is that we constantly tie it to an Islamic perspective. Islam teaches justice, Islam teaches equity. And in *seerah*, in fact, today we were discussing migration. How the Muslims, when they were persecuted, how they migrated. And I say, 'Why did we come to this country? Go and ask your parents why did they come to this country?' Because wherever they come from, they must have some kind of better freedom over here, better freedom of speech, the freedom to practise their *deen*, better opportunity. I mean, here you don't see class divisions as you see in some parts of the world. In the third world there's a huge class division, not everybody gets the same opportunity to learn, not everybody's voice is heard. Even the political elections, the election system doesn't work the same, so I constantly make them compare and think and make them see how lucky they are. I do it on an individual basis and I also do it on a macro scale. That's the part I enjoy. And it doesn't only happen in social studies, it happens in science, Islamic studies, everything is tied.

So, for Amani, instilling a critical yet faith-centred global worldview within students was an important aspect of their learning as Muslims and as Canadian citizens.

Developing Critical Literacy through World Issues

In my own teaching during the time I conducted fieldwork at Al Rajab, I tried to teach critical global literacy for my OAC-level World Issues course. I decided to teach a media literacy unit on the Persian Gulf War as a means to help students understand the politics of representational practices in the making of global crises and war. The course included the following: an examination of the political economy of war and the media; a study of propaganda and the manufacturing of consent for war; and issues of migrancy in postwar contexts, with particular attention on the differential impact of war on women. We also examined the conflicts in Kosovo and Chechnya, especially the effects of geopolitical conflict on Muslims in these regions. The course culminated in a school assembly, during which some students made presentations and there was a panel presentation featuring local and international community activists, who discussed refugee issues. Some of the students reflected on the critical lessons they gained from this course:

REHANA: Well, since we've been dealing with a lot of Islamic and Arab issues like that, I realized – you know, I had done a project on the Gulf War before, and I was always on the U.S. side. And now – yesterday I was reading this article about the media – you know, the one you gave us. It's just so unfair what happened in Iraq. But I wish Saddam Hussein would get a brain or something! I learned, like, how you taught us to read critically and things like that. Now when I read any article I'm like, 'Oh my God, look at this – Oh my goodness, look at that.' I just thought, 'Oh my gosh, I learned a lot.' And I'm really happy, I think I'm going to be able to use it in the future. Like, if I have any problems to do with Islam in my field, *insha'allah.*
AMAL: Before, I didn't even touch the newspaper. Now I feel like, 'What's going on – I want to see, I want to read this.' And the thing is, I was aware of everything, the problems we talked about, and

especially my dad. He's like, 'politics are politics' and we talked about it everyday.

REHANA: I think it would be much different if we were in public school, I think we'd get a whole different message. Before, I always used to be on the Western side, the American side, on the side of the U.S. Whenever I'd see any article I'd say, 'They are wrong,' the Arabs or whatever. Usually the wrong people now I think are the right ones. Because I've always grown up here so I'd think it was right – I was brainwashed by public school!

These students are describing how they developed a more critical consciousness and were less willing to take everything they read at face value. They were developing critical counternarratives to the hegemonic views promoted in the media and were learning to read between the lines and unravel the embedded interests and political motives behind global militarism. I encouraged them to take this knowledge from the level of awareness to activism by writing letters to the Canadian Foreign Affairs Minister about the Russian siege of Grozny, and by attending rallies and starting up petitions. These efforts introduced them to organized strategies for social resistance, which I hoped would be building blocks for future activism.

Examining Global Oppressions in Elementary Education: Avoiding the Minefields

It proved more difficult to develop social and political awareness among elementary school children. Ruqayyah was especially committed to addressing global concerns with her grade two students. We discussed how each year there was a new crisis in the Muslim world and how this sadly kept global issues in fresh relief. Ruqayyah spearheaded most of the efforts at Al Safar that were designed to respond to the local *and* global needs of Muslims affected by poverty, hunger, war, and displacement. Each year she organized the school's collection of food and money, which was then distributed in the month of Ramadan to local needy families. She also organized fundraising in the school to address global events affecting Muslims. Each year there was a new cause: Iraq, Palestine, Somalia, Bosnia, Kosovo, Chechnya, Afghanistan, and Iraq again. Each year, she would try to help her students understand what Muslims in these countries were experiencing, and she would find ways to promote activism among the student body. She described her frustration with such projects:

RUQAYYAH: Each year I have the same letter. I just draft it up and change the name [of the country]. And I'm like, 'Okay, why is this happening?' It's really sad, but the thing is, I want the kids to definitely know about it, *insha'allah*. It bothers me when people stay quiet about things like this because I think that's the least we can do. Again, being in a school like this, like I mentioned before ... being in a school period, you have the advantage ... You can mobilize the whole entire school population.

Ruqayyah spearheaded several efforts to mobile the children in her class and in the school at large. Every year she would have her students write letters to children in countries that were being affected by war and conflict, with messages of their support and solidarity. These letters would be posted on the walls of the school. One year, the students wrote letters to children in Kosovo. A prominent children's singer and songwriter in the Muslim community saw the letters and incorporated them into a song he wrote, 'The Letter.' The cassette was sold across North America to raise money for children in Kosovo. Later on, the children wrote letters to Iraqi children, and Ruqayyah sent those letters to a local newspaper in the hope that some of them would be printed. Unfortunately, the paper did not respond. Teachers like Ruqayyah viewed these activities as integral to Islamic learning and to developing an 'ummatic consciousness' – that is, awareness of the broader global community of Muslims.

Parents were generally in favour of these activities and were happy to support the school's efforts. Then one day Ruqayyah brought in a front-page article from a local newspaper that featured a photograph of a Palestinian boy who had been shot outside the Masjid Al Aqsa in Jerusalem. Many parents complained strongly about this, feeling that the photograph was too graphic for elementary children and might traumatize them. Ruqayyah disagreed that the picture was too graphic, pointing out that the image conveyed the global realities faced by Muslim children every day. She saw her action as a means of fighting injustice and creating awareness of the global plight of the Muslim world:

RUQAYYAH: We have to go against the injustice but support the people that are being oppressed whoever they are. That's what I'm trying to explain to them as well. But the unfortunate part is ... that it always happens against Muslims. I mean, who else is it happening against? Somalia, go anywhere ... It's happening against Muslims.

Yet I wondered whether this approach might also lead to a sense of victimization among these children, who would grow up witnessing the persecution and violence perpetrated against (and often by) other Muslims. In my interactions with youth in the community, I have noticed profound feelings of alienation – feelings that are a by-product of the 9/11 era and the ongoing imperialist military campaigns against Muslim lands. It is too early to tell whether Ruqayyah's lessons in global oppression will have such an effect on her students and whether they will result in greater social activism.

Ruqayyah mentioned one concern she had in her class as a result of bringing to light these geo-political conflicts, and that was the need to avoid the rise of feelings of anger among the children that were directed to specific groups that they felt were anti-Muslim. One parent complained that her child came home one day and declared, 'I hate Jews.' This was after he saw the picture of the boy who had been shot by Israeli soldiers. Ruqayyah was quick to debrief her students the next day. And she defended her strategies by reiterating that she had always promoted an anti-hatred platform. She reminded the children that she did not advocate hating anyone, and that many people from the Jewish community also opposed the occupation and were allies in the liberation process.

The Protest: Politicizing Spirituality

One of the most interesting and politically animating activities that the students at Al Rajab were involved in during the time I was conducting my fieldwork was a rally to protest economic sanctions against Iraq, which took place in September 2000. After gaining permission from the administration, Sakhina arranged for the students to be bussed downtown to march to the U.S. Consulate. In the week leading up, the girls prepared signs to carry; They also developed chants such as, 'One-Two-Three-Four! Sanctions only kill the poor! Five-Six-Seven-Eight! Stop the war! Stop the hate!' Sakhina explained why she wanted them to participate, and she spoke of some parents' fears regarding their daughters' participation:

SAKHINA: I'd like for them ... instead of being in their mental enclave, to actually extend it to the global. It's one thing to say, 'Okay, yeah, I'm really sad that they're getting killed in Chechnya,' but it's another thing to actually teach them how to do something about it.

Even like, for instance, the protest – a lot of them didn't even know what a protest was. I had parents calling me and asking me, 'Will they be safe? Will they get shot?'

JASMIN: Really? They were concerned about them being shot?

SAKHINA: Being shot because they're visibly Muslims, because they have to go in their uniforms, even those who don't normally wear hijab or *jilbab*.

The parents' fears were not so surprising, considering that many had come from countries where political protest can lead to violence. They needed to be reassured that their daughters would be safe, especially since their school uniforms would mark them as Muslims. In this regard, the students were more concerned about how they would be perceived wearing their abayas and hijabs than they were about their safety:

SAKHINA: The main thing that kept coming up with the students wasn't even about the protest. It was, 'But everybody's going to see us in our uniforms and then we're going to look so funny.' They worried how everybody else – those outside looking in – would look at them. I said, 'You don't have to worry about that. If you're going for the purpose, you're doing something for the greater community – the global community, your Muslim brothers and sisters across the world.' And even if they weren't Muslim, it's something that you should believe in. Nobody should be fighting people who can't defend themselves.

Sakhina was trying to help the girls overcome their self-consciousness about being at a public event in Islamic dress by reinforcing the broader political goals they were going there to advocate.

About one hundred girls attended the protest, all wearing the maroon abaya and white headscarf. They were the largest group at the rally. The protesters, who were predominantly Muslim, gathered for speeches at the Provincial Parliament and then marched a few blocks to the U.S. Consulate. This was a unique opportunity for the students to publicly express their solidarity with their fellow Muslims in Iraq and to voice their opposition to the violence of economic sanctions. They considered it their duty as Muslims to stand up against social injustice.

At the protest, the girls received gestures of support from passing motorists, who responded to one of their signs that said: 'Honk if you support us!' But they also encountered hostile and Islamophobic attitudes. I asked some of the girls to reflect on that day:

JASMIN: So what's your reflection on that experience?
SAFIA: Oh there was a lot of staring !
UMBREEN: I felt so uncomfortable!
SAHAR: A lot of people had negative attitudes!
SAFIA: And a lot of people would yell and they'd be swearing out the window and everything.
UMBREEN: Yeah, people were saying, 'Go back home!'
SAHAR: Yeah they were swearing at us and stuff!
SAFIA: Yeah, exactly. And I remember when I was walking I heard some man, you know how the men [in the protest], they were screaming really loud, right? So somebody went by and they said, 'Oh God, what's this all about? It's so loud they're going to break our ears!' They're causing so much noise and stuff. Yet if they were a bunch of other people that were protesting about something like, oh, women, 'We want to be topless,' they'd be okay about that. They'd say, 'Yeah, okay, protest all your rights, do what you want.' But when it comes to Islam, they're like, 'What are you doing? Go home!'
JASMIN: You thought the reaction was because you were Muslims and very visible?
SAHAR: Yeah, like, if we were out there saying, 'We want to be topless,' everyone would be saying, 'Okay, fine. Go for it!' But if you stick up for your rights and stand for what you believe in, then it's like: 'Who cares about you! What you say is not going to do anything so just stop talking!'

The girls felt alienated by the negative, racist, and xenophobic attitudes they encountered. They were certain that, had they not been identifiable as Muslims and had their cause been more consonant with what mainstream society would support, they would not have generated that kind of hostility from passers-by. As racialized and religiously minoritized women, they felt that their voices were not being validated as a legitimate exercise of political conscience. They had been positioned as foreigners and outsiders and as outside the broader Canadian narrative; indeed, they were being exiled by public hostility towards their Muslim identity.

Not all the girls remained silent and reticent during the verbal assaults. Some responded in kind, making the situation worse. This was not the decorum expected from 'pious Muslim girls,' but some of them were angry about being harassed while exercising their right to peaceful protest. The rally, overall, had a strong impact on the girls and their sense of identity as Muslims and Canadians. Many of them blamed their Islamic dress for provoking the negative reactions. For those who do not usually wear their abayas outside school, it was especially difficult:

SAFIA: I'm not used to it. Because I go out but I don't wear a maroon abaya that attracts so much attention, right? The teachers, they should have at least let us go in something that wouldn't attract so much attention. Okay, maybe we have to be covered, of course, but the maroon abayas, they made us look like turkeys on the street, so I think that's why we had even more attention. Because everybody kind of looks the same. But if we had had our own clothes on, okay, of course we have to be covered and represent Islam, but the turkey outfits did not go over well!

Safia saw their Islamic dress as too provocative for a public forum and felt that it overshadowed their voice, in a sense detracting from the message they were there to send. Instead of focusing on the racism and intolerance they faced, she allowed these attitudes to reinforce her personal sense of self-consciousness and self-blame.

The girls reported that at one point during the march, a woman who was stopped at an intersection became so incensed at the presence of these girls outside the U.S. Consulate that, in the words of Umbreen, 'She was about to get out of the car and hit somebody!' Some of the other students described this incident and had a different explanation for people's reactions:

LEILA: I think they were scared.
DEQA: I think they were surprised. They expect Muslim women to be oppressed at home, [and then they] see so many young Muslim women with hijab speaking up. You know, I think it sent out a good message.
LEILA: They were scared!
DEQA: And they were surprised. Some of them were surprised, some of them were scared, some of them were annoyed. It was just all mixed reactions.

LEILA: It was funny. That woman that stopped her car and said,
'What are you all doing? Go home! Go home!' She started like,
yelling out things and then the car behind her started honking at
her. And she had to leave. But it was funny!
JASMIN: So she stopped her car to yell out things?
LEILA: Like get a life!
DEQA: I guess she felt disturbed. 'What are they doing here?' and
stuff like that.
JASMIN: So would you like to do things like that as group again
through the school? Do you think it's important to participate in
events like that?
DEQA: It's important to support your people. Very, very, important.
And the more people that show up the more that you show people
that we are strong.

The rally served as a moment of politicization for these girls: they
now began to understand how space is racialized and delimited by
others. They had claimed that event as a space of spiritual praxis: from
now on they would link their actions to the desire to fight injustice
through public dissent. As young Muslim women, they had begun to
rupture stereotypes and to combat gendered Islamophobia by claiming a voice and defying those who cast them as voiceless and politically immature. For Leila, protests like these were a powerful avenue
for Muslim women to challenge the stereotypes associated with their
identity. She saw the rally as a means for empowerment and raising
not only the consciousness and solidarity of Muslims but also their
self-esteem:

LEILA: You're encouraging the girls over here to actually stand out.
Because they're getting the idea that the Muslim sisters have to
stay home, and so on. Because that's what they learn, from public
school and stuff like that – that Muslim women are oppressed. But
then they come here and they see that we're actually doing something and that encourages them to not feel low. It makes them like,
'Okay, I'm a Muslim and I'm not low. I'm standing up for my
people. I can do that.' You know? It teaches them that, in fact, you
have to go out and like, stop what people are doing. And then later
on *insha'allah*, they'll grow really strong, you know? And they'll
learn, 'Okay, yeah, we got the power.'

Therefore, field trips such as this were powerful pedagogical strategies that led these young women on a journey of political and self-awareness.

Towards a 'Pedagogy of the Oppressed': Public Protest as Education for Social Political Empowerment

Most of the girls found the protest an empowering and exhilarating experience, despite the negative feedback from passers-by. They framed their experience that day as building a stronger political and spiritual connection with the Muslim *ummah*; but they were otherwise sceptical of any impact that their protest had on a larger geo-political scale:

LEILA: I think it was like, really, really good. That was the first time I'd ever done anything to stand up against, like, what the non-Muslims are doing against our Muslim brethren back home. So it was like, a very good experience. And it taught you that, no matter what, you have to always stand up for your brothers. Even if you're alone, try it. Because like, the Muslims are supposed to be one body. So if one part is hurting then the whole part is hurting, you know?

DEQA: Personally, I enjoyed seeing so many Muslims coming together and all speaking as one voice. I didn't think it was useful, I mean, in my eyes it didn't affect anything that was going on back there [in Iraq], but it affected the unity here. And I think it was useful in that sense.

Similarly, Safia also did not feel that their efforts were validated by the powers that be or by Canadian society at large. Her views came from a space of alienation and disenfranchisement as she spoke of how she perceived society at large would react to their protestation against the plight of Muslims:

SAFIA: Everyone, all the Muslim people who were protesting, they were really into it. Even though in their hearts they knew it wasn't going to do anything. Because the Canadian people don't care, you could protest for like, years and years and they're not going to care. They're just going to ignore you. Or they'll send you home or threaten to send you to jail so that everyone will get scared off and

leave. Yet some people don't really care, they'll stay and then
they'll cause problems. And then it makes Muslims look bad
because they'll say they don't even listen to us ... because then
people think, 'Oh they're just refugees, they're taking welfare ...
immigrants this and that. They're illegal.'

Safia had developed a perception of how her dissent was positioned
by others in Canadian society. She felt repressed, owing to the negative
reactions the rally had generated. The negative aspects of the experience seemed to reinforce some girls' feelings of alienation – their sense
that they were not viewed as legitimate participants on the public
square. Fortunately students saw other benefits in attending the
protest that would hopefully keep this sense of despondency from
leading them into political paralysis or apathy.

Sakhina noted that some passers-by had honked their car horns in
solidarity with the protesters. She hoped this would teach the students
that there actually was some support to ending the sanctions, more
than what was suggested by the events of that day:

SAKHINA: And people honked. And, like, oh my God, this White
guy, he honked ... and in the cars and everything. People were
honking. They agreed with us. And that was, oh, interesting.
Because there are certain commonalities throughout humanity.
Like, you're against injustice and it was an eye-opener for them
in the sense that, okay, maybe just because everybody's not
Muslim doesn't mean they can't agree on things. So in that sense
it was eye-opening too.

There was a disturbing sense of 'surprise' in the girls' comments
about the passers-by, as if they had been *expecting* resistance to their
cause. It was distressing to see this level of alienation in their reactions
– distressing, but also understandable when one considers the racism,
Islamophobia, and social disenfranchisement that produce these sentiments. In this regard, Deqa viewed the rally as a catalyst for building
social awareness among the students. Until it was held she had not
realized that it was possible for them to organize and engage in public
dissent. She saw this experience as directly connected to Islamic education, which she felt included politics as an intrinsic aspect of social
life and Islamic epistemology:

DEQA: I think, like, most people in this school lack political awareness. They rarely know anything about what's going on. And basically their concern is about the hijab or whatever, but Islam is beyond that – it's a way of life, and politics is part of life, it is part of Islam. It's not just the school – Muslims in general avoid that part of Islam, because it's too dangerous, too confusing. But I disagree with that. Especially in an Islamic school raising young children – the future of the *ummah* – basically they have to give them that kind of awareness.

Thus, participation in this protest became an entry point into some of the more politicized aspects of Muslim identity. Students like Deqa were happy to take up the challenge as part of their identity as Muslim women.

As a follow-up to the protest, Sakhina had the students write down their reflections. She shared some highlights from these reports:

SAKHINA: What happened was they wrote essays on their trip. It didn't even have to be about the protest itself. Some of them actually wrote that 'Well, when I was going, I was so nervous about wearing the hijab and the *jilbab* and the uniform and everything but then we started marching and we started yelling and we started chanting, and after a while I forgot about anybody looking at me. I didn't care because I was there for a greater purpose.' That's their own words. It was just like, 'Wow!' So then afterwards we kind of had a debriefing the next day. On the Monday I talked to them and I said, 'So how did you feel about the protest and everything?' They were like, 'It was really cool to see so many Muslims and so openly. We all prayed *jumuah* [Friday prayer] at Queen's Park. It was just so cool. We all ate lunch together and we fought for our cause.'

Overall, the trepidation the girls felt about being in their Islamic attire and marching en masse at the protest gave way to feelings of unity and solidarity in a just cause, despite the negative responses. From a popular education perspective, I felt that the protest was an important pedagogical moment that opened up new critical vistas for understanding the world. I relate this to Freire's (1973) conception of *Conscientizacao* or 'conscientization, which refers to learning to perceive social, political, and economic contradictions and to take action against the oppressive elements of reality (p. 19). As these young women became aware of their racialization and their Islamization and all that is socially and politically embodied from that location, they were able to participate in a demonstration of resistance, using their Islamic spirituality to raise their voices against injustice. They rooted their actions from within a critical faith-centred vantage point, where religion is not only a site of oppression but also a site of resistance. In creating a pedagogy for the oppressed, Freire (1973) reminded us of this need to critically galvanize our consciousness in the direction of transformative possibilities: 'Every human being (no matter how "ignorant" or submerged in the "culture of silence") is capable of looking critically at his world in a dialogical encounter with others. Provided with the proper tools for such an encounter, he can gradually perceive his personal and social reality as well as the contradictions in it, become conscious of his own perception of that reality, and deal critically with it' (p. 13).

The Islamization of knowledge and praxis in Islamic schools, in the examples we have seen, attempts to provide students with a critical understanding of these local and global realities. Instead of isolating them from the world and confining them to intellectual ghettos, as critics of separate parochial schools charge (Gutmann, 1996; Callon, 1997; Jafri & Fatah, 2003), students are provided with opportunities to view a variety of physical, social, and political realities through a holistic lens rooted in a spiritual context that advocates social responsibility and action. Islamic education, when delivered from a critical faith-centred perspective, turns out to be essential for navigating the contradictions and complexities faced by diasporic Muslims who reside in culturally hybrid spaces. It provides a site of social critique, resistance, and transformation and is the entry point through which Muslims can access the broader public square. This aspect of Islamic education is an important pedagogical means for Muslim children and youth to locate their struggle to claim their identities as both Muslims and Canadians.

8 The Politics of Teaching and Learning in Islamic Schools

This chapter explores the politics of teaching and learning in Islamic schools by examining the curricular and pedagogical strengths and challenges identified by the various educational stakeholders. The primary challenges for Islamic schools are social, organizational, and economic. The narratives of teachers, students, and parents highlight the pressing issues facing these under-resourced independent community-based schools.

Academic Standards and Supports

As independent institutions, Islamic schools do not receive funding beyond the tuition they charge (which, at the four schools in this study, ranged from $250 to $300 per month). Nevertheless, many parents at Al Safar spoke highly of the academic standards at their school, which boasted among the best facilities of all the Toronto-area Islamic schools and which hired only certified teachers. Shahnaz, for example, felt that standards were higher at Al Safar than at many public schools:

SHAHNAZ: In this school, education-wise, I feel it's excellent. I feel education-wise that they're getting quite a bit, in fact, more than the other schools. I do hear my friends at work ... and their kids are in similar grades. When I talk about what Sohail and Amir are doing in school and when they say what their kids are doing in school, I think our kids are far advanced in the Islamic school. Even though the curriculum is the same, they have done more and over.

Al Safar was the only school in this study that participated in provincial standardized testing (EQAO)[1] for grades three and six.

Every year, results are posted prominently in the main hallway of the school; they demonstrate that Al Safar students are at least on par with when not more advanced than public school students. Few other Islamic schools have participated in EQAO provincial testing, owing to the costs involved to the schools. At Al Shawwal and other schools, parents have been advocating for these tests as a means of accountability and in order to see how their children measure up to provincial standards. Standardized tests, however, do not take into account social and cultural variables such as class and newcomer status. This would distinguish many Islamic schools from one another as well as from their public counterparts.

For example, Al Safar students are mainly from South Asian families, although many other ethnicities are represented at the school. Moreover, most of the parents there are professionals with good English-language skills who have already integrated well with Canadian society; this has allowed them to gain the necessary 'cultural capital' to help their children negotiate the educational system in Canada. At Al Shawwal, by contrast, most of the parents are recent immigrants from the Middle East and Somalia and have low incomes.

For many parents who are recent immigrants and refugees, English is a second language and their knowledge of Canada's educational system is highly limited. Because Islamic schools lack the resources to provide ESL support or special education, many children do not find the assistance they need. Such factors inevitably affect the results of standardized tests; the validity of such tests is rather dubious because those factors are not considered.

Special Needs Students

During my fieldwork at Al Shaban, I noticed that the school was accepting special-needs children despite the absence of special-education teachers. I spoke with the principal, brother Hashim, about my concerns for these children and suggested that they would be better off in public schools, where they would get the support they needed. He balked at this suggestion, feeling that it was an Islamic 'duty' to accommodate these children, not to banish them to the less desirable moral environment of the public schools. He felt that he could not turn parents down simply because the school did not have the capacity to assist these children. Yet, in my observations I found this to be a great disservice to these children and their families.

Two children in particular had very obvious special needs: an eight-year-old Arab girl with Down's syndrome whose parents were new to Canada and fearful of the public education system; and a nine-year-old Guyanese boy, also from a newcomer family, who appeared to have autism (in my lay opinion). Most often, I found these children wandering the hallways or sitting at the back of the class with nothing to do. Teachers were not equipped or experienced to deal with these children's needs, and many simply let them wander around the school (as opposed to disrupting classes). Other children did not play with them, and in the indoor play area (there was no outdoor facility), which was often unsupervised, I observed children harassing them. I intervened in these situations, and often a teacher would notice and come and chastise the children for their behaviour, but the children who were victimized were still left on their own. I was deeply saddened and disturbed by the situation of these children; whatever the principal's 'good intentions,' I felt it was an injustice as well as a display of arrogance: the public system was also underfunded, but even so it was in a much better position to help these children. All too often, Muslim school communities engage in unnecessary 'scare-mongering' against public schools, to the detriment of students who would fare much better in the public system.

Smaller Class Sizes and Strategies for Remedial Support

In other areas, Islamic schools did offer academic benefits. The students told me that the smaller class sizes allowed for more individual attention. Deqa and Iman from Al Rajab discussed this:

DEQA: Basically we study the same things other schools study. Academically it's actually better, because there are less students in a class, you know, more attention the teacher can give you. It's more comfortable this way.

IMAN: It's the same, basically, as my friend said, but also there is a smaller group and it's more helpful when you need tutoring or stuff like that. The teacher gives you more attention. It's very easy, but education-wise this school does not differ from any other school. We do exams at the same time and we learn the same topics so it's the same.

Farzana, another Al Rajab student, appreciated the fact that all secondary-level courses were at the advanced level. This was a benefit to these racially minoritized students, who in the public system would often have found themselves channelled into lower, non-academic streams (see Dei, Mazzuca, McIsaac, & Zine, 1997; Zine, 2001b). However, in such a curriculum there must be strategies to support students who are having difficulties coping with advanced levels. In this regard, the students at Al Rajab felt well supported. Because class sizes were smaller, there were more opportunities to get assistance from teachers. Students, both male and female, felt encouraged to excel academically.

One of the strategies the students cited that was designed to help support those who were getting lower grades was referred to as the 'Green Book.' This book was given to students whose grades fell below 60 per cent; the teachers, students, parents, and school administrators used it to communicate with one another. Each day the teacher would write comments about the student's performance, which were discussed with the student and then had to be signed by the parents and reviewed by the principal. This was a method of 'keeping tabs' on students who were not performing well academically. Students had mixed views about this system. Some felt that it did help keep them on track; others felt stigmatized by the Green Book and reported that it made them feel 'dumb.' Some commented that they didn't think that the boys in the school were given the book – an example of how they remained attuned to the school's gendered double standards.

Gender Equity in the Curriculum and Academic Expectations

As I discussed earlier, I did encounter double standards at Al Rajab at the social level. But at the academic level, the girls were very much encouraged to excel in all subject areas, including traditionally male-dominated subjects like math and science. The school also promoted public speaking contests, art competitions, and science fairs, all of which the female students dominated. I served as a judge during the public speaking competitions and was greatly impressed by the performances of the students, who ranged in age from eight to eighteen. It is important to encourage young Muslim women to become proficient public speakers so that they can claim a voice and gain the confidence to express themselves. Recently, Al Safar held its first public speaking competition. I attended the junior finals, as my son was a contender. Of the eight finalists in the junior division, six were girls, and three of the girls were chosen the winners. I was disappointed that my son lost, yet I was heartened to see these young girls claiming a voice in the public arena.

I was invited as a keynote speaker to Al Rajab's science fair, which is held annually at a nearby civic centre. I was greatly impressed by the projects the girls displayed, which were highly innovative. From my experience, I knew that while the teachers were supportive, much of the impetus to excel at these projects came from the girls themselves and from the culture of success and sisterhood they had developed. The boys also participated, but because there were fewer of them and they were less mature in many ways, they were usually eclipsed by these dynamic young women. It was heartening to see the girls in these Islamic schools excel academically and not face any obvious gender barriers. At the recent award ceremonies at Al Safar, girls were top among the winners at various levels of academic, artistic, social, and physical achievement.

These findings run counter to popular notions that Islamic schools relegate young Muslim girls to subjects that will enhance their 'value' as wives and mothers. The Swann Report on educational equity in Britain makes that very claim: 'From the statements which have been made by spokesmen of the Muslim community, however, it is clear that the form of single-sex education, which at least some are advocating for girls would entail a far more central focus in the curriculum on education for marriage and motherhood in a particular Islamic sense, with other subjects receiving less attention and with notions of career education as being seen as irrelevant to the pattern of adult life which the girls are likely to pursue' (Swann, 1985, p. 505, in Hawe, 1998, p. 135). Such criticism may be based partly on community attitudes but is perhaps also influenced by Islamophobia. Despite the conservatism in many of these schools, academically young Muslim girls in Canadian Islamic schools are not hindered in their academic pursuits.

Economic Barriers: Lack of Resources

As underfunded, independent, community-based schools, Islamic schools cannot afford all the amenities enjoyed by fully funded schools. The students at Al Rajab, for example, yearned for a proper library instead of the makeshift room with out-of-date books, which was all they had. Fortunately, since the time of my interviews, Al Rajab has moved to a new facility; now it does have a library, as well as a cafeteria and a large computer room. The school also leases space from a neighbouring building for a gymnasium, meeting hall, and congregational prayer room.

. Students also told me they wanted more course offerings as well as guidance counsellors to help them choose careers. Aliyah, for example, wanted to be a lawyer, but the school did not offer any law courses. Other students wanted more arts courses, such as drama. Rehana planned on a business career, so she wanted more courses in areas such as marketing. At the time, there was only one class in this area, and it was boys only, since there was less interest among the girls. Information technology courses were, however, available for both boys and girls, and many girls expressed an interest in working in that field. Many students were gravitating towards the sciences in the hope of pursuing a medical career. Some students complained that they did not have the opportunities that public students did to work in a co-op setting that would help provide them with opportunities to refine their career choices.

Because of financial constraints, course choices were more limited than those offered by the public system. However, Al Rajab is making progress in this and has even opened an accredited post-secondary college adjacent to its high school that offers a broad range of diplomas in medical, technological, and business-related fields as well as a liberal arts program. This demonstrates that progress is possible over time despite very real economic and social barriers. All the students I interviewed expressed a strong desire to continue on to post-secondary education. Many Al Rajab graduates had received university scholarships, and the school proudly displayed their acceptance letters and awards in the lobby. Some female students told me that their parents worried about sending them to a co-ed environment. At least one student, Farzana, had decided to go for a distance learning program as a result. The fact that Al Rajab has now expanded its academic enterprise to include post-secondary education means that families such as Farzana's will be less fearful about allowing their daughters to continue their education in a 'safer' social environment.

The Need for Arts and Extracurricular Activities

Some parents told me that their children's school could still do more to promote excellence. Rukhsana felt comfortable with the academic progress of her children but felt that there could be more emphasis on creativity:

RUKHSANA: Academic issues? No, I think they're doing fine. My kids like it. But they don't have enough arts and crafts. I find that you need the motor skills. They do have centres. I don't think they use them. I think they're more academic bound. I think that they need to use it. It's good that you know how to use your brain and to think and to do your math and your spelling. [But] you have to have some other creativity too. It can't be complete structure.

Other parents and students also complained that there was not enough emphasis on creative arts and that the schools needed extra-curricular activities. Shahnaz felt that children needed to develop in areas besides academic ones. In her view, schools needed to consider the physical and emotional well-being of students as well as their intellectual progress:

SHAHNAZ: I would like to see a running club. Like, you know, kids do something when they go out. You just don't go to school to study. You just don't go to build up your mental well-being. You have to build up yourself emotionally and physically too. Right? So intellectually you are stimulated there but what about your physical and your emotional? Emotional and physical needs are not being met in the school. Intellectually, yes. Okay, fine, intellec- tually, but there are two other needs which are lacked greatly in that school.

To boost children's self-esteem she suggested drama courses, debat- ing clubs, and public speaking courses. She felt that when her chil- dren participated in these activities in public school, they were more self-assured and confident, and she was concerned that they were becoming more shy and withdrawn. She strongly advocated more opportunities for children to round out their academic pursuits with other activities that would develop them in different areas of their personality.

Leadership development was another area for growth and development that was not well attended to in the schools. Nusaybah noted that at Al Rajab, there were fewer opportunities than in public schools to become involved in activities such as student councils:

NUSAYBAH: Student council is really fun. Like, I've been president twice in grade ten. And it's really fun. You get to be involved in so many things. You do fundraising and so many things. You're just a *part* of things.

Students like Nusaybah missed the leadership opportunities these activities offered. Aliyah described a yearbook project that students at Al Rajab initiated, which didn't come into fruition since the school administration didn't follow through on the project. She had taken pride in the initiative and was disheartened that it did not progress:

ALIYAH: That [yearbook project] was thought up by us. We wanted to do that. And we all worked on it. All the students that wanted to do it, we had a yearbook committee and everyone pitched in and did their part and everything and it was finished. But it never got distributed.

There was little support for student-based organizing at the school unless it was to raise funds to benefit the school. Students participated in weekly bake sales to help raise money for the school. Yet they wanted to see other kinds of activities that were based on *their* interests. While the schools did have parties for religious celebrations, some students recalled the social activities in their public school – for example, auctions where girls and guys were auctioned off for fun and to raise funds for the school. They recognized that these activities might not be appropriate for Islamic schools, but they wanted to have other halal (i.e., Islamically suitable) activities to engage in. Muslim youth in the community are seeking alternatives to mixed parties and raves. To address this, some Muslim youth organizations have begun staging 'alternative proms.' These are gender-segregated events that feature magicians, invited speakers, and comedy troupes. Such events are an outlet for Muslim youth who want to have active social lives while maintaining their Islamic sensibilities and boundaries.

Students also wanted more physical activities. They recalled the sports programs they were involved with in public school and spoke of the need for Islamic schools to develop extracurricular sports, especially for girls, who were constricted by their dress code. Saira explained:

SAIRA: I was in a couple of sport programs, and stuff like that. But sometimes it's kind of difficult because they're not all Muslim and you have to be dressed properly all the time, and ... you know, you have to be careful, you have to stay at your boundaries and at your limits, and you can't go wrong.

The girls at Al Rajab spoke of the activities they had participated in while attending the public system. At one time or another, Aliyah, Zarqa, and Nusaybah had been involved in everything from swimming to soccer to track and field. Their involvement in sports lessened as they grew older and faced family pressure not to engage in 'immodest' activities where they would have to be seen in public in inappropriate attire such as shorts or bathing suits. As a corrective to these prohibitions, these girls anxiously look to Islamic institutions such as schools to provide alternative programs that Muslim women can fully participate in and feel comfortable in terms of their dress. At present, Islamic schools provide little outside the physical educational programming mandated by the Ontario curriculum. Where schools lack adequate gymnasium facilities (such as at Al Rajab and Al Shaban), the opportunities are even more limited. Few teachers in Islamic schools have coaching experience or are specialists in physical education. Physical education is sometimes a 'free-time' activity during which the girls do whatever they want with little instruction or supervision. There is more emphasis on organized and competitive sports on the boys' side.

Nusaybah, Aliyah, and Zarqa lamented that they had grown 'lazy' because of the limited physical opportunities for young Muslim women:

NUSAYBAH: I think we should still do it [be active]. Even if it's not in school, then we should do it, like, after school. I mean, we're sitting and studying at home, we're being so lazy, just watching TV. We're not even going out for a walk. I used to go out for a walk every single day last year when I used to go to my high school. But now I don't even do it anymore, I've become so lazy.

ALIYAH: I really like swimming a lot. And we used to do that in my public school. We used to have a turn where we'd go swimming every day for gym. It was a lot of fun and we got a lot of exercise because swimming is such good exercise for the body. But here we feel like ... Do you guys ever feel tired?

ZARQA: I feel tired.

NUSAYBAH: I feel tired.

Iman was more patient with the school's lack of extracurricular activities and seemed accepting of the social constraints that made these activities difficult to arrange:

IMAN: Since the population of the school is very small it's hard to have extracurricular activities after school. It's also like, very tough, because that's the whole reason for coming to an Islamic school is to be surrounded by your friends, but at the same time, you have to be home by that certain time. Most of the parents try to keep their daughter well-guarded. We're not doing anything negative here, it's just that if we had any extracurricular activities that are positive ... at this time it's not open, but it will be, *insha'allah*. One day they'll open up.

In Iman's view, family pressure and the need to keep Muslim girls 'well guarded' were making extracurricular activities difficult. Yet she remained hopeful that these opportunities would materialize. She observed, accurately, that Muslim parents would feel more comfortable if their daughters' activities were organized through Islamic schools or mosques. Yet to date, the only such opportunities are a few 'women's only' swimming programs offered by the City of Toronto's public pools and a Muslim girls' soccer team that recently began (which is only for girls up to the age of puberty). Presumably, the organizers feel that after this age it inappropriate for 'pious Muslim girls' to be involved in public sports. Therefore, due to the practical and discursive constraints limiting physical opportunities for Muslim women, more efforts need to take place to create better opportunities for them to lead full and active lives. To ensure that they are physically fit, alternative programs need to be raised higher on the list of community priorities.

The male students at Al Rajab reported that they had cut down on extracurricular activities since entering Islamic school. According to Kamal and Daood, Muslim boys do not face the same dress restrictions, so there are more opportunities for them to get involved in sports and other activities outside the school. Even so, they had curtailed their activities in order to focus harder on their studies. While they noted that they had previously played basketball and joined hockey leagues, they felt that they now needed to concentrate on academics in order to prepare for university. For both boys and girls, however, it was clear that Islamic schools were not providing adequate opportunities for extracurricular activities that would enrich their growth and learning. A primary reason for this shortcoming is most likely connected to the lack of funding and resources that make it difficult for schools to pay teachers to take on the extra responsibilities.

Teaching in Islamic Schools: Benefits and Drawbacks

For teachers in Islamic schools, low wages are a major concern. As independent community-based schools, Islamic schools generally keep tuition fees as low as possible to make access equitable, particularly for low-income families. As a result, teachers' salaries suffer and this often leads to a high turnover. Teachers who have certification are sometimes compelled to transfer into public schools in order earn enough to support their families. And teachers who lack certification reluctantly accept low wages in order to gain experience that will help them qualify for teacher education programs, or they do so because they cannot afford to take time from teaching to enrol in a certification program that would qualify them to teach in the public system. Yet other teachers, even some with certification, prefer the Islamic school setting for a variety of reasons. I asked teachers about the benefits and drawbacks of teaching in Islamic schools and explored their reasons for being in an Islamic school setting.

Ruqayyah, who does have her Ontario Teacher's Certificate (OTC) and who did her practicum in the public system, admitted that she felt tempted to transfer to the public system. She enjoyed the diversity of public schools; in the end, though, she was drawn to the idea of working and teaching in a faith-centred environment:

RUQAYYAH: First of all, I love to do Islamic studies. That's one thing I really enjoy. I enjoy the fact that I'm able to relay to the kids whatever I learn, things about our history. Just the whole thing. For me personally, it's amazing just to hear the *adhan*[2] every day. The kids that graduated from here last year, they said that's one thing they took for granted, being able to hear the *adhan*, and now that they're in a public school, they don't hear it. I know public schools have a lot of pros as well. Being there would be amazing also ... I've always liked meeting people from different races or religions. Being with people of your kind is nice and everything as well, but I enjoy meeting other people too.

Besides being able to hear and respond to the *adhan* at appointed times throughout the day, Ruqqayah appreciated the cultural congruence in Islamic schools: she did not have to compromise her values and beliefs when she taught. In the public system Ruqqayah noted that she would have felt uncomfortable teaching things like Halloween, which she considered problematic from an Islamic perspective. She wanted to expose her students to broader cultural horizons by making them aware of other traditions and ways of life, but she wanted to do so without having to centre these, as is done in the public education system:

RUQAYYAH: We don't have to teach what we don't actually believe in, things like, Halloween, everything. We don't have to, but because it's in the curriculum, all these different traditions, I want them to know about it. I don't want them to live in a bubble or something and not realize what's going on around them.

Amira, a certified teacher with a Master of Science degree, also preferred teaching in Islamic school. She understood the challenges her students faced, having faced them herself, and now she wanted to contribute to the community by providing guidance and motivation to young people:

AMIRA: I guess the biggest reason was that I felt I wanted to put my energy towards Muslim children. I felt I had something to offer them, being a Muslim myself and understanding the issues and the struggles they would face, because I myself grew up and I went through the public system, and I knew the struggles. I thought, 'I'm a teacher,' and once I had my qualifications I wanted to just put my energy towards the Muslim children so that they would have an easier way, easier schooling experience, a more enjoyable one, too. And a motivating one as well.

Sakhina had graduated from university and was teaching at Al Rajab in order to gain experience for her application to a teacher education program. She was highly active in the Muslim community as head of a national youth organization, yet her motives for choosing Islamic school were at first mostly pragmatic:

SAKHINA: It wasn't like, 'I want to work with Muslim students' or something. It was more like I didn't have anything better to do, and a job opened. It's a different dynamic just because you have that basis of commonality. We're all Muslims. In a public school like where I grew up, you don't have the commonality so it was just different. I really enjoyed it in that respect.

Therefore, although she initially took on the teaching position for pragmatic reasons, Sakhina appreciated the sense of 'commonality' that existed within the school Similar sentiments were expressed by students, who described the Islamic school environment as offering a greater sense of 'family' and community.

Amira found a greater sense of religious freedom teaching in a more culturally congruent environment, where she could perform her religious practices free from external judgment and scrutiny. In an environment where her Islamic identity, beliefs, and practices were not an issue, she was able to concentrate more on her teaching, without constantly having to explain her lifestyle to others:

AMIRA: As a teacher, I guess the biggest benefit is being able to practice Islam – being able to pray on time, being able to celebrate the holidays to the fullest, and not feeling guilty or having to explain to everyone why you're fasting or why you're wearing this or whatever. The biggest benefit as a teacher would be ... I felt more open, you can express yourself more as a teacher, you don't feel like you're defending yourself all the time. So you're still moving forward, so not only are you practising your teaching, what you've learned in teacher's college or through your teaching years, but as an individual you're growing faster because you're moving forward, you're not always up against the wall trying to explain, trying to justify why you're doing certain things.

Amira preferred working with other Muslim teachers, and she enjoyed the camaraderie among her peers. She discussed how they were able to use a common Islamic framework to resolve issues and concerns that arose within the school. She commented that as a result, there was better understanding among them. She also felt a greater system of support among the teachers and enjoyed the fact that they were able to share ideas and resources.

Among the drawbacks identified was a lack of administrative support. Quite often, Islamic school administrators do not have a background in education; as a consequence, they cannot provide adequate support for teachers. Of the four schools examined here, only two had principals who were educators. None, however, had principal's certification. At Al Safar, sister Mehrun was a retired elementary school teacher who had taught in the local public school board for thirty years. But she was accountable to the *majlis shura* (the governors of the mosque), who had no background in education. At Al Shawwal, the principal was a teacher from Egypt. He was a newcomer to Canada and had difficulty with English; even so, he had been very accommodating of my request to do fieldwork. He later left to start his own school. His replacement was a former Iraqi soldier who was a refugee in Canada. He had no experience in school administration, yet he was in charge of the school's daily operations. The real authority at Al Shawwal was the *imam* of the mosque. He was the final authority on all matters, but he only came to the mosque on Fridays and was, therefore, difficult to access.

The other two schools, Al Rajab and Al Shaban, were family businesses, with husband-and-wife teams serving as administrators who had no previous experience in education. Sakhina sometimes felt that her school suffered from their lack of professionalism. For example, she noted that the principal did not act as enough of a buffer between teachers and parents when it came to complaints:

SAKHINA: I've talked to other teachers who work in other Islamic schools, and it's a common problem – the principal won't step in where they're supposed to step in. If a parent comes in with a complaint, you know, you can't have them talk to the teachers... or barge into the classroom. [Proper channels] aren't being maintained. That's how it was done back home. It's not done here. Like, it shouldn't be done here. It should be like how an organization is done. You go through this person and then ... It sounds bureaucratic, but there has to be some sort of system.

Teachers often complained that parents did not observe proper protocols and would simply enter and confront the teacher during class time. They felt that more leadership was needed to dealing with parents' complaints. Ruqayyah elaborated on this:

RUQAYYAH: Sometimes, if there is a complaint from a parent or not just from a parent but if there is a situation or an issue arising or something, sometimes the infrastructure or lack of infrastructure gets in the way. Because the teacher's there and she's doing her best and she's putting in so much effort and time and everything. But sometimes because not everyone on top is an educationalist, it's hard. Sometimes we need split-second decisions.

There is a clear need, then, for strong leadership based on sound educational knowledge and praxis. Yet that experience comes with a price tag, one that few independent schools can afford.

Lack of resources also affected teachers' salaries. Ruqayyah noted that most teachers were doing 'volunteer work' – that is, they were not being adequately compensated for their extra time and effort. Amira complained about the lack of adequate financial compensation and security, despite the extra effort and commitment on the part of teachers:

AMIRA: The biggest drawback, and it's a fact of life, is the money, the salary. And with the salary comes the benefits and the pension – you know, we don't have any of that. So that is a big drawback. You feel it. For some reason it feels like you're working extra hard in the Islamic school when you try to do certain units, you just want to do more because you're with the Muslim children, it's an Islamic school, so you stay extra long or you go the extra mile, you know, talking to parents or with the children, you know somehow they just seem they're like your own children. So you put in so much effort but in terms of financial return, there is very little. That is the biggest drawback.

Ruqayyah pointed out that low salaries especially affected women teachers, given that many were primary breadwinners:

RUQAYYAH: The two things I would say, one would be the pay. It is tempting to want to leave only because of the pay, especially if you are supporting your own family. It's a myth if anyone thinks it's only the men supporting it, especially because there are all girls in my family. Right now, I'm not the married one so I'm the oldest in my family, so it is hard. But I struggle, and *insha'allah*, something will be worked out.

For certified teachers, staying on and teaching in Islamic school is a testament to their commitment to Islamic education and to developing faith-centred learning environments.

The lack of resources had an impact on education quality, as Sakhina noted:

SAKHINA: I wanted to do Internet stuff. I couldn't because there's no Internet link-up. All this stuff costs money, right? The library was inadequate, but I'd still make an appointment – let's go to the library to do our research because students need to [learn] research skills because that's what they're going to be doing later on … Like, the library there was basically one room with a wall filled with books, but these books could be like, forty years out of date.

Few Islamic schools have libraries, and many do not have proper curricular materials. At Al Shaban, one of the teachers was borrowing her daughter's grade seven textbooks from public school for use in her classroom. Because students did not have their own texts, they had to write notes as the teacher 'lectured' on the material in the textbook. Other teachers were buying workbooks from local bookstores with their own money; these served as their core curricular materials. During my fieldwork, there were no books to be seen at Al Shaban. The lack of resources affected other areas as well, such as arts and crafts, which suffered greatly in the more underfunded schools, where materials were at a premium.

During my fieldwork, parts of Al Shawwal were under construction, and teachers often had to work in makeshift conditions without proper facilities or resources. Maha acknowledged these challenges as a teacher but felt that she would be able to cope with them for a time. She was more concerned about the parents and students and the standards they had a right to expect. She was unhappy with the way the administrators were dealing with the problems:

MAHA: Like, if I feel I can teach, no matter where I am. It doesn't matter even if I have a lot of materials or not. Like, of course we need all these things but they are caring about the walls, they are not caring about the material, they are not caring about subjects, they are not caring about the books. Whenever the teachers are ordering books, and he is telling, 'Okay, you can share together, no problem, we don't have budget' and so all this. This is a *school*. You are taking money from these people, we should be honest. What is this Islam? If I'm not honest with the parents ... and it's not easy for them even to pay this money. So they want, something out of their children. Why are they sending them to Islamic school? Just not for learning, they can learn. He can learn English. Arabic, it's not a problem – even the mother can teach him. Like, we need an Islamic way, Islamic manners, practicing Islam, this is what we need.

For Maha, then, the school was sacrificing the parents' trust by not providing the quality they had a right to expect. Many families had to struggle to send their children to the school, and they deserved an adequate return on their investment. As Ruqayyah noted, other schools were able to afford better resources:

RUQAYYAH: In terms of resources, we have no problem. *Alhamdulillah,* I can't complain about [resources] because even ... one of the public school principals said that we get a lot more than even they did actually. So in terms of that, *alhamdulillah,* the kids' program is enriching. We never stop. We always keep enriching it more and more.

Al Safar was in a unique position to afford up-to-date resources, unlike many other schools that were less established. The school often boasted of their resources and achievement as being even above and beyond the public school system. As such, they were able to provide better resources and curricular materials as compared to other schools in the study, which had lower tuitions and catered more to lower-income families.

Teachers as Role Models

Beyond the benefits and drawbacks of teaching in Islamic schools is the actual significance placed on being a teacher in an Islamic school. They are expected to exemplify Islamic values and behaviours in all they do. One parent, Khadija, told me that teachers' are the 'mirror of the children':

KHADIJA: When you see a group of children and the teacher is inter-acting with them, she or he is forcing their own persona onto the environment. And [children] catch on to that and they behave as they have seen their teacher. They are pretty much the mirror of the children ... For me, they are the second mothers of the child.

The role of teachers was held in high regard and along with that came high expectations, especially from parents. For Shazad, teachers were 'ambassadors of Islam.' to their students and had to model Islamic behaviour for the students to follow. He also felt that they needed to be Islamically knowledgeable and able to convey that knowledge in a youth-friendly manner:

SHAZAD: Well, the most important thing is the role model. That includes in the classroom, in the hallway, and also in the mosque. You have to live Islam completely. So, just like the parents suppos-edly practise Islam, the teacher has to do the same thing in all that the child sees. So [teachers'] practice of Islam is very important – their knowledge of Islam and so forth. And also their ability to deliver the message.

Rukhsana also noted that teachers should act as positive role models and they, like parents, are responsible for helping children differenti-ate between Islamic and un-Islamic forms of behaviour. She felt that Muslim educators had a primary role to play in shaping the morals, values, and ethics of Muslim children.

Zahra pointed out that in their interactions with children, teachers must follow the example of the Prophet Muhammed. She acknowledged the strong influence that teachers have on children, in that they spend more time with them than the parents do:

ZAHRA: Islam is a way of life. They [teachers] have to be really kind, they have to be really nice to the kids, they have to be role models to the kids, they have to handle them in a nice, loving and caring way. You know how Prophet Muhammed treated the kids. He used to treat them kindly, he used to respect them. If they want to be respected, they have to respect the kids. Not like, you know, king and landlord and peasant or something. We don't want the kids to learn that thing, that's not why we send the kids there. From this age they have to learn love and sharing and caring. Because they spend most of the day in school. We [parents] see them a couple of hours.

Zahra also rejected authoritarian models of classroom management that she referred to as the 'king' or 'landlord' and 'peasant' structure and reminded teachers that respect was a mutual undertaking.

Nadia worked as a parent volunteer at Al Shawwal. She maintained that teachers must model a good work ethic. For her, a good work ethic was part and parcel of good Islamic training, and she felt that many teachers at her children's school, largely owing to their inexperience, were not modelling this adequately. She felt that some of them needed to be more organized and prepared as an example to students and that they needed to work together more as 'team players.'

The students, too, saw teachers as role models. In that regard, they had high expectations of them as models of Islamic behaviour and action. Leila and Iman discussed this:

LEILA: It's like a role model. We should act the way she is acting. Because the students will be looking up to the teacher. If the teacher does something bad, then the students would be like, 'She's not doing the correct thing so how do you expect us to?'
IMAN: Yeah ... part of the reason why we come here is not only to get Islamic knowledge, but also the teachers. Like Leila said, we have to look up to them and they can't really act different ... they just have to be very, you know, Islamically good people.

Deqa added that teachers need to help students navigate the difficult terrain between culture and religion – that is, help them differentiate between community cultural practices and the Muslim faith – so that their knowledge of Islam is not confused by cultural practices that have no basis in the faith.

Saira and Noora were well aware that their teachers were making a financial sacrifice by choosing to teach in Islamic schools rather than in the public system. They appreciated them for it. They saw their teachers not only as important role models but also as guides for their future:

SAIRA: The teachers play a very big role ... They're our role models, they're the ones who give us our knowledge and tell us everything we need to know. The teachers in the Islamic school are just exceptional. I have no words to describe them. They do so much work, and even though they might not get the fair amount of money they're entitled to get, still they would give up anything to help us, and we can always go to them with our problems or any questions we have, and we can be sure they'll always be there for us even when we leave the school and go out into the world. If we ever ... need anyone to talk to, they're always here and they play a very important role because they basically help us in every way they can, they're always there for us, and you know, I guess they love us very much.

NOORA: The teachers play a very big role for our school. Because they provide us with enough knowledge, Islamically as well as in other subjects. And the teachers are not only like teachers, as in public school teachers – they're also like parents to us. They teach us and they guide us to the right way.

The notion of the Islamic school being like a 'family' is continued in these references to the teacher's role being like that of a parent. Kamal expressed similar sentiments and appreciated the fact that he received more individual attention from his teachers:

KAMAL: Teachers are totally cooperative. I got more attention in here than I got in [public school name]. Because you have a limited number of students and the teachers are all for you. Every teacher, at least every teacher I have had till now, cares for me as a son.

The students' references to Islamic school teachers being more caring and attentive are in stark contrast to the alienation that some racially minoritized children and youth experience in the public school system (see, for example, Dei, Mazzuca, McIsaac, & Zine, 1997; Zine, 1997, 2001). Smaller, community-based schools, in which most people know and interact with one another outside the school, inject familiarity and comfort into both teaching and learning.

Some students remarked on the downside of this dynamic: too much familiarity meant that teachers could easily relay information back to parents when they saw them in social settings outside the school. According to some students, this often led to breaches of trust. In the public system, students could confide in teachers on certain issues and be sure the information would remain private. In Islamic schools, teachers are often regarded as surrogate parents and sometimes report such confidences to parents. Nusaybah offered an example:

NUSAYBAH: Like, you are afraid. Like, at public school you told your teacher everything … Here, there was this girl and she told the teacher about this guy she loved and wanted to marry. And she asked for advice. And the teacher turned around and told her parents.

Especially where issues concerned potential damage to the 'honour' of the student or the school, teachers were likely to intervene. Many of these teachers were older and viewed as 'aunties' in the community. However, students did note that there were other teachers – generally those who were younger and who had grown up in Canada – with whom they felt free to talk about anything without fear of disclosure or negative judgment.

Teacher Qualifications

Few Islamic schools demand that all of their teachers have the Ontario Teacher's Certification (OTC). As a result, the vast majority of these schools lack formally qualified teachers. It is difficult for these schools to require certification, since (as discussed earlier) few can afford salaries that are competitive with the public system. In addition, provincial guidelines for private schools in Ontario do not require that certified teachers be hired; in other words, there is no government regulation or standard relating to private-school teachers' qualifications. As a consequence, these schools find it difficult to maintain educational standards. The Islamic schools in this study that were not able to hire certified teachers usually required that at a minimum, their teachers be university graduates. In this study, only Al Safar hired teachers who had obtained the OTC. In the other schools, the teachers did not have this qualification. Some teachers had, however, taught in their home countries and had obtained a letter of permission from the Ministry of Education that allowed them to teach in Ontario schools. After accumulating two hundred hours' teaching time, they would be able to apply for their OTC.

Others taught in Islamic schools as a transition after leaving university until they found better jobs or entered a teacher education program. As a result, there was often a high turnover of teachers at the end of each school year. Many educated professionals from abroad did, however, stay on in Islamic schools, since they found it difficult to receive accreditation for their degrees in Canada and were otherwise shut out of the labour market except for low-skill, low-income jobs. They, therefore, found teaching in Islamic schools preferable to driving taxis or other jobs that were not commensurate with their experience.

Rima did not have her OTC but had taught back home in Egypt. She felt that many unqualified people were applying to Islamic schools because teaching offered more prestige than other low-wage jobs in the labour market:

RIMA: The school itself … the salary … it ranges very low. One sort of teachers come here because they're motivated … the other sort of teachers because they can't find anything else to do. When they come into the *masjid* [they're told] 'Oh, come on, we need you, we'll hire you.' They feel they find a job to fulfil their ego. Do you understand what I mean? You come in and you can't find a job anywhere else so you come in here for that prestige instead of McDonald's.

Rima saw herself as one of the 'motivated.' She was committed to being an educator, as she had been in her native country. She felt badly that she did not have her certification, but as a divorced single mother she could not afford to stop working to attend a teacher education program. She believed that if she did acquire certification, she would stay teaching in Islamic schools. The OTC, however, would allow her to bring better experience and knowledge into her pedagogy:

RIMA: The fact that I don't have my teachers' certification is something that bothers me very much Not that I would go and teach in a public school system. It's just something that I feel I want to be able to give the kids the right way plus that extra moral support and knowledge of Islam.

Students complained of the lack of qualified teachers. Farzana, an eighteen-year-old at Al Rajab, discussed her experience at another Islamic high school for girls, which she attended before transferring to Al Rajab. I had asked her previous school to participate in this study; the authorities there had declined. From my observations I could see that the school was extremely substandard; it consisted of a series of small rooms into which the girls were herded like cattle. There were no outdoor facilities, nor a gymnasium for physical activity. According to Farzana, the teaching was substandard as well. The teachers and administrators were all immigrants of South Asian origin, and they modelled the schooling after the methodology used 'back home.' Farzana noted that the teachers may have been educated, but they did not necessarily know how to teach:

FARZANA: I feel that the worst thing is ... like, teachers who are educated and stuff, but sometimes they don't know how to teach. They might have a degree but they don't have a teaching degree ... teaching skills. So that's the biggest challenge for me ... finding good teachers ... They bring teachers from anywhere, [as if] anybody who has a degree can teach, which is not true. So that's why I like this school better, 'cause we have all the teachers, so far, and they're a bit better organized.

Farzana preferred Al Rajab, which though not ideal was better organized than her previous school. Parents, too, complained that 'anyone' could get a job teaching in some Islamic schools. Nadia discussed the hiring criteria she wanted to see:

NADIA: I want them to be focused, organized. I want them to be involved. I want someone who is education oriented. I don't want someone as myself, a homemaker, coming into the school and doing a teacher's job. That's just ridiculous.

Zahra felt that some teachers in her children's school lacked not only educational qualifications but also the social skills to deal with young people. She felt that they were bringing their training from 'back home,' which was more authoritarian and not conducive to the cultural context of teaching and learning in Canada:

ZAHRA: First of all, most of the teachers don't have qualifications, and they don't have the personality … you have to have. Teachers, the way they were brought up [is] the way they're teaching our kids. You know, it's just like one way. They're not investigating, they're not thinking okay, this kid may be suffering from something, he's too shy to talk. You know, something is lacking from the teacher [if] they don't have social … skills.

Zahra was vocal in her concerns about how the teachers related to the students. She had encountered problems with her own children at school and felt that teachers needed to examine their own practices and ways of assessing students and the difficulties they might be having.

Qassim worried that the often high staff turnover in some schools was affecting quality and standards. He noted that at Al Shawwal, part way through the school year they were already on their third principal. He was concerned about the overall standards in these relatively new schools, including the lack of certification:

QASSIM: I believe that the best thing is for us to operate at least minimum-level provincial standards, right? But I know with a lot of Islamic schools, they're fledgling. They're now beginning and so they can't afford that. So I don't have a big issue with teachers who aren't [OTC] qualified but who may have taught somewhere else, as long as the school is committed to upgrading their skills, is committed to training them. So that [teaching is] not like what we talked about before … linear training where they're all sitting behind a desk and the teacher's saying, 'This is what it is,' and they all sit there and say, 'Okay, no problem, that's what it is.' Critical thinking is something that as Muslims we value from the very beginning until the end, right?

Qassim, then, was willing to be patient with the 'fledgling' schools so long as they were committed to ongoing teacher education that promoted active modes of learning and critical thinking skills, as opposed to more didactic methods of teaching that characterized many classrooms. In this vein, he was pleasantly surprised and very happy with his son's kindergarten teacher; he found her highly professional, organized, and creative in her pedagogy even though she lacked Canadian credentials.

Even some students expressed patience and understanding when assessing their teachers and the quality of the education they were receiving. Saadi and Sabbir noted that many teachers did not have certification, but they also recognized that the school was in a nascent stage and that it would improve over time:

SAADI: Quite frankly, the academic standards ... I mean, they're trying to keep up. Like the material they're giving you, I think it's up to the standards but the teachers are not as qualified as you get in the regular public school. There are a few teachers that are not as qualified. They don't have degrees in teaching.

SABBIR: Everything gets better over time, and this is like a new thing. It's been like two or three years that it's been open. So just like the public schools. They've been open for twenty-five or fifty years, a hundred years, they have a good establishment. Just like that, our school can grow and develop and they can get qualified teachers over time.

Clearly, some parents and students were willing to be patient with the school's growing pains. They were confident that over time, with better resources, the standards would improve. With at least one of the schools in this study, that is in fact what has happened. Since my fieldwork at Al Rajab, the school has relocated to a new site, which has greatly elevated the school's physical standards. It has also been working with a private technical institute, which has provided the students with computers and computer training. This shows that with time, tenacity, and patience, Islamic schools can embark on a process of professional and institutional development.

Other students recognized that Islamic schools in many ways involved a trade-off. Many compared their Islamic school teachers favourably with their previous teachers in the public system, whatever their qualifications:

TASLEEMA: For me, it's the teachers basically. They're really nice and they explain to you everything. They don't just tell you to be quiet – 'Okay, that's it. I can't explain to you anymore.' You can ask twenty times and they'll reply back, they have a lot of respect for us. And I think it's the whole, again, community sense, like we know each other, and even if you get mad at each other, we ignore it. In [public school] I don't think they are as understanding. So I think they're more understanding here, it's better.

AMAL: And it feels like the teachers care about you more here.

REHANA: Yeah, like you're encouraged.

TASLEEMA: Yeah, and if you have a problem, you can talk to them, and they'll understand and say, 'Okay, if you can't manage then we'll do something about it.' Like, it's not 'You have to do it.'

REHANA: And there's always an Islamic view of things, like the response to the problem. So we don't have to get all these other views of what to do before you can get a proper view that you can follow.

For these students, the pros of Islamic schooling outweighed the cons with respect to the benefits they were receiving. The social and cultural impact of the Islamic school environment must not be under-estimated. Students' emotional and spiritual well-being is an important component of learning and growth. For many students, a community-based faith-centred learning environment gave them a sense of being respected and supported.

Language Issues and the Lack of Specialist Teachers

The teachers noted weaknesses in the school's standards that they hoped would be addressed over time. Sakhina pointed to the lack of ESL teachers. Al Rajab took the same approach as the public system, placing newcomer students according to age, whatever their facility with English. Yet it did not have ESL teachers to provide support for these students. This posed difficulties for teachers:

SAKHINA: You'd have students coming in from other countries who didn't even know the language. They're in my grade ten course and they can't speak English properly. What are you supposed to teach them? And it wasn't just a case of one or two. In a class or thirty-six there could be five or six. So what do you do then? The only thing I could come up with is you'd have to pair them up with students who were excelling so that they wouldn't be lost.

Sakhina also pointed out that Islamic schools relied solely on tuition fees and so could not afford to turn down ESL students. And Ibrahim, a community education activist, noted that many of the teachers in Islamic schools were also ESL speakers:

IBRAHIM: I don't think any of them ... they probably have some qual-ifications, but I would say that 99 per cent of these teachers are from outside of Canada with English as a second language. And so that by itself poses a problem because with the kids that are going here, pronunciation might be an impediment to comprehension. So just talking to them, you know, some of them were struggling to express themselves. Basically the teachers overwhelmingly speak English as a second language.

Students discussed similar concerns when it came to some of their teachers. They often found teacher's accents difficult to understand. This led to frustration and misunderstandings on the part of both teachers and students:

NUSAYBAH: Okay, the accents you notice, but when you try and ask, 'What did you say?' they flip out on you! They'll be like, 'What am I speaking, French?' And you'll be like, 'No, no, no, I just want to know what you said,' you know? Or 'I don't understand.'

ALIYAH: Because before, we were used to, like, the white accent. All our lives we go to public school and we know that accent. And when I came here, and all the teachers were talking so weirdly, it was really hard to understand what they were saying. Because they also have like this British way of talking. And you can't really understand because you're not used to it. And when you ask they think you're making fun of them. And you really just want them to repeat it.

Aliyah noted that many of the teachers at her school came from a British system of education in South Asia. This affected their 'Britishized' South Asian accent and their pedagogy and praxis as well.

Reproducing the Colonial Classroom

Many of the teachers in the Islamic schools I examined were products of colonial education systems in South Asia or the Middle East. I noticed a specific style of pedagogy among teachers who had grown up in British schools in countries such as Egypt and in South Asia. These teachers were highly authoritarian and led teacher-directed classrooms that produced mostly passive learning. In these classrooms the teacher was the 'giver' of knowledge and the students were to 'receive' this knowledge in an unquestioning manner. There was little emphasis on arts, drama, or any creative pedagogical strategies, as lessons were strictly 'by the book.' Students were expected to work independently and quietly. The seats were organized in straight rows facing the teacher rather than in the mixed groupings favoured in child-centred classrooms.

In these 'colonial' classrooms, work was expected to take place in silence, and anyone fidgeting was quickly taken to task. The elementary classrooms were unadorned by the usual brightly coloured displays of student work and posters, and teaching strategies rarely included visual aids. The delivery of lessons was dry and formal. The secondary classrooms were equally austere: the teachers lectured, and the students were expected to write or copy notes. There were no creative or interactive activities. Learning was a one-way process, with the students as passive rather than active participants.

The teachers in this style of classroom were from education systems in Egypt and in South Asia, where many attended the elite British convent schools. As educators, they embodied the strict, severe, and austere manners into which they themselves had been socialized. They perceived the Canadian school system as too 'loosey goosey' and as lacking proper discipline. Canadian students were used to a different kind of school culture where they were accustomed to talking and joking around with teachers, were unable to develop a rapport with these teachers. After observing one such classroom for some time, I offered advice to the teacher that she 'loosen up' a little and perhaps smile and be a little friendlier. The students might then find it easier to relate to her. She seemed taken aback by the idea, telling me that she was there to be their teacher, not their 'friend.' From her perspective, teachers were there to impart knowledge and uphold rules and regulations; whether or not they were engaging or affable was irrelevant.

The pedagogy and style of these teachers was reminiscent of a colonial mentality where students were socialized to be obedient and subservient subjects of empire, and to acquiesce to authority rather than question it. Colonial education was a means for creating docile and subjugated bodies, for producing indigenous loyalists who were graciously 'uplifted' by Western knowledge, values, and mores. In this way they would be raised from barbarism to a state of civilized collusion with the hegemony of empire building. Willinsky (1998) describes how colonial education systems reinforced the 'right to rule': 'This aim of colonial education was to transform natives into colonial intermediaries, turning schools into civil service training institutions intended to support the administration of the empire. The schools formed an integral part of the governing apparatus, creating a class of half-proud, half-ashamed bureaucrats to serve in that shadowy space between the colonizer and the native, schooled in tattered textbooks devoted to scenes and lessons from the unapproachable motherland, lessons that were thought to make obvious Britain's right to rule and the natives duty to serve' (pp. 99–100). The legacy of these systems remains embedded in many educational programs in the postcolonial context. Teachers in Islamic schools who model their pedagogy after their own training in these institutions are in effect reproducing the colonial classroom in Islamic schools.

Parents who were familiar with this style of education complained that it was not conducive to the culture of teaching and learning in Canada:

KARIM: Most of the teachers are from outside Canada. The way they grew up, the way we grew up, the relationship we used to have with the teachers, [they] used to be like masters, they had the whole control over everything, not only the class, but even you could say the soul. They could do anything, they could hit, they could do anything, and they [students] didn't have any say. I mean, from that kind of environment, unless there is a way to change that behaviour, that's what you see.

The idea of the 'teacher as master' was rejected by parents like Karim. Although their own upbringing had reflected this style of pedagogy, they did not feel it was an appropriate way to engage their own children. Even though they did not approve of the rigid authoritarian manner of teaching that they were subject to they did concede that under the education system 'back home,' students were generally better behaved and more disciplined and that they had greater respect for teachers. They wanted their children to absorb these attitudes but felt that different strategies should be used.

Having attended convent schools in India, Shahnaz had first-hand experience with the type of teaching that some teachers from that system were implementing in Canada. She noted the mismatch that students encountered when they were confronted with that style of teaching:

SHAHNAZ: I find our method of teaching and learning is different back there than here. There, in India, the child can read at four ... Kids go to school with big, big huge bags – little kids like JK and SK – big huge bags. And they learn so much. Here, with one book, they learn A-B-C-D in SK. [In India] they talk and they teach, talk and teach. So when the kids have been born over here, brought up over here, and they have gone to public schools before and now they're going to the Islamic school ... when they find the teacher is like that they just don't know how to settle that in their mind.

Shahnaz went further, complaining about the teaching style she had encountered in some classrooms here and arguing that foreign-educated teachers were manifesting inappropriate attitudes and personalities:

SHAHNAZ: Again, I'm saying ... nothing is personal in all these things, it's just that everybody cannot teach. Not everyone who has a background in teaching from India or Pakistan can teach. In fact, they're worse teachers sometimes. It is a very different system there. And I try myself because I've been educated in India and I find that when I teach the kids I'm very rude to them. I'm just a mean mother. I just can't teach them.

Shahnaz was the product of a postcolonial education system, and she worried that that system was being reproduced in her children's classroom in Canada. Some students expressed similar sentiments. They also saw that their parents were more reluctant to complain or advocate on behalf of their children than they were when they attended public school:

NUSAYBAH: In public school if a teacher yelled at you or threw something at you or hit you, your parents would be in there like, attacking them, being like, the authority. Here, the teachers will tell you to shut up and call you mean things. In public schools your parents would come in and be the authority and say, 'Have some respect for my child.' Here parents let them say it.
IMRANA: They treat us like it's India or Pakistan.

Therefore, for some parents as well, the role of the school as a site of unquestioned authority was also reproduced when the structures for teaching and learning were modelled after the colonial-style systems in which many of them grew up.

During my fieldwork, I sometimes tried to make critical interventions. Colonial-style approaches were evident at Al Shaban and Al Shawwal and among some teachers at Al Rajab. The pedagogy at Al Safar provided a better example for these schools to follow, so I arranged for two teachers from Al Shaban to observe Ruqayyah and Amani's classes there, so that they might learn new teaching techniques. Ruqayyah and Amani had excellent rapport with their students and taught in an engaging, interactive, and creative style. I wanted the other teachers to observe how they structured and conducted their classes so that they might become inspired to follow suit. These teachers found their visit helpful and informative but added that they lacked the resources that Al Safar had, which made it more difficult for them to take more creative approaches. I encouraged them to focus on strategies they could adopt that did not involve additional resources but simply more creativity on their part. I also reminded them that traditional Islamic education was based on the Prophet Muhammed's example, and that he had suggested that learning through play was the best way for children up to age seven. To decolonize teaching and learning practices in Islamic schools, it will be necessary to reclaim parts of the traditional Islamic educational heritage, which is relevant even in the twenty-first century. These teachers found it sobering that their methods contradicted traditional Islamic pedagogy, which had been interrupted and derailed by colonialism.

Discipline as Islamic Praxis

Al Safar, the most established of the schools in this study, was also the only one that had developed a code of conduct for students. For

Amira, discipline began with inculcating a faith-centred consciousness that emphasized accountability for one's actions:

AMIRA: We teach them in Islamic studies that you're accountable for everything, that there's good consequences and bad consequences. Ultimately it's heaven or hell, so you know, they're taught that for every action, if you do something good the consequences are very good. But if something is done that is not right, then you have to learn, you have to change, you have to try. A lot of what we talk about is repentance. When we do the attributes of Allah,[3] right in the beginning I start with the attributes of Allah. You talk about these concepts, accountability ... Because sometimes children, when they do something wrong they're afraid to admit it. They lie. So we talk about repentance, how Allah is most forgiving, most merciful, and we talk about, again, their relationship with Allah. You know, you can lie to your teacher, you can lie to your parents, but Allah knows.

Thus, discipline was not viewed simply as punishment; rather, it was understood as part of a student's growth and learning. Students were made aware of school's expectations regarding behaviour and of the consequences for misbehaving, but they were also taught that Islam emphasized repentance and forgiveness.

From a faith-centred perspective, accountability involves responsibility to Allah the Creator, transcending existential notions and boundaries. Amira reported that in their journals, students often asked for forgiveness for specific things they had done. This was a sign of their *taqwa* (consciousness of God) and of their fidelity to the high moral standards expected of them as Muslims. Each year, the school's award ceremonies honoured students for exhibiting good Islamic behaviour as well as excellence in academics.

According to Mehrun, the principal, Al Safar's philosophy of discipline was simply following Islam, which as a way of life inculcates the foundations for self-discipline:

MEHRUN: Islam is discipline. Like simple prayers, prescribed times, that is discipline. Fasting is discipline, all this is discipline. So Islam is discipline, and *alhamdulillah* on the whole I find that there are not as many discipline problems, they are very minor discipline problems. And most of the time the parents cooperate. We don't have that much trouble. Sometimes parents do get a little sensitive about it, but on the whole, we don't have that much fighting and things like that. You know, when they are playing games they get a little rough sometimes, and then, it escalates, a little bit of pushing but no hitting, kicking, *alhamdulillah*, not that much really. Very rarely.

Abdus-Sabur (1995) noted the infrequency of antisocial behaviour in Islamic schools. Similarly, Mehrun encountered fewer serious discipline problems in Al Safar than outside the school. Islam helped inculcate self-discipline, which, she argued, was the foundation for proper behaviour in children.

Teachers at Al Safar used a variety of classroom management strategies; all, though, were faith-centred. Ruqayyah showed me the stickers her students earned for good behaviour; in her classes there were also awards for 'student of the week.' She also reinforced rules by citing specific hadiths, thus adding religious weight to her classroom's norms for conduct:

RAEESA: Something as basic as sharing or even whispering ... It happens a lot in primary grades when they'll *psss-psss-psss*. And I'll be like, not again. So I told them, 'If there's three people, two of you can't whisper.' And I said, 'That's not a rule, that's a hadith.' I just tell them everything is in Islam, every single thing. You wake, you go to sleep, everything, having etiquette when they're eating. Not saying 'no' to food, or if you're offered something, just politely say 'yes.' Or like, 'Yes, please' or 'No, thank you' or something but not completely refusing it or whatever. And I tell them a lot, because I'm big on not wasting food. So I tell them a lot of things like, 'There's a lot of kids starving.'

Classroom rules, then, were lessons in Islamic values. Lessons in etiquette and life skills reinforced Islam's central teachings. On the hallway walls, students pinned up hadith posters that contained messages about Islamic manners – 'be truthful' and 'don't backbite' – as well as other hadith relating to the importance of learning and of performing good acts such as alms giving. These serve as a reminder of the broader spiritual rules of conduct in the school and shape their behaviour not just as students but as Muslims.

Amani in her classroom presented an exemplary model of the *adab* (etiquette) of Islamic teaching. She was very friendly and gentle with her grade seven class, and they all seemed to like and respect her. She always listened to her students and was caring and attentive to them on an academic and personal level. She never shouted or got angry with individual students or with the class as a whole. Instead, to control the class if they got out of hand, she would follow a hadith of the Prophet Muhammed where he counselled people in a state of anger to sit down and take sips of water. Amani would do this as a silent gesture, letting her students know she was angry. She would sit down, sip water, and recite verses from the Qur'an quietly to herself as a way of calming down and reserving her anger. The students would quickly pick up on her action and realize that this meant she was unhappy with the class, and they would quiet down. In this way, her attempts to follow the sunnah (teachings of the Prophet Muhammed) and not lose her temper became a method of classroom management.

Bilquees taught her kindergarten students Islamic ways of controlling their anger and dealing with conflicts:

BILQUEES: Just teaching them 'Okay, if you're angry what do you do? Do you go hit someone or yell at someone? How do you control your anger? If you're really furious, how would you handle your anger in an Islamic way?' Especially with kindergartens, they get angry. Kids go into temper tantrums and things like that. And I just talk to them. I say, 'Okay, what do you say?' And they know what to say: 'Oh, we say, "aoothoobillahi minashaythan nirrajeem" so we send the *shaitan* away first.' So this is how they learned about that, and in different ways.

The Arabic phrase that Bilquees taught her students is an invocation to banish the devil, or *shaitan*, who is causing them to be angry and destructive. This faith-centred approach incorporates the metaphysical into both anger management and classroom management. In this way, students gain interpersonal and life skills based on an Islamic epistemology in which the spiritual and physical realms are intrinsically connected.

Redisciplining Discipline Strategies: Towards a More Democratic and Engaging Classroom

Yet not all schools took this approach to discipline. Teachers and parents at Al Shawwal, for example, were constantly complaining about discipline problems at their school. Because of the recent turnover in principals, they did not yet have a cohesive set of rules for conduct and behaviour. Also, teachers did not spend enough time developing appropriate and consistent class rules; thus, expectations were not clear to the students. When I began fieldwork at Al Shawwal, half the school year had already passed yet only one teacher had developed any classroom rules. I was assisting in Rima's grade four class, a small but unruly group of nine students – eight boys and one girl. Rima was having difficulty with their behaviour: they were inattentive and often acted up during lessons. I suggested creating a more democratic classroom structure where students would be responsible for co-creating the rules that would facilitate the development of a learning community in the classroom. They would also be responsible for co-developing the consequences for transgressing the rules. I hoped all of this would give them a greater sense of responsibility toward one another and greater regard for managing their behaviour. I helped the teacher brainstorm some class rules with the students and develop a strategy for determining fair consequences for breaking the rules. The idea was to shift the teacher's pedagogy and praxis away from the current authoritarian mode, which seemed to create more tension in the class, towards a more democratic organization in which the students could feel a greater sense of ownership.

This seemed an effective strategy at first, but after my fieldwork was completed, I feared that the teacher would lapse back into her more authoritarian mode. Rima was fearful of losing control of her class and maintained a rigid structure, which she felt would deprive the students of opportunities to act out. This made for a highly teacher-directed and didactic pedagogy in her classroom. To model some alternative teaching possibilities for her, I conducted some interactive activities with the students for the Medieval Times unit. I included lessons examining the Islamic medieval world as well as the European one, based on a curriculum guide I had co-authored for grade four Ontario students (see Zine and Muir, 2000). I took the students out of the cramped classroom downstairs to the gymnasium so that we would have room to do the drama and role-play activities I had planned. The lessons focused on social hierarchies and examined the class-based systems in Europe and the Islamic world during the medieval period. The students were excited about the change of pace, which removed them from the tedious monotony of pencil-and-paper work that they normally did in the class. The activities were highly successful, and the students cooperated well. Moreover, they were excited to be learning in an active rather than passive mode. Throughout the lessons, Rima was nervous that at any moment the class would fall apart because of the far less structured setting. In fact, the opposite happened: the students were deeply engaged and did not act bored or restless. I doubted, though, whether Rima would feel comfortable enough to take such 'risks' with the class in my absence.

According to Maha, some of the discipline problems at Al Shawwal were related to the need for teachers who were new to Canada to become accustomed to the cultural context for teaching and learning:

MAHA: It's a problem because some of the teachers can't handle it, like, they can't deal with students. And when we just be firm, its like, maybe ... we are getting hyper and we are taking it out on the students ... Different cultures, different environments.

Maha herself was a newcomer from Kuwait. I observed that in her preschool classroom she had different cultural expectations regarding the attention span of young children – expectations that were not generally viewed as reasonable in Canadian early childhood education. While the preschool room did have good resources, such as educational toys, a play centre, and arts and crafts materials, Maha still used a direct instructional method at certain times of the day, when she expected the children to sit and listen to her lessons and answer questions. These sessions were often fifteen to twenty minutes long – too long for preschool children's attention span. Maha was a pleasant, caring, and patient teacher, but her unrealistic expectations of children this age made classes more frustrating for both her and her students.

Differential Treatment and Nepotism in Disciplinary Measures

Teachers at Al Shawwal and Al Rajab had concerns about nepotism – specifically, privileged treatment was being extended to certain students, making discipline policies hard to enforce. Sakhina and Rima talked about situations where they felt 'favouritism' on the part of school administration made the enforcement of the rules unfairly malleable:

RIMA: I find that discipline ... needs to be taken care of but there's a lot of nepotism regarding discipline. Because we don't have that many children in the school, these things are obvious.

JASMIN: When you say there's nepotism regarding children, you
mean children are treated differentially?
RIMA: Depending if their mother's working there, who their father is,
who their mother is.

Similarly, Sakhina complained that occasionally some students
would receive preferential treatment and avoid being disciplined for
transgressions for which other students were held accountable.

At Al Rajab, some of the boys were often very noisy and unruly; at
times, they could be heard all the way to the girls' section of the
school. When Sakhina was teaching the boys and they misbehaved,
she would force them to sit in the girls' section of the classroom,
which they disliked but nevertheless made them more subdued.
When she had no choice but to send boys to the principal's office, the
philosophy was 'punish now and talk later' or, depending on who the
student was, they might not face any consequences. This inconsistency was a problem when it came to developing uniform standards
and expectations.

Disciplining Wayward Students:
Punitive and Corporal Punishment

As noted earlier, Islamic schools are often seen as places where
wayward students are sent to be rehabilitated and resocialized, and, in
this way, they serve the function of providing 'behaviour modifica-
tion', as Nawal explained:

NAWAL: I even heard parents saying if the child is being bad, 'I will
put you in Islamic school.' For them it's a disciplinary thing. Kind
of like a punishment and also to discipline – 'My child is not doing
very good in the public school; he's mean, he's rude, there's a lot of
behavioural problems that he's facing so let's put him in Islamic
school so he will be more ... properly socialized.'

Many parents feel that their children pick up bad behaviours in
the public system. Being threatened with Islamic school in this way
results in the perception that these schools are punitive environments. It is disturbing that some students and teachers reported corporal punishment being used as a means of discipline. Certain teachers resorted to pinching, hitting, and ear pulling to keep students in
line:

NAWAL: As a teacher I try to be firm. I've worked with various teachers with different discipline strategies. In Islamic school I've noticed hitting, beating, telling them to leave the classroom, different kinds of things. I personally think that in Islamic school we have to be more attractive to attract the children towards Islamic education, not let them just leave and run and think, 'Islamic school was the most horrible experience of my life.' We're ... competing with public education. And if you go and see the public education, even though the results will be the worst, the outlook of it is so nice that our children are automatically attracted towards it.

For Nawal, corporal forms of discipline were likely to turn students away from Islamic education and make them more attracted to public schools, even though, in her view, this would lead to an even more destructive outcome.

The use of corporal punishment is a serious concern. While it was not common practice, isolated incidents were reported at Al Rajab, Al Shaban, and Al Shawwal. As noted earlier, these schools also had more rigid, authoritarian-style classrooms. No incidents involving physical punishment were reported at Al Safar, which had a more positive, Islamically based approach to discipline and where corporal punishment was forbidden. In traditional Islamic approaches to education, which are based on the sunnah of the Prophet Muhammed, corporal punishment is rejected. The Prophet was famously patient and tolerant with children and never resorted to physical punishment. Corporal punishment, then, is forbidden by Islam besides being illegal. No school where I conducted fieldwork sanctioned corporal punishment as a policy, but isolated cases were reported.

Parents, teachers, and students reported specific instances of corporal punishment and other inappropriate disciplinary measures. Zahra was critical of Al Shawwal's approach to discipline. She was receiving constant complaints about her two boys' behaviour there and was angry when they reported being slapped or having their ears pinched:

ZAHRA: And they bring letters, complaint letters. When they come, we have to talk to them, we have to ground them because every single day they have to bring letters: 'They did this, they did that, they went into the office.' We are not sending our kids to be grounded, we are not sending our kids to be pinched or slapped, *honestly*.

Punitive and destructive forms of discipline led to negative attitudes towards school and created what Zahra referred to as a 'cat and dog' relationship:

ZAHRA: I want to add something. What I see nowadays is the teachers and kids have a cat-and-dog kind of relationship. My kids, they hate to go to school now. They know that they are going to be in trouble. They say, 'Mommy, he's gonna send me to the principal today, I know he is going to do it.' Having that fear to go to school, at this age, is really frustrating.

Such stories evoked memories of my own experiences growing up in Canadian public schools. Not so long ago, students in the public system were threatened with 'the strap,' which was administered in the principal's office. In the Islamic schools in this study, however, corporal punishment was not meted out in the principal's office but rather by specific teachers who lacked the skills to cope with difficult students.

Bilquees reported that her school's principal had no effective strategies for discipline. Physical punishment was never used at her school, but neither was there a consistent approach to discipline. The problem was compounded by the fact that Al Shawwal had three different principals in one school year. No surprise, then, that the school had trouble maintaining clear and consistent discipline strategies:

BILQUEES: The principal would talk to them, and for my kindergarten, they used to give them to write their names a hundred times, or give them some work to do. They will get yelled at. And with the other principal, they have to stand with their hands up or against the wall or something. He used to do that quite a bit. But the kids really had problems. It was really bad.

The fact that the principals were inexperienced exacerbated the discipline problems the school faced. With one of the principals at Al Shawwal, I discussed my concerns over the incidents of physical abuse that had been reported to me during the interviews. He was a newcomer to Canada from Iraq and spoke little English. He had a military background and no experience in elementary education, and his attitude towards schooling and discipline had been shaped by his own upbringing under a highly authoritarian regime. Yet even he was against corporal punishment at the school. I encouraged him to discuss this with the teachers and pointed out that the school might be shut down if the parents raised the issue with the authorities. Surprisingly, however, the parents did not escalate their concerns to this level. Doing so would have been seen as a betrayal of the community; better, it was felt, to deal with such matters *within* the community. It was clear that the principal and the parents wanted to protect the students, but they also wanted to protect the school.

I observed one incident of ear pulling during my classroom observations at Al Rajab, in a grade four class. The teacher, an older woman from South Asia, wanted me to observe her doing a 'model lesson'; she preferred this to my usual spontaneous requests to sit in classes. I agreed to observe her lesson the next day; to my disappointment, it was simply a textbook lesson, and I sat at the back of the classroom writing notes. The class was very well behaved, but I noticed that at one point a boy in the front row was talking and the teacher tugged his ear and accused him of being disruptive. I was shocked by her action and by her accusation against him. Authoritarian teachers like this make rigid and unreasonable demands for silence and stillness that were incompatible with children's needs and attention spans, especially in lessons that were less than engaging. After the class, the teacher was anxious to hear my assessment of her teaching abilities. When I confronted her about the ear-pulling incident, she seemed embarrassed, justifying her action as an almost unconscious reflex. I reminded her that this was not an appropriate or Islamic means of discipline and that she should find other strategies. Clearly, this teacher was drawing on her own upbringing under the harsh disciplinary standards of schools 'back home.' I hoped she would realize that this was not an acceptable practice to reproduce.

Among high school students, there was less concern about physical punishment, though threats and some physical assaults with chalk did take place. Nusaybah and Zarqa discussed this:

NUSAYBAH: One of the girls said, 'If you touch me I'll hit you back.'
ZARQA: My parents don't touch and I don't want people –
JASMIN: Are your teachers physical?

NUSAYBAH: No. But I got whipped at with a chalk once. That was funny. I couldn't stop laughing cuz it came right at my face!

ZARQA: They wanted to put tape on my mouth because I ask too many questions!

These students thought the incidents were funny; nevertheless, they reveal inappropriate methods for dealing with students.

The students also noted that male teachers knew how to be strict with boys but were at a loss when it came to disciplining girls. How were they to do so while maintaining appropriate Islamic guidelines, which forbade physical contact? Imrana talked about the male computer teacher's frustration in this regard:

IMRANA: He gets frustrated very easily. He doesn't have patience with us. With the girls. With the guys he'll like fight and say, 'Sit down!' With the girls, he'll smile. He doesn't know how to control us.

Because this teacher lacked training in classroom management, he was unable to develop appropriate strategies to deal with either the boys or the girls.

Other teachers noted that the problem of out-of-control students was related to the students' backgrounds. Many of them were from refugee camps and war-torn countries and had seen and suffered violence. Rima maintained that families coming to Canada to escape these harsh realities were breeding grounds for domestic discord and that the parents lacked appropriate parenting skills. She added that the children of these families did not respond to more gentle or reasoned types of discipline, since they were accustomed to a harsher tone. And she pointed out that in some schools, such as Al Shawwal, there were more children of refugee families struggling on low incomes. The students at Al Safar were more affluent:

RIMA: You're getting these kids that have been raised [in harsh circumstances] ... They come from different backgrounds where they maybe had to beg to eat, it had to be really rough to survive, [parents] are rough with their kids. These kids are not used to, you know, being, 'Oh, this is wrong and this right and you should respect this' and that sort of talking in that tone. They are used to a harsher manner. [So] if you use that kind of way with them, that's not going to be reinforced at home and you're going to lose those kids. They're going to think you're wishy-washy. That's where I think there's a difference between Muslim kids … You don't find that maybe at Al Safar. You don't have that problem because these kids come from a professional background … The parents come from a Muslim background, middle class, where they're treated the way the public school system does. You have to show respect and you can't say that and just a look would get them straight. You have a certain standard behaviour respected in their community. But the kids that we're dealing here with are different. They're from families that were mistreated in their lives and they mistreat their kids somehow.

Bilquees suggested that weak parenting skills were contributing to students' misbehaviour. She blamed abusive households for contributing to children's acting out at school. Clearly, student behaviour was a complicated issue that touched on the social and economic hardships faced by families. That said, the schools lacked strong approaches to discipline and in some cases simply reproduced the destructive, abusive, and punitive measures in children's families.

Rima pointed out that many teachers were struggling with discipline and were not receiving support and guidance from the school administration. She added that many teachers simply fell back on the disciplinary strategies they remembered from their own schooling experiences and that they needed help to reframe their methods:

RIMA: We, as teachers … because we're not educated in that … we need support, too. Because we also come from that background. We don't know where and when to stop or how we can get the support that we want. How do we get the point [across to] the child without losing it ourselves? Without having to raise our voice? We need training in that, you know what I mean?

Parents were concerned about the emotional costs of harsh discipline. Qassim worried that such discipline would compound the self-esteem issues that Muslim children already faced as racialized and religiously minoritized young people:

QASSIM: Talking down to children as opposed to talking to them, and stuff like that. Those kind of things I really worry about … because a lot of our kids – I mean, in the Muslim community – have self-esteem issues. They're growing up fighting a self-esteem battle. And if our teachers aren't empowered to try and help them overcome those issues, especially at this level, they'll grow up with that inferiority complex.

Therefore, Qassim feared for the long-term effects that negative treatment would have on these children and their psychological and emotional well-being.

In Asma's view, the onus was on the school administration to set behaviour standards and to ensure that appropriate policies were in place. She felt that this leadership was lacking in most Islamic schools:

ASMA: I think there has to be a leadership factor in a principal – someone who's going to take responsibility for a school, whether it's on a volunteer basis or a paid basis. Whether that person is self-appointed or selected by the community, there still has to be an element of leadership. And to me, leadership is somewhat of a magical attribute, in which that person can command the behaviour of his or her followers. And in this case the followers are the teachers and the students. It is a presence. It is moral and ethical behaviour in that principal himself or herself. There's a quietness. There doesn't have to be any yelling. There doesn't have to be physical punishment, either. What I have learned from the public school, where there is a real mish-mash of stories – household stories, single parents, poverty, what have you – is that the children are treated with self-respect. Their own self-respect is drawn upon to deal with certain situations that come up. Children don't have the judgment to deal with situations and that's why they go to school to learn. When people do not behave according to the rules of the environment, they have to be taken out and they have to be made to understand what behaviour is not accepted.

She felt that the principal at Al Shaban provided such a role model. Without resorting to yelling or threats, he was able to command respect from students:

ASMA: I believe that [at] the Al Shaban school ... as that school is becoming more and more a success story, brother Hisham, the

principal, is more actively involved. If you pop in there, you will
see him with the children. And they know in his presence that
there is no reason to fool around; that he actually loves them. He
has a commanding presence.

Qassim did not have the same confidence in the administration at Al
Shawwal, which was headed by the imam of the mosque. He felt that
the instability of the school administration was making it difficult to
develop and maintain any continuity in standards and practices. He
wanted to raise these concerns at the next parent meeting:

QASSIM: I'm seriously considering writing a letter to the imam of the
    Mosque and to the school about their hiring practices, especially
    with regard to the principal. Because I think if you have a good
    principal and you have people who are qualified ... Maybe they're
    not fully qualified ... I hope eventually they'll make provincial
    standards – at least their minimum standards – because ideally our
    Islamic schools should be even surpassing. That's how it's sup-
    posed to be. I want to go to the next meeting and I want to raise
    this because it's ridiculous that we're spending one term with three
    principals. What kind of continuity, what kind of long-term plan-
    ning do they have? What kind of vision? Who are the people?
    Where are they coming from? All those things are big issues.

The lack of vision and planning was disturbing for parents like
Qassim, who hoped that Islamic school standards would one day
surpass those of public schools and who felt that currently some of
these schools were struggling to keep up even the minimum standards
set by the Ministry of Education.

School administrators, for their part, felt that families had to show
more responsibility for disciplining their children at home and that
lack of discipline in the home was causing problems at the school.
Raeesa, the vice principal at Al Rajab, told me they would soon be
starting a process of acclimatizing new students to the Islamic school
environment and making them aware of the rules as well as the behavioural standards expected of them:

RAEESA: So, *alhamdulillah*, now discipline is not a big issue. And now
    what we do for the newcomers, at the time of admission we inter-

view the child with the older ones. Young ones, like parents, will know the rules and regulations, they will talk to the child. Honestly speaking, younger kids are much easier to discipline than the older ones. Of course you find that. So for the older kids, we specially interview them and we make them aware of all the policy and rules and everything, and if they're violating any of them we give oral warnings, then written warnings, and then that's it, we say, 'Bye bye, we can't deal with you anymore.'

Raeesa also felt that Islamic values and practices were missing from many households, making it more difficult for students to adapt to school rules, such as wearing the Islamic uniform:

RAEESA: I was just telling you, environment plays a big role. Let me give you a simple example of hijab and abaya. Okay, never mind, let them take it as we impose on them, the abaya, the *jilbab*, and the hijab. I know most of them, still they don't wear it outside, but they do wear it to the school, and properly, they wear it very properly, but [not] when they go out with the family because the families don't wear what their kids do. I never blame them, sister, I've never blamed these kids, because they've never been brought up how they're supposed to be, and still, still, they're learning the things here, but they have no cooperation at home.

So in her view, the lack of congruence between Islamic practices in the home and in the school was contributing to the discipline problems the school was facing. Raeesa also felt that students coming from the public system were importing negative behaviours and manners and that they needed to be resocialized and disciplined to conform to the expectations of the Islamic school:

RAEESA: We had a very hard time in the beginning of the school years, you know, disciplining the kids, because even though they were all from the public school system, they were very rude, talking back to the teachers, and you know, like, language sometimes, they had no control on the language. But *alhamdulillah*, slowly by slowly, with the reminders, with some detentions, now they're in control and they're learning the discipline.

Therefore, Islamic schools face many present and future challenges. Maintaining appropriate academic and disciplinary standards is a matter of self-regulation, as the Ministry of Education does not regulate private schools at present. This means that the community must serve as an educational watchdog to ensure that schools are achieving appropriate standards and providing adequate social and academic services.

9 Weaving the Strands of Discourse and Praxis: Mapping Future Directions for Islamic Schools

> The most honest men of future generations will carry this *'ilm* [knowledge], they will purify it from the falsification of the extremists, and the assumptions of the liars, and the misinterpretation of the fools.
>
> Hadith of the Prophet Muhammed, narrated by Abu Hurairah[1]

I began this study by stating that I support the ideal of Islamic schooling, though not necessarily the present realities of many Islamic schools. I have witnessed a great deal through this research that has made me hopeful that the ideal is worth pursuing. At times, however, I fear that realizing this ideal will mean swimming against the strong tide of puritanical and patriarchal religious authority. My goal was to provide an ethnographic account of these schools that allows the participants, as primary stakeholders, to situate their experiences and speak to the realities they have encountered. I mean this study to be a testament to the real possibilities inherent in a critical approach to faith-centred learning. I also mean it to present the consequences of uncritical adherence to puritanical faith-based ideologies, which threaten to prevent the advance towards more progressive Islamic educational ideals.

To conclude this study, I want to revisit some of the ideals that I hope can be achieved for Islamic schools as sites for developing empowered spiritual ontologies and for promoting social justice and academic excellence. To this end, I will re-examine some of the broader sociological and ideological imperatives for Islamic schools. I will also analyse the discursive function of Islamic schools in order to map out how Islamic epistemology informs the development of Muslim ontologies in the context of Islamic educational institutions. Finally, I will make some concrete recommendations for fostering the social and academic development of Islamic schools.

For this investigation I have attempted to integrate a critical faith-centred epistemological framework as a means to unpack a new set of discursive possibilities that may help guide Islamic schools out of their social, structural, and political malaise and preserve these schools' potential. The liberatory goals of this research have been to highlight the challenges and possibilities of Islamic schooling in a diasporic context, with a view to better understanding how Islamic schools can serve as avenues for social, spiritual, and academic development in Canadian Muslim civil society.

Revisiting the Possibilities:
Islamic Schools and Canadian Muslim Civil Society

Civil society has been described as separate from both government and the private sector. The constituents of civil society include NGOs, religious organizations, schools, civic associations, and charitable groups, as well as individuals and families. These bodies have specific, diverse missions that contribute to the quality of life in a given societal context. As a minoritized diasporic community in Canada, Muslims have developed institutions that not only contribute to the development of the broader infrastucture of Canadian civil society but also constitute a microcosmic Muslim civil society. In the Canadian Muslim community, these organizations and institutions contribute to the integration and betterment of Muslims. Islamic schools play a key role in this order. According to Ahmad (2000), religious institutions and schools have a huge potential to effect positive and progressive social change, provided they become truly open sites for intellectual freedom and deliberation:

> After the Mosques, there come the schools and then later social service agencies and civic groups aimed at social betterment. The schools are the key element in the chain. It is through education that massive social change is wrought. But unless the schools themselves are structured as marketplaces of learning rather than as means of simple indoctrination, we engage in a self-defeating process. The students must be approached as independent agents being taught the essentials of independent original thought, rather than vessels to receive the pureed contents of our conclusions. (p. 1)

Ahmad advocates the civic and Islamic education of diasporic Muslims, who, he suggests, could serve as catalysts in Muslim societies by providing role models for grassroots communities to strengthen their own advances towards 'bottom up' civil society. Wedding a good civic education with a strong critical faith-centred Islamic education might at the same time reduce the fears of liberal critics, who argue that independent religious schooling works against the development strong civic engagement and undermines the goals of deliberative democracy (Gutmann, 1996; Callon, 1997). While Ahmad is looking at the transnational benefits of exporting good, civic-minded Muslims to countries 'back home' to help encourage civic engagement and develop a critical mass of democracy-seeking grassroots activists, there are also social and political benefits to be accrued right here.

For example, I have argued that, from a critical faith-based perspective, spirituality is a vital component of social and political activism. Islamic schooling can, therefore, do much to assert Muslim identities in the public sphere, by promoting civic engagement. We have seen how some of the schools in this study supported the involvement of students in public protests and other political processes; others, though, remained socially and intellectually isolated. Yet when viewed through a critical faith-centred lens, it is clear that religion and spirituality have the potential to revitalize local grassroots movements as spaces of resistance to injustice and oppression (see also Dei, 2001a). A critically focused Islamic education is, therefore, key to inspiring strong levels of local and global civic action and counteracting claims of 'ghettoization.'

Independent religious schools can contribute to the development of Canadian Muslim civil society by encouraging greater immersion in faith-based discourses and by providing a pedagogical medium in which faith and spirituality can inform daily social life and personal and political development. While responding to local diasporic needs, these schools struggle to develop new discursive foundations on which to build a pedagogical framework that reflects the culturally hybrid space in which they reside. As alternatives to public secular education and as sites of social reproduction, these schools are constantly challenged to find ways to help Muslim children and youth negotiate positive identities as Muslims and as Canadians.

Avoiding Authoritarianism in the Islamization of Knowledge

Islamic education provides an entry point for faith-centred knowledges and understandings to become valid ways of knowing and making sense of the world and for allowing faith-centred voices to become integral to social, academic, and political processes. Islamic schools produce oppositional knowledge that subverts dominant secular, Eurocentric discourses, which for too long have been viewed as the only valid basis for compulsory education and learning. In this way they enable alternative thinking and non-secular articulations of knowledge and ontology. This path opens the possibility of ideological reform; it also offers a chance to reclaim the hermeneutical spaces of theology and Qur'anic exegesis from patriarchal and authoritarian orientations. As I have emphasized earlier, moving from a faith-centred perspective to a *critical* faith-centred perspective involves avoiding rigid dogmatic thinking; it also requires that spaces be opened for contestation and debate. In addition, it involves re-examining many taken-for-granted aspects of Islamic tradition on the basis of new scholarly perspectives, many of which have not yet gained currency in mainstream Islamic thought. In other words, it is not enough simply to integrate Islamic knowledge; close attention must be paid to what *kind* of knowledge is being imparted and whether it sustains the core values of justice and equity in the Qur'an or has become subservient to patriarchal and authoritarian orientations. Hefner (2007) summarizes the problems facing contemporary Islamic schools:

> Here then is a dilemma, arguably *the* dilemma, at the heart of Islamic education today. Is the purpose of Islamic education to teach fidelity to a fixed and finished canon? Or should religious education offer a high minded but general religious ethics that looks outward on creation and encourages a plurality of methods for fathoming and engaging its wonder? For a Western public shocked by images of terrorist violence and convinced that madrassas may be a big part of the problem, the suggestion that the fault line in Islamic education lies astride this question of scholastic unitarianism versus epistemological pluralism may appear ludicrous. In Muslim educational practice however, there is no more decisive a contest. (p. 35)

In these volatile political times, then, the core problem in Islamic education is an epistemic one. It has become necessary to critique and negotiate the boundaries of faith, knowledge, and identity through this unsettled discursive terrain in order to shift from the path of narrow literalism and dogmatism towards broader and more cosmopolitan epistemological and ontological possibilities.

The Anatomy of Discursive Function in Islamic Schools: Unpacking the Ideological Pathways

In this section I map out how discursive practices function in Islamic schools. This requires us to unpack the textual and rhetorical processes by means of which the discursive practices rooted in Islamic epistemology frame and reference the production of specific kinds of subjectivities in Islamic schools. This process involves a complex articulation of discourse, praxis, and subjectivity, which is carefully woven and entwined within the normative functioning and day-to-day life of Islamic schools.

The ideological worldviews espoused in Mosques and religious institutions play a central role in shaping the way the local diasporic Muslim community, including its Islamic schools, is structured and organized socially, culturally, and politically. The pervasiveness of religious ideologies and culture within the Muslim community impacts everyday life, as well as social and political practices. Too often, these ideologies are premised upon patriarchal and authoritarian discourses. These discourses are contained within specific (often literal) narrations of Islamic epistemology. Other, more progressive Islamic orientations proceed from different readings of the broad corpus of knowledge that constitutes Islamic epistemology. These alternative narrations, which are framed by the values of social justice inherent in Islam, provide a different lens through which these discourses are read, understood, and taken up.

Within Islam's multiple and varied traditions, various discursive formations are produced. All of these proceed from the same epistemological foundations. These foundations are based on a combination of revealed sacred knowledge in the form of the Holy Qur'an, historical narrative based on narrations of prophetic knowledge and wisdom (hadith); and hermeneutic interpretations of these sources, from which Islamic systems of *fiqh* (jurisprudence) are derived. A large part of Islamic epistemology is based on hermeneutic processes. For example, the broad corpus of sharia (Islamic law) is based on scholarly legal interpretations of the Qur'an and hadith, and *tafseer* (exegesis of the

Qur'an) is based on an interpretation of the sacred text. Within these hermeneutic spaces, possibilities exist for alternative readings of these primary epistemological sources. Some contemporary scholars are providing new interpretations based on feminist readings; other scholarly perspectives emphasize social justice as the primary lens for deriving meaning from these textual sources (see, for example, Abou El Fadl, 2001a, 2002; Wadud, 1992).

In the context of Islamic schools, Islamic knowledge is generally based on traditional readings that are not informed by the newer discursive understandings posed by contemporary scholars. As a consequence, certain issues, such as narrow, patriarchal views of women, remain uninterrogated and uncontested. As we have seen, the schools in this study take different approaches to gender equity. While all of these schools promote academic achievement for girls as well as boys, the gender-based social relations and interactions in the schools reveal that girls are more highly regulated as sources of public honour.

A school's ideological orientation, as it is informed by particular readings of foundational Islamic sources, largely determines how such issues are taken up in school policy and practice. Schools informed by alternative discursive understandings would, therefore, operate within different kinds of epistemic boundaries, which would result in different types of polices and practices that have the possibilities of being more 'progressive' with respect to issues of gender and equity.

In envisioning new possibilities for Islamic discourse and praxis, it is important to first understand how discourses operate in schools as central organizing principles – that is, how they inform pedagogy and practice and affect (often strongly) the Islamic subjectivities that are produced. The way in which knowledge within these schools becomes hegemonic and ultimately shapes the social ideological and pedagogical practices of the school needs to be analytically deconstructed to understand how critical interventions and reforms can be made. I contend that this process begins within the discursive foundations I have outlined and is framed by the school's specific religious orientation. For example, within the Sunni Islamic tradition there are four primary *mahdabs* (legal traditions): Maliki, Salafi, Hanafi, and Hanbali. All four were founded by ninth-century Islamic jurists. Islamic schools and religious centres are often aligned with a particular juristic tradition and base their ideology and praxis on the rulings made within that branch of thought. Two of the schools in this study followed a Salafi[2] orientation, which is one of the most conservative religious traditions. Another followed the Hanafi school, while the other did not officially align itself with a particular doctrine.

The specific doctrinal orientation of the school provides a vantage point through which Islamic knowledge is filtered. Islamic epistemology, being the combination of revealed sacred knowledge, historical narrative, and prophetic wisdom, is subject to various interpretive practices, as discussed earlier, including Qur'anic commentary or exegesis and the various forms of juristic knowledge (*fiqh*, sharia) derived from the foundational texts, as represented within the four *madhabs*. These doctrines combine to form the broad corpus of official religious knowledge on which all teaching in the Islamic tradition is based. A large part of this knowledge is then filtered through particular ideological lenses, then disseminated in mosques, schools, and the Muslim community at large through specific rhetorical and textual practices. For example, specific religious messages are communicated through *khutbas* (sermons) and taken up in men's and women's study circles known as *halaqas*. These messages are also circulated as religious texts (i.e., books and magazines), which are sold in Islamic centres and bookstores. They are also found on countless websites.

The Formal and Hidden Curriculum of Islamic Schooling

The religious messages of mosques and Islamic schools present specific normalizing discourses that affect the educational pedagogy and socialization practices at those sites. The knowledge drawn from those discourses is disseminated through the formal curriculum as well as informally. The formal curriculum includes the knowledge presented in the official school curriculum, which Islamic schools reinforce in the classroom through specific texts as a means of guiding students' social and spiritual development. As we have seen, integrative practices that lead to the Islamization of knowledge weave religious knowledge into various aspects of an otherwise secular curriculum and allow this knowledge to become more organically connected to different facets of learning. Through this process, the formal curriculum of religious education becomes broadened in scope and integrative content.

The informal or 'hidden' curriculum is informed by the same discourses as the formal one but operates in less tangible ways. The hidden curriculum is a means through which the implicit assumptions of teachers and other school agents are relayed – assumptions that silently structure social discourse and educational praxis (see Anyon, 1989). Student's behaviour is also affected by their interactions with teachers and by the silent expectations and perceptions that discipline their actions to accord with the school's governing norms. The gen-

Figure 9.1. Anatomy of Discursive Function in Islamic Schools

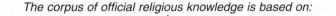

The corpus of official religious knowledge is based on:

↓

---

1 Epistemology: Combination of revealed sacred knowledge, historical narrative/prophetic wisdom, hermeneutics (knowledge based on interpretive reasoning)

---

which is disseminated through:

↓

---

2 Rhetorical and textual practices: e.g., sermons (*khutbas*), study circles (*halaqas*), religious conferences, religious instruction, religiously based texts, etc.

This informs:

↓

---

3 Educational pedagogy, socialization: official educational discourse, hidden curriculum, counselling practices, gendered socialization/expectations, Islamic behaviour, etc.

This knowledge frames and mediates:

↓

---

4 Everyday practices of schooling: e.g., governing rules, regulations, gendered space, ritual practices, etc.

All of these discursive practices structure:

↓

---

5 Subjectivity/ontology: e.g., how students give meaning to themselves and others and how they position themselves within the world.

---

dered boundaries at the Al Rajab school, for example, were maintained and regulated not by physical barriers or written policies but through a disciplining and watchful gaze that could be likened to Foucault's notion of a panopticon (as discussed in chapter six; see also Haw, 1998).

The hidden curriculum also helps govern socialization practices. For example, in some classrooms boys and girls are segregated; this hierarchical organization of social space then reinforces the dominant discursive norms circumscribing gender relations and interactions. But the hidden curriculum can have positive effects, such as when students describe their school as a 'family.' Such feelings of social cohesion and belonging are cultivated not through lectures and texts but rather through verbal and non-verbal interactions among teachers and students.

So the epistemological and ideological foundations on which a school is built inform its everyday practices, including its spiritual and devotional practices as well as social interactions and methods of socialization. Through these ideological and social processes, the discursive practices in Islamic schools produce specific types of subjects. Muslim children and youth begin to frame their identities and subjectivities through the discourses and narratives made available to them. The normative boundaries of what is halal (permissible) and haram (forbidden) constitute the framework on which they erect their spiritual and social lives. Their ways of assigning meaning to themselves and others and of positioning themselves in the world are shaped by their school experience and by the discursive narratives within which they are socialized (see Figure 9.1).

Discourse and Agency

I do not mean to imply that rigid and deterministic forces are at work in Islamic schools that completely subvert independent thought and free will. I am saying, rather, that the avenues through which we express our agency are mediated by specific social, cultural, and discursive practices. In Islamic schools, as in other schools, these practices have both positive and negative outcomes with respect to how they structure specific types of subjectivities. We have seen how Muslim students who have struggled in public schools with negative social influences, such as drug and alcohol use, have embraced the alternative discursive norms in Islamic schools, which promote spirituality and sobriety. We have also heard the narratives of Muslim students who were subjected to negative Islamophobic discourses outside school and who found a greater sense of empowerment and spiritual identity on transferring to Islamic schools. The student-based culture promoted a positive faith-centred perspective; but some students felt that their school's narrow boundaries needed to be challenged. This reminds us that within these discursive spaces and practices resides the power and spirit of critical agency.

From the vantage point of the critical faith-centred epistemology I am proposing, critical agency is vital if we hope to address the systemic oppression that often operates within Islamic institutions. I base my proposals on the epistemological values of social justice that are integral to Islam. By allowing these values to serve as the central ideological lens, as a 'check and balance,' we will be opening up new discursive orientations and practices that have the potential to make Islamic schooling more relevant and viable in a pluralistic society.

Developing a Multicentric Framework for Islamic Knowledges

To reform the (at times) oppressive discursive norms of Islamic institutions, such as schools, we will have to introduce counter-discourses that are capable of mediating and shaping ontological development. Alternative Islamic narratives need to be inserted in order to provide discursive options. As Dei, James, James-Wilson, Karumanchery, and Zine (2001) have argued, inclusive educational practices decentre hegemonic knowledges to make room for other ways of knowing. This forms the basis of 'multi-centric' education that creates a plural centre within educational discourse and praxis. I propose that Islamic education should also be based on the same multi-centric principles that would effectively de-centre the hegemony of authoritarian narratives and present students with the broader discursive possibilities that exist within Islam. Rather than imparting a single authoritative narrative, Islamic pedagogy must widen its discursive boundaries to include alternative epistemological understandings that provide students with the opportunity to investigate these multiple truth claims on ideological, rational, and empirical grounds. Students will then be able to accept or reject options from the various discursive possibilities presented to them.[3] This in turn would foster a more deliberative and less indoctrinating educational environment.

By advocating a more plural centre I am not proposing an 'anything goes' approach to Islamic education. Rather, I am calling for the inclusion of scholarly perspectives that are legitimately derived from valid epistemological sources but that have long been marginalized by the conservative scholarly status quo. These 'subjugated knowledges,' such as Wadud's (1992) feminist exegesis of the Qur'an and the brilliant work of the Islamic legal scholar Khalid Abou El Fadl (2001a, 2001b, 2002), are relatively unknown to local religious authorities, yet these scholars present Islamically valid discourses that are not only intellectually rigorous and engaging but also spiritually inspiring. It is unfortunate that conservative mainstream scholars, whose authoritarian[4] discursive powers are threatened by these intellectually subversive counter-knowledges, view these important and necessary counter-hegemonic discourses as illegitimate and invalid.

If we are to create a more pluralistic centre out of which Islamic discursive knowledges can be disseminated and debated, we will have to move these alternative discourses from the margins to the centre in Islamic institutions. Islamic schools can become a powerful site for deliberating on these emergent scholarly sources, which are revitalizing critical intellectual engagement with the epistemological foundations of Islam. Yet introducing these discourses is easier called for than accomplished. Whenever a source of epistemological authority is challenged, the established vanguards of Islamic knowledge will resist and attempt to delegitimate these counter-narratives. The gatekeepers of Islamic authority have closed the door on critical thought and engagement and have led Muslim culture into a state of intellectual paralysis and decline (see also Abou el Fadl, 2001b, 2002). Attempting to beat down these doors and unsettle the sense of security that many have derived from these static norms and seemingly axiomatic truths is a difficult but necessary task. Breaching the barriers behind which the discursive boundaries of faith frozen in an often de-contextualized and ahistorical space is paramount to the task of achieving the ideals of Islamic schooling based on a critical faith-centred framework.

Recommendations and Strategic Interventions

During this research, several recommendations emerged from the data and my direct observations. I discuss these next, as concrete suggestions for improving Islamic schools and help them better promote academic excellence within a framework that serves to correct the institutional power structures that limit more equitable possibilities.

School Governance

School governance was one of the key areas cited by participants as a space for educational reform. Leadership was seen as lacking in many schools; too often there was a high turnover of unqualified principals. Limited financial resources make it difficult for Islamic schools to attract qualified principals. As a result, many schools hire either retired teachers or people with no educational experience. Many schools are started by individuals and institutions (such as mosques) that lack experience in education. As a result of the growing demand for Islamic schools, the number of these schools in the GTA is increasing every year. Capitalizing on this demand are non-profit institutions, such as mosques, and private businesses. In non-profit schools, the same board that runs the mosque or community organization generally administers the school. The (exclusively male) representatives of these organizations generally lack any experience with education and fail to develop independent school boards.

Over the past two years, Al Safar has established a school board, whose members are appointed rather than elected. Its members are all male elders from the same ethnic group and have backgrounds in fields such as business (at least one member, though, does have a background in education). The school board excludes women and does not reflect the community's ethnic diversity. Because of the composition of the board, it is out of touch with the realities of children and youth. Moreover, the board has failed to include members of the community with strong backgrounds in teaching and school administration, who could contribute knowledge and expertise. Community 'politics,' referred to as a divisive form of 'tribalism,' contributes to these exclusionary practices.

Recently, I was approached by one of the male parents at Al Safar with whom I had worked on the parent committee. He was now a member of the *majlis ashura* (the mosque's governing body), and he wanted me to join the school board, since he was committed to making the board less gender biased. I was pleased with this initiative but declined the offer, suggesting other candidates. I had many pragmatic reasons for not getting involved, and I was also admittedly irked by the fact that, as a parent working in education, , in the past eight years that I had been involved with the school, I had never been asked to provide input on the basis of my knowledge and experience. I hoped that other women (perhaps less jaded) would step up to the plate instead. It is often difficult for women to disrupt the patriarchal standards that are entrenched in these institutions; too often their positions are marginal, ad hoc, and tokenistic.

Creating More Democratic Structures: Parent Associations

An issue related to the authoritarian patriarchy that perpetuates gender-based inequality in school governance is the fact that these institutions lack democratic processes. Schools run by non-profit organizations do have elected representatives; where school boards exist, they are generally appointed. Also, parent associations are often restricted to fundraising activities and have no voice in school policy and practice. (The 'advisory' capacity of parents is limited in the public system as well.) The Islamic principles of *shura* (consultation) call for a stronger commitment to collaborative engagement between parents and school administrators.

The two non-profit schools in this study, Al Safar and Al Shawwal, had parent organizations. The other two, Al Rajab and Al Shaban, were private businesses and did not have parent committees, though parents did serve as volunteers and also helped raise funds on an ad hoc basis. Parents from these schools discussed their involvement in Islamic schools and offered recommendations for overcoming the challenges faced by parent committees.

Shazad complained about the limited role of Al Safar's parents' association. He accused the mosque administration, which governed the school, of attempting to contain the role of parents:

SHAZAD: One of the major problems with Islamic organizations is the power structure. Sometimes the parents' association comes to the level of being just, 'We need funds.' That's their only role. Therefore, it frustrates the parents because most of the parents' overriding concern is for the Islamic school's environment. That's my major concern. So sometimes it's very difficult mobilizing the parents. And because of the power structure, people or groups of people, they like to be in the helm of control and they will maintain that control at all costs at the expense of the frustration of the parents and so forth. And that is not healthy for the child, for the parent, for the community, whatsoever. If they are not doing a good and efficient job, fine; get another person who can do a good job, and let them be; let them have some level of accountability. Maybe to some level of the parents, or some other body, and move forward.

In Shazad's view, the closed power structure of the mosque and the school had consigned parents to marginal roles such as organizing school events, volunteering on field trips, and raising funds; those parents lacked input when it came to school policies and practices. Many parents felt that, in a community-based school where families paid fees for their children to attend, parents should have a stronger decision-making role.

Sobia discussed the parent committee at Al Shawwal. She wanted to be more involved in the school and felt that bake sales and hotdog days were not the best use of her time and experience:

SOBIA: The one sister goes to me, 'How come you didn't come to the [parent association] meeting?' I remember I was asking them, like, 'What do you guys do?' And she's like, 'Oh, you know, we organize bake sales and, you know, we treat the teachers to coffee and donuts and we meet in the mornings.' And I'm just like, 'Well, I'm not available at that time. It won't be a convenient thing.' I don't want to say I'm going to be committed and then not be able to participate. So I said, 'Well, you know, if something comes up, I wouldn't mind getting involved but not in terms of baking cookies or whatever.' For me, that's not how I could use my time most effectively.

For my own experience in a parent organization, I know that parents are underutilized, given the talent and experience available in the school community. There was often an antagonistic relationship between the parents and the school, a result of parents' frustration that their concerns were not being appropriately addressed as well as the inexperience of the school administrators in dealing with those concerns.

Parents had played a strong role in the formation of Al Safar and felt cheated when they were marginalized after the school was founded. Asma and her husband had been highly active in starting the school, and both were involved in the parent association. Yet Asma was disheartened that parents who were so instrumental to the founding of the school, were now shut out of the decision-making processes:

ASMA: We had from near the beginning a parent association. The purpose of that was for the parents to know each other. It was a friendly thing. It was all of us patting ourselves on the back, saying, 'Hey, we did establish this school, and we're very proud of it, and brother, do you have a problem? Maybe we can help.' But as the school grew and there came a volunteer principal, that principal appeared to become very defensive towards her teachers and she appeared to want to control the teachers. There was absolutely no place for a parent in the running of that school. Parents were not allowed to provide input. They were physically removed from school premises. They were insulted. So that was a sad day when I realized that I could not stay there any longer.

Asma removed her children to public school and to another Islamic school. Many families move in and out of the Islamic school system in the hope of 'finding the grass greener' in public schools. In Asma's case, she later re-enrolled her son at Al Safar after two years in the public system. Many parents are frustrated in the short term with the situation in Islamic schools but remain committed in the long term to the benefits of faith-centred learning that they feel ultimately outweigh their frustrations and the shortcomings of Islamic schools.

Ibrahim, a community-based education activist, consulted at Al Shawwal and was asked to recommend ways to improve the school's structure and functioning. He shared with me the directives he gave the imam in charge of the school's administration:

IBRAHIM: Most of the problems we face in Islamic schools are political. I said to the imam, 'First of all, what we need is to strengthen the parent council, and we have to have a board of trustees to run this school so that you, the imam, don't have to be called every minute to tell you what is happening. The board of trustees will be empowered to hire the principal and the teachers and pay them. They will be empowered to raise the funds needed to run this school to make sure there is enough equipment to improve the quality. But let the people who have knowledge in education run the board so that when it comes to appointing a principal, there will be a number of candidates that will compete for the job and be hired based on their experience and knowledge. The trustees will do things to enhance the quality of education in the school.' That was my recommendation. And I still believe that all Islamic schools must have these kinds of board of trustees, a strong parent council, and a strong teacher council.

Ibrahim also felt that the board of trustees should include women in leadership roles. He lamented the patriarchal structures that exiled women from public and political spaces. He criticized the divisive ethnic- and gender-based politics that were thwarting the development of Islamic schools as exemplary institutions. He felt that a 'model school' needed to be developed that would transcend cultural politics and demonstrate the possibilities of Islamic schools:

IBRAHIM: But at the end of the day we are talking about ethnicity, about ego building, you know, and this, by itself, has impeded any effort to produce a good Islamic school. But I still believe that maybe one experimental school can take the lead and try to demonstrate to the others ... You know, "Come and see what we are doing here.' And I think if parents know that there is one good-quality Islamic school, all of them will go there. They will be ready to make the necessary sacrifice in order to give their children a good Islamic education in a good school.

Other parents also felt that greater professionalism was required from school leaders. Qassim felt that in itself, Islamic knowledge was not sufficient qualification for administering a school. An administrator also needed to be able to work with parents and help Muslim children and youth develop a strong sense of identity in the diaspora:

QASSIM: I'm very much against just hiring somebody who they might consider to be Islamically qualified. Like, they might have graduated from Medina University or wherever, but somebody who graduates from Medina University doesn't have the skills of administration. You need to have somebody who has administrative skills, who is able to think long-term and plan long-term and be able to see the need for fostering children who grow up with positive identities; who grow up strongly rooted in what their culture and their belief system hold, and who is able to value the parents as being an important – an integral – part of the whole school system.

Clearly, more work needs to be done to improve parent–school relations and create more democratic governance in Islamic schools. The voices and experience of all stakeholders, including educational specialists, need to be heeded.

From Conflict to Cooperation:
Developing a Federated System of Islamic Schools

At present, Islamic schools in the GTA operate independently and are not part of any organized system. Informal attempts have been made to organize Islamic schools into a federation; in such a system, they would retain their individual autonomy but would also be part of a coalition operating under standardized guidelines administered by a central coordinating body. The educational advocacy group that Ibrahim represented had met with school administrators across the city to discuss the advantages to such a system:

IBRAHIM: There must be a central governance. I think the Jewish schools have that kind of governance. They have what is called the Jewish Federated Schools so that all schools are registered under one kind of board of education. It would be a federation of Islamic schools so every school has to register there and this is the governing body.

Attempts to develop such a system have so far failed, owing to the varied nature of the schools and the competition among them. Schools that are run as businesses do not want to be subservient to outside authority and align with their competitors. Also, competition between non-profit schools impedes any attempts to develop even strategic alliances. For example, the possibilities of developing buying coopera- tives to purchase textbooks at reduced rates or arrange teacher devel- opment workshops were cited as specific economic advantages to building more cooperative alliances, but these benefits have not per- suaded the schools. Qassim, an Islamic school activist, shared his pes- simism about this sort of cooperation:

QASSIM: Because of the nature of our community, I don't see it being an easy process of them [Islamic schools] coming together to try and work collectively towards that ... There's a competition there where, you know, Al Safar has to be better than Al Shawwal, you know what I mean? It's taking something that should be healthy and making it become unhealthy. But collectively, what is the goal? Is the goal to be able to say, 'So and so is the best Islamic school'? Or is it to say, 'We're producing children who will go out there and change society'? And that I'm not sure that they're up for.

Therefore, in Qassim's view the potential for competition and con-flict could divert from the true goals of Islamic schools to guide chil-dren to become good Muslims and good citizens.

Ibrahim believed that an Islamic school federation would result in more uniform educational standards. In the United States, the Council of Islamic Schools of North America (CISNA) had been given author-ity in some states to accredit schools that meet government criteria. Unless Canada's Islamic schools develop a self-regulating system to ensure high standards, community representatives may be compelled to lobby the provincial government to conduct more oversight. At present, there is minimal regulation and accountability, and this has led to divergent standards. In Ibrahim's view, if Islamic schools do not develop a system to regulate their standards, then government inter-vention may be called for:

IBRAHIM: Maybe I think this is where the Minister of Education has to come down very hard to say, 'Look, we are very concerned about ...' You know, to visit these schools and do an evaluation and give them a licence just like a restaurant. If you're running a restaurant, you get a visit every year. You have to renew your licence. To run a school, you've got to be licensed to run a school.

He also suggested a rating system for Islamic schools based on spe-cific criteria, much as universities are ranked every year. The criteria might include whether the schools had certified teachers; whether they participated in provincial standardized testing; and whether they had a library and a gymnasium. This would inform prospective parents about the schools they were choosing for their children. He also argued that the Ministry of Education should be sent copies of this annual report, especially if schools were receiving funding in the form of tax credits, to ensure greater public accountability.

Funding and Public Accountability

Tax credits for parents who send their children to private schools is a highly contentious issue. Opponents argue that tax credits will erode an already underfunded public system. Proponents reply that their taxes are supporting a public system they are not utilizing and that tax credits will allow them to channel their taxes to schools of their choice. A more nuanced analysis of tax credits needs to be undertaken. Supporters of public education have every right to contest the channelling of public money to private institutions; but a distinction needs to be made between elite private schools and not-for-profit, community-based schools. Many Islamic schools are not-for-profit, and most of them charge only nominal fees to ensure that lower-income immigrant and refugee children can attend them. Thus, they have limited resources to pay teachers and buy materials. Future governments may need to consider whether these not-for-profit schools merit funding, provided that they comply with mandated criteria.

Many Islamic schools lack sufficient funds to meet ministry guidelines. Qualified not-for-profit schools should be able to access government funding – indeed, they already can in every other province: Quebec, Manitoba, Saskatchewan, British Columbia, Alberta, and the Maritime provinces all provide per pupil grants or partial funding to schools that meet specific criteria – for example, to schools that follow provincial education guidelines and hire certified teachers (see Canadian Education Association, 1992). Shapiro's (1985) report proposes ten funding options for private schools. Representatives of Islamic schools have endorsed the 'associated schools model' as a viable option. These schools would receive partial funding and operate under the auspices of local school boards. Shapiro (1985) explains this alternative vision for funding: 'Goals of this model would be to bring many private schools under the umbrella of a public system, and, at the same time, provide a large variety of public choice. In time, some associated private schools might become alternative schools within the system' (p. 131). This model would open the possibility of accommodating various types of independent schools, such as Afrocentric schools and faith-based schools, under the umbrella of the public education system, thereby maintaining public accountability. It would also provide more options for students in a diverse society. Broadening the purview of public education to accommodate some of these schools would result in a greater diversity of educational possibilities.

Teacher Development

Another important issue for Islamic schools is professional development. Many teachers in Islamic schools lack certification. Some have had experience teaching 'back home' but are new to teaching in Canada. A critical intervention in this area was made through MENTORS (Muslim Educational Network, Training, and OutReach

Service), a registered charitable organization that promotes community capacity development through educational services. MENTORS developed a teacher education institute for teachers in Islamic schools. It also formed a partnership with the Ontario Institute for Studies in Education at the University of Toronto which provided seminars for participants on how to apply for the teacher education program. Most teachers in Islamic schools are not certified, so these seminars were an important means for them to learn how to qualify for and enrol in teacher education programs.

The seminars were scheduled over two days in the summer of 2001 and were attended by 135 teachers from 16 Islamic schools across Ontario. The event included an 'education fair' that showcased books and software. Twelve workshops were delivered each day by professional facilitators on topics such as the following: classroom management; child-centred classrooms; lesson planning; students with learning problems; critical literacy; teaching to multiple intelligences; creative problem solving; educational leadership; art in the Qur'an; Islamic art; and integrating Islam with the curriculum. These topics addressed many of the gaps I had observed in Islamic schools' pedagogy and practices. There were also roundtable discussions where administrators could discuss school governance. This was a unique opportunity to provide pedagogical support to teachers in a forum that allowed them to share knowledge, experience, and information with one another. As a result of popular demand and continued need, the teacher education institute is becoming an annual event, with different post-secondary institutions hosting the institute each year.

Teachers were also appreciative of the opportunity to learn more about the teacher education program, although the criteria for admission were prohibitive for many who were unable to access original transcripts from their universities back home, due to situations of war and their displacement as refugees. Academic institutions should take these factors into account; specifically, they should view the geopolitical climate as a mitigating circumstance, not as a basis for exclusion. It is unfortunate that those who are fleeing war-torn countries cannot apply for admission to certain post-secondary programs because they have fled war-torn countries and no longer have access to original transcripts.

Many Islamic school teachers cannot afford to leave their jobs to attend a teacher education program full-time. A part-time program (i.e., weekends and nights) offering core topics covered in the full-time program would make this kind of training possible. Also, the teaching practices of these student teachers could be observed on site rather than in a practicum setting. These types of flexible learning situations for prospective teachers in community-based schools would go far to promote equity and access for marginalized communities.

From my perspective, these interventions showed the 'catalytic validity' of my work that Lather (1986b) proposed as one of the hallmarks of critical ethnography. Catalytic validity refers to the ways in which research can become a catalyst toward social change and transformation, through a process of 'conscientization,' as proposed by Freire (1973) that allows participants to critically engage in activities to improve their conditions. The teacher institute served this purpose of developing a critical awareness and providing a response to specific needs in the community that were necessary for educational reform. This research was instrumental as the catalyst for these important developments to take place.

Gender Equity: Reframing Gender Discourses

The final key area of reform in Islamic schools is gender equity. Islamic schools are often constrained by puritanical discourses framing gender relations. This has led to various constraints for female students, albeit at a social rather than an academic level. Female Muslim students have complained about the lack of physical education opportunities for them, both in schools and in the broader community. The practical and discursive constraints limit opportunities for Muslim women, who are discouraged from being physically active in public spaces. Better opportunities need to be created for them to lead full and active lives. To ensure that Muslim girls are physically healthy and fit, alternative programs need to be moved higher on the list of school and community priorities.

Muslim girls need to have more empowering narratives available to them that will frame their sense of possibilities for the future. Muslim women generally are subject to double alienation: gendered Islamophobia in society, and restrictive gender-based patriarchal norms in their communities. To rewrite these scripts in more empowering ways will require a remapping of the discursive boundaries that circumscribe and define their identities. Opening up broader, more empowering narratives for Muslim women will involve reforming the normative discourses in key sites in the community, such as mosques and schools, by providing alternative narratives. Gender-based reform must also involve letting women take on key leadership roles in the community, both on school boards and on the governing councils of mosques. This will allow for greater representation of Muslim women on terms they themselves define.

The Way Forward

This study has provided a new vantage point for critically interrogating the role of Islamic schools in a diasporic context. It has provided new ways to understand the social and discursive construction of gendered identities and gender relations in these schools. It has also outlined the ways in which the Islamization of knowledge plays an integral role in how meanings are constructed in these educational sites. I hope this investigation has represented the realities of my participants in ways that do justice to their commitment to faith-centred learning and to leading spiritually-based lives, and that it has given voice to their concerns relating to the often challenging present-day conditions in these schools.

Islamic education, delivered from a critical faith-centred perspective, is essential to Muslim youth if they hope to navigate the contradictions and complexities of the culturally hybrid spaces they inhabit in the diaspora. For youth who choose a faith-centred path, this type of critical engagement provides a site for social critique, resistance, and transformation and is the portal through which Muslims can access the broader public square. My analysis has highlighted the challenges and possibilities of Islamic schooling, as narrated by the stakeholders who have offered their stories. I have been especially inspired in this work by the Muslim youth who shared with me their struggles to claim their identity as both Muslims and Canadians, struggles that are their entry point to their journey on the 'straight path.'

Notes

Chapter 1

1 For example, Azmi (2001) describes events in the 1970s, when the Muslim community in Toronto began to organize around the distorted manner in which Muslims and Islam were being portrayed in the public school curriculum. In the mid-1970s a Toronto-based group, the Canadian Society of Muslims, began a campaign to counter the anti-Muslim and anti-Islamic bias in school textbooks. It prepared a report, *On the Image of Islam in School Textbooks in the Province of Ontario,* and submitted it to the Ontario Ministry of Education on 16 May 1975. This report listed eleven history textbooks approved for study in Ontario schools that were deemed offensive to Islam and Muslims and called for their removal from schools. When the government did not act on the report, a public campaign lasting almost two years was launched. During that campaign, a six-thousand-signature petition was gathered, a spirited protest was held at Queen's Park, a letter-writing campaign was undertaken, and efforts were made to attract support from Muslim political leaders and the UN. In the end, seven of the books listed in the report were removed from the curriculum, but the other four were not. Azmi reported that the effort to eliminate these few books from the educational canon was met with 'significant resistance and considerable hostility, both from public education authorities and the local media.' Moreover, 'from the perspective of the Muslim community, this incident confirmed that there existed only a token willingness to accommodate Muslim concerns on the part of public education authorities, no matter how passionately these are perceived by sizeable sections of the Muslim community' (p. 261).

2 Halal food means food that is permissible according to Islamic tenets. Muslims are forbidden to eat products that contain pork or alcohol or

their by-products. As well, meat must be slaughtered according to Islamic specifications that render it halal (i.e., beginning with the name of God, slaughtering with a sharp knife in a humane manner, and draining the blood).

3 Ontario's Muslim population has doubled over the past decade, largely as a result of immigration. Visit http://www12.statcan.ca/english/census01/Products/Analytic/companion/rel/on.cfm.

4 It is important to distinguish between 'Islamic schooling' and 'Islamic education' (albeit the two are not mutually exclusive). By Islamic *schooling* I mean a structured system of Islamic learning that takes place in organized sites such as full- and part-time schools and home schooling environments. Islamic *education* I use more broadly to refer to the dissemination of Islamic knowledge through formal and informal channels, both within and outside structured sites of learning. Thus, Islamic education takes place within sites of Islamic schooling, but it is not confined to those sites and can be transmitted informally through families as part of the 'pedagogy of the home,' or through dialogue with community sites and with the non-Muslim community.

5 *Madrassah* in Arabic simply means 'school.' In North America, however, the term often refers to part- time after-school or weekend schools for Islamic education. Azmi (2001) describes three full-time *madrassahs* in Ontario that operate on different ideals than other Islamic schools in that they ignore or reject outright the public school model, viewing it as an inappropriate site for Islamic education; they favour more 'traditional' knowledge and practices of Islamic learning. These schools also place greater emphasis on Arabic and Qur'anic memorization and recitation and pay limited attention to 'secular' subjects. Azmi notes that proponents of *madrassahs* and Islamic schools have competing ideologies relating to the role of Islamic education in Canada. Supporters of *madrassahs* contend that Islamic schools reproduce the secular public school model to the detriment of a more 'authentic' Islamic way of learning. Also, these *madrassahs* hold a more segregationist social ethic than Islamic schools, which generally promote integration and model their institutional practices and curriculum on the public education system.

6 It is interesting that in 2006, when seventeen young people in Toronto were charged with alleged terrorism activities, this did not open a discussion of how conditions in public schools (which all of the accused attended) might have led to their plans to commit violence.

7 'Imam' is an Islamic term for anyone who leads a congregation in prayer.

It is traditionally used to denote Islamic scholars and religious leaders in the community.

8 The term fundamentalism is contested by many Muslims as a Christian-centred term that does not apply to Islam. However, I use the term to denote the narrow and rigid conceptions and worldviews attributed to a literalist reading of Islamic doctrine. Alternately, I use the term 'puritan' interchangeably with 'fundamentalist.'

9 For example, a group of Muslim activists in the Greater Toronto Area (GTA) have recently begun to develop a 'think tank' and social justice reference group to consider the strategic engagements and interventions that Muslim intellectuals and activists should be involved within to further develop a positive and proactive Muslim presence in the North American diaspora.

10 An *ijaza* was not a formal insititutional diploma. Rather, it was a kind of certification that an individual had studied in some fashion a particular text or body of knowledge with a particular *shaykh* (Berkey, 2003, p. 225).

11 Berkey (2003) notes that while Islam is not inherently antirational (as evident in the flourishing of the physical sciences during the Islamic Golden Age), many religious scholars or *ulema* were suspicious of knowledge drawn from pre-Islamic sources. The thirteenth-century Ayyubid sultan al-Malik al-Kamil prohibited the *ulema* in Damascus from studying or teaching anything but religious sciences and expelled students of logic and the 'sciences of the ancients' (p. 230).

12 Where gender-biased language arises, I will acknowledge its inappropriateness with '[*sic*].'

13 Imam Al Ghazzali explains the concept of the 'heart' in terms of its Islamic meaning: 'When we speak of the heart, know that we mean the reality of man [*sic*], which sometimes is called "ruh" [spirit] and sometimes "nafs" [soul]; we do not mean that piece of flesh which lies in the left side of the chest; that organ is not worthy for the cattle possess it; as do the dead. It can be seen by the ordinary eyes, belongs to this world, which is called the visible world [shahadah]. The reality of the heart is not of this world; it has come to this world as a stranger or a passer-by, and that visible piece of meat is its vehicle and means, and all of the bodily features are its army, and it is the king of the whole body; the realization of God and the perception of His beauty and its function' (in Sharifi, 1979, p. 79).

14 In supporting multicultural education as integral to Islamic learning, Shamma quotes the following verse from the Holy Qur'an: 'Allah has created you from a single male and female and made you into nations

and tribes so that you may know one another. Verily the most honoured
of you in the sight of God is the most righteous of you' (49:13). This, she
writes, is in contrast to the status quo in American education, which privileges the knowledge of the dominant culture. She argues: 'It stands to
follow that if only America's history is emphasized and mostly (White)
American scientists, inventors, writers and humanitarians, and other
notables are taught, then the inescapable conclusion is that Americans, by
virtue of being (White) Americans, are better than everyone else' (p. 281).

15   American Islamic educator Dawud Tauhidi (2006) has created a program
for developing a holistic Islamic curriculum based on a *tawhidic* framework rooted in seven key principles: *tawheed* (God consciousness) and
moral, intellectual, physical, interpersonal, cultural, and social literacy.
The document further outlines a model for Islamic education based on
character development, which Tauhidi regards as necessary to fill the
spiritual void created by secular modernity, which he argues has lead to
a variety of societal ills.

16   Al-Fatiha is the opening verse of the Qur'an and one that is traditionally
read to begin activities.

17   The term hijab refers to the headscarf traditionally worn by Muslim
women. The term *veil* is also used to refer to the headscarf, while niqab is
the term for a veil covering the face.

18   *Bradari* refers to the extended kinship network or clan.

19   The notion that public schools are truly secular is contested. Blumenfeld
(2006), for example, discusses the Christian hegemony and privilege operating in American public schools through celebrations of Christmas and
Easter – practices that are also common in Canadian schools. Blumenfeld
describes a symbiotic relationship between Christian privilege and the
religious oppression of non-Christian minorities: 'oppression towards
non-Christians gives rise to Christian privilege in the United States and
Christian privilege maintains oppression toward non-Christian individuals and faith communities' (p. 196). Celebrations of religious traditions are
supposed to be carried out in a secular manner, and schools are not
allowed to proselytize; even so, Christian symbols are prevalent in the
form of Christmas trees, as well as in school assemblies where Christian
themes and carols are presented. The ubiquity of these practices renders
them invisible and therefore unscrutinized. As Blumenfeld notes: 'Christian dominance is therefore maintained by its relative invisibility, and with
this invisibility privilege is neither analyzed nor scrutinized, neither interrogated or confronted' (p. 206). Joshi (2006) further argues that Christian
privilege is characterized by the power to define normalcy: 'That which is

associated with the Christian norm is considered religious or spiritual while that which is not is rendered exotic and illegitimate and relegated to cult status' (p. 122). Christian hegemony and privilege therefore render the secular nature of public schools questionable.

Chapter 2

1 According to Taylor (2002), secular notions of spirituality stem from '*neo-colonizing* spirituality,' where 'notions of spirit are subordinated in a more secular worldview, such that it is human will and mind that form the primary opposition to matter' (p. 1). Spirit, in other words, is subordinated to intellectual faculties. Concerns may arise that this strips spirituality of any metaphysical connotations. While it is important to develop broad notions of spirituality (perhaps including secular notions) it is equally important to ensure that such moves do not empty spirituality of its metaphysical, divine, or cosmological grounding.

2 For example, the Prophet narrated the following statements: 'Make peace between one another for enmity and malice tear up heavenly rewards by the roots.' 'Do not say, that if people do good to us we will do good to them; and if people oppress us we will oppress them; but determine that if people do you good, you will do good to them; and if people oppress you, you will not oppress them.'

3 Another hadith defines 'excellence' as actions that work towards social justice: 'What actions are most excellent? To gladden the heart of a human being, to feed the hungry, to help the afflicted, to lighten the sorrow of the sorrowful, and to remove the wrongs of the injured.'

4 For example, liberal notions of the 'good life' are believed to be best determined through an individual's own moral convictions and autonomy, rather than a set of predetermined precepts (see McLaughlin, 1992, p. 118).

5 In Canada, according to a report by the Toronto Police Service, there was a 66 per cent increase in hate crimes in 2001. The greatest increase was against Muslims. Of the 121 hate crimes linked directly to 9/11, 45 were perpetrated against Muslims, 20 against Jews, and 38 against other groups.

6 Refugee Housing Task Force Meeting Minutes, 16 October 2001.

7 In Islamic tradition, *jinn* are created from the fire of hot winds (Qur'an, 15:27) and from smokeless fire (Qur'an, 55:15).

8 For example, interest in spiritual cosmology led to scientific breakthroughs such as the solar and lunar calendars.

Chapter 3

1 In the Muslim community, members are commonly referred to as 'brother' and 'sister' to denote a fellowship of faith and as a form of fictive kinship.

2 An abaya is a long overcoat worn over street clothes.

3 Student interviews took place after my period of teaching in the school so as not to place the students in an awkward situation that could have resulted in having them simply 'telling me what they think I want to hear.' I was concerned about minimizing the relations of power within the research encounter.

Chapter 4

1 *Shalwar khameez* refers to the long tunic and baggy pants worn traditionally by South Asian women.

2 For example, some relevant hadith regarding neighbours have narrated the following: 'He who believes in Allah and the Last Day let him not harm his neighbour; and he who believes in Allah and the Last Day let him show hospitality to his guest; and he who believes in Allah and the Last Day let him speak good or remain silent.' And also: 'The best of companions with Allah is the one who is best to his companions, and the best of neighbours to Allah is the one who is the best of them to his neighbour.'

3 'RRSP' stands for 'registered retirement savings plan.'

4 'Allah' is recognized as the name of God by Muslims. In Arabic it is neither masculine nor feminine, which conforms to the notion of God in Islam as being neither male nor female, but rather transcending notions of gender and other anthropomorphic characteristics.

5 Here Nusaybah is referring to the Islamic notion of *dunya*, or material world, which according to the Islamic world view is temporal and transitory, compared to the *akhira*, or hereafter, which is eternal.

6 The term *mashallah* means 'by the will of Allah' and is used by Muslims to praise specific actions.

7 The term *jazak Allah* is used in the Islamic lexicon in place of 'thank you' as a means to confer blessings on another.

8 The term *insha'allah* means 'God willing.'

Chapter 5

1 Other recent examples of gendered Islamophobia: An eleven-year-old girl
   in Quebec was forbidden to wear the hijab while playing soccer. FIFA
   (Fédération Internationale de Football Association) later ruled that the
   ban was appropriate on the grounds that the scarf posed a safety risk.
   The xenophobic 'Citizens' Code' in Herouxville, Quebec, banned the
   burqa, the niqab, and the stoning of women in response to debates on
   'reasonable accommodation' in that province. In both incidents, the
   Muslim woman's body was scripted as a 'dangerous foreigner' embodying fears that represent not so much personal risk as they do a kind of
   civilizational danger.
2 The burqa is a long cloak or overcoat worn by some Muslim women.
3 'TTC' is the acronym for the Toronto Transit Commission, which operates
   buses, subways, and streetcars.
4 'Hijabi' is a colloquial term used among Muslim women to refer to those
   who wear the veil or headscarf.
5 A *jilbab* is a long overcoat worn by some Muslim women (also referred to
   as an abaya). It is the official school uniform for girls in some Islamic
   schools.
6 Controversies over the full face veil or niqab were ignited recently in
   Britain after a teaching assistant who wore it was suspended for refusing
   to remove it. The school authorities contended that students who were
   non-native speakers of English were having trouble understanding her
   without seeing her face and mouth. Debates surrounding the face veil
   have since unfolded in the British political arena. Jack Straw, leader of the
   House of Commons, criticized the niqab as being 'such a visible statement of separation and of difference' as to jeopardize British social
   harmony. He added that he refused to speak to women at his North
   England constituency office who donned the face veil. These sentiments
   were echoed by Prime Minister Tony Blair, who called the face veil a
   'mark of separation' that 'makes other people from outside the community feel uncomfortable.' A spokesman for the opposition Conservative
   Party also weighed in on the debate, arguing that some British Muslims –
   who comprise almost 3 per cent of the country's population – had set
   themselves on a course of 'voluntary apartheid,' leading separate and
   isolated lives outside the mainstream of British society (Cowell, 2006). In
   a post-9/11 context, fear and suspicion are being mapped onto Muslim
   women's bodies, which are seen as bearing a foreign, alien, and poten-

tially dangerous culture and way of life that threatens the status quo. Questions of whether Muslims are capable of truly 'embodying' citizenship by assimilating with Europe's mores, customs, and dress codes continue to spark xenophobic reactions.
7 Muslim women use the term 'niqabi' to refer to women who adopt the niqab or face veil.

Chapter 6

1 Roald, 2001, discusses female circumcision as a pre-Islamic cultural practice that still exists in some parts of the Muslim world, as another extreme form of controlling female sexuality (p. 251). The practice is a drastic means of disciplining the 'dangerous feminine.'
2 CRLO is the acronym for the Permanent Council for Scientific Research and Legal Opinions, the official institution in Saudi Arabia responsible for issuing Islamic legal opinions.
3 In Arabic, *iman* refers to faith; *hayah* refers to modesty and is applied to both males and females.
4 In Arabic, *salah* refers to prayer; *dua* refers to supplications made following the prayer.
5 'Imam' refers to the leader of the prayer.

Chapter 7

1 This phrase is known in the Islamic lexicon as the *shahadah*, or declaration of faith, which states, 'There is no God but Allah and Muhammed is his messenger.'
2 This phrase means 'peace be with you' and is used by Muslims as a salutation or greeting and when parting.
3 The term *subhanallah* is used to praise God. Amani is using it here to draw attention to the wonders of creation that she explains in her science lesson.

Chapter 8

1 EQAO is the acronym for the Education Quality and Accountability Office, an arm's-length agency of the Ontario Ministry of Education that designs and administers standardized tests.
2 The *adhan* is the call to prayer.

3 There are ninety-nine different attributes of Allah in the Islamic tradition.
   Learning the various names given to Allah based on these attributes is an
   integral part of Islamic teaching and learning.

Chapter 9

1 From Al-Khatib Al-Baghdadi, Sharaf As/hab Al Hadith; At-Tabrizi,
   Mishkat Al-Masabih.
2 Salafism ('predecessors' or 'early generations') is a generic term that
   refers to a school of thought that takes the pious ancestors (Salaf) of early
   Islam as exemplary models.
3 I would also propose that other sectarian discourses be included as a
   means to present the epistemological variety of Islamic traditions.
4 In *Speaking in God's Name*, Khalid Abou El Fadl (2001a) powerfully outlines how authoritarianism is constructed. He sees authoritarianism as 'a
   fraudulent claim whose natural effect is to usurp Divine Will' (p. 141). He
   continues: 'Authoritarianism is the marginalization of the ontological
   reality of the Divine and the depositing of this Divine Will in the agent so
   that the agent effectively becomes self-referential' (p. 141). He argues that
   only Allah, the Qur'an, and the Prophet are *authoritative* and attempts to
   usurp and subvert this authority and replace it with one's own will
   become part of an authoritarian narrative.

References

Abdul Rauf, M. (1983). The future of Islamic tradition in North America. In E.H. Waugh, B. Abu Laban, & R. Quereshi (Eds.), *The Muslim community in North America* (pp. 27–280). Calgary: University of Calgary Press.

Abdus-Sabur, Q. 1995. The infrequency of antisocial behaviour in Islamic schools in North America. *Muslim Education Quarterly, 12*(3), 56-61.

Abou El Fadl, K. (2001a). *Speaking in God's name*. Oxford: Oneworld.

Abou El Fadl, K. (2001b). *Conference of the books*. Lanham: University Press of America.

Abou El Fadl, K. (2002). The place of tolerance in Islam. In J. Cohen and I. Lague (Eds.), *The place of tolerance in Islam* (pp. 3–26). Boston: Beacon.

Abu Laban, B. (1983). The Canadian Muslim community: The need for a new survival strategy. In R. Quraishi, E.H. Waugh, & B. Abu Laban (Eds.), *The Muslim community in North America* (pp. 75–92). Edmonton: University of Alberta Press.

Abu-Lughod, L. (1991). Writing against culture. In R. Fox (Ed.), *Recapturing anthropology* (pp. 137–62). Santa Fe: School of American Research Press.

Abu-Odeh, L. (2000). Crimes of honor and the construction of gender in Arab societies. In P. Ilkkaracan (Ed.), *Women and sexuality in Muslim societies* (pp. 363–80). Istanbul: Women for Human Rights, New Ways, and Women Living under Muslim Laws (WLUML).

Ad-Darsh, S.M. (1996). Islam and the education of Muslim women. In *Issues in Islamic education* (pp. 24–7). London: Muslim Educational Trust.

Afshar, H. (1989). Education: Hopes, expectations and achievements of Muslim women in West Yorkshire. *Gender and Education, 1*(3), 261–72.

Ahmad, I. (2000). Building Muslim civil society from the bottom up. Paper presented at the American Muslim Social Scientists meeting, October 2000, Georgetown University, Washington.

Ahmed, L. (1992). *Women and gender in Islam*. New Haven: Yale University Press.

Al Hibri, A. (2000). An introduction to Muslim women's rights. In G. Webb (Ed.), *Windows of faith* (pp. 51–71). Syracuse: Syracuse University Press.

Al-Jabri, H. (1995). Profile: Double youth, the split personality syndrome. *The Message* (Canada), *19*(8), 28.

Alloula, M. (1986). *The colonial harem*. Minneapolis: University of Minnesota Press.

Al-Naquib al-Attas, S.M. (1979). Preliminary thoughts on the nature of knowledge and the definition and aims of education. In S.M. al-Naquib al-Attas (Ed.), *Aims and objectives of Islamic education* (pp. 19–47). London: Hodder and Stoughton and Jeddah: King Abdul Aziz University.

Al Otaibi, M.M., & Rashid, H.M. (1997). The role of schools in Islamic society: Historical and contemporary perspectives. *American Journal of Islamic Social Science, 14*(4), 1–18.

Al-Qaradawi, Y. (1960). *The lawful and prohibited in Islam*. Indianapolis: American Trust.

Anderson, G. (1989). Critical ethnography in education: Origins, current status, and new directions. *Review of Educational Research, 59*(3), 249–70.

Anwar, M. (1986). *Young Muslims in a multicultural society*. London: Islamic Foundation.

Anyon, J. (1989). Social class and the hidden curriculum of work. In J.H. Ballantine (Ed.), *Schools and society* (pp. 257–79). Mountain View: Mayfield Publishing.

Azmi, S. (2001). Muslim educational institutions in Toronto, Canada. *Journal of Muslim Minority Affairs, 21*(2), 259–72.

Bammate, H. (1963). *The Muslim contribution to civilization*. Takoma Park: Crescent.

Barlas, A. (2002). *Believing women in Islam: Unreading patriarchal interpretations of the Quran*. Austin: University of Texas Press.

Basit, T.N. (1997). 'I want more freedom, but not too much': British Muslim girls and the dynamism of family values. *Gender and Education, 9*(4), 425–39.

Baum, G. (1987). *Compassion and solidarity: The church for others*. CBC Massey Lectures. Montreal: CBC Radio Canada.

Berkey, J.P. (2003). *The formation of Islam*. Cambridge: Cambridge University Press.

Berkey, J.P. (2007). Madrasas medieval and modern: Politics, education, and the problem of Muslim identity. In R.W. Hefner and M.Q. Zaman (Eds.), *Schooling Islam* (pp. 40–60). Princeton: Princeton University Press.

Berns McGown, R. (1999). *Muslims in the diaspora.* Toronto: University of Toronto Press.

Bleher, S.M. (1996). A programme for Muslim education in a non-Muslim society. In *Issues in Islamic Education* (pp. 61–65). London: Muslim Educational Trust.

Blumenfeld, W.J. (2006). Christian privilege in the promotion of 'secular' and not-so 'secular' mainline Christianity in public schooling and in the larger society. *Equity and Excellence in Education.* Special Issue: Beliefs and Biases: Ethno-Religious Oppression in Schools, *39* (3): 195–210.

Borland, K. (1991). 'That's not what I said': Interpretive conflict in oral narrative research. In S.B. Gluck and D. Patai (Eds.), *Women's words* (pp. 63–75). New York: Routledge.

Borovoy, A.A. (1996). A key reason to bar funding to more religious schools. *Toronto Star,* 18 January.

Bullock, K.H. (2000). The gaze and colonial plans for the unveiling of Muslim women. *Studies in Contemporary Islam, 2*(2), 1–20.

Bullock, K.H. (2002). *Rethinking Muslim women and the veil.* Herndon: International Institute of Islamic Thought.

Burgess, A. (1990). Co-education: The disadvantage for schoolgirls. *Gender and Education, 2*(1), 91–5.

Callon, E. (1997). Discrimination and religious schooling. Paper presented at the Canadian Centre for Philosophy and Public Policy Conference on Citizenship in Diverse Societies: Theory and Practice, University of Toronto, October 1997.

Canadian Education Association. (1992). *The public funding of private schools in Canada.* Toronto.

Castellano, M.B. (1999). Updating Aboriginal traditions of knowledge. In G.J.S. Dei, B. Hall, & D. Goldin-Rosenberg (Eds.), *Indigenous knowledge in global contexts: Multiple readings of our world* (pp. 21–36). Toronto: University of Toronto Press.

Clarke, L. (2003). Hijab according to the Hadith: Text and interpretation. In S.S. Alvi, H. Hoodfar, & S. McDonough (Eds.), *The Muslim veil in North America* (pp. 214–86). Toronto: Women's Press.

Cooke, M. (2001). *Women claim Islam.* New York: Routledge.

Cowell, A. (2006). Behind the veil debate: The British debate over full-face veils worn by some Muslim women raises a bigger issue: How well are Muslims assimilating in Great Britain and the rest of Europe? *New York Times Upfront,* 27 November.

Davies, B., Dormer, S., Gannon, S., Laws, C., Rocco, S., Taguchi, H.L., & McCann, H. (2001). Becoming schoolgirls: The ambivalent project of subjectification. *Gender and Education, 13*(2), 167–82.

Dei, G.J.S. (1996). *Antiracism education: Theory and practice.* Halifax: Fernwood.

Dei, G.J.S. (1998). Why write back? The role of Afrocentric discourse in social change. *Canadian Journal of Education, 23*(2), 200–8.

Dei, G.J.S. (2001a). Anticolonial thought and the challenge of subversive pedagogy. Paper read at the Transformative Learning Conference, Ontario Institute for Studies in Education/University of Toronto, 3 November 2001.

Dei, G.J.S. (2001b). The resistance to amputation: Spiritual knowing, transformative learning, and antiracism. Keynote address, Transformative Learning Conference, Ontario Institute for Studies in Education/University of Toronto, 3 November 2001.

Dei, G.J.S., & Azgharzadeh, A. (2001). The power of social theory: The anticolonial discursive framework. *Journal of Educational Thought, 35*(3), 297–323.

Dei, G.J.S., Hall, B.L. & Rosenberg, D.G. (2000). Introduction. In G.J.S. Dei, B.L. Hall & D.G. Rosenberg (Eds.), *Indigenous knowledges in global contexts.* Toronto: University of Toronto Press.

Dei, G.J.S., James, I.M., James-Wilson, S., Karumanchery, L., & Zine, J. (2001). *Removing the margins: The challenges and possibilities of inclusive schooling.* Toronto: Canadian Scholars' Press.

Dei, G.J.S., James-Wilson, S. & Zine, J. (2002). *Inclusive schooling: A teacher's companion to removing the margins.* Toronto: Canadian Scholars' Press.

Dei, G.J.S., Mazzuca, J., McIsaac, E., & Zine, J. (1997). *Reconstructing 'dropout': A critical ethnography of the dynamics of Black students' disengagement from school.* Toronto: University of Toronto Press.

Driscoll, E. (1997). Hunger, representation, and the female body. *Journal of Feminist Studies in Religion, 13*(1), 91–104.

Durkee, N. (1987). Primary education of Muslim children in North America. *Muslim Educational Quarterly, 5*(1), 53–81.

El Guindi, F. (1999). *Veil, modesty, privacy, and resistance.* London: Berg.

El Habti, R. (2004). Laïcité, women's rights, and the headscarf issue in France. Retrieved from http://www.karamah.org/docs/Veil_Paper.pdf.

Essed, P. (1991). *Understanding everyday racism.* Newbury Park: Sage.

Essed, P. (1996). *Diversity: Gender, color, and culture.* Amherst: University of Massachusetts Press.

Foucault, M. (1975). *Discipline and punish.* New York: Vintage.

Foucault, M. (1982). The subject and power. In H. Dreyfus & P. Rabinow (Eds.), *Michel Foucault: Beyond structuralism and hermeneutics* (pp. 208–28). Chicago: University of Chicago Press.

Francis, B. (1999). Modernist reductionism or post-structuralist relativism: Can we move on? An evaluation of the arguments in relation to feminist educational research. *Gender and Education, 11*(4), 381–93.

Freire, P. (1973). *Pedagogy of the oppressed*. New York: Continuum.

Freire, P. (1997). *Pedagogy of the heart*. New York: Continuum.

Game, A. (1991). *Doing the social: Toward a deconstructive sociology*. Toronto: University of Toronto Press.

Giroux, H. (1983). *Theory and resistance in education: A pedagogy for the opposition*. South Hadley, MA: Bergin and Harvey.

Glazer, B., & Strauss, A. (1967). *The discovery of grounded theory*. Chicago: Aldine.

Gorder, C. (1996). *Home schools: An alternative*. Mesa, AZ: Blue Bird.

Gutmann, A. (1996). Challenges of multiculturalism in democratic education. In R.K. Fullwider (Ed.), *Public education in a multicultural society: Policy, theory, critique* (pp. 156–79). Cambridge: Cambridge University Press.

Hajjaji-Jarrah, S. (2003). Women's modesty in Qur'anic commentaries: The founding discourse. In S.S. Alvi, H. Hoodfar, & S. McDonough (Eds.), *The Muslim veil in North America* (pp. 145–80). Toronto: Women's Press.

Halstead, M. (1991). Radical feminism, Islam, and the single sex school debate. *Gender and Education, 3*(3), 263–78.

Hamdani, D. 1999. Canadian Muslims on the eve of the 21st century. *Journal of Muslim Minority Affairs, 19*(2), 197–209.

Hammersley, M., & Atkinson, P. (1983). *Ethnography: Principles and practice*. London: Tavistock.

Handa, A. (2003). *Of silk saris and mini skirts: South Asian girls walk the tightrope of culture*. Toronto: Women's Press.

Haw, K. (1997). Why Muslim girls are more feminist in Muslim schools. In M. Griffiths & B. Troyna (Eds.), *Antiracism, culture, and social justice in education* (pp. 43–60). Stoke-on-Trent, UK: Trentham Books.

Haw, K. (1994). Muslim girls' schools – a conflict of interests? *Gender and Education, 6*(1), 63–76.

Haw, K. (1998). *Educating Muslim girls*. London: Open University Press.

Hefner, R. W. (2007). Introduction: The culture politics and future of Muslim education. In R.W. Hefner & M.Q. Zaman (Eds.), *Schooling Islam* (pp. 1–39). Princeton: Princeton University Press.

Hofmann, M.W. (2002). Has Islam missed its enlightenment? *American Journal of Islamic Social Sciences, 19*(3): 1–10.

Hoodfar, H. (1993). The veil in their minds and on our heads: The persistence of colonial images of Muslim women. *Resources for Feminist Research, 22,* 5–18.

Hoodfar, H. (2003). More than clothing: Veiling as an adaptive strategy. In S.S. Alvi, H. Hoodfar, & S. McDonough (Eds.), *Muslim veil in North America* (pp. 3–40). Toronto: Women's Press.

Huntington, S. (1993). The clash of civilizations. *Foreign Affairs, 72*(3), 22–8.

Husain, S.S. & Ashraf, S.A. (1979). *Crisis in Muslim education.* London: Hodder and Stoughton, and Jeddah: King Abdul Aziz University.

Jacobson, J. (1998). *Islam in transition: Religion and identity among British-Pakistani youth.* London: Routledge.

Jafri, R., & Fatah, T. (2003). Muslims oppose funding. *Toronto Star,* 14 July, A17.

Jones, A. (1993). Becoming a 'girl': Post-structuralist suggestions for educational research. *Gender and Education, 5*(2), 157–66.

Joshi, K. (2006). *New roots in America's sacred ground.* New Brunswick, NJ: Rutgers University Press.

Karumanchery, L. L. (2003). The colour of trauma. Doctoral diss., Department of Sociology and Equity Studies in Education, Ontario Institute for Studies in Education, University of Toronto.

Kelly, P. (1997). Integrating Islam: A Muslim school in Montreal. MA thesis, Department of Islamic Studies, McGill University, Montreal.

Keung, N. (2002). The hijab and the job hunt. *Toronto Star,* 18 December, A7.

Khaf, M. (1999). *Western representations of the Muslim woman.* Austin: University of Texas Press.

Khan, S. (2000). *Muslim women: Crafting a North American identity.* Gainesville: University Press of Florida.

Khan, S. (2002). *Aversion and desire.* Toronto: Women's Press.

Khan, S. (2003). Why does a headscarf have us tied up in knots? *Globe and Mail,* 26 September.

Khan-Cheema, M.A. (1996). British Muslims in state schools: A positive way forward. In G. Sarwar (Ed.), *Issues in Islamic education* (pp. 83–90). London: Muslim Educational Trust.

Khanum, S. (1995). Education and the Muslim girl. In M. Blair & J. Holland with S. Sheldon (Eds.), *Identity and diversity: Gender and the experience of education* (pp. 257–77). Philadelphia: Multilingual Matters.

Kimmel, M.S. (1994). Masculinity as homophobia: Fear, shame, and silence in the construction of gender identity. In H. Brod & M. Kaufman (Eds.), *Theorizing masculinities* (pp. 119–41). Thousand Oaks, CA: Sage.

Landsberg, M. (2002). Muslim feminist focuses on roots of extremism. *Toronto Star,* 15 December, A2

Lather, P. (1986a). Research as praxis. *Harvard Educational Review, 56*(3), 257–77.

Lather, P. (1986b). Issues of validity in openly ideological research: Between a rock and a soft place. *Interchange, 17*(4), 63–84.

Lazreg, M. (1988). Feminism and difference: The perils of writing as a woman on women in Algeria. *Feminist Studies, 14*(1), 81–103.

Lazreg, M. (1994). *The eloquence of silence: Algerian women in question*. New York: Routledge.

Lenk, H. M. (2000). The case of Emilie Ouimet: News discourse on hijab and the construction of Quebecois national identity. In G.J.S. Dei & A. Calliste (Eds.), *Antiracist feminism*. Halifax: Fernwood.

Mabro, J. (1991). *Veiled half-truths*. London: I.B. Taurus.

MacLeod, A.E. (1991). *Accommodating protest: Working women, the new veiling, and change in Cairo*. New York: Columbia University Press.

MacMaster, N., & Lewis, T. (1998). Orientalism: From unveiling to hyperveiling. *Journal of European Studies, 28*(109/110), 121–35.

Mahmood, S. (2005). *The politics of piety*. Princeton: Princeton University Press.

Mandaville, P. (2007). Islamic education in Britain: Approaches to religious knowledge in a pluralistic society. In R.W. Hefner & M.Q. Zaman (Eds.), *Schooling Islam* (pp. 224–41). Princeton: Princeton University Press.

Mascia-Lees, F.E., & Johnson Black, N. (2000). *Gender and anthropology*. Prospect Heights, IL: Waveland.

Mazrui, A. (2002). Is globalization a clash of civilizations? An interview with Ali Mazrui. *AMSS (Association of Muslim Social Scientists) Bulletin, 3*(2), 9–11.

McCloud, A. B. (2000). The scholar and the fatwa. In G. Webb (Ed.), *Windows of faith* (pp. 136–46). Syracuse: Syracuse University Press.

McDonough, S. (2003a). Perceptions of hijab in Canada. In S.S. Alvi, H. Hoodfar, & S. McDonough (Eds.), *The Muslim veil in North America* (pp. 121–42). Toronto: Women's Press.

McDonough, S. (2003b). Voices of Muslim women. In S.S. Alvi, H. Hoodfar, and S. McDonough (Eds.), *The Muslim veil in North America* (pp. 105–20). Toronto: Women's Press.

McHoul, A., & Grace, W. (1993). *A Foucault primer: Discourse, power, and the subject*. New York: New York University Press.

McLaughlin, T. (1992). The ethics of separate schools. In M. Leicester & M. Taylor (Eds.), *Ethnics, ethnicity, and education* (pp. 100–13). London: Kogan Page.

Memon, N. (2006). Colonizing Muslim schools from within: An analysis of neoliberal practices in Toronto's Islamic schools. Paper presented at the Rage and Hope Conference, OISE/University of Toronto, 24 February.

Mernissi, F. (1987). *Beyond the veil: Male–female relationships in modern Muslim society*. Bloomington: Indiana University Press.

Mernissi, F. (1991). *The veil and the male elite: A feminist interpretation of women's rights in Islam* (Trans. M.J. Lakeland). Reading, MA: Addison-Wesley.

Metcalf, B.D. (1996). Introduction: Sacred words, sanctioned practice, new communities. In B.D. Metcalf (Ed.), *Making Muslim space in North America and Europe*. Berkeley: University of California Press.

Miller, B.D., Van Esterik, P., & Van Esterik, J. (2001). Anthropology and the study of culture. *Cultural Anthropology* (pp. 8–20). Toronto: Allyn & Bacon.

Mire, A. (2001). Skin bleaching: poison, beauty, power and the politics of the colour line. *Resources for Feminist Research, 28*(3–4), 13–38.

Misbahuddin, K. (1996). The lingering hijab question. *The Message, 21*(3), 29.

Mohanty, C. T. (1991). Under Western eyes: Feminist scholarship and colonial discourses. In C. T. Mohanty & A. Russo (Eds.), *Third World women and the politics of feminism* (pp. 51–74). Bloomington: Indiana University Press.

Moghissi, H. (1999). *Feminism and Islamic fundamentalism: The limits of postmodern analysis*. New York: Zed.

Moors. A. (1991). Women and the Orient: A note on difference. In L. Nencel & P. Pels (Eds.), *Constructing knowledge, authority, and critique in social science* (pp. 114–122). London: Sage.

Murad, K. (1986). *Muslim youth in the West*. London: Islamic Foundation.

Muslim Canadian Congress. (2007). Statement: MCC rejects John Tory plan to fund private religious schools. Retrieved 24 July 2007 from http://www.MuslimCanadianCongress.org.

Mustafa, B. (1999). Education for integration: Case study of a British Muslim high school for girls. *Journal of Muslim Minority Affairs, 19*(2), 291–8.

Myers, W.D., & Jenkins, L. (2000). *Malcolm X: A fire burning brightly*. New York: HarperCollins.

Nyang, S. (2000). Islam, American society, and the challenges. *The Message*, 25 (1),15.

Ornstein, M. (2000). The differential effect of income criteria on access to rental accommodation on the basis of age and race: 1996 census results. Report, Institute for Social Research and Department of Sociology, York University, Toronto.

Osler, A., & Hussain, Z. (1995). Parental choice and schooling: Some factors influencing Muslim mothers' decisions about the education of their daughters. *Cambridge Journal of Education, 25*(3), 327–98.

Parker-Jenkins, M. (1995). *Children of Islam: A teacher's guide to meeting the needs of Muslim pupils*. London: Trentham.

Parker-Jenkins, M. (1999). Islam, gender, and discrimination in the workplace. Paper presented to the Nationalism, Identity and Minority Rights: Sociological and Political Perspectives Conference, September, University of Bristol.

Parker-Jenkins, M., Hartas, D., & Irving, B.A. (2005). *In good faith: Schools, religion, and public funding*. Aldershot: Ashgate.

Parker-Jenkins, M., & Haw, K. (1996). Equality within Islam, not without it: The perspectives of Muslim girls in a Muslim school in Britain. *Muslim Education Quarterly, 3*(3), 17–34.

Patai, D. (1992). U.S. academics and Third World women: Is ethical research possible? In S. Gluck & D. Patai (Eds.), *Women's words* (pp. 137–53). New York: Routledge.

Patai, D. (1994). When method becomes power. In A. Gitlin (Ed.), *Power and method: Political activism and educational research* (pp. 61–73). New York: Routledge.

Proweller, A. (1998). *Constructing female identities.* Albany: SUNY Press.

Quantz, R.A. (1992). On critical ethnography. In *The Handbook of Qualitative Research* (pp. 447–503). Thousand Oaks, CA: Sage.

Quraishi, A. (2000). Her honor: An Islamic critique of the rape laws of Pakistan from a woman-sensitive perspective. In G. Webb (Ed.), *Windows of faith* (pp. 102–136). Syracuse: Syracuse University Press.

Quraishi, M.A. (1970). *Some aspects of Muslim education.* Baroda: Sandhana.

Qutb, M. (1979). The role of religion in education. In S.M. al-Naquib al-Attas (Ed.), *Aims and objectives of Islamic education* (pp. 48–74). London: Hodder and Stoughton and Jeddah: King Abdul Aziz University.

Ramadan, T. (2001). *Islam, the West, and the challenges of modernity.* London: Islamic Foundation.

Raza, M. (1993). *Islam in Britain, past, present, future.* Leicester: Volcano.

Read, J.G., & Bartkowski, J.P. (2000). To veil or not to veil? A case study of identity negotiation among Muslim women in Austin, Texas. *Gender and Society, 14*(3), 395–417.

Reay, D. (2001). 'Spice girls,' 'nice girls,' 'girlies,' and 'tomboys': Gender discourses, girls' cultures, and femininities in the primary classroom. *Gender and Education, 13*(2), 153–66.

Refugee Housing Task Group. (2001). Meeting minutes, 16 October 2001. Metro Hall, Toronto.

Rezai-Rashti, G. (1994). Islamic identity and racism. *Orbit 25*(2), 37–8.

Roald, A.S. (2001). *Women in Islam.* London: Routledge.

Robertson, H.J. (1997). Must girl-friendly schools be girls-only schools? *Orbit, 28*(1), 4–7.

Safi, L.M. (1999). The transforming experience of American Muslims: Islamic education and political maturation. In A. Haque (Ed.), *Muslims and Islamization in North America: Problems and prospects* (pp. 33–48). Beltsville, MD: Amana.

Sahadat, J. (1997). Islamic education: A challenge to conscience. *American Journal of Islamic Social Science, 14*(4), 19–34.

Said, E. (1979). *Orientalism*. New York: Vintage.

Saiyidain, K.G. (1992). *Iqbal's educational philosophy*. Lahore: Sh. Muhammad Ashraf.

Sarwar, G. (1996). Islamic education: Its meanings, problems, and prospects. In G. Sarwar (Ed.), *Issues in Islamic Education* (pp. 7–23). London: Muslim Educational Trust.

Sawicki, J. (1991). *Disciplining Foucault*. New York: Routledge.

Scrivener, L. (1999). Secrets and lies: South Asian parents usually follow tradition, but sometimes their children don't. *Toronto Star*, 16 May.

Scrivener, L. (2001). Islamic schools a 'safe space.' *Toronto Star*, 25 February.

Selby, K. (1992). The Islamic schooling movement in the United States: Teacher's experiences in one full-time Islamic school. *Muslim Education Quarterly, 9*(1), 35–48.

Shaikh, S., & Kelley, A. (1989). To mix or not to mix: Pakistani girls in British schools. *Educational Research, 31*(1), 10–19.

Shamma, F. (1999a). The curriculum challenge for Islamic schools in America. In A. Haque (Ed.), *Muslims and Islamization in North America: Problems and prospects* (pp. 273–96). Beltsville, MD: Amana.

Shamma, R. (1999b). Muslim youth in North America: Issues and concerns. In A. Haque (Ed.), *Muslims and Islamization in North America: Problems and prospects* (pp. 323–30). Beltsville, MD: Amana.

Shapiro, B. (1985). *The report of the Commission on Private Schools in Ontario*. Toronto: Ontario Ministry of Education.

Sharifi, H. (1979). The Islamic as opposed to modern philosophy of education. In S.M. al-Naquib al-Attas (Ed.), *Aims and objectives of Muslim education* (pp. 76–117). London: Hodder and Stoughton and Jeddah: King Abdul Aziz University.

Simon, R., & Dippo, D. (1986). On critical ethnographic work. *Anthropology and Education Quarterly, 17*, 195–9.

Smith, D. (1990). *The conceptual practices of power*. Toronto: University of Toronto Press.

Smith, D., McCoy, L., & Bourne, P. (1997). How are schools working for female students in Ontario? *Orbit, 28*(1), 2–3.

Smith, G. (2002). Muslim garb a liability in job market, study finds. *Globe and Mail*, 18 December, A10.

Smith, Linda Tuhiwai. 1999. *Decolonizing Methodology*. London: Zed Books

Spinner-Halev, J. (1997). Extending diversity: Religion in public and private education. Paper presented at the Canadian Centre for Philosophy and Public Policy Conference on Citizenship in Diverse Societies, University of Toronto, October 1997.

Stephens, J. (1990). Feminist fictions: A critique of the category 'non-Western woman' in feminist writings on India. *Subaltern Studies, 6*, 141–61.

Sweet, L. (1997). *God in the classroom*. Toronto: McClelland and Stewart.

Tauhidi, D. (2006). *The Tarbiyah project: A renewed vision of Islamic education*. Abiquiu, New Mexico: Tarbiyah Institute.

Taylor, M.L. (2002). Decolonizing spirituality. Paper presented at annual meeting of the American Academy of Religion (AAR), Toronto, 23 November.

Thiessen, E.J. (2001). *In defence of religious schools and colleges*. Montreal and Kingston: McGill-Queen's University Press.

Todd, S. (1999). Veiling the 'other,' 'unveiling ourselves': Reading media images of the hijab psychoanalytically to move beyond tolerance. *Canadian Journal of Education, 23*(4), 438–51.

Vashti Persad, J., & Lukas, S. (2002). *No hijab permitted here. Study on the experiences of Muslim women wearing hijab applying for work in the manufacturing, sales, and service sector*. Toronto: Report by Women Working with Immigrant Women.

Wadud A. (1992). *Quran and woman*. Kuala Lumpur: Penerbit Fajar Bakti.

Wadud, A. (2000). Alternative Qur'anic interpretation and the status of women. In G. Webb (Ed.), *Windows of faith* (pp. 3–21). Syracuse: Syracuse University Press.

Webb, G. (2000). Introduction, may Muslim women speak for themselves please? In G.Webb (Ed.), *Windows of faith* (pp. xi–xx) Syracuse: Syaracuse University Press.

Willinsky, J. (1998). *Learning to divide the world: Education at empire's end*. Minneapolis: University of Minnesota Press.

Wright, O. (2000). Multicultural and antiracist education: The issue is equity. In T. Goldstein & D. Selby (Eds.), *Weaving connections* (pp. 57–98). Toronto: Sumach.

Yamani, M. (1996). *Feminism and Islam: Legal and literary perspectives*. New York: Ithaca.

Yegenoglu, M. (1998). *Colonial fantasies: Toward a feminist reading of Orientalism*. Cambridge: Cambridge University Press.

Yousif, A. (1993). *Muslims in Canada: A question of identity*. Ottawa: Legas.

Yusuf, H. (1994). Lambs to the slaughter: Muslim students in public schools. Speech given at OISE/UT, October.

Yuval-Davis, N., & Saghal, G. (1992). *Refusing holy orders: Women and fundamentalism in Britain*. London: Virago.

Zine, J. (1997). Muslim students in public schools: Education and the politics of religious identity. MA thesis, OISE/University of Toronto.

Zine, J. (2000). Redefining resistance: Toward an Islamic subculture in schools." *Race, Ethnicity, and Education, 31*(2), 293–316.

Zine, J. (2001a). Developing a critical faith-centred epistemology for antiracist feminist praxis. Paper presented at a roundtable session on Anticolonial Education, Transformative Learning Conference, OISE/University of Toronto, 1 November 2001.

Zine, J. (2001b). Muslim youth in Canadian schools: Education and the politics of religious identity. *Anthropology and Education Quarterly, 32*(4), 399–423.

Zine, J. (2001c). Negotiating equity: The dynamics of minority community engagement in constructing inclusive education policy. *Cambridge Journal of Education, 31*(2), 239–69.

Zine, J. (2002). Muslim women and the politics of representation. *American Journal of Islamic Social Sciences* (Special Issue: Islam and Women), *19*(4), 1–22.

Zine, J. (2003). Dealing with September 12: Integrative antiracism and the challenge of anti-Islamophobia education. *Orbit* (Special Issue: Antiracism Education), *33*(3), 14–16.

Zine, J. (2004). Creating a critical faith–centred space for antiracist feminism: Reflections of a Muslim scholar-activist. *Journal of Feminist Studies in Religion, 20*(2), 167–88

Zine, J. (2006). Unveiled sentiments: Gendered Islamophobia and experiences of veiling among Muslim girls in a Canadian Islamic school. *Equity and Excellence in Education* (Special Issue: Ethno-Religious Oppression in Schools), *39*(3), 239–52.

Zine, J. (2007a). Deconstructing Islamic identity: Engaging multiple discourses. In A. Asgharzadeh, E. Lawson, & A. Wahab (Eds.), *Diasporic ruptures: Transnationalism, globalization, and identity discourses* (pp. 111–30). New York: Sense Publishers.

Zine, J. (2007b). 'Safe Havens or Religious "Ghettos"? Narratives of Islamic Schooling in Canada.' *Race, Ethnicity and Education, 10*(1), 71–92.

Zine, J., & Bullock, K.H. (2002). Editorial. *American Journal of Islamic Social Sciences* (Special Issue: Islam and Women), *19*(4), i–iii.

Zine, J., & Muir, S. (2000). *Islamic medieval world*. Toronto: Pathways.

Index

abaya: defined, 334n2 (chap. 3); and
school uniforms, 86–7, 98;
wearing of, 164–5, 167–8, 174,
253–5. *See also* hijab; Islamic
dress; niqab
Abd' al Wahab, Muhammed Ibn, 61
Abdus-Sabur, Q., 32, 128, 293
Abou El Fadl, Khalid, 52, 60–1,
191–2, 317, 337n4 (chap. 9)
Abu Laban, B., 5
Abu-Lughod, L., 80
Abu-Odeh, L., 207
academic standards, 261–2
academic success, 126–7, 129–30,
132
accountability, 51–3, 292
activism, 250–2, 309
activists, 331n9
adab, 147, 233, 293–4
Ad-Darsh, S.M., 17
adhan, 272, 336n2 (chap. 8). *See also*
prayer
Adler v. Ontario, 38
administrators, 15, 274–5, 277,
302–4, 322
administrators, interviews: on curriculum, 235–6, 240–2; on disci-

pline, 292–3, 304–5; on double
standards, 218; on Muslim identity, 111; on need for school, 83–4;
on public schools, 123
advanced level classes, 264
affair du foulard, 154
Afghanistan, 162
African-American Muslims, 30
African-centred schooling, 7, 40, 72
Afshar, H., 191
agency, 227
ahl al-kitab, 115
Ahmad, I., 308–9
Aisha, 18, 24
akhira, 334n5 (chap. 4)
algebra, 238
Ali: on friends, 142; on Islamic
schools, 133–4; on role models,
141; school as family, 107, 127–30,
141; on single-sex schooling, 204;
on teachers, 132; on un-Islamic
behaviour, 125
alienation, 252, 257–8, 327
Aliyah: on extracurricular activities,
268; on gender interactions, 223;
on holidays, 102; on Islam, 146;
on Islamic dress, 98, 164–6; on

traditions and celebrations unit, 241–2
tribalism, 106, 318
tuition, 85–7, 261, 325
Turkey, 154, 162
tyranny of beauty, 161

Umar ibn al-Khattab, 23
Umbreen: on counselling, 149–50; on peer pressure, 140; on political protest, 254; on racism, 170–1; on reputations, 205; on single-sex schooling, 203; on stereotypes, 169–71
ummah: community identification, 16–17; connection with, 257; desire to create, 35; and political protest, 246, 252–60; ummatic consciousness, 251; and unity, 52
un-Islamic behaviour, 125–8, 135–6
United States, 28–30
unity, 51–2
University of Toronto, 326
UN Tribunal, 38
U.S. Consulate, 252
'us *versus* them' thinking, 115

Valentine's Day, 104
values, 120, 148, 157–9, 235
veils: defined, 332n17; and *fitnah*, 192; and Islamic identity, 171–2, 177–8; multiple meanings of, 157–9; politics of, 153–84; as resistance discourse, 178; stereotype of veiled Muslim women, 181–2. *See also* abaya; hijab; Islamic dress; niqab
violence, 127–8, 251–2
voluntary apartheid, 335–6n6

Wadud, Amina, 18, 316

Wahabi movement, 60–1
water cycle, 235, 239
weekend schools. See *madrassahs*
Western educational philosophies, 26–7
Western imperialism, 21–2
white accent, the, 287
white washing, 102–3
Willinsky, J., 289
windows, 214–15
women, historic role in education, 24
Women Against Fundamentalism, 33
women's dress. *See* Islamic dress
workplace discrimination, 156–7
World Bank, 21
World Issues course, 249
world religion courses, 114
worldviews, 55–7, 249, 311
World War I, 5

yearbook, 268
Yuval-Davis, N., 33–4

Zahra: on discipline, 298–9; on stereotypes, 149; on teachers, 279, 284; on un-Islamic behaviour, 135
Zarqa: on discipline, 300–1; on gender interactions, 223; on holidays, 102; on Islam, 148; on Islamic dress, 164–6; on Islamic identity, 177; on isolation, 112–13; on peer pressure, 139; on physical activity, 269–70; on public schools, 129–30; on single-sex schooling, 201; on surveillance, 213–14, 222; on veiling, 177
Zine, Jasmin, 8–9, 316
Zuleikha, 135, 137